# south of my dreams

# south of my dreams

## finding my american home

· *a memoir* ·

# F. K. CLEMENTI

THE UNIVERSITY OF
SOUTH CAROLINA PRESS

Published by the University of South Carolina Press
Columbia, South Carolina 29208

uscpress.com

Printed in the United States of America

Library of Congress Cataloging-in-Publication Data
can be found at https://lccn.loc.gov/2024026137

ISBN: 978-1-64336-495-7 (hardcover)
ISBN: 978-1-64336-496-4 (ebook)

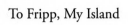

To Fripp, My Island

Some of the characters' names and other identifying details were altered to preserve their privacy and to hide the identity of those who don't deserve one.

This is a true story.

# CONTENTS

# PART 1

# Chestnuts

# 1

I had a farm in Africa
at the foot of the Ngong Hills.

—Karen Blixen

Outside the United States, the world is divided into two categories: those who love America and those who hate America. I have never met anyone who is indifferent to America. If I heard the phrase "I am completely indifferent to America," I would know that the utterer is masking with irony an ineluctably negative judgment. One must be pretty simpleminded to miss that America exists and demands a position: "Oh right, America! I always forget it's there."

I loved America very much. Then I came to America. And I understood that love can be like white hair: better than baldness, but just as dreadful.

I also loved Rome. I was born there. Same place where my father, his father, their forefathers were born. If those people could talk, they'd tell worthy stories of varying miseries and triumphs along a line that spans, I am told, at least fourteen generations . . . and dead ends with me. I loved my family home, its imposing building with a balcony that ran all around the perimeter of the house, polished marble floors, long corridors, long libraries, windowless halls, sun-drenched rooms, playrooms, unused rooms, old bathrooms with views and the glorious bidets. I remember the bakery downstairs; the air we breathed announced when the *pizza bianca* (focaccia) came out of the oven with its scent of olive oil, salt, and herbs. I remember the *supplì* at Franchi's in Via Cola di Rienzo on Saturday afternoons. I remember the tiny butcher shop, whose only two interior colors were aged white (for the walls, counters, and attendants) and sanguine red (for meats and aprons). There, one could still receive that conscionable yet by now obsolete answer, "We are out of chicken today. Try us again on Wednesday." Such an answer would spiral America into a national crisis. What I don't remember is paying any special attention to any of this: it all just was, and I believed it had to be the same all over the planet, anywhere, everywhere. I didn't know, growing up, life could subsist without these comforts, this beauty. Empirical reality refutes me. My crown for a paper cone of roasted chestnuts and a cappuccino at Castroni's! My crown will die unclaimed. I am in America: none of this exists around me. Only in me.

Sure, one could drive—never walk—to the nearest Starbucks and only half-knowingly compromise one's health with those half-toxic, half-unaffordable coffees. But, honestly, no thank you.

In any case, as I type this, there is no time for flights of fancy or the reemergence of subconscious drives, because a tornado is coming. I feel it, rather than see it, from the window where I sit, in this old southern home. (Southern as in un-northern United States, not Sicily.) The wooden structures of the windows tremble, the glass clinks, the light and the air change even inside the house. These southern storms are somewhat sadistic storms: they arrive slowly, don't look like much at first, and end up annihilating everything in their path. A minute before, the birds stop flying, the squirrels stand petrified in the middle of the garden with the front legs folded on their chests, the crickets dare not rub their wings, only a few old and dry leaves complain with a desperate rustle frrr frrr frrr. A second later, the air is sucked away, the sun disappears, and the sky turns completely green.

These frightening minutes before the storm have a sedating quality too. When you understand that you cannot do anything against forces bigger than yourself, you give in to an almost Zen strength that holds no illusion of control. Inside, the adrenaline takes a holiday. Outside, the sky lowers, thickens, the heat becomes oppressive, the oxygen turns into stone. The hysteric warnings from news outlets make no sense: what happens is so different from the way they describe what's expected to happen. Tornados, the fireless dragons of the Great Plains, the prairies and the American highlands, are always surprising. So monstrous that, in 1887, the government banned the use of the term itself because the panic it infused once announced caused more victims than its actual passage. Tornadoes have a dark sense of humor: they can lift up a bunch of chickens and return them back in the same spot, whole and healthy but completely plucked of feathers. Dorothy and her little dog Toto in the *Wizard of Oz* are taken away by a tornado. Dorothy comes from Kansas, the state where, historically, the entire Pottawatomi tribe was swept away by a deadly tornado near the Kaw River where they were all subsequently buried. Their spirits were to ensure that the area would never again be attacked by the Great Wind; however, the dead must have held a grudge against the place or simply gotten distracted over time because Kansas is regularly ravaged by this and other bizarre types of natural phenomena on an American scale, that is, humongous. Ninety percent of all the tornadoes in the world occur in America, so it's no exaggeration that at least 80 percent of the fabulous stories about them originate here. For example, the story of the elephant-shaped tornado, which for half an hour slammed its proboscis left and right, causing a catastrophe in lives and properties in Salina, on June 6, 1876: while the elephant twister moved away sinuously on the horizon, a gentleman stood at the door of his north-facing house admiring it, when an unannounced second tornado came from the south side and hit the man and his house, obliterating both.

Laura Ingalls Wilder, the writer of *Little House on the Prairie*, remembers that Pa, the beloved father interpreted in the television series of my childhood by Michael Landon, told her that one day he was in South Dakota where a tremendous twister had just swept away the property, including the animals, the work tools, the shack, and the stables of a Midwest settler whom Pa was visiting. Everyone gathered to assess the extent of the devastation, and when they looked up, they saw a black thing circling in the air and starting to descent toward them: at first they thought it was a bird, but once the object got close enough they realized it was a door. The door of the peasant's hovel, which no longer existed. From the now blue and serene skies, the door came down slowly, slowly, and settled at the feet of the dumbfounded bystanders. It did not have a scuff and was returned with the hinges still attached.

America can be discovered also thanks to a tornado observed from one's own window. A personal America, different from the images embedded in movies, news, and songs, and different as well from the place this European teenager fantasized about moving to in her outlandish dreams. This teenager, me, dreamt of living in New York, the state-of-the art *Caput Mundi*, the matrix of glamor and poshness. Fuck poshness! Here poshness has no room to breathe. Here, one finds out, the prairies extend into Manhattan. America is a state of mind. You see what your imagination inspires you to see. When you stop dreaming, though, you realize that neither floods of money nor crates of San Pellegrino water (that pricey green bottle that screams "I'm not a Republican!") will never wash away America's rusticity, it runs too deep in its veins. America is also Fifth Avenue, but that's because Fifth Avenue at bottom is still Dorothy's Kansas.

I am 25 years old, and it is 1995. An extremely cold winter is underway in Jerusalem, where I am too. It is raining; wind is blowing mixed with sand; it is miserable. My parents send a couple of survival packages inclusive of some clothing items such as romantic long woolen coats, soft-brimmed hats Alexandra Fyodorovna-style, and a pair of burgundy lacquered shoes, with black laces, rather chic as if fashioned for an English Milord of another era, perfectly masculine. In short, I look like an androgynous German diva of the 1920s . . . think Marlene Dietrich. Except that Marlene Dietrich would not have set foot in a kibbutz. And like her, I'm completely out of place here, dressed like this. The beautiful burgundy shoes refuse to walk on these harsh grounds. They don't look shiny anymore. I don't know what to make of these worn-looking shoes. I've never known worn shoes. I always had new shoes. New clothes. Beautiful things. As a child, come September, my father would take me to buy school supplies for the new year. Everything new, even when the things of the previous year had not been unwrapped. New *grembiulino* (a buttoned smock—white for girls, blue for boys—topped by a broad cravat knotted in a front bow), new cravat, new binders, new erasers, new pencils, new notebooks, and all the necessary textbooks. It was a fact of life taken for granted in my family, just like having bread on the table. There must be bread on the table!—even if the menu of the day featured pasta, fried chicken, panino with frittata, and a slice of strudel. One needs a loaf of bread. One needs new school supplies every year. One needs a flaring Max Mara neck-to-heel coat and cashmere scarves in a kibbutz. Everything new. It is a miracle when something survives the frequent wardrobe purges imposed by my mother's bon ton.

My mother is a unique case of insanity and care. Her origins are unknown to me, because they are unknown to her and, since she lies, I couldn't believe a word about any story she would relate if asked. Her roots started somewhere in Vienna and stretch all the way to Rome, via Trieste, when her father moved to the eternal city to study *belle arti* and paint. The man was rich and had nothing better to do. I suppose he would have liked my lacquered shoes. They say we look identical. I have no idea. He died when my mother was still a small child.

I begged my mother not to chuck my burgundy shoes. She had her judgmental eyes on them. I wore them last year, in Poland, and they looked the part on those Romantic promenades and totalitarian boulevards. You ask: What has Poland got to do with anything? It does, because the current Israeli interlude in my life was preceded by a Slavic interlude; Picasso had the blue period, and I a Slavic one.

Before moving to Israel, I was living in Poland. After high school, I enrolled at university, threw myself heart and soul into Slavic Studies, and moved to Warsaw. I fell madly in love with the subject matter and the places I roamed for five years with burning curiosity: St. Petersburg, Moscow, Prague, Kiev, Lvov, Vilna, Odessa . . . I believed that I could live happily forever in any of those regions, with unsolvable inferiority complexes hidden inside overblown egos, anywhere between Vienna and Gorki. I could have but didn't. I mistook geography for purpose. Then I mistook my purpose altogether. My purpose for living in those days was the love of a young Pole, Janusz Budulec. My love for Janusz Budulec made sense of everything in those days.

When, after an intense three-year relationship, Budulec vanished, my life blanked out too. I lost interest in life and in any part of the cruel and boundless Slavia. I left Poland (which was now loaded with my pain) and came to Israel. I hadn't considered that the pain would follow me here. And here, like a wreckage from the past, my lacquered shoes wrinkle, exfoliate, split in the dry desert air. And here they'll remain, in a black dumpster, full of rejected furniture, rotten lettuce leaves, and cigarette butts. Shalom.

Having these catwalk clothes is a real problem in the kibbutz because I cannot lose sight of them for a moment: if they end up in the laundry facility, the Russians and some old acrid Israeli woman will steal them; if I leave them unattended, the Americans, the only righteous ones around, will redistribute them equally among the members of the community following the fundamental rule of this place which requires that nobody own or desire more than anyone else. The kibbutz is a kolkhoz of sort, that, just like its Soviet relative, was obviously not ideated by Italian or French Jews. In fact, me and my two French friends, Sonia and François, although socialists, have no intention of redistributing anything of our own, let alone receiving the hygienically suspect stuff of others. We found ourselves the cushiest jobs. Sonia and I are sheltered from the torrid heat and the frozen rains in the nursery. François works in the laundry facility, where he leaves the bulk of the effort to his colleagues while he reads French newspapers and other intellectually stimulating materials, coopting the only bench near the only heater.

The harshest tasks have been left to the Russians and to the Americans: to the Russians precisely because they're Russians, and therefore the kibbutz director, Roy, has no qualms in discriminating against them. To the Americans because they asked for them, wanting to experience the true reality of the place to the fullest, not wishing to avoid (like the Italians and the French) any aspect of this adventure. We, the West Europeans, on the other hand, promptly withdraw from any repugnant adventure: Americans, who grew up in ugly places, with fattening, carcinogenic foods, but also with a great sense of justice, meritocracy, and equality in that little bit of healthy blood that still flows in them, gleefully clean the chicken coops (with consequent irritation of the eyes and respiratory tract infections, and above all a 5 AM wake-up call each morning); Sonia, François, and I count on the fact that experiences can be absorbed intellectually, not merely physically. The only exception to this geo-spiritual archetype is a French *oleh chadash* (new immigrant), Michel (pronounced Mishel): this one is determined to pass for an American, starting with his name which he insists on pronouncing in English "Michael" although it comes out of his tightly protruded Gallic mouth as "My-kòll."

My-kòll has a nonchalant cigarette hanging from the side of his meaty lips (Americans collectively stopped smoking around 1970), he wears his button-down shirt sleeves elegantly rolled-up (Americans only wear T-shirts), and he ends up picking cotton in the fields with his beloved gringos. He immediately gets a second-degree sunburn, an erythema, and is debilitated for days.

I share a tiny room with a Belgian roommate, the oldest among us (meaning, the closest to thirty), a bit hippie, largely minimalist, and ready to immolate herself for who knows what subconscious sense of guilt toward the Chosen People. I say this because, weirdly, she is not Jewish. The Belgian girl left Europe with merely her backpack. My parents paid a hefty overweight fee for my suitcases at the airport, and I have occupied every accessible corner of our room: guitar, violin, books, loads of impractical clothes. The Belgian girl does any work she is given without batting an eyelid. Exemplarily, and unlike all others, she never complains. The rest of us do nothing but. It's a national trait. She likes to plant things that grow, and she works the land with her bare hands. She is an archaeologist by training, but she never speaks in such a way that the terms of her discipline would crop up and make her appear superior or snobbish. Her name is disarmingly Christian: Krista. "The last Kristos over here became quite famous," I cheer her on. "Vell," she says without smiling, with a cute accent, "I'd like to live past 33." She has a point.

I'm curious to see if the Belgian girl will stay, or if at some point she'll beat feet and declare defeat. She is severe in a Flemish way that blends together quietude and moderation into a kind of noble monasticism, and this can be a disadvantage in the countries along the Mediterranean basin, where the modus operandi is aggression. I am so tired of aggression. Maybe I should move to Bruges.

I make friends and I guess I make enemies too. Krista moves, untouched by others, like a holy spirit among the campfires of our young, fragile psychologies. I would like to talk to Krista about my problems (like friends do), because she strikes me as someone who would never give you wrong advice. But her Cistercian abstention from emotionality makes me uncomfortable, makes me feel stupid: what with my paranoias, my phobias, my anxiety about all sorts of diseases, my over-accessorized wardrobe, and my not knowing when to shut up. I would like, for instance, to hear her take on this one "pioneer" in the kibbutz whose erratic, clingy behavior has been bothering me since I arrived. But I shut up.

Luckily, the problem seems to be taking care of itself, as I receive a momentous call early one morning. It happens around 4 AM: the phone in our room rings and we jump up to the rational thought "We are at war!" I pick up the receiver and hear on the other end the calm and cultivated voice of a gentleman who is looking for me: "This is Professor Antony Polonsky from Brandeis University." He must have disregarded the time zones. Polonsky is reaching out in his capacity of director of the Near Eastern and Judaic Studies program to extend me the invitation to join the graduate body of Jewish history students in his department. "If you'd do us the honor," he says. Is this a prank? No, I know it isn't. I really know. But "honor"? And there is more: for the trouble, I am offered a lavish scholarship to cover university fees and life expenses. In the fog of my nightly drowsiness, I hear him talk of tens of thousands of dollars. This is how my life makes a 180.

"Think about it and let us know."

Think? Polonsky calls me twice more to make sure I am thinking about it and do not accept similar offers from competing universities. I wonder, perplexed, if there is a fight going on in America to win me, The Great Me, while I, unaware, am here, in this place out of this world, a wonderous yet psychotic country, stuffing myself with schnitzels and chickpeas. Not only am I invited and compensated for the opportunity, recompensed for accepting the gift of a future out of here, away from aggression, but they also make me feel as if it were their honor and not mine, all mine and mine alone to be one of them. Think? Done.

I go.

In movies, things usually go like this: The hero hangs up the receiver—cut! The hero walks unhindered through a stress-free airport—cut! A young lady with crow-black hair tightly pulled up in a chignon, neckerchief, and unworldly white teeth greets him cordially—cut! Zoom broadens to outside of the aircraft, plane takes off (not a minute of taxiing) and we understand, led by the musical crescendo, that our hero has just turned a page and is about to write the next triumphal chapter of his life. Cut!

I hang up the receiver. I take off. I leave Jerusalem behind, with the bombs, the fear of dying or, worse still, the fear of killing. But nothing happens like in the movies. Cut!

This story, like most stories, hides a long, extravagant, and confidential genealogy.

Let me start over: Rome, 1969–1988.

When I was a little girl, I went around asking my mother, my father, all my uncles and aunts and whomever had ears to lend, "Where was I born? Are you sure it wasn't Noyorc?" (my toothless way of pronouncing New York). The answers were sometimes humorous, often dismissive, always shattering. "We found you in a dumpster, maybe an American tourist ditched you there." "Nowhere near New York." "Go play outside, you need fresh air." They did not let me dream in peace. My dream situated me in Noyorc. It wasn't my only dream of course: but the others too were met with the same disappointing improbability. For example: "Could I be Queen one day?" "Never." How outrageously sad. The idea had come to me from the fact that a soupçon of aristocracy runs through my maternal line. At some point, someone along that line owned a castle. A castle that my grandfather, the Count (yes, my spitting image), lost at cards in the early 1900s: a castle to visit which, they informed me with the satisfaction of those who know how to whip up bad news and enjoy the reaction in the recipient, "We would have to pay the ticket like everybody else," they laughed so hard. "How about a prince then? Can I have a prince?" it was my next best option. As an only child, I was always sourly aware of how horrible loneliness is. There was no doubt in my mind that one day I would look for LOVE, legendary love, the greatest romance ever experienced in human history. I wanted someone from whom to receive eternal and unconditional love (unlike my mother's—that was nothing but conditional), and who (unlike my weak father) would save me from my reality and make a different reality possible. The kind of love only American silver-screen heroes seemed capable of. At length, I got over the loss of my heraldic bearings; I archived for later use my romantic fantasies; but I didn't let go of my New York dream as easily. That, it seemed to me, had a real chance.

My mother was not exactly an Anglophile (she didn't care for Australia,

Canada, or England), but she loved America, where she had never been. She made up for the real with films and books by American authors to which she persistently exposed me. I owe my imagination to Hollywood. My father, a trumpet player, added the soundtrack to my childhood through the music of Glenn Miller and the old American standards. In our house, all day long, you could hear anything from Brahms to Bob Dylan, Mendelssohn to Joan Baez, Christopher Parkening to T-Bone Walker. My father had arranged the score of *The Man I Love* for solo trumpet and played it in a way that even then, even as a small child, made me go weak in the knees: *He'll build a little home, Just meant for two, From which I'll never roam, Who would, would you?* . . . I could not know the lyrics then, yet I got the message loud and clear through the eloquence of those Gershwin's notes.

To be clear, all young Europeans in those days were totally Americanized —from the blue jeans they wore, to the rock & roll they danced to, and the lingo of badly pronounced Anglicisms they used. This context created the condition for my love for New York: a different sort of arrangement.

I was mesmerized by the America that culture projected onto my eyes. When I looked away, I hated what surrounded me. I couldn't possibly be from "here"! On the split screen of my life, this is what I observed: There: Cary Grant who, hilarious, builds the most gorgeous home for Myrna Loy, his wife in *The House of Our Dreams* (1948); Burt Reynolds (the only man I can stand a moustache on), who quaffs a whiskey at 10 AM with distinct Anglo-alcoholic elegance and the marvelously confident outspokenness of a Doris Day or a Katharine Hepburn. Here: the public housing on the outskirts of Rome, the saucy portions of spaghetti Alberto Sordi and Anna Longhi voraciously gorge themselves on in *Vacanze intelligenti* (1978), the violent slaps that Monica Vitti receives from the man she loves and the passionate kisses with which she regales her victimizer afterward. On the one hand, there was the glamor exuding from the students in the TV series *Fame*, their beautiful white teeth, their talent always rewarded proportionally to their merit. On the other, I looked around and saw *morti di fame*, wretched guttersnipes—("fame" same spelling for two totally different words in English and Italian)—intermingling with the children from "good families," as the old bourgeois generation used to call themselves, in the public schools: we all had crooked, yellowish teeth, we were pale, skinny, none of us was particularly athletic. We were all in school together, rich and poor, and our different social classes were supposed to be concealed behind the white and blue *grembiulini* but were instead loudly announced by them: spotless smocks, with starch-ironed cravats versus faded smocks whose frayed ribbons dangled flabbily. Then, also in this world (not Hollywood's), there were the fascist, racist, antisemitic, homophobic punks.

One day, just outside my school building, a classmate, Mimmo Lattanzi, two years older than I, charged against me full steam with all the strength of his teenage, testosterone-packed body: chest first, mouth bent downward like a maddened bulldog, forehead lowered to better aim at mine. "*Ebrei di merda! Tutti ai forni!*" he yelled. His crude poetics was inspired by the golden Magen David, the Star of David, I unwisely wore around my neck. "Shitty Jews! You should all burn in the ovens!" Dumb with equal parts surprise, curiosity at what was happening (as if to someone else), and terror, I watched his arm rise up in the sky, above both of us, thick and muscular like Michelangelo's David. I did not see it come down. But I felt something clobber the top of my head so hard that I heard the inside of my cranium thud like a ripe watermelon. Mimmo was flogging me with a long black umbrella. It ended only when the umbrella broke. I walked back home, my hair all messed up in a cluster of dirt and blood. While in American films the villain dies or apologizes in scenes full of pathos, Mimmo felt not an ounce of remorse. In fact, no one thought much of the incident. The school administrators agreed on the diagnosis: the child had a crush on me and that's how boys express their love for girls. It all ended there. But the lesson sank in: men who love you beat you up.

Unlike the American model, our parents never went anywhere. Their lives were physically one with their children's. We were always together. We had our own rooms, but no one would have dreamed to hang the sign "Stay out" on the door—the American mother respects the privacy of her child and with tears in her eyes retreats quietly to the kitchen when said door is banged on her nose . . . the Italian mother ends up on the 8 o'clock news. The concept is so incompatible with our nature, that we don't even have the word "privacy" in Italian. If I had diarrhea one day, I would become the commentary of the whole marketplace. Everybody would be told, and no one would refrain from a loud fun joke at my expense. Parents liked it, adults liked it, children just had to get used to belonging to the community.

What I saw around me bothered me because it seemed provincial and pitiable, even though it was in the very heart of Rome, cradle of something admirable if not quite a standing civilization. I felt that my world lacked energy or imagination; it had no élan left to improve itself. My world had just survived the deadliest war in human history. Of course, it was exhausted and half dead. America had won the war; America was always on the right side of things. America had reasons to be cheerful. Or so I thought.

As a child I wanted to change everything around me. I wanted white fences to paint, like Tom Sawyer. I wanted to be Jo March of *Little Women* who works, studies, writes, and saves the whole family with her stubborn ingenuity and independence. Jo March who, despite being from Boston, goes to live in New York, marries Professor Fredrick, and has two sons. I wanted to write my own story and make it about the most fantastic things. To hear people say, "Fania, you cannot!" Or "Darling, don't be silly, these are all fantasies!" was unbearable. I wanted to be from New York. Jo March, minus the two children. (A concept, that of motherhood, that never figured in my imagination . . . neither then nor now.) So I kept asking, "Are you sure I'm not from Noyorc?" hoping that maybe someone would suddenly recall an accidental switch of cribs at birth, and my peculiar case could be solved by a swift return home. Only much later, I learned the perfect English expression for this: wishful thinking. It does not exist in Italian: without knowing it, I had chosen a culture that even idiomatically presupposes the possibility of miracles.

The fact is, I had to have worn out everyone with my fussing and mewling about New York. So for my eighth birthday, my uncle, *zio* Adriano, engineered a reverse-psychology intervention by way of a brilliant gift, or the first brick in the edifice of the most formidable castle in the air: a check. I was handed a rather daft piece of paper, clearly the product of some mechanical office machinery, holding no human warmth, resembling nothing cheerful or celebratory as the occasion seemed to dictate. Zio Adriano explained: "Your aunt and I opened a bank account for you. Now you have 50,000 lire in there and if you keep adding money, when you're eighteen, you can use it to go to New York." Maybe other children my age would not have grasped the enormity of the suggestion and would have been disappointed: not me. I got it. I forgot even to look at the corner in the room where dolls, clothes, a bicycle, roller skates, jewels, chessboard, Walkie-talkies, Aurora pens, a cassette player, and other presents laid piled up. Influenced by my beloved *White Fang*, *The Last of the Mohicans*, and *Little Big Man*, I launched myself into a stomp dance around my uncle as if he had become a sacred fire. If it was meant as a mockery, it wasn't received that way. This was a plan. Everyone eventually collaborated to the making of my dream by generously contributing to my fund. (How did they think this would cure me?)

All the while, my mother undividedly kept her focus on my *Bildung*. The ideal of cultivation wasn't to be entrusted exclusively to the school system. She did not want me to be like other people's daughters. She despised most people. And she despised the way in which they brought up their children. She fundamentally never liked children. She liked only one: me. For the longest time, I saw the world through her eyes and myself in that world. I had to be larger than the place I realistically occupied in life: how to do that in Rome? Not doable. We travelled a lot as a family and as soon as it wasn't complete madness to do so, she put me on an annual diet of foreign trips by myself. Since the age of 12, I was signed up for study-abroad programs in countries far better than my own to be exposed to what my mother defined "different worlds." Cologne, Paris, London . . . there I saw clean streets, garbage cans used for garbage (rather than garbage used as street decoration), luxuriant public parks (unlike in Rome, where my parents could no longer take me to Villa Pamphili Park because it had become a barren desert of parched earth, whose leafless trees were garnished with used syringes by the drug addicts hanging about there).

I loved what I found "out there," in those other worlds. My mother beamed at my reports. My father didn't see her point of these exercises in fate, of his only daughter alone in the world risking who knows what. My mother knew no fear: "Nonsense. She'll handle it!"

I traveled, I read, I saved. My curiosity grew. My bank account grew. And

I with them. But when I turned 18, I did not go to New York City. It took me ten more years. Eight to get to Boston and two to fight my way, tooth and nail (and an iron will), to Manhattan. Nothing happens like in the movies. Mine is the story of a girl who basically wanted three things from life: living in New York, being queen, and finding her prince who would never leave her side. Preferably in that order.

# 2

1988. I'm 18 years old, I do not celebrate, and I do not undertake the longed-for trip to New York, either. However, in my personal annals, 1988 goes down as Freedom Year! A time awaited like manna from heaven. Until now, I etched the days in little marks on my bedroom walls, like a forlorn prisoner in an abandoned cell: 6570 marks. In Italy, the age of 18 brings you a driver's license, the pleasure to vote, and the right to get drunk. My mother, on the other hand, experiences my looming coming-of-age as the looming end-of-her-life: like a caged lioness, she has been scratching, biting, roaring, menacingly pacing about the ephemeral perimeter of my existence of cum-laude high-school student. Up until this fateful birthday, all my dresses are bought by her, haircuts decided by her, holidays organized by her, friendships approved by her, my thoughts controlled by her, self-confidence crushed by her. Now the wires of the mesh relax, the threads come loose, and the mouse, if it's quick, should be able to sneak away before the lioness pounces. *Mors tua, vita mea.* (You die, I live. More or less.)

All through high school, I've had no life of my own. No boyfriends, no parties, no time for anything but study and educational travels. At age 18 years and three days, I remedy the omissions, thanks to the timely birthday of a classmate, whom my mother detests, who celebrates with wild dances, alcohol, and marijuana. I do not distinguish the latter from dried oregano. I never touch this sort of stuff due to a mildly maniacal fear of transmissible diseases, including death, and because I set up a completely different mission for myself: I seek literal escape, not figurative oblivion.

At the fête, I fall in love with the first guy who speaks to me. Stefano. Stefano is the wealthy son of transalpine parents, who divides his life between Switzerland and Italy. (*You said Switzerland? I mean, non-Rome all year round? Hmmm . . .* ) It is upon him—this gorgeous boy who looks like Avigdor in the film *Yentl*—that falls the honor to be the first man to kiss me. I warn him that I do not know how to do it; I make mistakes; and I burst into tears. French kissing is not at all self-evident. It is neither natural nor logical. He grants me a make-up attempt. I'm lost in love. If he asks me to marry him, I'll accept. And I'll move to Switzerland. Instead, the day after the kiss, Avigdor goes away: he communicates this fact to me in a postcard illustrated with idyllic snow-covered peaks, once he is already in Lausanne, and I will never see him again. First romantic heartache. They say love is important. All right, but what exactly it is, nobody can tell. Everyone must figure it out on their own, I suppose. I imagine Love as the angel who will help me cross the Jabbok River, without dying in the process. A saving force that will facilitate my escape, that will protect me and shelter me, while I dedicate myself to growing my own voice. I imagine Love as the opposite of what my mother's love for me is. Love, the way I dream of it, is a third lung, by which to breathe better, rather than a pillow on my face under which I asphyxiate and die. I need a man-bridge, a man-Pegasus, a passepartout-man to open all locked gates: an earthly savior, an omnipotent Doppel . . . helper yes, but no master. I do not want to belong to anyone. That'd be death: and if death were my drive, it could be aptly fulfilled by my mother. If I wished for death, all I'd have to do is to remain in this drab cisalpine region. *I* pine after life.

At the battle cry "Freedom!" as soon as I turn 18 and finish school, I put myself at the helm of my own life: I confidently step into the vast and open oyster that is society, and I discover what neither the books nor the movies nor the pop songs, nor the Sunday inserts of the national newspaper *La Repubblica* have prepared me for: Every man between the age of 35 and 93 will try to get into my pants.

I also discover that I am afflicted by a chronic psychological handicap, a condition that blocks the "No" mechanisms. Perhaps contracted in childhood during the excessive exposure to the maternal warning "Fania, don't be difficult, or no one will ever want you!" I am incapable of saying "No" to others. It is not other people's fault, of course, it is my fault that I don't say "No." Even when a "No" happens to escape my mouth, it automatically translates itself into "Yes" somewhere between my lips and the addressee's ear. Even when I repeat it several times, and unmistakably, "No, no, no," it gets ignored. Every man who gets it into his head (or is it another organ?) to shag me—regardless of power imbalances, working hierarchies, age differences, decorum . . . and, worse still, my emphatic "NO"—will just proceed as planned. I am besieged. I'm afraid I'll never get anywhere based on my merits: nobody seems to care about my merits. Perhaps, as a rule of thumb, women's merits do not matter to anyone in a universe topped exclusively by men who take advantage of talented women even more than silly women, because first, there is more satisfaction in it, and second, because the smart women are also at their core really stupid if they think that in the end their brains will vindicate them. They'll have no rematch, no vendetta, no matter how high up the ladder they climb. From underneath them, there will always emerge a man who'll raise a tyrannical, accusing, violent little finger and pull them down. At the precise moment I enter the grown-up world, I must deal with the indigestible lesson that there are people with whom you choose to go to bed and people with whom you cannot choose not to go to bed. I struggle to navigate these two destructive currents. I hope, secretly, that this is only a baptism of fire, necessary for reaching distant and shining goals. Once my value will be demonstrated, no one will allow himself to put my body before my mind: I will be in a position of total self-determination and freedom. (*Wait, am I a stupid or intelligent one?*)

I read that in America they take cases of sexual harassment in the workplace extremely seriously in court and that over there they even created a category for the crime of "marital rape." America may be militaristic, imperialistic, and hypernationalistic, but it recognizes the right of "No" for women. I vaguely recollect a dream that had to do with Noyorc. . . .

I quickly assume the role of sexual object established for me centuries before I was born. It works like this: You are at a new entry-level job as a journalist in which you place all your hopes for economic independence and highest professional consummation; if your 40-something boss invites you out for dinner—"All within the norm! Don't fret! Just a quick bite"—Do you go? You go. And if he asks you, with the same nonchalance, to swing by his downtown *pied à terre* from where you'll walk together to that folkloric trattoria he thinks you'll like so well—"All within the norm! Don't fret! I'll show you my place and we'll go from there!"—Do you go? Of course you go! And do you know how I know? Because otherwise you wouldn't be the somebody you've become, I would not know your name, I would not read your weekly pieces in the magazine (*kudos, such a meteoric rise at such a young age!*), you would have remained in a thick shadow for the rest of your natural life.

*I* am *leaving* the shadows. Only 18 and I am a rising star at the most prestigious publication in the nation, *Politicus*. I landed this job fortuitously, at a diplomatic party to which my university professor brought me and where he introduced me to a 40-something Polish Jewish exile (married, not out of love but for citizenship requirements, to a much older Italian divorcée) who tells me "Come see me." Where?! After I figure that out, I do go see him in his office, an office at *Politicus*, the most important political weekly, and the man, Gwidon Goldblatt, gives me the first of many more freelance writing assignments. When my byline appears in *Politicus,* my mother sits down, closes her eyes, takes a deep breath and nods; my father tears up; my friends lose their minds. They joke that I am some kind of miraculous being: they touch me, rub my knee, my head, my hand saying they expect to be "healed" and their wishes to be realized. They joke, but not entirely. What I don't tell them, my parents, or anybody else is that the position comes with the obligation to allow my boss to have me off the books. "Allow" is a big word. I am young, not brain-dead. I get it. *Boss, got it?* He is the reason why my byline is in print. That, and my own brilliance, of course. He becomes my lover and my mentor (ancient Greek style, I suppose). He must have an arrangement on the matter with his wife, who lives in a different town, in a different region. But the writing came first. I do not write at *Politicus* because I sleep with my boss, I sleep with my boss because I write at *Politicus*—a sophism that few would appreciate, so I keep the sophism (and the affair) to myself.

I spend these first years of freedom basking in new cool experiences, adventurous travels, prodigious encounters, and unimaginable opportunities . . . and I say plentiful *Yeses!* and loads of *Noes!* identical to the *Yeses.*

*Politicus* brings money, prestige, and a relationship that *is* important to me. I seem born for this. My multilingualism comes in handy. The years I spent segregated at home, reading predominantly foreign literature instead of leafing through low-brow photo-story magazines, practicing music instead of smoking a spliff with friends, broodily philosophizing instead of French kissing, are yielding the sweetest fruits. My mother's devotion to exposing me to the news—and our habit of fighting, foaming at our mouths, every day over our divergent political viewpoints—is paying back. There are no twenty-year-olds capable of discussing the world socioeconomic stage the way I do. Not only can I throw a dart at a map of Romania to show you where Timişoara is, but the name itself rolls off my tongue as if it were the most natural thing in the world to know what the hell Timişoara even is. Older journalists squint perplexedly at having to place Taiwan's current governmental metamorphosis, while I sit back relaxedly as I enlighten you on the migration routes of the Han masses in the seventeenth century, the importance of the Hoklos in relation to the colonial travesty, and (of course) I'll unpack for you how this passage to democracy under Lee Teng-hui is happening, trust me. Like a well-trained monkey at a nineteenth-century Science Expo, I can pick up a newspaper in at least ten languages and tell you directly what kind of headline a particular country is waking up to this morning. I reason and debate like a man. While other women often listen quietly while the guys are haranguing a roomful of brilliant male minds, I, Fania, sanguinely jump in to add, reframe, correct, and contradict. And I can write. *This girl can write, I'm told a corridor whisper goes.* Gwidon is patient and indulgent. He brims with pride at having discovered me. He has great plans for me.

If I really had to nitpick and focus on the half-empty glass (a bad character flaw for sure), I'd say that Gwidon, our affair, his family in Tuscany, my reputation, ethical questions on the matter, and so on are the least of my problems. I'd even say we love each other. I will never, ever, ask for anything: he will always ask for this one little thing only. *You're welcome.*

The worst of my problems is someone else . . . A senior journalist, a legend of foreign correspondence, well over ten years older than my father, a man with extraordinary credentials, as well as loads of sex appeal and such an intelligence-fueled sense of humor as to come through as aggressive; an exquisite writer and refined thinker, who actually read and *understood* the western canon. He is also a Don Juan, the alias of a psychopath. In itself this would be a minor issue were it not for the association of this trait with a criminal propensity to physical assault. I'll call him Inferno. I take Inferno, as I do Gwidon, as a statistical rule: if two out of the two people I work the most closely with harass me all the time, I must assume (even I, the last of the stupid) that a third or fourth man would do the same. I therefore keep away from other colleagues as if I were affected by some form of social dementia. More wisely still, I complain to no one, I report nothing.

Inferno's preferred means of torment: phone calls. Daily. For hours. I press the receiver with my shoulder against my ear, while I sit on the balcony, warming myself on the hard bricks under the late-spring sun, or while I lie on my bed, or while I perch myself on the windowsill admiring a winter sunset over the Roman cupolas, or while I climb a step ladder to reorganize the bookshelves in my room, and he, from his house or the office, talks from the other end nonstop. My father quietly comes in to call me to dinner and, not to disturb this conversation which must be important (*such a daughter! Such a rising star!*), moves his lips soundlessly and gestures in that unique Roman way that is a language onto itself, "We are about to sit down to eat." I raise my right hand with an equally explanatory gesture and roll my eyes to heaven, "Yes, give me five minutes . . . you know how it is . . . work!" But after a quarter of an hour, Dad returns, and the metaphorical gesticulation is now signaling a frustrated "For crying out loud, what does he have to talk about at this time!" And I, in response, mimic great frustration to him in what says: "I know! Bugger! This stupid work stuff, right?" My father and I understand each other, we sympathize with each other (I know how much he cares about eating! He hasn't gotten over his 1943–1945 starvation stint) and we laugh in our silent insult at the expense of the intruder.

What I do not say either to my father or anyone else is that this important and recognized intellectual on the other end of the line daily holds me hostage for hours on sex calls, to jerk himself off at the sound of his own voice that endlessly recites fantasies evidently arousing to him, in which my role is to contribute apropos with an occasional monosyllabic moan.

"When I see you next time I'll show you my cock."

"Uh-hu . . ."

"It's so hard, you know . . . Will you take it so wet and hard?"

"Mm-hmm . . ."

"% $ # @ & *% $ # @ $%"

"Mm-hmm . . ."

"Listen, how I'm wanking it . . . You hear it?" It's impossible not to: that sustained thudding, audibly misted by the lubrication, produced by his choking member slammed against the telephone receiver as if its little dumbfounded mouth could add something of its own to the conversation.

"Mm-hmm . . ."

The hours of precious life wasted this way do not mean much to the twenty year old who hopes to have all the time in the world to make up for them. But under Inferno's pressure, the risk of losing the job of my dreams is serious. The fastest route to survival must be travelled with a snake pace: glide below radar, slither over obstacles, sneak (*nervously*) between office floors, in and out of bathrooms, to avoid interception. Until one day, Inferno, physically thrice my size, jumps from fantasies to facts: in the middle of a workday, he calls me into his office, locks the door behind me, and assaults me. Like in a Laurel and Hardy farce, he chases me, and I run round and round his desk, hoping that Gwidon—only a couple of office doors away—suspicious of my absence will come look for me. Then I conclude: "If I let him touch my boobs, maybe it ends there." "OK, I'll let him put his hand between my legs . . . what do I care! I make him happy with this little treat and he'll go away . . ." Meanwhile I say "No," but kindly as one does to refuse a cucumber sandwich over tea. The "shout!" option does not cross my mind. What crosses my mind, however, is the counterconcern that Gwidon could actually come look for me *now* and suddenly this late intervention seems less desirable: if he catches us this way, who will be thrown out, me or the national legend of journalism?

In newspapers, books, Hollywood movies, and my mother's reports, there are plenty of references to the very tough system that exists in America to protect women from the macho brutality of those around them at work, at home, in society. Not even a President in America can afford to pass the threshold of decency and law, neither with his secretaries, nor with his cook, or his masseuse. Didn't I want to move to New York once? Are you all sure that I was not born in Noyorc?

But besides the super powerful ones, there are also very ordinary common civilians to fear, like, say, my friend Gillo. Gillo, a university mate of mine with a fancy sports car, who lives with his parents in a luxury apartment in the Parioli neighborhood, still served and worshipped by his old nanny who is still on payroll, despite her charge now being almost twenty-seven years old. He looks like a young Jeff Goldblum, including thick-rimmed glasses and the slow way of pushing them up his nose with long, deft fingers. He likes me, I feel safe in his environment of upper-bourgeois refinement. We are cut from the same cloth that way. At the first attempt at intimacy, to which I offer myself with enthusiasm and hope, who knows, for a great liberating love affair, Gillo tries to ingest me. He bites deep into my flesh, everywhere; I start bleeding and screaming before I can push him with all my strength to the ground and run away. My reaction to this traumatic surprise is *not* to confess but to break up my relationship with the circle of friends to which we belong together. I choose retreat over battle. I do so out of cowardice: because I couldn't bear it if the group of friends, knowing the facts, chose Gillo over me, if they did not believe me or, worse, if they believed me and it still wouldn't matter. To sum up: My mother loves me and is violent; boys who love you are violent; my senior colleague, Inferno, doesn't love me, yet he is violent. *Is there a position I can occupy to which the others' reaction isn't violence?*

I go see my doctor, a feminist who insists on being called only by her first name—no titles or formalities with her—an Athena with the balls of her father Zeus. Maybe she'll give me some pointers. The doctor skillfully pretends not to recognize the marks of Gillo's teeth surrounded by bruised swollen skin. She does not call the police, she does not send me to get an anti-rabies shot. (Human teeth, I already read on it, carry more germs than those of a dog.) There's a lesson in this, not dissimilar from previous lessons . . . all these lessons point to the same fact: there is no recourse for those who end up in the wrong hands here. "Each for himself, all against Fania, and Fania as far away as possible from everyone." I think it is the admirable Oprah Winfrey who said that there are only two possible answers to the question "Have you ever been harassed?": "Yes," and "I do not remember."

I keep on going because going leads somewhere, I do not know where, but over there is where the future is. And I have every intention of dragging myself to that elsewhere, like a crocodile shambling out from the deep swamp.

For as wild and painful as it is, the outside world is still better than home. Here, I am at the mercy of my mother's hysterical reactions to every single move I make—even before I make it—if my moves don't adhere to her will. She owns me. And she makes sure to exert her power of ownership without mercy. Let me exemplify: Summer of 1987, a friend invites me to go with him on an archaeological expedition to Israel. I consult the astral alignments: (1) Don't I belong to the socialist/Zionist youth movement *tzair chadash* and (1B) happen to be expediently attending right now a course of modern Hebrew language at the synagogue's cultural center? (2) Isn't my mother ardently pro-Israel? (3) Doesn't my mother demand that summers be devoted largely to learning experiences abroad? (4) Isn't it a fixation of my mother's that I live only on cultural-academic interests that will lead straight to the best career track and social ascent? (5) Won't dad be on my side on this one? Yes, yes-B, yes, yes, yes, yes. The Sun transits in the Ninth House, Mercury is trine to spiritual Neptune, Moon thickens into waxing. My mother says no to the trip to Israel. She didn't choose this particular friend for me (and hence doesn't like him), she hasn't herself come up with this particular destination, the timing is off with her own phases: No.

Instead, she ships me to sailing school on Ventotene Island. I suffer from motion sickness, and boats hold the top place of honor in the list of vomit inducers. I am also phobic about open seas. Furthermore, being as keen on a good tan as she is, my mother deliberately omits to pack for me sunscreen lotions. ("So you'll be more beautiful when you come back," she says.) I learn what "hoist the mainsail," eye splice, and cabotage mean and not much more because by the third nautical idiom my body burns to an atomic crisp. From the hospital where the sailing teacher transports me, I call dad begging him to come pick me up. He does not, of course. He too is a prisoner of that *force majeure* that binds us all: some by acts and words, others by a single glance. My mother: The Medusa who doesn't kill, unfortunately, but lets live in agony.

The same dynamics will sabotage the traditional *pizzettata* to celebrate the end of high school, and my trip to New York when I turn 18. She finds a way

to abort my trip to New York (1978–1988: ten expectant years . . . *pooofff.*)
When the time comes for me to go to New York, as a tourist, as a present for
an excellent high-school graduation in the summer of 1988, my mother decides that *that* summer, of all summers, irrevocably, the whole extended family must (MUST!) go on a long tour of northern Italy, southern Austria, and
Yugoslavia. If it kills us (and it almost does, but I won't get into that), we must
all go. No New York, if I intend to still live "under her roof." (Which I don't.
But she sabotages every attempt of mine to rent myself a place in Rome.)

My mother loves to tell of an episode that *she* thinks exemplifies the essence of *my* character: On one of those Saturday afternoons when, as per routine, she brought me on a long walk downtown, to shop, people-watch, and
try out all the delicacies Rome can offer, I had been making a fuss because I
craved roasted chestnuts (amply available at every street corner on that October day). She kept piling up gifts and treats but refused to get me what I was
asking for: a few chestnuts. My litany of unnerving tantrums over it ruined
my mother's afternoon and frayed her nerves. So she stopped in the middle of
the road and pleaded with exasperation: "Fania, be reasonable! Mom bought
you a new skirt, a lovely shirt to go with it, we ate ice cream, tonight we
plan on having fried mozzarella-stuffed bread for dinner, your favorite . . . I
brought you twice on the escalator, that you enjoy so much . . . So why are
you whining? What could be missing, what do you lack?" To which, pouting,
I had replied: "Chestnuts."

With my mother it is always her way or the highway. It is as she says or else
no money, as she says or else no holidays, as she says or else no clothes, as she
says or else no help, as she says or you'll unleash a Sophoclean tragedy. Greek
tragedies are not only unavoidable but become eschatological in our family.
I am an only daughter, long-awaited, last-born in the family, the center of
great love, and the privilege of this affection comes with the cross of a crush-
ing sense of guilt (*you are not the way I had planned you*) in which my mother
hammers a new nail each passing day.

My mother is a special type of crazy. The epicenter of our Bentham Tower.
You fear her eyes, whether she is there to surveil you or not. She is so much
fun from the outside. You have to experience her from the inside, to be close
enough to her that you finally spot the contorted mechanisms behind the

obscuring façade, inside the black box of her mind. Her narcissism operates through me. She does not wish or attempt to be herself beautiful, successful, extraordinary, at the center of grandiose things. She demands all of it but vicariously, through me. A coward, in the end. And like most cowards, abusive. She is the divinity at the center of my father's and my existence. Everything she gives, and she gives loads, she can take away, and she does, any moment . . . leaving dad and me suddenly cut out from the source of all goodness, stranded, forlorn, deadly injured, and most of all, uncomprehending. *"Where did I go wrong"* ceases to be a question very early on for me. The unspoken diktat is: *"Ingratiate yourself again!"* The sooner I repair the tear, the faster I will be loved, seen, *given* again. There is no "being loved for who you are" when one is not allowed to be. The extent of my freedom is: be hers or be her enemy. My choice.

Ally and arch-nemesis. Dispenser of either gifts or thrashings depending on my compliance to her rules: until I end up perceiving both (the good and the evil face, the rewards and the punishments) as a double version of one same thing . . . the two sides of one coin.

My mother buries me under the avalanche of her gifts. The gift of life, the gift of cultivation, the gift of taste, the gift of aspirations, horizons, love of reading, love of talking, and pure literal gifts. (*God, the gifts! The stuff! Stuff I like and don't like, stuff I need but truly could live without, it doesn't matter, stuff upon stuff upon stuff.*) Add everything together and you get the gift of Gifts: an appetite for independence, a cult of my own personality. From her standpoint, a move bound to backfire.

She manipulates me. She controls me. She spies when she thinks I am hiding something (how could I?) and then she does what she wishes with whatever information she obtains: my private treasures (small things, little things, the irrelevant cornerstones of a child's life) become the objects of public conversations and derision with her friends. I can complain, of course, kick and shout. And so the gifts go away, the smile on her face goes away, even the good mornings and good nights . . . embargoed. Until I crawl back, of my own volition, under her boot.

My childhood is 50 percent undiluted happiness and 50 percent death wish.

The relationship my mother established with me since my B&B days in her womb is like the part of the iceberg beneath the sea surface. There is no problem visible from above that doesn't start at that base below. Seeing (I asked) a psychotherapist is (she answered) categorically out of the question. She fears, correctly, that I intend to whine about her. My last resort: fleeing as far as possible, into the jungle or the tundra, no matter, as long as I don't owe every breath I take to the grace of others and no one holds any debt over me. *Sì, grazie.*

The first lifeboat the universe sets afloat in front of me so that, if I'm smart, I can jump on and save myself from these corrosive dynamics, is university. I choose Slavic Studies. When it comes to studying, my parents put no limits on financial resources, incentives, and support. The important thing is to wrap an idea in an attractive educational or cultural package, and everything is allowed. Slavic Studies require that I explore the immense Slavia: they do not require it however in the protracted, uninterrupted, and intense way I embrace—moving there for five years, returning home only for the exams.

I apply for all sorts of fellowships, grants, and study-abroad programs in every single East European country with an embassy in Rome. And they all have an embassy in Rome. Their personnel get to know me well: the young applicant, a tad off her head, who voluntarily wishes to stay where desperate prime ministers cannot convince their diplomats to go. I am sure they set their full spying apparatus on me and still I couldn't care less: what I have to hide is a question for psychoanalytic therapy, not national security. And if I can avoid surveillance from my mother, I can effortlessly handle the KGB or the Stasi. I obtain scholarships to study in Wrocław, Vilna, Kiev, Prague, St. Petersburg, and in a burst of originality I ask the Polish embassy and La Sapienza University in Rome respectively to allow me to attend the University of Warsaw and let my work there be counted toward my Italian degree. That's how the most beautiful years of my life finally begin: I meet Janusz Budulec, my best friend Galina, and also Brett.

While I admit that a university degree is paramount, deep inside I know that a university career will never do for me. I lack the necessary intellectual rigor: I am a *bon vivant,* one who does one thing while already dreaming of the next one, someone who pretends *to be* but who *is* not, because *being* demands exertion and assertiveness—two things for which I'm ill-equipped. Then one must consider the enslavement an academic career requires. I am not cut for that either. Decades of lackeying for some bureaucratic scholar who, perhaps, will come through with his promise to leave you his post one day; and without the insider's support, no tenure track will ever be granted.

So while I enjoy my days as a self-exiled scholar in any foreign country that will have me, I also nurture my career as a journalist and cultural correspondent for *Politicus,* keeping all my contacts in Rome—where I return periodically to take exams as a nonattending student. I additionally make money tutoring people in pretty much any humanistic subject matter. This way, my New York funds grow, but the distance between me and New York does as well. Perhaps America is truly off the plate.

Aside from the excruciating presence of my mother in my life, however, the years between 1989 and 1995 are very full and fulfilling. My true friends are here in Europe; *Politicus* puts me on an exclusive career track (harassers aside); I begin to move in the intellectual circles that count; I collaborate at establishing a publishing house with Janusz Budulec in Warsaw and another in Rome in collaboration with my friend, Marco Cassini. These are years of exotic travels, historical evolutions—from the Berlin Wall that almost fell on my head as I rushed there from Prague to see it come down one night, to meeting Spielberg who was shooting *Schindler's List* in Krakow just outside my ground-floor apartment window—and getting to hang out with lovely people like Seamus Heaney (pre-Nobel), Andrew Motion (pre-PEN presidency), and Krzysztof Kieślowski (premortem).

The more I expand, the tighter Europe fits, and Rome doesn't fit at all. I am at the center of these movers-and-shakers groups, intellectual communes with an unholy power over the shaping of the local cultural and political worlds. We dress hippie-retro chic (tree huggers, free-love practitioners, humanity friends that we are), but our greedy expansion is Victorian. "Our" group mentality stifles and terrifies me. I'm not safe here. My body is not safe here. My persona glitters, while the real person shrivels. My ideas are not safe: they are not always appreciated, or rather they are not appreciated when they have the *chutzpa* to diverge from the group opinion. Lefty group. Intelligentsia group. The Group's group. In principle, I'm with the group: I like the group; we have a similar formation, the group and I. Except I have traveled more than the group, lived abroad away from the group, I speak more languages than anyone else in the group and therefore I have access to books not yet translated in Italy, which helps me reach horizons outside of the group's grasp; and I have a different subjective experience that I would like the group to take into consideration from time to time. Unthinkable: one must disappear, one must dissolve into the group, like a sugar cube under the pouring tea. So I learn to bite my tongue when I am with the group. What the group says wounds me, but they do not know it because the group thinks only as such, disregarding differences within itself: the group homogenizes, and when we homogenize we agglomerate everything into the greatest common factor. The women homogenize to men, the disabled to the physio-obvious, the non-Europeans to the Westerners, the different types of all kinds to the hetero-Whites . . . mainstream phagocytosis. No one however phagocytizes the Jews, it must be said—Jews are indigestible and the permission for them to exist is expunged with a fervor known only to the very righteous every time a debate lamentably veers toward the subject "Israel." Without any consideration for those present in the group. The group hates Jews. Exocytosis.

I'll spell it out: I know the group loves me, but only as long as the small peculiarity of my peculiar Jewishness is kept hermetically under lock. Between Mimmo Lattanzi's fascist simplicity ("Jew-swine!") and the Socialist affiliates' sophisticated repudiation of the Jews, as "something" that ought not even to subsist in society anymore—it's hard to appreciate the difference. No matter which side you take, you give yourself to your enemy.

Like a noose around my neck, I feel my breath taken away more and more by misogyny, racism, anti-Semitism . . . and have I mentioned the furious quarrels with my mother? All things I cannot change or join allies in fighting. I back up . . . back up . . . back up . . . When my back is against the wall, it's time for me to make a run for it. I graduate *summa cum laude* in record time, pack my stuff, and move to Israel. I'll call it Lifeboat #2. After all, what is Israel but a paroxysmal mixture of Italy and America, of über-Kultur and wilderness? I'll be fine there.

But I will not be fine in Israel. If I minded continental machismo, what of the pathological phallomilitarism of these parts?

I am having lunch in the kibbutz cafeteria, a quiet, sunny day, with hardly anybody around. Maybe they are all swimming in the community pool or visiting friends in town. I sit alone by the large window that overlooks the main road to the entrance gate. There, on the dusty gravel path, a black limousine slowly rolls in. A limousine from which only one man comes out. An unexpected visitor. An ambush. It's my colleague from *Politicus,* Inferno, who has kept on sex-calling me even here, and who has now been sent to Jerusalem to cover the Intifada and me. He checkmated us all. The Knight is upon the Queen. I empty my plate into the garbage bin and biting my lower lip to a bleed, hoping to stop the tears, I hold my head high and go out to greet him. This time I won't escape his fantasies.

In a room at the King David Hotel (I guess I'm worth it), he'll make me wish for terrorists to blow up this building right now. He finally does to me everything he ever wished for. King takes Queen.

If even the whole Mediterranean basin is too tight for me, and if, as suggested by Moses Hess, Rome and Jerusalem are in the final analysis a reversed mirror of each other, perhaps it is time for me to scan the horizon for yet a third way out of here. Lifeboat #3. Galina and Brett invite me to New York. New York, NY. Noyorc. I may have no plans, but I have plenty of excuses.

I rush to the American embassy to inquire about visa matters: the secretary behind the desk tells me that tourists do not need a visa. I beam. This worries the secretary who starts adding details about deportations, arrests, muddy criminal records for those who dare stay on US territory for more than three months . . . as if he wished to stop me by this, or to prevent some machination he is decoding on my happy face. Well, he has a point. I don't care about his dreary warnings: I received exactly the answer I hoped for, and now I have a dream to chase, sir . . . move out of my way! Life, not to mention the day, is short and I must go shopping for my departure. *Grazie, arrivederci.*

I use my money to buy a roundtrip ticket to New York. This time, I don't have to answer for it to anyone. Seven years after my dismissed eighteenth birthday, I have considerable savings, experience with travels, and above all an Olympic practice in announcing my decisions to my mother only after they've already been taken and implemented. When, in other words, it is too late for her to derail the course of the events.

The illusions about America I had as a child are gone (thank you, Ronald Reagan!); of course, I know that life is not what you see in films. (Even if I still hope it is a bit.) But unfulfilled curiosity is hard to kill. I yearn for a chance to start all over, in a place where no one knows who I am, where I can put to good use the lessons I learned in my European phase and avoid making the same mistakes in the upcoming American phase. *Orpheus was offered a second chance but screwed it up:* I *will have no problem not looking back.* Who knows, America may teach me to say NO! My friend Galina did it. One day she was in Warsaw, the next in New York. She's the type who has never even used the word "compromise": she's the type who slept only with two men in her life-time, one of whom, Brett, just married her. She's all brain. Me, I'm the type to whom the Parcae apportioned a different organ, not as vital.

My grand entrance into America happens in a circumvoluted, labyrinthine way. And both things, the arrival and the labyrinth, I owe to Galina.

Galina moved to Manhattan to do her doctorate in Jewish Studies at Columbia University. Then Brett too moved to Manhattan. And they got married at City Hall. Both, like my lacquered burgundy shoes, are a vestige of my Varsovian days. She, Polish; he, Canadian. They invited me to visit them for a week to thank me for introducing them to one another. Yes, I played Cupid . . . but accidentally, really. Never mind all that, I am ecstatic to be granted an opportunity to come, even if only as a weekly tourist, to New York, finally, for the first time. I buy a TWA round ticket. My friends assure me they'll chaperone me around. I couldn't ask for more. (*Or could I?*) I set the past aside, and I throw myself into the present moment. Geronimo!

"Every man gotta right to decide his own destiny," says Bob Marley. Not that taking cues on life from Bob Marley is a great idea, but more refined quotes on destiny from Marcus Aurelius are presently escaping me. In any case, here I am, ready to briefly visit my friends Galina and Brett in New York. It is 1995.

There is only Brett waiting for me at the airport when I arrive. I automatically start to the taxi area, but Brett stops me, adding a smile that says "I know you!" This embarrasses me a little, as if I have fortuitously revealed an inclination to commit a crime. Brett says, almost spelling the words to make it clear that his plan is not negotiable, "We are taking the subway." Spending money on a cab, he implies, would be unscrupulous. I pretend to be absolutely on the same page. I am not. I am tired, I am carrying tons of heavy stuff—the ridiculousness of which is underlined by Brett's simple act of not helping with it—distributed inside a number of suitcases that exceeds the limbs I have available to drag them. Besides I was going to take a cab because I always take cabs from airports. That's what they're there for, for those like me, I thought.

I observe, wide-eyed, like a child at the zoo for the first time, an extraordinary world. We are on the subway line Ⓐ (the same as per Duke Ellington's song): we are on it for a really long time, and, from what Brett explained, there is still far more to go. Suddenly he says, "I've got an idea: let's get off here." I wish to scream NO! but I smile agreeably even if I don't understand the change of plans or where we are since I did not bring a map or study any tourist guide before coming: I thought that all the films I watched on this place would suffice. Agonizing under my load, I follow him. We are enfolded in a sea of people that swings, flows, opens up, closes down on you, backs off, following an inner syncopated rhythm of its own, and it seems a miracle that nobody bumps into everyone else . . . And me, me here! I am in this flow . . . I see myself as if through the lens of a camera, an out-of-body experience, I see myself from the outside: I am an anonymous indistinct part in this foreign yet nonthreatening mass. Look, that's me walking among New Yorkers! I see what they see, I hear their voices and they hear mine. My heart beats fast. Brett and I walk through a tunnel that ends in a long escalator at the top of which I can now distinguish the natural light from outside. *Orpheus, don't look back, lead me there!* We must be near the exit. We exit: Times Square. Times Square under the sun of a day like any other, in the middle of the workweek. I am besides myself with joy, I want to scream, I want to cry, I need to hug someone! But I daren't hug Brett, out of loyalty to Galina, and no one else around gives me the impression of being sufficiently clean. I must control the instinct to throw my bags in the air as Mary Tyler Moore does her hat in the opening theme of the eponymous TV show. Although today Mary Tyler Moore couldn't hold a candle to me: she was in Minneapolis (whatever that is), I in New York! Inside me a little voice bursts into song *"You're gonna make it after allllllllll!"*

Meanwhile, Brett has been enjoying my reaction without saying a word. *Am I being that pathetic?* "I thought you'd like the surprise," he says. I am plentifully repaid for any imagined debt they thought they had toward me. May their marriage be a triumph, may the three of us always be bonded like brethren, I forever bless them and us. Although now I realize the sad temporality of my presence here: I am visiting New York, they're staying. If, by hypothesis, I was the one who had married Brett, say, it would be me today benevolently inviting friends to come for short visits. But I did not want Brett: it is here that I am meant to meet the right person for me . . . and this dream has to happen in stages: the first being New York, and then all the rest will follow. I always took for granted in my reveries that I would get here alone, on my own efforts, not thanks to this or that Prince Charming. I prefer not to be indebted to anyone. I am overcome with emotions. Soon I will be reunited with my friend Galina. Brett brings us back underground and we continue our journey to their love nest: an apartment not much bigger than a literal nest, in Inwood, the northernmost Manhattan neighborhood, at the edge of the bridge that leads to the Bronx, along the red subway line ①. A place never featured in any film as far as I can tell, more akin to the Mokotów district in Warsaw than my Trastevere stomping ground in Rome. I am happy. And I really should have thrown these damn suitcases in the air and left them in Times Square.

As soon as she sees me, Galina lugubriously intimates not to set foot outside: they are expecting riots any day now far worse than those in Crown Heights in 1991. I was with her in Warsaw in 1991 and I do not remember any riot in Crown Heights. (What is Crown Heights anyway?) The jury's verdict on the case of some O.J. Simpson, an African American football player, is about to be announced: if they find him guilty, my friends explain and the news corroborate, Black people will start breaking everything, burning shops, attacking White people on the streets, in their homes, on public transportation. *Every Black person in this rather large country?* A pogrom, in sum, but more heterogeneous. And I thought I had left behind pogrom-oriented Europe! On the other hand, the idea of witnessing such a historical event, of finding myself amid a scene from *The Pawnbroker* or *Zoot Suit,* does intrigue me. Galina and Brett always expect only the best from minorities: the panic with which they welcome this news seems contradictory. I, on my part, am shocked to hear for the first time both my friends and an entire nation ("the most powerful in the world," as American presidents never omit to add) talk of "blackness" and "whiteness" as if they were real things, not just incidental biotypes of the human landscape.

Nonetheless, psychological terrorism always works wonders on me. So I stay put and no one will ever know I even arrived. On October 3, the jury declares Simpson innocent, despite his absolute guilt. The decision is polarizing, but my holiday can proceed undisturbed, without topical microgenocides.

Galina, with whom until not long ago I was studying at Warsaw University, explains to me that a PhD is the only way to land in the United States: you must enroll at university. *Again. Seriously?* I always imagined myself simply packing, hopping on a plane, and once at JFK, even before getting into a taxi, buying a newspaper to scan the real estate ads. Instead, I learn now that "You cannot do that, Fania!" that there are insurmountable visa issues, that you have to take another degree. This is a major bummer, but let's not allow anxiety the upper hand. Everything seems fabulous beyond expectations, after all it's not a big deal to readjust my vision and update it to the following new version:

> Me: books under my arm, floating Max Mara coat, and Tuscan leather bag, I go to class, through poetically snow-dusted paths, at Columbia University.
> Me: walking down familiar streets, I greet with a wave of my hand dozens of friends who smile and call my name.

I am Barbra Streisand in *The Way We Were*. I am Juliette Lewis in *Husbands and Wives*. No problem: I can easily do this PhD. Where do I sign up?

Considering that my vacation lasts only seven days, I have about twenty-four hours at most to formulate this PhD plan. First of all: "Galina, what is a PhD?" And how does one figure out what all the acronyms Americans use mean? As I was learning English, growing up, I found no indication anywhere in my textbooks that Americans speak by abbreviations. Abbreviations become actual words, used as nouns, conjugated as verbs: take NASA, ATM, radar and sonar, no one even remembers that they were originally acronyms; TCB; "Kit!" and hundreds of others including the full medical gamut of syndromes, disorders and diseases (OCD, COPD, ADD, ADHD, PTSD, MS, ALS, IBS . . .). In their laziness, Americans contract the already short version of the phrase *as soon as possible* and, to avoid the extra exertion of having to name all the letters (*a.s.a.p.*), they recompose it into a noun "aysap" . . . who does that? Who has ever found to be too much of a mouthful the words OMG?! Ignorant of these linguistic shortcuts, I miss 65 percent of what's being said to me.

"Doctor of Philosophy." Her tone says, "you, cretin!" I watch her mouth as she invests thirty minutes of my vacation into a detailed explanation. It sounds as if Galina had this lecture ready in her pocket. What clarity, what precision: she is really amazing.

"And what do I do to apply?"

Disdainful laughter: "Good luck with that! It's not that easy. But go ahead and try."

There seems to be loads of procedural steps: there is an application to fill out, upon which a selection committee reviews the applicant, but their decision is extremely selective. Good news: the application forms can be obtained for free by visiting the university department one wishes to apply at. (Well, then there's a fee to actually apply, but what are a couple of hundred dollars for a dreamer so close to her dream?)

When she sees my resolve, Galina insists that the ideal place for a PhD for me is Brandeis University. For me. For her, it is Columbia. We are in New York; Brandeis University is in Boston. And Boston is a four-hour drive from New York, 220 miles, 354.056 kilometers. Galina must have misunderstood my dream. Galina herself, with the zeal of those who do not take "no" for an answer, calls Brandeis to announce my interest in their doctoral program. Indeed, she, who knows how to do it, takes an appointment for me with important scholars and heads of departments. It looks like a project dear to her heart, I surmise; it seems important to her that, now that I got it into my head to enroll in a doctorate here in America, Brandeis should be where I end up.

Brett puts me on a Greyhound bus at Port Authority, waves *ciao ciao!* with his hand, and I'm not sure what's supposed to happen next. I don't have a map, and I have only the vaguest clue of where I'm headed. Loaded with stuff, as if I were going to live in Boston starting today, I search my handbag for my Walkman and try to relax. Paul Simon's words in my ears suddenly make all the sense in the world . . .

*I've gone to look for Ameeeee-ricaaaaaa. . . .*

*Laughing on the bus . . .*

something something *over an open field . . .*

*All come to look for Ameeeee-ricaaaaaa . . .*

I am so euphoric, I cannot breathe.

I am short of breath, additionally, because when the Greyhound bus gets to its destination, I am neither *in* Boston proper nor anywhere near Brandeis. I read on the note with the instructions that Galina composed in her crystal-line handwriting and Brett pushed in my trench coat's pocket, that from here I must look for the 70 bus, then something something, then a stretch on foot. I neatly fold their instruction leaflet, free one arm from the grip on my luggage, raise it high in the air, and hail a taxi. I instruct the driver to take me to the main entrance of the Department of Jewish Studies, I negotiate an extra fee for him to wait there until I'm done, and I promise myself to never admit to Brett and Galina the affront to frugality I just committed. The fact is that I find fatigue to be indecorous. Not to mention the fear that, to save money, one runs the risk of getting lost or being killed, or, worse, of being raped and left alive with the memory of it. *Taxi!*

I see nothing of Boston, not even the gigantic golden cricket on the dome of Faneuil Hall. No young Harvard students in white uniforms rowing for the Head of the Charles Regatta (you know, the kind you see in *Dead Poets Society*). All things I know from books, not from this impromptu visit. However, on top of the lusciously green hill, where the university building I am headed to is located, I see a bunny. Born and raised in Rome, I only know rabbits from encyclopedias and menus. It takes me a moment to focus and recognize what I'm looking at. I am transfixed—perhaps this much enthusiasm is a bit vulgar, but I can't contain it. I must make others aware! I look around trying to establish some kind of contact with the humans passing by, and I stage-whisper from my throat pointing an expressive finger, "A little bunny!" but quietly not to scare the rabbit (or the passersby) who ignores me while I believe the passersby are a bit scared. Nobody pays attention to me. Are rabbits that common around here? Perhaps, this is a good reason not to discard this place a priori. Would I really discard it simply because it is not New York . . . or Boston, for that matter? Galina says it's perfect for me, doesn't she? I also see a squirrel. No, not one, tens! What an extraordinary coincidence! I'm so lucky today! It's like Richard Adams's *Watership Down!* To spot all these wild animals on my first visit . . . What are the chances? Who would have thought?

After being introduced to loads of people, my visit climaxes with the two most important meetings: with the head of the department, Antony Polonsky, expert on the history of Polish Jewry, and with Alan Mintz, no one. The latter is a small man, with a neatly trimmed beard, two lively judgmental eyes and the unmistakable air of someone who has already decided to subject me to an examination and fail me. My ornery determination shields me and somehow allows me to go through with it without drowning in a pool of my own urine. This is also because I do not know who he is . . . yet. Ignorance *is* bliss. He asks me questions about Alberto Moravia, as if to verify that I am truly Italian (my accent never gives it away). Then he moves on to list obscure names of intellectuals and late-nineteenth century unpublished diarists—whom even Asor Rosa, the lion of Italian academia, has never heard of, I'm sure. I do not let myself be intimidated. Either I claim to know them (I lie), or I feign amazement (a bit over the top, admittedly) at his knowing Italian literature better than I. I don't think he liked me. Polonsky does, though, and it is Polonsky who rules here. He, the chair of the Near Eastern and Judaic Studies Department, wishes to put together an *ad hoc* team of students with whom to work on Polish Jewish history and who are fluent in several Slavic languages. He's hard pressed to find such people in America where he just moved himself. I embody his dream. I make his dream a step nearer. He is quite distinguished, dressed in the best London couture, with the sharp humor of the English upper-class: funny, intelligent, polite, and extraordinarily kind, he is not one to be fooled by anyone, though.

On the way back to Manhattan, I play more Paul Simon and my thought stream starts flowing against the tide. Instead of focusing on the future, I focus on the past. On the jostles of fate that, one turn after another, led me to

a Greyhound bus which speeds along highway I-95 South through Massachusetts, Connecticut, and New York State.

*Many's the time I've been mistaken*
*And many times confused*
*Yes, and I've often felt forsaken*
*And certainly misused*
*[la la la la]*

. . .

*and sing an American tune.*

# 3

Brett and Galina are people with great common sense, if it ever existed. They never make mistakes, they never fail, they know precisely what to choose, what to do, which way to go without ever getting lost. They form a two-entity nucleus, unassailable. Even their names are always pronounced together as if they were the title of a legal office: Brett & Galina Associates. They cast a guru vibe, there to dispense advice and protection (or—spirits forbid!—the opposite) to their selected circle of friends. Perhaps exactly for this reason, I hold myself at a certain reverent distance, abashed. They have no money, life as newcomers and as students here is hard, and so they live frugally. They do not have a bed, they sleep on the floor, hugging each other tightly. I know this because they piled my pallet under the table practically at their feet. My head lies surrounded by dust balls and spiderwebs in the only free corner in the room, with my right cheek dangerously close to the cast-iron radiator from the 1930s. Their lifestyle demands minimalism because their ideology rejects consumerism *tout court:* they recycle everything, make bread at home, exchange clothes with each other (since they have similar physiques), cut each other's hair. When I met them, Galina had golden curls cascading down her shoulders, and Brett sported a beautiful woolly head the color of dry straw in the autumn fields. Today they both have hair cropped like Tibetan monks. Brett resembles Benedict Cumberbatch. Now Galina resembles Benedict Cumberbatch as well.

*Yes, yes . . . there was that brief fling between Brett and me* (I believe he proposed marriage), *so many years ago (so many in the mind, not on the calendar, though) . . . but in the end he chose the absolute best girl in the world: the one who's not me.*

Another thing that Brett & Galina do together is bicycling. They have clusters of bikes hanging on the walls of their one-space apartment, including one tandem, a unicycle, a tricycle with the huge front wheel and two tiny back wheels, and another contraption in which one sits almost at ground level and stretches one's legs forward in order to pedal—practically a canoe on rollers. The two of them belong to a cyclists' club and they regularly ride hundreds of kilometers together with their co-hobbyists. Brett rides his bike to work to the Bronx in the morning, and so does Galina, who now boasts a massive gastrocnemius and pulmonary alveoli as large as broccoli stalks. Galina is committed to saving libraries (*wow*), cleaning city parks (*huff, she's good!*), helping women (*I don't get this one*), and fostering abandoned children for a couple of days (*this I get, though it disconcerts me*), and her list of extracurricular activities extend to rescuing stray cats, stray dogs, and stray bums, not counting grassroots action to demand cycling lanes and healthy drinking water. I, who do not help anybody or anything in particular, feel uncomfortable around them. I say little about what I do because suddenly I realize that there is no angle under which I could put it that would not reveal the overly bourgeois side (*a curse!*) of who I really am. They, on the other hand, are not me: they are strict vegetarians, they fight the Hollywood vampire by refusing to go to the cinema, they don't just have a cup of coffee wherever, they patronize only certain places and boycott others, and they look down upon you (me) for unthinkingly going for what you (I) like. Every single minority or alterity (apart from the Jews) is inherently better than the majority to which they belong. (*Except for that minute, during the O. J. Simpson debacle, when, it seemed to me, they lumped the minority into an indistinguishably threatening group.*) When I met her in Poland, Galina took buses and ate pork *bigos*. She wanted to escape the teeny mountain town she came from and her father: she was ambitious and set on becoming someone. But she was already someone, or she wouldn't be here, in New York, today. All I did was introduce her to Brett: but it was her wisdom to pick the winning horse. I ought to keep closer to her, I wish to hide inside of her and learn all the things about life that I fail at deciphering on my own.

Looking out the window, as the Greyhound bus rolls on, I have no reason to doubt that a glorious tomorrow is unfolding before me as well. I'm confident.

What I see of New York in just a few days is enough to draw all necessary conclusions. Like Rome, New York is a place that is best discovered on foot. No need to waste time in museums or other attractions that involve queueing and a ticket. Those can come later. Both cities' beauty is rooted in their architecture, and while Rome's splendor resides in its placid eurythmy, New York's is to be found in its vital arrhythmia.

One day, Brett, a fanatic of winding paths and less-travelled routes, brings me on a tour that leaves me quite disorientated and, above all, through which I see nothing of what I think of as Manhattan. He hasn't considered that a tourist visiting for the first time wishes to see the Empire State Building, the Brooklyn Bridge and Ellis Island. Brett avoids the Empire State Building, Ellis Island, Broadway and the rest like the plague. Instead, he takes me on a walk around their Inwood neighborhood before heading south to Margaret Corbin Drive, where we explore the Hudson Gardens and admire Fort Washington, and only thanks to the fact that the pedestrian stretch along River Side Drive which the city intends to build has not been built yet, I am spared the twenty-kilometer-long endurance march along the western flank of the town. Flank, not middle of the city. The middle is Broadway. To add to the general impression of surreality, here comes a medieval manor, plopped in the middle of our labyrinthine journey, between Fort Washington and West 190th Street, called The Cloisters. We go inside. Founded in 1624 by Dutch merchants, New Amsterdam, like the rest of America, has not known the Middle Ages. So to explain the hoariness of these stones, one must follow the whereabouts of George Gray Barnard, a curly-haired and cross-eyed sculptor who, in the early twentieth century, left Chicago to study *beaux arts* in Paris and while in France started collecting beautiful things, including whole chunks of monasteries in ruin. Old stones that no one wanted. Except for Madame Baladud de Saint-Jean, who apparently was very much attached to her ten Gothic arches, which came from the abbey of Saint-Michel-de-Cuxa and with which she had decorated her French baths.

Barnard began to court the French noblewoman who did not have to think twice when the extravagant American offered her a considerable sum of money for her antiques. Unlike Madame Baladud, the French government took very poorly the news that a Yankee had arrived to loot France, and they quickly moved to pass a law for the protection of cultural assets. Barnard, shrewder than his enemies, packed up, wrapped his lot (comprised of legally acquired pieces of art—from statues to fireplace mantelpieces, arches, pilaster capitals, whole abbeys, cemeteries, and a sculpture in stone of the Christ which a family of peasants in the Pyrénées-Orientales had been using for centuries to prop up a pile of dung in the farm) and exported everything to America just before the new law came into force. It was December 1913.

Back home, Barnard built a manor made of huge antique pieces to protect the smaller antique pieces displayed in it. Their new purpose was to infuse in his students (who had only seen pictures in books) a passion for ancient-gothic art. The Cloisters therefore bear the plural name because this "convent" is in fact a compilation of various convents, the main bulk of which belongs to the abbeys of Saint-Guilhem-le-Désert, Bonnefont-en-Comminges, Trie-en-Bigorre, and indeed Saint-Michel-de-Cuxa. After all, how many of us would have had the opportunity in our life to take a dump in one of Madame Baladud's bathrooms? This way, however, millions of people can edify themselves and even shed an emotional tear before the absolute loveliness of this bizarre architectural patchwork, on the hills overlooking the Hudson River, surrounded by orchards, birds' songs, a persistent breeze, and where no noise from the city can penetrate to disrupt the composition. As if 10,000,000 people in frenetic motion a few steps further down the road did not exist.

I am grateful to Brett for having shown me this place and for having remained the respectful delicate and poetic Brett of old. He had ambitions as an artist when we met. I remember him slumped on the ground, in those Italian cathedrals, replicating in his small notebook the ornamentations of the grids and grates that decorate the churches' floors and through which pilgrims can take a glimpse of the ancient sarcophagi underground. He caught these details and reproduced them so neatly and prettily in tiny pencil drawings, which he later mounted in little wooden frames he made himself. He leaves me to my reflections while he goes explore some new addition in the Nine Heroes room. I feel at peace: maybe it's the scent of the luxuriant herbs, spices, and flowers surrounding me, or maybe it's because I am finally where I was always meant to be, in New York. I read in the leaflet that these plants are the same that Charlemagne had wished to plant in his imperial gardens in Aachen. I've been in Aachen, Germany, before, but I feel so much better at the Cloisters in Washington Heights. I like it here, even if it's not the Empire State Building or the Brooklyn Bridge. It's as if Brett understood exactly why I came and conveyed without stating explicitly: If I want to test New York out, I should fall in love with those aspects of it that are really worth loving.

From Galina, a day later, I receive a different gift, but one just as important. She sets me on a more obvious path to discover New York: granted that the "obvious" in New York is still extraordinary. One morning she declares: "Come with me to Columbia. From there you'll start your tour of the town proper." We reach West 116th Street by train: once we emerge from the subway, she takes me by the shoulders and gently turns me 180 degrees pointing me southward: "This is Broadway," she says, "Keep walking straight on this road until you see the Statue of Liberty." "OK."

I put food before sightseeing. I must eat. It is no exaggeration to say that Manhattan's food and architecture go together perfectly. You cannot love this place unless you love eating here as well, since New York offers more than simply food: it offers a way of eating. Eating on the street, eating in plain sight, eating while walking, eating on public transportation, and above all eating alone in public without any embarrassment or inhibitions—an unthinkable proposition where I come from.

My friends already brought me out one evening to allow me to taste something that I would never have had the opportunity to try elsewhere—world cuisine being this city's true forte, and perhaps it is precisely here that world cuisine lives its best hour. (In Rome, you eat Italian—if you want foreign food, that's what a passport and a train are for.) They chose an ethnic restaurant: not one of those restaurants plainly visible from a busy street, well-publicized, widely known, and to a certain extent assimilated, but a restaurant for connoisseurs, harbored underground, whose only customers were us, and whose attendants did not speak a word of English. A restaurant from one of those corners of the world where the alphabet letters are circles, knots, and aesthetically cute doodles. A restaurant from one of those corners of the world where they likely don't have a restaurant like this, given the famine they suffer. I find comfort in the thought that both the restaurant's nationals and Brett &

Galina are vegetarians: we would not accidentally eat a forbidden or forbidding animal.

Had Galina not set me off on this "Grand Walk," though, I wouldn't have discovered the New York food *experience* I was hoping for. I enter a place a few blocks from Columbia University, southeast corner, between Broadway and West 103rd, that doesn't feature regular chairs but long benches with a high back, made of hard and creaky leather, like those I saw in the movies. This is the Diner. Short for dining wagon, the diner is the most American of all eateries. Invented in Rhode Island at the end of the Civil War by a certain Walter Scott (just a homonym of *Ivanhoe*'s Scottish author). Scott used to drive around all day long in his cart pulled by a horse called Patient Dick, selling greasy but tasty sandwiches to those poor souls who, while wealthy families sat at their well-dressed tables attended by well-trained servants, were still out and about breaking their backs working and had no way to make it home for a meal. The same Scott is also recorded in history for the invention of the "chewed sandwich" which he added to his menu for the less affluent and stuffed with leftovers and small pieces discarded from the various cuts from previous preparations.

I immediately fall in love with the Diner. It's like entering the set of *Frankie and Johnny:* instead of Al Pacino behind the fat-frying grills, I distinguish from afar a Puerto Rican man who has a mustache that looks drawn with kohl along his upper lip; my server is a middle-aged lady reminiscent of Laverne from the sitcom *Laverne & Shirley* rather than of Michelle Pfeiffer.

She hands me a laminated menu, as big as Moses's tablets: my English is great, but the menu may as well be printed in ancient Tamil since I cannot recognize a single item. For example, I understand "pig," I understand "blanket," but what the heck is a "pig in a blanket"? Luckily, since this is a city of foreigners and strangers like me, they made sure to illustrate every dish with large, succulent, eloquent images that render literacy a mere surplus. I see omelets, potatoes of all shapes, steaks drowned in brown sauces, huge smoothies, banana splits that, if the figure is to scale, must be transported to the table by at least two people. The lady with her pinafore—order pad in hand, chewing gum in her mouth, and pencil behind her ear—helps me decide what I want. I would like to order everything.

Caught between curiosity and hunger, I am assailed by the desire to impersonate the Rockefeller type and command: *One of everything, please! (Hold the piglet in the blanket, though.*) My choice falls on the classic breakfast: "Western omelet" (*we'll see*) with three types of cheese and mushrooms, grilled potatoes (*my the onions*), toast (*they bring me a bready Leaning Tower of Pisa*) with butter and jam, and also a sweet round bun, golden brown on top and crumbly inside that they identify for me as a "biscuit" . . . when I read the word I expected a cookie (*what do cookies have to do with my omelet?, I had wondered*) basing my assumption on my French and what I learned in London during the study-abroad programs my mother enforced when I was a young girl: instead the American *bisck-it* is bread, grainy, buttery, with a salty aftertaste. It is the national food of the South: the quintessence of the confederate kitchen.

My breakfast is augmented by some coffee: technically, "some" does not begin to describe the ludicrous amount of coffee I get. I take a sip of it, Laverne sees it and immediately arrives with the carafe to fill my mug up again, "Here you go, hon." (*What's "hon"?*) I have a quiver of irritation: how much will all these coffees cost me? I'm sure I ordered only one. They're screwing me because I'm a foreigner, and they know it. When the bill arrives, under the coffee item, the sum adds up to only a few cents. It's the law of the "free refill"! In America, you order a drink and you are entitled to a full glass of it until you say enough, until you can't take it anymore, or until you pay the bill and leave—if you can still get your weight off the chair and stand on your legs, that is.

I could be wrong, but I think that, pointing the finger at the food in front of me that I did not have the strength to finish, Laverne is asking if I want to take it to go. Is she out of her mind? Perhaps she mistook me for a beggar! I blush and even if I am not entirely clear on what the word "leftovers" means, I shake my head resolutely—No, no, no, no, thank you, you're mistaken!—and leave both a very generous tip and the Diner.

I'm not going to tell Brett & Galina that I didn't put my capitalist money to work for a single minority entrepreneur! That I contributed to the implosion of the planet with my not-so-vegan breakfast. Or it could be the end of *our* friendship for good. I don't set foot in a museum or even obliquely look at a single one of the tourist guidebooks they lend me. I'm just not that kind of tourist. Brett wouldn't talk to me anymore if he knew.

Instead, I walk. I consume my feet, insatiable for these streetscapes and the energy vibrating in the air. I'm in a womb, I reached a safe haven, *I am home.* I fully feel it as soon as I eye the Statue of Liberty. I'm not *at* the Statue of Liberty, which is rather ugly per se. No, I just see it in passing. When I reach the southernmost tip of the island, I find out that the city offers those who live on some island off of Manhattan a ferryboat service that shuttles back and forth every thirty minutes and on its path it sails by the famous lady with the torch and its neighboring hallmark, Ellis Island. I am perfectly happy to sit on this ferry, with other commuters, enjoying the cold wind, the stench of oil, the sound of the waves. The only thing one can envy those wretched masses from the past who landed here by boat is certainly this first view they got of New York. The skyline that seems to emerge from the waters, imposing, signaling with sparks of glittering silver the promise of a future. What a pity that immigrants' first impression today is but a frigid airport.

Standing on the dock aft, I do not even notice the biting temperature, so overwhelmed am I by the way what enters my eyes shakes my soul to the core. I dare not blink. Next to me, a small lady with a large head of bristly black hair and penetrating green eyes touches my arm lightly and begins to narrate, as if this were part of the deal, in a markedly Yiddish accent: "We came after the war. When we heard that we were about to arrive, I came out of the cabin and saw this"—she points to the Manhattan skyline that fills up to burst the horizon—"I will never forget it. Since then, once a year, every summer, I force my family to take the ferry. My children never complained about it. And now they bring their children. I promised myself to make this trip at least once a year to remember the blessing that touched us." My eyes meet hers: and together with this grandiose scene, we also take in the past and the future. I tell myself that were I to live here, I would take the ferry on today's date, every year, to remember. In fact, I would do more: I would take the ferry and tell everyone about this lady, so that this lady's story does not die. "You see, I lost the whole family at Bergen-Belsen," she adds.

I return to the base after 10 hours, 7½ miles, or about 12 kilometers one way (I walked both ways). At this point, however, I have no doubt: this is my home. It's not because of Hollywood or the 1970s cultural influences. There is something else in this connection, nay, this cosmic attraction between me and New York City. Yes to the PhD, and I'll do it at Columbia. It is decided.

Inevitably, the week ends. Israel awaits me and so does an indefinite future. I leave. Strangely enough, I'm not sad. I feel that this visit has helped me: it measures a start, not a finale. *Veni Vidi Vici*. I have come, I have seen. I will work on the victory later. It's not *Arrivederci*, but *Ci vediamo*.

It's Sunday. On Sundays, at the crack of dawn, Brett & Galina join their cycling group and bike their way along large and small interstate routes, through naturalistic areas, along harsh coastal or mountain tracks. It is perfectly right that they should keep their rendezvous and not make an exception today just because I am here *and* leaving. Yesterday evening, they gave me instructions on how to safely lock, where to leave the keys, how to call the shuttle that will take me back to JFK for a mere few dollars. I am alone in their rather overheated studio apartment, a bit bored and with no idea how to kill time. And most of all, I am hungry. I'm really hungry. Everything is so pleasantly quiet. Who would have thought New York can be quiet? This is not part of the myth. How strange being here, like a package abandoned to its own destiny. I imagine them with their friends, weightless (no loads or luggage), in total freedom, with their shaved heads, in perfect shape, all muscles, no fat, whizzing on the road in single file, each an island, total independence. I wouldn't have become a cyclist, all steel muscles, useful clothes and practical shearing, for Brett's love. He did well not to choose me. It is totally worth it, for the love of Galina, to give up being an artist, to work and pay rent. I feel lonely. But when I live here, I will also have my circle of friends: they will be conversationalists who smoke, drink, and make love in an inconsiderately promiscuous way, occasionally retreating to some artist colony where they'll invite me too, or they'll have beach houses where we will spend wonderful summers and holidays all together. It will be just like *The Big Chill* (Marvin Gaye's *Ooh, ooh, I bet you're wond'ring how I knew* in the background included), the film that marked my imagination and my love for America, perhaps more than any other.

I notice the yellow pages on the telephone shelf. I look for pizza. The volume is gigantic and full of advertisements and unfamiliar entries: I do not know how to navigate this sea of images, promises, addresses that are obscure to me. I dial a random number from what seems the right section. The first ring hasn't finished echoing when someone picks up. An abrupt, hurried voice, clearly of someone who has no time nor patience for my hesitations and rhetorical formulas: "Excuse me, good morning . . ." "What do you want?" "I would like to know if by any chance you also deliver to home addresses and if I could place an order by telephone because . . ." "Yup, what do you want?" Brief but evidently terrified pause on my part. He went straight to the point. "I don't have a menu in front of me . . . so, I'll have to ask, do you have . . . ?" "Pizza." "Right," I agree stupidly. I sense that the guy is busy, he has no time to teach the latest human arrival (they call it "greenhorn" over here) the rules of the game. "Don't worry, people learn by themselves," he probably tells himself a million times a day to avoid empathizing with the rest of humanity." No one taught *you* nothing. Where was the kindness when you had to figure it all out on your own?"

"A pizza, please," I say.

"Regular," the pizza chef decides for me. (Regular . . . *regolare* . . . in the sense that it is not *irregolare*, irregular, rhomboid?) "Small, medium, or large?" he inquires. There, now he speaks the language of my empty belly! I giggle, I relax, I feel confidence grow in me for my ability to function in an unknown world: I am very hungry.

"A really big one, please." I think of the little pizzas, a few centimeters in diameter, shrew restaurant owners in Rome serve their baffled customers.

"Extra large, for the young lady, then" he says as he probably writes it down. Me and this dude are practically bonding by now.

"And loads of mozzarella," I venture, daringly. This is paradise, and I reached it without having to die. Absolutely ideal! I remember Peppinella Trattoria, in Rome, with its tables dressed with white paper, cloth napkins, the simple grub always perfect. It was my family's favorite destination: *nonna* Binde, my grandmother, offered us dinner at Peppinella's, on the 27th of each month, the day she collected her pension money. Then we all congregated there for birthdays, anniversaries, meetups with friends—any excuse was good to go to Peppinella's, where the *maestro* at the oven, Eugenio, made a special pizza just for me, and after many years of frequentation, the owner included it on the menu: Pizza Fania. To those who asked, she explained in tight dialect, "It's named after the daughter of Mr. Mario, the gentleman who plays the trumpet: it's basically a pizza margherita with lots of cheese." Eugenio was the rarity, not the rule: ask for any variation to a dish in a Roman restaurant and you are inviting the owner to treat you in the vilest of ways: "Sure, because you're special! Yeah, we'll improvise, no problem, we always custom-make our dishes for the first asshole who comes around," they'll tell you either with words or facial expressions. Instead, seemingly, "extra mozzarella" is a possibility contemplated by the order of things in the Bronx. I say the Bronx, because that's where my friend here, my pie whisperer, is answering from. Evidently, I must have called outside the area where I'm staying, although, undeterred, the guy immediately cuts me short saying that it's not a problem and they deliver in Manhattan as well. I give him the address and I wait. Meanwhile, now that I have familiarized myself with operating the phone, I also call a taxi. (I don't know exactly what a shuttle is: but I understood it's not a taxi.)

Someone rings the downstairs bell: "Delivery!" I hear a man's yell made metallic by the old-fashioned intercom. I buzz him in and wait for the elevator to arrive, as I start wondering whether this is not one of those fatal mistakes about which Brett & Galina warned me: I do not remember, did they say anything about the mortality rate for home deliveries? Too late. The elevator doors open, the delivery man is here. I drop the money I hold in my hands. My fingers aren't functioning properly, my knees bend under me, my mind and body are exclusively focused on one function and one function only: the gaze. A young man, muscular, stocky, in comfortable clothes, emerges from the elevator with a square cardboard box in his arms measuring at least 150 centimeters per side. "24 inches, regular, extra cheese?" The delivery man asks and thrusts the monster box at me. I nod with my head because words do not come out. If I do not hurry and stretch out my arms, as if to catch a child who just dropped from a tenth-floor terrace toward the sidewalk, the delivery guy would let the pizza plunge on the ground—without checking if I'm ready to take it or not (*wow, they are seriously in a hurry here*). That's how you learn in New York: quickly or too bad for you. I barricade myself inside (deadbolt, hasp latch and padlocks) just as Brett & Galina request, and balancing the enormous weight of this hot box in my hands, I step toward the only available room.

Where do I put this box now? I'm afraid to damage something. And they have no dining furniture. I sit on the floor; the box in front of me; I open it. *Mamma mia!* I clap my hands at the sight of this masterpiece. I talk to this pizza, I introduce myself, I keep clapping like a child or a gravely demented adult. I have never seen so much melted mozzarella in my life. The round pie is presliced to surgical precision, and each slice is a huge triangle, which I do not "bring" as much as "lower" from above into my mouth, like a sword swallower . . . if the sword were a cheese-topped Damascus cleaver. It's getting ugly. Oil everywhere. Hands red with sauce. God, this is good!! I am making love to this thing! They even put a mini plastic "table" in the middle of it . . . It takes me a moment to understand: it stops the flap of the box from collapsing over the cheese. Haven't I known all along that I am born for New York?

After about a slice and a half, totaling eight hundred pounds of carbs and fats, I slip into a digestive coma. I don't want to leave my pizza, but I can't pack it either. It's hands down the best pizza I've ever had in . . . *Driiii-nnnng!* They ring again. "Who is it?" "You call a taxi?" My suitcases are ready, but I am covered in grease. I have cheese debris between my teeth, and above all—ABOVE ALL—I have a giant box with a ton of uneaten pizza and a 2-liter bottle of Coca-Cola (an homage from the Bronx guy to the young lady who will beat the pizza-binging record of all times). Brett & Galina ought never, ever, to find out. If they do, my already feeble reputation with them would be ruined.

I grab my suitcases, I hang souvenir bags from my shoulders, I shove the unopened Coke into the fridge, irreparably contaminating my friends' psycho-alimentary environment, I close the pizza box, that is by now soaked in food juices, and I head downstairs. I signal the taxi driver to wait a second while I run to the nearest garbage can. I smile my goodbyes to my pizza. My heart is bursting with joy. I will come back. If anything, to order one more time before I die a pizza delivery from the Bronx. I gently deposit the box above the bin . . . not inside of it, because its diameter is infinitely smaller than this pizza container. As I walk to the car, I turn to look one last time at that bundle of indigestible joy and see that a homeless man has already approached the trash can, is opening the box and makes the same face I must have made earlier: he lights up in jubilant disbelief. There it is, my kindred spirit, by a trash can, at the end of my first week in Manhattan. I'll take it.

# PART 2

# Bitter Herbs

# 4

Polonsky calls again at the kibbutz to pressure me to accept Brandeis's offer. I think hard. I am a coffee drinker with no tea leaves to read. An inner voice tells me that until I receive a definitive answer from the New York universities I applied to, I shouldn't accept other invitations . . . that if it is not New York, it's a no deal. Deep down something tells me to wait. But my generation in Italy was not brought up believing in "inner wisdom" or the "power of the universe." I grew up in an environment of pure madness, at the center of which stood like the Chimera my multifaceted vengeful mother. Any chance to escape can't be worse than a life sentence on the same continent with my mother, I tell myself. The only exception being where I just escaped to Israel, that is, where terrorists blow up busses every day and death is all around. Here I am a terrified soldier; at home I am a terrified prisoner. A chance is exactly what Polonsky is offering me, beating to it Columbia University and New York University which have not yet replied. I have not yet learned that, although the end justifies the means, the means is more important than the end and we must concentrate on the means more than anything else, because *how* we get to an end is more vital than arriving there. Fleeing one's family and one's world at all costs is the wrong parameter for making good decisions. Add to this my propensity to grab every opportunity that comes around, to accept everything for fear that in the selection process I may end up discarding precisely the one thing I should have held tightly instead. The one thing. Which one is the one thing?

I do not listen to the inner voice. On the contrary, I believe that if my friend Galina thinks that this offer by Brandeis is the most extraordinary thing that can happen to me, it must be so: I must trust her. I have to trust her, since I do not know whether I can trust myself and certainly I oughtn't pay heed to the siren song, to the objective and dispassionate opinions of my relatives. I want my future now. I am twenty-five; I am fed up with the mental and physical violence that overshadows everything—from the microworld of family to the entire globe.

I do not listen to the inner voice.

August 14, 1996. At the Leonardo Da Vinci airport, I hug mom and dad. One violin, a carry-on bag, three checked suitcases (and fourteen boxes of books that will arrive in three weeks by boat to an address not yet determined), I am flying to Boston, not New York.

The Bostonians are often thought of as the founding fathers of the nation (though not by Virginians). The real deal in American aristocracy. No doubt they are real, but it seems to me that they all look like Irish rascals, or failed boxers, or drunken laborers who lost their jobs ten days ago. Henry James, returning to Boston in 1904, comments sourly on the appalling procession of the populace strolling (like he was) in the Boston Common on Sundays: "For no sound of English, in a single instance, escaped their lips; the greater number spoke a rude form of Italian, the others some outland dialect unknown to me . . . No note of any shade of American speech struck my ear . . . the people before me were gross aliens to a man, and they were in a serene and triumphant possession." In short, nothing to do with his homogeneous Boston of better times, James assures us. Would James see me too as a gross alien? I would like to reassure him that I do not feel comfortable—neither triumphant nor serene.

The American élite, what people here call "old stock" (the opposite of our *nouveaux riches*), is geographically associated with the state of Virginia, the Carolinas, *and* Boston. While everyone arrived in patched-up caravels or oxygen-free ship's holds as part of the malnourished and unwashed multitudes, the élites' ancestors navigated comfortably on beautiful vessels, served with white gloves, and a hand stretched out to help them off at the docking— so that their steps would be secure from the first. Since then, they have never stopped being *in cima,* on top of everyone else.

Many of these patricians have periodically lost face, especially because of the political kerfuffle between America and England, later because of that moral lapse known as slavery, then because of the snafu between secessionists and Yankees, and so on. But their names are still there, and so are their possessions. Inevitably, and not without the notables' resistance, newer families eventually made it into the ivory tower, people of lesser "stock," in short, *brodaglia* (watery broth)—people like the Rockefellers, regarded with great disdain at first and called out as vulgar peddlers. But what is *nouveau riche* today, becomes old money a century later. The Rockefellers, the Vanderbilts, the Astors made their fortune in America in the nineteenth century, but they also made America's fortune. Their names are engraved wherever their pockets helped erect something: buildings, parks, hospitals, museum wings, laboratories, orphanages, bridges, streets, libraries, and even dishes—General Lee's cake, rice and apricots *à la* Jefferson, and eggs Benedict, commissioned at the Waldorf Hotel in New York one morning in 1894 by a millionaire to rid himself of a massive hangover—and all this to monumentalize their passage through history forever.

Meanwhile, I have nowhere to live. Apart from the first few nights in a quaint Back Bay hotel.

I wonder why a city on the Charles River isn't called Charleston or Charlestown. Boston has its name because of an English Pilgrim who namesaked it after the place he hailed from. Strange, considering that he had escaped his own town to save his neck from the religious persecutions in the first Boston: I would have called it at most Great Boston, to distinguish it implicitly from the "insignificant Boston," out of contempt for the compatriots who had thrown me out. The original British Boston (of which, let's face it, no one has ever heard) still exists, 150 kilometers from London, in Lincolnshire: it would be funny if the great President Lincoln got his name from the English region. But it's just a happenstance of history and of onomastics.

In any case, the American Boston was born in 1630, only ten years after 102 Pilgrims disembarked from the Mayflower. It is said that the captain of the Mayflower was lost, so he made a quick decision to get everyone on land as soon as possible rather than risking staying afloat without finding Virginia where they were originally headed. The haste of this decision was determined by the fact that the crew had run out of beer—which the pious albeit not abstemious Puritans onboard preferred to water and drank by the gallons every day, children included. At that point, the captain could see clearly that his sailors, now parched and exhausted by months of navigation in the company of arrogant zealots, would have no scruples about mutinying if they had to face another day without the comfort of alcohol. In short, the story of the new America, the white one, was christened with a mug of amber brew.

Although I missed it on my first visit to Boston, Faneuil Hall is quite a central part of this town's identity and an embodiment of patriotic pride: often referred to, a dash pompously, as "The Cradle of Freedom," it was erected in 1742 and it is in this building that Samuel Adams and other patriots set the masses' hearts afire with their anti-English, anti-monarchical discourses, until the fuse of the Revolution finally reached the powder keg . . . an inexplicably creepy building. At some point in history, Faneuil Hall burned down but unfortunately it was rescued and patched up. They restored its original name too, even though Mr. Faneuil, a champion of democracy and liberty, who generously donated his money to erect this building with the intention of providing the worthy citizens of Boston with a public space in which to discuss and express themselves democratically, had himself made that money trading in slaves.

Boston is disliked by most people; perhaps because it's a bit snobbish, with its Harvard, its Paul Revere, its dusty history—Americans do not seem big fans of the past. If you came to Boston during the colonial times, sooner than later you'd end up eating beans cooked for hours in a dense molasses: so the rest of America jumped on the opportunity to nickname this hub of sophistication, "Beantown." Not a compliment.

During my one-day visit more than a year ago, I did not realize that Boston, erected on the Shawmut Peninsula, is surrounded by water. Between the seventeenth and eighteenth centuries, it became not only the largest city in New England but a port and a vital industrial center for the whole nation, with thousands of people flocking here to seek refuge, work, a new chance, and escape from slavery. I feel I have nothing in common with this long line of migrants that winds up along history's four-hundred-year-long umbilical cord: could I be wrong? Nevertheless, Boston's human and urban profile have not radically changed in the last two centuries, no matter what Henry James thought. And its two main classes remain the proletariat and the "aristocracy" —with almost nothing in between. The rich still live where they have always lived: in the elegant and spacious, green and bucolic, neighborhoods of Back Bay and Cambridge. And the others? I'm afraid I am about to find out empirically by myself.

It took me a while to understand why everyone corrects me when I call the whole city drawn on my metro map Boston. I must have been wrong all my life for saying Boston, New York, Chicago. I learn the hard way (kind correction after unkind correction after annoyed correction) that Boston and New York are a mosaic of "mini-towns" in their own right. That is, "Boston" is only part of a vast urban entity that includes the city of Cambridge, Brookline (*no foreigner wouldn't pronounce this Brooklyn!*), Watertown, Boston proper, Newton, Somerville, and so on, just as "New York" is made up of five boroughs: Manhattan, Bronx, Queens, Brooklyn (*Jeez!*), and Staten Island. (Not to mention that the appellation New York means New York State, not Manhattan, as the rest of the world thinks.). *How am I supposed to know all this beforehand? How not to make a fool of myself every time I open my mouth here?* If at a party you introduce a friend who lives and works at Harvard saying "McShmo here is from Boston," he will correct you calmly, but shooting one eyebrow up to his hairline, with "I'm from Cambridge." If snobbism were a sound, it would be this one word: Cambridge. McShmo says Cambridge but he is actually implying "Harvard": if it only made sense to say "I am from Harvard," I am sure these people would say it. That's why no one likes Beantown.

Another big warning for foreigners: Don't assume (foolishly) that just because a town is famous all over the world, it must be a capital. Americans choose their states' capitals based on their equidistance from the borders of their respective state. Yes, I know, no one else does this: it's as if, despite the center of commerce, education, medicine, and the arts being in New Delhi, Asarganj were the capital of India. (*Is it because America is such a young country, and they don't know how to do things yet? Why don't they ask around?*)

Louisa May Alcott grew up in Boston. Now that I see with my own eyes the colorful brick houses, on four levels, along the tree-lined avenues of the

Back Bay area, with chimneys on top of the gray roofs and skylights that illuminate the mysterious habitable attics, I understand from where Alcott drew inspiration for her refined environments, in which girls keep a pristine purity despite their rebellions . . . girls who can afford to put Virtue before Money because . . . of money is there aplenty.

Boston was founded in 1630; the first house was constructed in Cambridge in 1631. Where the newcomers slept that whole first year, I have no idea. I land at Logan International Airport, not at Plymouth via the Mayflower but neither at some dingy bus station turned makeshift homeless shelter. Where I will sleep during this first year here, I have no idea.

Here I am. Disoriented and with all the possible imaginable paths unfolding before me. Which one do I take?

There is only one thing to do. Put one foot in front of the other and . . . *Uno due, uno due, forward.*

I'm back on Brandeis soil. This time around it is not for a one-day visit, this time around I take public transportation: I must get into the habit of acting like a local. It takes a while to reach the campus, because Brandeis is far outside the boundaries of the actual city. At breakfast, I study the situation: I'll take this bus, clearly marked on the map in front of me; I see that I'll have to switch to a different one at Newton Corner, and after that the map loses all traces of what I think is the last bus to Brandeis. No need to panic, I will follow step by step the directions contained in the welcome package that the university sent me a couple of months beforehand in anticipation of my arrival and my complete disorientation. In fact, today is Orientation Day, which means that someone will bring the arriving students on a tour of the entire university, someone will take pictures for our identity cards, and someone else will give us a two-hour workshop about rules and regulations, and from what I understand we will be offered lunch. Fear mounts. On second thought, it may be prudent to call a taxi today.

I arrive on time (cab money well spent) and find a festive atmosphere: it's as if the entire university were looking forward to meeting us, as if they had been holding their breath expectantly until now. Everyone knows exactly what to do and what to say: they behave gracefully, they have every imaginable piece of information at the tip of their finger, no one appears stressed or worried. They smile and are extremely accessible: when our guide (another student volunteering for this role) shows us the main offices, the secretaries hop up from their chairs ecstatic to welcome us and shake our hands. They tell us that "We are here for anything you need." I am stunned, incredulous. It feels as if I was transported into some high-definition science fiction movie. Maybe these are automatons programmed to appease the Earther that would otherwise freak out if she saw the real shape of the aliens under the mask. (The only unexpected element is that they do not wear white coats here.) I mentally wink at my literary soulmate, Gregor Samsa.

Of La Sapienza University, I remember an infinite labyrinth of abysmal corridors: and, during the exam sessions, these corridors packed with students bivouacked on the floor, noisy, messy, waiting for their name to be called. Evanescent pieces of papers, handwritten, pinned on some dirty wall with fundamental information scribbled on them about, I don't know, the day and time *your* name will be called by the examining commission or the fact that the day and time indicated on a previous illegible scrap of paper had been changed. I remember the hours spent queuing at the registration office, hoping to reach the tiny window behind which the state employee at the desk could arbitrarily and at any point decide it's time to leave and shut his service window closed. A truly Kafkaesque hell.

I remember my very first experience at the Departimento di Lettere (Italian Department)—it must have been late August. I recall being very excited on the way to the very first university lecture of my life. It was Asor Rosa's class: I arrived and found the *aula magna* (the grandest lecture hall) cordoned off, with a sign "Tutto Pieno" (Full). All the seats had been taken. But the lesson had not even started, there was not a living soul around. I was early. A janitor who was propping himself up sleepily on a wooden broom explained to me that, for a tip, he could reserve a seat for me in the room next time. He told me that that was how everyone else did it: there were people who showed up at the most absurd hours of the night and taped a piece of paper with their name on a chair to claim it. But only a "well oiled" janitor had the ultimate power to swap, unglue, make appear or disappear those "reservation" notes. I left and never went back. I did the entire university track without ever following a single lesson in person. (The regulations allowed for such arrangement, and I availed myself of my right to not stoop low enough to bribe the broom personnel for a seat in a classroom.)

The last time I was at La Sapienza was the day of my dissertation defense. A family contingent was there in the audience. My father, overwhelmed by emotions and happiness, gave (on request) 100,000 lire to a random guy standing in the corridor outside the defense room who had assured him that *it* was the official procedure for obtaining a printed copy of my diploma (that dad could later proudly frame and show everyone). The official procedure. To date, almost three decades later, we have never obtained the printed copy of my university degree. Those were the early 1990s, and this was the sad state of La Sapienza's administration: a surreal maze designed by Hieronymus Bosch, a mammoth system whose individual parts were all broken or corrupted. I took all exams as a "nonattending student." I lived in Poland at the time and returned to Rome a few weeks before the exam sessions to prepare. I always passed with flying colors.

Except once: The exam was on theater history with Professor Santini. A success: I had very much loved the dozens of books assigned, and I had been able to carry on an intelligent, coherent, interesting, inspiring conversation with the examiner, proposing at every turn original conclusions of my own. I had answered everything. I had dazzled the examiner. She told me, in fact, that I had just earned myself a 30 *cum laude*—the highest possible grade. The university had recently switched to a digital system and our old grade books—physical booklets in which the various professors scribbled their grade by hand at the end of an exam—had been replaced by hi-tech electronic cards that the examiners scanned on their computers getting immediate access to the entire academic history of the student in front of them. Santini inserted my electronic card in the computer reader to type in my mark, looked at my records, and said, "Ah, I see . . . You got only 30s and 30s *cum laude*. An exemplary student. Then it is time to teach you a little humility. 27." I stood there, frozen in place. It took me a moment to realize that, in the noisy room where so many were being grilled by various other examiners, a grave silence had fallen all around me: everyone had heard her. The students, Santini's colleagues . . . everybody was stunned, heads lowered, no one dared look at me—perhaps for fear of contracting the invisible toxicity that had just enveloped me. Her colleagues stared at her as if to say, "Come on, you can't be serious!"

Neither opposing her nor showing my tears, I took back the electronic card she handed me and headed toward the exit; I might have peed myself, I can't tell. The shock was too great. The students standing by the door and along the corridor whispered kind words of encouragement as I filed past them, but I could not react. This is without a doubt the most vivid memory I have of my days at La Sapienza. And in a certain way, this incident faithfully reflects a general atmosphere that applied at the time to all areas of life in my country. Life in Italy was without appeal: whatever happens to you cannot be disputed, you accept the worst as a fait accompli because you're taught from a very young age, even if not in so many words, that at the end of the long corridor of your existence, through which you struggle in the dark to find your footing, there lies not the door you expect, but a wall, or another stretch of corridor, less illuminated even than the previous one.

Brandeis hits me as a very bright place. Maybe it's because of the green hills on which it is spread out, or its buildings with large windows; no locks at the doors; no cordoned-off classrooms; giant metal signs properly affixed at each entrance, in every hallway, next to the elevators, above doors, that indicate where to find the people or places you need to find. Here people do not conceal themselves behind a witless bureaucracy that entitles them to get away with murder, here people sit behind modern desks, in offices cheerfully decorated with plants, and with an inviting coffee aroma lingering in the air on every floor—because every floor has a small refreshments area with a pot of free coffee available to whoever desires a cup. There are modern elevators that work, without cigarette butts on the ground or push buttons scorched with cigarette lighters. And only now do I understand why people had thought I was crazy when, on my first visit, I got so excited over a squirrel. They are everywhere. They are the equivalent of stray cats at the Roman Imperial Fora . . . only less approachable.

The entire campus is in bubbly ferment, students enjoy their time here together, they learn, socialize, experiment with life. I so wish to edge in, to become part of this human landscape. The place is plastered with flyers, posters, post-its, announcements of all kinds. Courses, events, parties, study groups, support groups, reading groups, sport groups, cooking groups, pet-owners groups, animals-lovers and animals-eating groups, but also invitations to join music bands of all genres—from classical orchestras to jazz duos. In particular, my eyes fall every time on notices regarding an association called Hadassah— clearly for women. I read "Feminism" between the lines. I can't put my finger on what it really means to be a feminist: equality, work, freedom, abortion, divorce . . . Sure. But where do these miracles come from? It is more likely that storks bring them than men spontaneously dispense them to women.

I think of Inferno, who's still pestering me with his sex calls and threatens to ask the magazine to send him to America to cover this year's presidential elections, and who defines as "lesbicona" (ugly dike) every woman with a voice—from Oriana Fallaci to Golda Meir to Empress Maria Theresa. I suspect he throws the epithet at all those who hang up on him. I am not a *lesbicona:* I still let him wank on the phone. But despite what I say (parroting my mother), I am not a feminist either. The internalized echo of centuries of men booing (before stoning) women reverberates in me . . . I join Hadassah.

I also enroll in a program called Women's and Gender Studies. Never heard of it before. We don't even have the word for "gender" in Italian, other than as a grammatical concept. The crates of books finally arrived from Rome. Before I left, I grabbed, without much of a plan, all my Natalia Ginzburg, thankfully. There is also Simone de Beauvoir. And Eliza Orzeszkowa. Come to think of it, maybe I did not choose entirely at random, maybe the universe had already fated this PhD to turn into an opportunity for me to rediscover women, to find my way to feminism, to celebrate us. Screw men! (*If only.*)

Brandeis offers free internet: it is a telematic system with which you can do digital research, but more importantly if someone has the right programs on their computer, they can write to each other in real time. I think they call this electronic post or electronic mail. They already assigned me a user ID (*Id . . . as in Id, Ego and Superego? No idea, but I nod as if I knew what this one-hundredth acronym stands for*). This ID (not pronounced *eed* apparently) turns out to be the key to accessing Brandeis's computer system. I absolutely must tell everyone in Italy! They must do this internet thing! It's so cool. No more expensive calls at inopportune hours. (God, could this rid me of the phone wanker?) This is the future! My ideal future in any event: a system that allows me to stay here without feeling completely alienated from the people I left behind.

I immediately propose the internet to everyone back home.

My old friends make fun of me and, although they do not understand what I'm talking about, they tease me for my xeno-loving and futuristic internationalism *à outrance*: "Rieccola con le americanate!" (Here she goes again, with her *America-knows-best* ideas!) My father is the most recalcitrant: "No! What's this new fad you got into your head now? Daddy prefers to talk to you over the phone, to hear your voice. We are too old, we don't need this stuff." Perhaps I'd better alienate myself from these people. Much healthier. Perhaps it's better if they never discover the internet.

It is 1996. Computer screens are black, the words you type are white, one typeface for all. To connect to the internet, they use a dial-up modem that goes something like this as it dials itself in: *teee teee teee teee teeeeeee . . . shteebong shteebong!* You are online.

I do not own a computer, but this doesn't faze me because I can use the machines the university puts at my disposal and those at the public libraries throughout Boston. Public libraries are open seven days a week until late at night: this would make my researcher friends back home weep tears of envy and disbelief. The university here in America is not a place where one enters with leaden feet, heart apprehensively beating in one's throat, hoping to make it out having suffered the least possible humiliation. Here university is the intellect's playground, a grand laboratory of thought: everything is set in place to cater to the students' needs, it all orbits around them. I am not used to this yet; I still have massive palpitations every time I approach the entrance.

One does not easily scrub from one's subconscious over twenty years of a medieval regime. Is one supposed to flirt with the professor, as a good-will investment? Where's the trick? They say that in order to pass a course you have to write a final paper. Are we sure that's how everybody does it? I must figure out as quickly as possible if there isn't a special "course" to follow (*wink wink*) to ensure the desired results . . . If I need a *raccomandazione* (such a loaded concept in my language) to get things done, I'm done for. Recommendation and its sister *raccomandazione* were separated at birth: one was adopted by the

English language and the other by the Mafia. *Raccomandazione* in Italian is that essential patronage without which no one can make it in a social order like ours entirely hinged on clientelism. Coming from a family of perfect Nobodies, I have never been on the receiving end of a *raccomandazione*. I came here without one: but can I keep going without that special blessing that only an influential protector can bestow on my future? I'm fretful: I try to take deep breaths, to tell myself "what you see is what you get" (nothing up their sleeves, magicians say), but I cannot believe it; there must be some passage I skipped, a secret map I didn't receive of the mines in this field I unsteadily walk on . . . as soon as I put my foot in the wrong spot, it's the end. If indeed "what I see is what I get" then this would be *il paese del Bengodi* (Pinocchio's Shangri-la): a place where, if you follow the rules, if you put one foot in front of the other, you simply discover that you are able to walk, without having to crawl, and without having to duck behind the bushes to avoid invisible, unexpected snipers. This is simply "a university." I wasn't prepared for "simply."

Brandeis was built in one of the worst and economically most devastated areas of Boston, Waltham. Waltham's wealth used to come from its industries; but with the change in production, foreign investments, and other socioeconomic transformations, at one point it lost everything, unemployment pushed the workers to earn their bread elsewhere, and Waltham became a ghost town of sorts, with empty, barred buildings. I wouldn't live here if my life depended on it. However, its famous university remained. The campus is an expanse of green hills and classroom and office buildings that recall the blocky architecture of the Hebrew University in Jerusalem, but without the rosy stones characteristic of the holy city. To be fair, it is not geography that makes a place: Brandeis was not built on these hills, or in the ugly and forlorn town of Waltham, nor along an old railroad stretch, or forty-five miles from Cambridge . . . these are only physical coordinates that per se don't signify much: Brandeis is not built in a place but on an ethos. A bit like America: it is not so much the sum of its individual geographical points, but rather the unshakable fabric of its moral identity.

After the Holocaust, the surviving Jews rushed to make two urgent things: a State in the Middle East (*see Bible for details*) and a university in America, one without *numerus clausus* against them like Harvard had; a liberal and nondenominational university, with the Hebrew motto stamped on its elegant seal: "Emet" (Truth). In 1948, its founder, Abraham Sachar, chose for this new institution the name of a man of integrity, who had won the esteem of the entire nation, the first Jewish associate justice on the Supreme Court, Louis Brandeis. Open to all students, but attended disproportionately by Jews, Brandeis University follows the Jewish calendar as far as holidays (innumerous) and above all it follows the ethical dictates of Judaism. Liberal, humanitarian, humanistic, egalitarian, secular, pacifistic, inclusionist, with the imprimatur of that Jewish culture that appreciates and protects the dialectical *pilpul* to arrive, if not to an agreement, at least to a better understanding of each other's differences . . . and to live with them. That same culture—half utopian, half materialistic—through which Jews from the *shtetlekh,* the rural villages of Galicia, Lithuania, Poland, brought to America a wave of rationalism and humor, of enlightened creativity and vital imagination, that the gray, self-restrained Anglo-Saxon culture needed as a cactus needs water in the desert. (*I think of the Jews of Italy . . . the fear, the discomfort, the camouflage . . . living in the certain knowledge of being hated.*)

Sometimes I think that it was especially the oppressed who gave the best to this nation. Not that the poor have more imagination than the wealthy— that's bollocks. I do not believe it is material poverty, but rather oppression that makes of people tireless fantasists. In the case of the Jews, for example, inspiration comes directly from the Jewish community—a desperate community, for most of history, but one in which the entire village takes responsibility for everybody's survival. Surrounded either by the walls of the ghettos or by the invisible walls of hatred, injustice, and betrayed trust, the Jews survive by turning the group into a single unit, keeping people attached to the community like limbs to the body, elaborating mental escapes when physical escapes are unattainable: from the mysticism of the Baal Shem Tov to the communism of Karl Marx, from the cinescapism of Hollywood to that of the Superman comics . . . all inventions of those who replace the material power (which they haven't got) with an imaginative power that frees the spirit of everyone.

That the poor are treated horribly everywhere is not news: it's an unbroken rule. However, to the starving immigrants, whose fingertips were consumed by the soil and burnt by the sun, whose cracked skins on their cheeks made them look like scared animals on the run, America—maybe also with a good thrashing every now and then, let us have no illusions—ultimately said: "Let me see what you can do." Who has ever heard such a thing where I come from?

I know something about Jewish imagination. I know how to recognize at least its main ingredients. Recipe: Galician meadows and a dash of Hungarian steppe, a handful of birch forests; mix together and dip in the mighty rivers of the Voltava or the Vistula, the Volga or the Danube. Jewish fantasy travels on magic letters. Each letter of the Hebrew alphabet contains all of Creation. Connected with the others, each letter gives life to secret combinations: for some, the formula obtained can be fatal if one can't stand it. The combination is happiness. The kind of happiness that comes at nobody's expense; a happiness married to justice. And riding an *alef* or a *gimmel*, clinging to a *kof* or a *lamed*, the Jew floats weightlessly in the air or on the ground, but never alone . . . always at a short distance from another Jew, on his own letter, because the combination is made up of people not just words, the magic of the alphabet per se is not enough. One must put compassion, intelligence, and humanity into the Logos; a quality that only the Created possesses and can use to shake the imperturbability of the Creator who, having abandoned His most trusted companion, Man, and His most beloved invention, the Word, is sulking all alone, in the far distance where the only existing sound is the hollow echo of His footsteps when, thoughtful and half-repentant for his crimes and bouts of anger, He paces back and forth through the dark and precious corridors of eternity.

*This* is the spirit of Brandeis.

In order to make a living, my department gives me a job that will justify a plump monthly check: I'll be a TA. (*Do they read it on my face that I have no idea what TA stands for?*) Even if I figured out what the acronym means, I still wouldn't know what kind of job it refers to, but never mind . . . no point in second-guessing myself: like a born impostor, I slip into these roles I understand nothing of and, with my intuitive antennas tuned in, I try to capture signals, every microscopic trace, any clue I can gather from the surrounding world that indicates how I must proceed. What if I ask too many questions and they realize I am not the person they need for this role? Practically choked by the fear this thought inspires, I keep silent, and I move forward blindly.

They make me fill out a huge pile of forms. I see now that bureaucracy, even in the most advanced country on earth, does not relent. I write incorrectly at least twenty times my date of birth. (In America, the month precedes the date, according to the same counter-world-wise logic that wants the thousands to be separated by a comma and the decimals by a period.) In all these forms, the word "race" constantly comes up. I had never thought of myself in terms of race before. Here, on the other hand, they don't miss an opportunity to ask you to identify and disclose yourself. I'm puzzled: a secretary asks if I need clarification and I explain that I do not know which box to check. "Caucasian," she suggests. I respond rather haughtily: "Caucasian? Dear lady, Italy ends nowhere near the Caucasus, even if you fold the map!" She squints and examines my face north-to-south and east-to-west: the only brown pigmentation on it is the copious freckles (not exactly an Azerbaijani complexion, I'd say) while the rest looks like a pale rag—in part due to the utterly unexpected conversation about race we are having. "White?" she asks out of a sense of rhetorical sarcasm, not because she doubts the accuracy of her blue eyes: "So, Caucasian," she checks the box for me with a flourish. It appears that Americans call White people Caucasian, despite the actual skin tone that characterizes the Euro-Asiatic regions. However, I do appreciate the kindness with which they treat you poorly here.

As part of the orientation program, there is also a workshop to attend in order to be prepared for the *actual* workshop scheduled for tomorrow. I participate in this pre-workshop or workshop on the workshop. I seemingly take notes: it's not meticulousness, it's that I am so scared that busying my fingers pretending to do something constructive is turning into the only constructive thing I can do. I understand around 60 percent of what is being said; a tide of new terms rises to my ears, and a great deal of them are insidious acronyms. Quietly, I continue to write in my notebook to give the impression of having the situation under control. It transpires that TA stands for teaching assistant. The trainer says that a TA is associated to a professor who lectures twice a week, while the TA meets once a week with the same group of students to clarify sibylline points, answer their questions, teach new material, and above all administer the exams and grade them. Fuck. So "assistant" does not mean the person who makes photocopies, perhaps a cup of tea, for the professor and rearranges his books on the shelves. I must teach a class of undergraduates. And I also learn the word "undergraduate."

Had I already learned at this point the expression "when the shit hits the fan," it would surely be the ideal moment to use it. Because now the crap is really flying in all directions and there is no angel in heaven that can help me from ending up covered in it from head to toe. Me, teaching? Now they'll find out that I am but a poseur, that they made a big mistake accepting me here, and they'll send me back home, to my father (*I could think of worse punishments*) and my mother (*here's one*). The thought that I could escape to Canada does cross my mind.

This first day started with a beautiful sun in the sky, welcoming smiles from welcoming folks, a positive energy through and through . . . and it quickly turned into a nightmare for my nerves. I realize that my life is truly no longer the same: its general parameters have radically changed. Like a flash of light, the memory of my last few years in Europe passes before my eyes. If I wished to be a translator (why not?), I was immediately offered a well-paid project to work on by this or that publishing house. Journalism? (why not?) I get a job at *Politicus*—to the tune of millions of lire per published piece. Should I switch to theater? No problem. I am invited to join Krzysztof Kieślowski, who is holding a seminar for drama students in Wrocław. And how about films? Why, just ask! And I end up on the set of a film by Nikita Mikhalkov (secret lover of a friend of mine fourty years his junior) who also brings along Miša Baryshnikov. A drink? See you all at *U zlatého tygra* (The Golden Tiger pub), where I'll be having a coffee while Bohumil Hrabal finishes his beer. Guess who lives next door to me in Krakow? Wisława Szymborska—who, by the way, praised my interpretation of her poems. She is my friend! There were dinners with Ryszard Kapuściński in Warsaw before he left for Africa and tapas with Roman Polanski in Spain. There was an insouciance to life that I sense will never manifest itself again, not here in America. Not for me. Back then, it was my home game. Played gingerly thanks to a sense of belonging as well as a network of who-knows-whom that I don't have in this new place.

Back there, I could risk falling, because I could only land on my feet. What's the worst that can happen, when you have your safety net in place to catch you? Even if the safety net was my parents and our troubled relationship.

Here I don't even have that. Here, I am a fish out of water, a trout stranded on the top of a mountain. Here it is about working hard, demonstrating what you're made of. And what am I made of? Part Mr. Magoo, part . . . jellyfish? In America, at Brandeis, they do not care about my aristocratic flair, the existential *je ne sais quoi,* the air of mystery that actually hides only one secret: the emptiness behind the mesmerizing façade. Here they demand proof; they want results; they apply transparency. I notice only now that none of the girls around me wears makeup, or stagy shoes, or diva leather bags. They wear eyeglasses, for goodness' sake! And they are unadorned, wrapped in large deforming T-shirts that don't require ironing, Bermuda shorts, not even a little showy ring. My mind rushes to the mountains of stuff I brought with me: I must have expatriated with more accessories, parfum bottles, and lace bralettes (Agent Provocateur, thank you very much) than these peers have seen in their whole lifetime. Here, rightly, they don't give two farthings about *looking* smart, they demand you prove you are. I'm about to throw up.

The semester begins and I marvel at the plasticity of human adaptability . . . specifically my own. I do not know how to read the campus map, and yet I get to my classrooms; I do not know the procedure to get a hold of textbooks, yet I stumble into the right place and receive a pile of books as if they were there ready to drop into my arms and no one else's; I don't know yet that they don't have the *quarto d'ora accademico* here (that very sweet deal based on which Professors, with capital Ps, are entitled to arrive as late to class as it suits them), yet I fortuitously arrive fifteen minutes earlier than I would in Italy and that means just in time. "Please, take a copy of the syllabus," says the professor, and I, who have never heard the word before, take the pile of stapled pages and make a mental note: "SYLLABUS." I also see that the marks here are not from 18 to 30, the totally arbitrary range used by Italian universities (18 being the worst, 30 the best), but F to A (passing through a crescendo of nuances —D, C, B . . . like a musical scale). Another mental note: "RELEARN EVERYTHING!" I make mental notes about everything, my brain is an overloaded bulletin board; not a thing looks familiar, but, instinctively, I gather that the only way not to be crushed by the new situation is to flow with it without offering resistance. I allow myself to be modeled by the surrounding forces: I absorb and bend malleably to the power of what's happening, from the manners to the language, to the accents and the attitude, from the architectural forms to the natural and human compositions. At home, I read the syllabus carefully. There are no oral exams, only papers (the exact opposite of what I was accustomed to). This may sound unthreatening to me if I were born here, but since I was not, it sounds utterly disturbing: what is a paper? The heart palpitates menacingly. I retch.

When it is time to deliver my first term paper, I have the foresight to go to the Writing Center to get it read over by a second pair of eyes. My work is returned to me unrecognizable. The predominant color on the page is red, just like in elementary school . . . except that I was an excellent pupil in elementary school. How did I get worse?

"It's not that your reasoning is invalid," expounds the graduate student, probably younger than me and certainly with less experience of writing and everything else: "It's that the reasoning is completely lost in a tangle of useless sentences, which do not serve the purpose of developing any additional ideas." *Ouch.*

"They embellish," I attempt a self-defense.

"They weigh everything down," she cruelly points out. She erased every parenthetical, all hypothetical conditionals and also every "We think, we believe, we suppose." "Who is the co-author of this work?" she disingenuously asks.

"I wrote it myself," I say proudly.

"So why 'we'?"

Once the nauseating humiliation has subsided, I sit down at an isolated library table where no one can as much as glance at my execrable typescript and review her corrections, line by line. I admit that if I removed the pomposity, the text would gain in fluidity and clarity . . . and modernity. I indeed have noticed that Americans do not speak like me. They do not use cheesy rhetorical forms of false modesty, self-criticism, and self-doubt. The American researcher does not "believe," he affirms. He "would (not) like to illustrate," he illustrates. He does not "think," he demonstrates by assuming that the interlocutors will agree, and if they don't, it would be due exclusively to a flaw in their mental processes and not in those of the author. In effect, Americans avoid expressing negative opinions, let alone doubts, about themselves and whatever regards them. Everything is positively superlative: the university campus, its distance from home, the teachers, the programs, the experiences in this or that class—even when they fail; the winter frost, the summer torridness, and when placed in front of an overwhelming monstrosity—a genocide, say, or the collapse of the planetary ecological system—first Americans emit the empathic bleating *mmmmmmmm,* visually marked by the arching of their eyebrows and the dropping of their razor-thin lips, but then their expression immediately lightens up again, they put that frown upside-down, and spot an angle that allows them to throw a brighter light on any such circumstances: "OK, but imagine the powerful memoirs by those who survived the massacres," or "OK, but I read that, at some point, relocating on Mars will be an option." Hurray.

"Negative" is the worst adjective you can attach to a person here: "you are so negative" equals to labeling you as toxic and therefore, in order to avoid the risk of contamination, one must, with good manners, jovially but positively avoid you.

The only ones who have no qualms in staring straight into the belly of that dark abyss Americans call negativity are foreigners. We foreign students are pretty negative about everything and cannot refrain from burdening everyone with our insecurities or sharing with others our comments. Americans cannot handle comments: comments are to Americans as rude as silence is to Italians. In any case, when foreign students get together, the most pressing theme of conversation is the green card. I appreciate how terrible it must be not to have a residence status for those poor souls who, should they be sent back home tomorrow, would face certain imprisonment, torture, death, or else infectious diseases eradicated in the First World but not back home. I discreetly keep to myself when these conversations occur, and they do often. I do not wish to flaunt my luck, completely random, as luck always is, to belong to a country that gets along very well with the United States and with which the whole visa thing is amnestied:

"I'm Italian, you see," I explain with elegant humility.

"It makes no difference!" A derisive chorus arises in response. "Even if you come from a country that does not require an entry visa to the United States, once you finish your PhD, if you do not have a green card, they'll throw you out after two weeks." No exceptions.

Gérard Depardieu's hurt-puppy-like expression as he tries to charm Andie MacDowell into becoming his accomplice in a marriage of convenience in the romantic comedy *Green Card* passes before my eyes. So that was true? I thought it was made up. I thought we were not supposed to believe Hollywood films!

"You get married or find a job where they accept to sponsor you" *Ah! Then there are other means: do not always be so defeatists, compañeros!* "But nobody sponsors you"—*blimey*—"American companies don't want to run the risk of paying thousands of dollars in legal fees to sponsor an employee who, as soon as he has the permanent status, resigns and . . . goodbye, fools!"

How to give this demoralizing piece of information a positive spin? Putting myself in step with American optimism, I find a solution: I will stop hanging out with foreigners and surround myself with Americans instead, both with the hope of finding a husband–sponsor and in order to keep away from funereal atmospheres.

In the morning, I often go to the library to write emails to a small group of correspondents I have from across the world: from America to Canada, Israel and Russia, absent Italy of course. I sit myself in the big main hall, at one of those long tables full of IBM monitors that look like huge interplanetary insects.

I am welcomed by a message from Galina. Brett & Galina write regularly, and receiving their virtual letters delights me to no end. This morning, among the thousand directives and warnings, Galina instructs me to get in touch with an acquaintance of hers who is a graduate student in my program and whom she and Brett think it's important I meet. Someone who passed their approval test: I approve. I answer immediately, grateful for the advice, but as I type I stumble into a word I'm not sure I am spelling correctly. I turn to a guy sitting to my right, and I ask a little abruptly, due to my haste, "Excuse me, how do you spell 'undoubtedly'?"

Americans never know how to place me, as I don't sound stereotypically Italian at all: New Zealand, South Africa, Kiribati? Taken aback, the young man, with a very intelligent face and a strong resemblance to actor Alec Baldwin, first smiles and then gives me the answer without letting transpire that he probably thinks I must be an idiot for not knowing something so basic. (*How did she get to study here?*)

"Thank you," I say cordially and swivel back to type the word correctly before I forget it again. But Alec Baldwin continues to look at me and smile: he sits there with his right index finger raised, as if asking for permission to ask a question. He solemnly waits for me to finish my message to Galina and then gently interjects: "Sorry," he begins, with that finger still raised in front of his face like someone who thinks long before revealing his ideas but also who is demanding total attention from the interlocutor. The interlocutor is me at the moment. And naturally I begin to fret a dash that he may be about to put me on the spot with some complex highly academic question which I will not be able to answer. "I could not help but pick up an accent. Where are you from?" I think a moment: what answer do I give him? I consider a white lie. What answer adheres best to either the truth or inner reality? Can I say Italy?—a country I don't identify with and I've been trying to escape since I can remember. Do I have the right to say Israel? After all, technically, I just left Israel to come here. (No, I have zero right.) Five years in Poland would perhaps authorize me to say Poland . . . not a chance. Sticking to the strictly biographical, I say: Rome.

"Are you Fania?"

I almost blurt out, "*Who the hell are you?*" in full aggression mode *à la Rome.* Instead, I nod, tentatively, as if I weren't that sure myself anymore. He is out of himself with amusement. "Do you know Galina?" he asks. My eyes grow wide. He points to the screen of his computer: "I was responding to her email right now! She told me about you and wanted me to contact you. I am Yonah."

I show him the email I was about to answer too and for which I needed the word "undoubtedly" as in "*undoubtedly, I'll have a chance to meet Yonah around.*" Undoubtedly. We shake hands: a remarkable, strong, loyal handshake.

This is how I meet Yonah Hausmann: thanks to Galina, and with her blessing. (In the end they managed to repay me.)

# 5

Yonah knows Galina because both are Jewish Studies scholars, and so they cross paths at conferences and other professional events. He hasn't met Brett in person yet. However, "I talked to him on the phone," Yonah explains, "and he told me that you and he were a couple once." I stare at him blankly. What turn could a conversation with Yonah have taken for Brett to feel compelled to throw in this obsolete piece of information? I'm pissed off—on my own, on Yonah's, and also on Galina's behalf who must have been next to him as Brett unnecessarily overshared. Yonah has a humorously mischievous look in his eyes . . . I like him.

We immediately fall in love. It would be absurd not to. We are perfect for each other. If there were a past life, in that one Yonah and I had to have been in love with each other already. I feel as if we've been chasing each other for centuries, and only at the end of the twentieth we finally got to live out the happy ending of our preordained fairy tale.

Yonah and I are Polonsky's pet students. He has placed great hopes in us: this is because, with him, we are the only two researchers who know Polish very well and intend to work on Poland's Jewry. During the years I was gingerly sashaying around Warsaw, playing a part in the last encore of its dying intelligentsia, Yonah was there doing the same thing. We never met in Warsaw; our roads never crossed, not even in the circles of foreign exiles among whom I had met Brett. I am from Rome, Yonah from Coronado Beach, California. We were both in Warsaw, and now both on the green hills of Waltham.

Yonah is the human equivalent of *They Can't Take That Away from Me* played by the Ted Rosenthal Trio. One of those melodies you recognize at the first note, and from the first phrase it puts you in a good mood and makes you feel happy and cozy.

We go out with his friends. We go shopping. We are almost always at this or that cinema. First film seen in Boston: *The Mirror Has Two Faces.* The selection this year is inexhaustible: *The English Patient, Fargo, Jerry Maguire, Hamlet* (with Kenneth Branagh enacting a Christological portrait of himself as Prince of Denmark), and *Trainspotting.*

We eat at the Durgin-Park and the Union Oyster House, two restaurants very close to each other, right by Faneuil Hall Marketplace, competing for the title of Boston's oldest eatery. Durgin-Park dates back to 1742; the Union Oyster House, which is reminiscent of a London Southwark pub, to 1826. However, it is the latter that features the coveted plaque from the US National Tourism Office (I might be making this office up) attesting to its seniority. This is because the founding family of what is today the Durgin-Park sold their dining hall in 1827 to John Durgin, John G. Chandler, and Eldridge Park, who restored it and turned it into the establishment Yonah and I visit 170 years later—thus screwing up the timeline for the trophy.

But let's move on to the menu. I puzzle at the dozens of pages in my hands. Someone like me should arrive at 8 AM to have enough time to read and decode the whole menu and still be able to order by 8 PM. From what I can tell, the typical New England dishes are, by and large, all things lengthily overcooked, either stuffed with or wrapped in pork. I don't eat that. I do not eat oysters, nor the renown lobsters (poor creatures!); I do not touch crab cakes or scallops, all new words—*no, grazie!* However, I see "cherry stones" . . . we're getting somewhere! We are not, because presently I find out that they have nothing to do with cherries, but they are giant mollusks in boatlike shells—*grazie, no.* There are so many types of salads on the menu, but I am not a fan of raw vegetables, so *passo, grazie;* shepherd's pie? *No;* the waiter, running out of stamina, suggests "Indian pudding?" At this point, I feel obliged to say Yes.

The recipe for the Durgin-Park baked Indian pudding is as follows:

1 cup yellow granulated cornmeal
½ cup black molasses

¼ cup granulated sugar

¼ cup lard or butter

¼ teaspoon salt

¼ teaspoons baking soda

2 eggs

1½ quarts hot milk

*In a well-greased crock, mix all the ingredients thoroughly with one half of the hot milk and bake in very hot oven until the mixture boils. Then stir in remaining of hot milk and bake at very low heat for five to seven hours.*

Best dessert, with worst racist name, I've ever had.

We hike chunks of the Appalachian Trail, visit Rhode Island, and pick apples in Vermont. When he proposed this last activity, I knew we were not going to help any grower in particular, but I still wasn't sure what the journey entailed either, since there was clearly no mention of the supermarket. Apple picking is the art, I now know, of getting in the car and taking any mountain road until you run into a scribbled cardboard sign announcing that those who wish can help themselves to all the apples they like: they give you a basket and, when you come out of the orchard, you pay based on the weight of the apples you intend to bring home. This is moving. It signals a trust in the honesty of Man; a trust Europe has lost a long time ago. I cannot imagine Italians trusting others with the task of paying for what they could enjoy for free if they only hide artfully among the trees or fill their pockets undetectably before getting back to the car. I feel again the pangs of shame and embarrassment I used to experience as a child for the second-rate spirit of my country.

We try restaurants of every imaginable ethnic group. We read. We visit museums. Yonah introduces me to the Isabella Gardner Museum, and it becomes our favorite place. I tell myself that one day, when we no longer live in Boston, we will return here to visit and we will make sure to sit in the Isabella Gardner Museum's inner courtyard, surrounded by plants and the dripping of water fountains, and remember today's happiness. We talk about our dreams for the future. We share a distaste for all Republicans, for religion, and for

*Schindler's List*—to be fair, in this order. Normally, atheists can be unlikable: but Yonah is one of those rare agnostics who puts such gentleness, tolerance, and open-mindedness into his Voltairean enlightenment to be more righteous than the purest of believers. We both love Woody Allen, passionately; classical and Klezmer music (Yonah plays the clarinet); *Seinfeld;* cheesecake; coffee at any time . . . and New York. It turns out that living in New York is a dream he's had since he was a child. We weave together imaginary paths that lead us to Manhattan, where we wish to move—together, but we blush to say it—as soon as we're done at Brandeis. Yonah also loves how I speak, how I write, how I think. He gently incites me to fulfill my dreams without judging, controlling, or putting them into question.

I end up living in Waltham. Yes, drab Waltham. I have a huge attic space, all to myself, but I can stand upright only in the very middle of it because of the steep roof. It is an unusual place, and most unusual is the cheap rent I pay for it ($300 plus electricity and other common expenses that we divide by three). Indeed, just like in a 1980s TV sitcom, I live with two guys, who were here before me, and have been occupying the second floor of this large suburban home for years. One is Charles Fisher, a guitarist, tall, dark-haired, and very sexy. He is 39, recovering from a divorce he didn't initiate. He is the boss around here: he is extremely reliable, correct, responsible, and therefore manages our group's accounting and payments: he is serious to the point of being gloomy, with a solid head on his shoulders. He does not drink, he does not smoke, and he spends a lot of time at home, where he keeps a neat environment and makes no noise. I never met the actual owner of this house, but I gather that he completely delegates the management to Charlie, from whom he regularly collects checks from the rotating tenants every month. The other one is Tim: younger than Charlie, Tim is the one with his head in the clouds, two-thirds hippie and one-third white trash. Tim is a good guy too, despite not being a father-husband type like Charlie. Tim collects in his room a thousand licit and illicit plants: various cacti, exotic saplings, medicinal plants, stuff with which he produces smelly teas. Luckily, he doesn't do drugs and he doesn't drink because he's an eco-maniac, vegan, and dedicated to yoga and spiritual health. I am the youngest, an alien and faux pas incarnate, so Charlie and Tim are very protective of me in a brotherly manner.

Comes the cold. Extraordinarily early and intense even for icy Massachusetts. I take a picture of Charlie as he shovels the snow after a huge snowfall that made the newspapers headlines all over America: Charlie is a Goliath, and yet the snow reaches almost to his chest. He and Tim warn me not to go out on the street because they would not know how to fish the "piccola Italiana" out of the tall snow. What they did not warn me about, though, when I took the room, was that the attic is not climatized, has no radiator or AC (I must wait until the summer to learn this new acronym). The cold in my room is unbearable and I run to Harvard Square to buy a goose-feather comforter. I hide myself under it, head too, like a turtle, and when I wake up in the morning, I am alive but the water in the glass on my bedside table—a milk crate reborn as nightstand thanks to Tim—is frozen solid. I bring it for a laugh downstairs to show it to my friends. When I hand Charlie the icy cylinder, he first pales then reddens with an apoplectic flush. He stammers, apologizes—as I begin to sneeze—and by the evening, when I return from my classes, I find an electric heater planted in the middle of my now cozy attic. A gift of contrition from Charlie, who tells me that this month I am exempted from paying electricity. I sneeze and give him a hug Italian-style. I think he likes me: not like a sister. But I already have a big mess in my life right now, it's better not to play with fire. I'll settle for the space heater. Let this little crush freeze in the bud like everything else in this house.

Charlie, with great patience, teaches me the most obvious things, not only for my benefit but also because I think he is afraid that I will do some damage to "his" kitchen and "his" house. So he shows me how to use the American coffeepot—the one that produces a thin brew, burnt-flavored, and full of germs, because it doesn't boil the water; he explains to me how to use the microwave—an instrument of death that certainly causes brain cancer; and especially how to shower. In order to have a hot shower, it is necessary to ignite a special boiler placed in the bathroom, inside the shower cabin itself. Here, in America, in the homeland of the Massachusetts Institute of Technology (MIT, *yet another acronym*), in the country that sent the first man to the moon, if I want to wash myself, I must manually strike a match, bring the flame close to a gas nozzle and hope not to blow up the whole bloody wooden house (the one the second little piglet builds).

Charlie is very patient with me. Although I wonder if he does not associate (as it is often the case even with the kindest people) the stranger to the idiot, or thinks that, after all, I come from a vanished civilization where I rubbed two stones together to light the fire until a minute before I boarded the plane to Boston. He is right about many things, but on many others he does not so much underestimate me as much as he overestimates his own lifestyle. The fact that I am bewildered by the antediluvian mechanism of the hot-water boiler in the shower says a lot more about the underdevelopment of this place than of my origins. As for the microwave, he can laugh as much as he likes: I do not even step near it for fear that the radiations will reduce me to a domestic version of Silkwood.

My attic has three skylights and loads of unusable space, but it's deliciously private. I found it by myself: I answered an announcement in the newspaper. Before this, I visited other places and learned quite a bit about "Houses of Boston: Typologies and Inhabitants, from Deluxe to Slum" (*perhaps this should be my next term paper*)—they were all undoable. Including one, much closer to the university, which was wrapped in a spicy cloud of curry, occupied by fifteen graduate students from India, and the only space available for me was the covered porch. An inexpensive room was available in a nineteenth-century house on three floors, plus a habitable attic and basement, in the East End, entirely populated by medical school girls and an unregistered number of cats. I even lived there for one week, but the heaps of human and nonhuman hair in every shower drain, sink, dishwasher, and cutlery drawer weakened and eventually broke my resolve. In any case, I learned something important there, from Bess, one of the medical students, whose clinical specialty was schizophrenia. The more she talked about it (the schizophrenia, that is) the more I seemed to recognize its symptoms in me and, in the end, I implored: "Please, take me to your laboratory to diagnose me!" She explained that schizophrenia does not occur in people who simply hear about it, nor in individuals older than twenty-eight. I am twenty-six so now I just have to live the next twenty-four months, scrupulously analyzing each and every bizarre move or thought of mine. I couldn't stay there.

I also explored au pair situations, more to visit the homes of the rich than out of a heartfelt vocation to raise the children of others. I received numerous offers, the most attractive of which was from a family in Newton Oak Hill with three children and a dog living in a colonial revival home with an interior décor from a page of Architectural Digest. I had a premonition: by the end of the first month with these people, I would end up poisoning the brunette wife, after serving her their three children for dinner, and marrying her unsuspecting husband. Mary Poppins's life was never in my plans.

In the Sunday edition of the *Boston Globe*, I found the announcement for a "shared living" accommodation at 69 Orange Street, Waltham, MA 02453. I showed up, without references of any kind (even if these were specifically requested in the announcement). It was good of Charlie to give me this chance—he even came to pick me up by car where I was staying in that transitional period and helped me move. This suburban home has none of the charm of the Bostonian brownstones or typical New England mansions. It is a mediocre house, in a depressed town, which exudes an air of "hard-work and no-cheer" typical of the proletariat who build what they have with their naked hands and blood under their nails. And yet I like that it does not have the Gothic patina à la *Arsenic and Old Lace*, nor that stale opulence which (perhaps because I'm envious) plunges me into an inane melancholy rather than igniting the fire of proactive ambition. With Charlie and Tim, I feel happy and safe. It is certainly a favorable sign.

Charlie helps me navigate the complex ritual of Halloween's trick or treat. It is not that complex, but judging from how hard Charlie lends all his strengths to this teaching opportunity, I begin to fear that there are dangerous sides to this infantile tradition more malicious and covert than meets the eye. When the first group of children knocks on our door, we go open (me, excited at the idea of this new experience, Charlie excited at witnessing a foreigner's reaction in person). "Nooo!!!" he shouts, agitated, scaring the children to death, as soon as he notices that I am about to pour in their baskets a portion of M&Ms from a large jar I bought wholesale for the occasion. One only gives wrapped and individually sealed sweets. I am harshly reprimanded. Once upon a time, Halloween treats were candied apples and other home-made desserts. But since then America's parents have entered into a collective paranoia about the possibility that their children may receive apples with hidden razors in them or sweets made of rat poison. Apparently, what does not worry them is to send their children at night to knock on the doors of perfect strangers in exchange for candies.

America is a country of inordinately trusting people. They nurture paranoias about things that will never happen, but when it comes to real dangers, they seem to pay no attention. These people have newspaper distributors! They put a coin into a metal box on the street that contains a stack of newspapers, the coin unlocks the door of the box, they pull the door open, take one copy of the newspaper, and close the door which automatically locks back in place. This would be a nonstarter where I come from. It wouldn't last a day in Naples or Rome! Any scumbag worth the name would set his alarm clock early, go downstairs, open the vending machine, take out for the price of one coin all the newspaper copies, and sell them for a profit at the next street corner. That in a country of over 200,000,000 people no one, ever, thought of committing such a pitiful act of incivility simply dazes me.

Another feature that by comparison puts my troglodytic country to shame is the American impulsion to co-participation in the common good. I notice it in every small detail. Take recycling: it's a religion. This new faith, that I embrace wholeheartedly, gives me a chance to add the word "compost" to my vocabulary. Well, never mind that initially I had taken that "s" in compost as an American variation on the French compôte, so that when Tim asked me one morning "Would you like to contribute to the compost?"—meaning, if I wanted to combine my food refuses with his in the big garden bin outside where stuff stinks and ferments endlessly and *not* help him cook something— I answered in a spirit of camaraderie, "Sure, teach me how! It'll be such a treat to swirl it into my yogurt for breakfast!"

I like to have breakfast at the slightly clattered table by the kitchen window overlooking the street. I learn to eat monumental blueberry muffins I buy at the nearest Purity Supreme. The Purity Supreme alone occupies an area as large as the town of Pisa, yet I can hardly find anything to buy in here. I search through the microscopic pasta aisle, but the only brand I find is called "Mueller," which looks overcooked before having touched boiling water. I gander at shelves full of products that I don't recognize. And those I recognize don't help much because my diet has always been very limited and disproportionately dominated by cheese. America, immense country of cowboys and hamburgers, hence with enough cows to justify the existence of both, produces only two cheeses: actually, a cheese in two colors—white and orange: harder than a Philadelphia cream cheese, limper than hand soap but with the same taste. If you melt it, it vanishes instead of clumping into elastic strands, leaving behind a beige or orange smudge on your food. The orange one is called cheddar, like the English village in which it was born. When they first brought it to the New World, they must have tied it to a rope hanging outside the ship and dragged it in the ocean, out of consideration for the passengers' olfactory receptors: once arrived, they must have rinsed it under fresh water, thrown the resulting washout on a wagon and transported it all the way to Wisconsin, a remote and landlocked state, and by then they had utterly forgotten what this thing was supposed to taste like and kept making it wrong ever since.

I wander into the Deli area (short for delicatessen), our *pizzicheria*. In a wicker basket, I notice a stack of plastic bags containing what look like pieces of cheese. Waste cheese. Better still: charity waste cheese. A bag of 500 grams of discarded pieces of imported cheese, 50 cents. And my favorite: Parmigiano rinds. 40 cents for over half a kilo. This is inexplicable. They do not sell Parmigiano nor Emmenthal, yet somehow the rinds of these phantom cheeses, or their faux version, end up in these bags. Throwing behind me the last remnant of dignity, I grab an armful of cheese baggies. Bothered by remorse, I immediately write to my mother for a quick ethical check: with her typical aplomb, she finds only positive angles to this experience. America, already a near-flawless paradise in her estimation, shines even more glorious in her eyes.

My parents (who share a keychain with the effigy of JFK, whom they loved and over whose assassination they cried inconsolably) are enamored of America. Americans to them are and will forever mean Liberation, their eternal April 25, 1945. The idea of not throwing the peels away every time the grocer starts cutting into a new form of cheese and of selling them instead for a symbolic sum so that the poor, who cannot afford the Deli products, can at least afford its waste, appeals to my mother as one of the highest expressions of justice and social charity. To me, it strikes me as yet another slap on the emaciated face of poverty. Between not eating cheese at all and eating it *as* off-scourings, what would the poor prefer? I'll never know. With my Max Mara

coat, and the elegantly light step of a purebred feline, I will nonchalantly return many times to the Purity Supreme to empty out the wicker basket, thus
taking away from the poor even the scraps option.

A stone's throw from my attic, on Moody Street, I discover Angelo's House
of Pizza, where Angelo and his family make a dizzyingly good pie. It's been a
long time since Angelo and his wife have had a chance to speak Italian with a
fellow citizen: they love when I show up. Their children were all born in Massachusetts. They also work in this *pizzeria:* they take turns for their one day off
a week, except for the father who is never absent. They are good people. They
work from morning until night. They tell me about the great wealth they
managed to accumulate in America, thanks to hard work, of course, and they
feel obliged to assure me that, one day, I too will be just like them. The wife
tells me that they live on a ranch, many miles from here, with acres of land
and horses. "But when do you enjoy your ranch? You're always here! I mean,
if you spend two hours in the car every day to get to the pizzeria and back,
and you stay bottled up in this oven from 9 AM to 1 AM, seven days a week, the
ranch with the horses, the acres of land, the Jacuzzis in each of the seven bathrooms you own, do not really make sense any longer, do they?" I ask unwisely.
I read an expression of sincere shock on the face of Angelo's wife. I would give
anything to put the hands of the watch back half a minute to retract my question, which was utterly rhetorical but instead hit the literal channels of this
exhausted woman's brain, who may be reconsidering her entire life right now
. . . she who emigrated with nothing about thirty years ago and now has
horses and a jacuzzi all of her own. She is probably thinking that I am not
American-dream material: that this country is not for me.

Nonetheless, their pizza is divine. Almost like the one from the Bronx. I
eat until I feel sick. I cannot order small portions, I like taking home the giant
carton of a large pie, with the tiny plastic tables to hold the lid, with its huge
slices collapsing under four pounds of mozzarella. Perhaps it's an attempt
to recreate that last magical moment at Brett & Galina's house. Despite my
undiminished appetite, I find myself losing weight and vomiting a lot these
days, because of the great anxiety and stress I am under. I also notice a suspicious tremor of my hands, to the point that it becomes hard to bring the fork

straight to my mouth; even more unusual for me, I sweat a lot despite the icy weather, and I'm always so sleepy.

In the course of a few months, I learn tons of new customs and cultural curiosities. Some stun me. For instance, Americans have undefinable table manners. They must have been taught that the left arm is held under the table, stretched between one's legs, as if one were pulling up a sock between mouthfuls: the very few who choose the use of silverware, stab the food with the fork in the left hand, so as to be able to maneuver the knife with the right one, then at each bite they put down the knife, switch the fork into the right hand and finally bring it to their lips. It is evident to them that those who (like me) never put down fork and knife are not representative of an alternative and superior civilization, but simply left-handed.

Surprisingly, the eating culture here remains extraordinarily uncomplicated. Americans eat everything and eat it all the time. And they love to do it in public, on the street, on public transportation, and especially while driving their cars. And here is the crazy part: If they do not finish something, they throw it away, and they throw away food even just because they've decided to try a different one. No one cares about prices: no one seems to lack money to afford every gluttonous whim.

Another social peculiarity is their way of meeting and mating. "Date" (noun and verb) is not, as I had been taught in school, the number on a calendar (or at least not only) but, in everybody's daily parlance, the word refers to two people going out romantically with the prospect of having sex and getting married. (*Getting married: very important in America.*) The first time I hear the word I have no idea what it means, and my first mistake is not asking. It will take getting a couple of guys enraged before the concept becomes less elusive to me. As soon as I land here a few fellow students invite me out and I think nothing of it, it's what people do—like me and my friends Marco or Alessandro used to do in Rome. We are young, we're colleagues, we are well-adjusted adults, let's go eat something together . . . nothing more, nothing less. Instead, when "less" happens, it irritates these American guys who had no intention of killing an hour in good company (mine), for the heck of it, but who instead were weighing me out as a possible matrimonial prey and a future vessel of children. If you make them invest money on a meal for you without some kind of return, they resent you and they never talk to you again. There is a rule for everything here. I am lost. I will have to learn empirically, get bruises and wounds on the battlefield: the space between theory and practice is a dark closet full of pain, in which I move stumbling against this or that blunt object.

I feel obliged to open this parenthesis about dating (and the fixed steps it requires) because it embodies perhaps one of the most incomprehensible American oddities for me. Fundamentally, systematized dating is integral to a controlling mindset: America is affected by control freakiness. Love, marriage, and passion are managed on a par with career, athletic regime, or the planning of one's children's academic future: nothing is left to chance.

People make it their purpose to help single friends mate: it's practically a mitzvah, a religious obligation. One earns a special place under the sun in Eden this way.

Pretty much anywhere else in the world (where women have gained a modicum of freedom and control over their bodies and time), it's not unusual for a friendship to become a sex affair, a sex affair to turn into a lasting friendship, a sex affair never to grow into a friendship, and for a love story to vanish into smoke—I have seen and experienced a combo of them all. It's a bit like dancing by music you hear for the first time: you follow the rhythm, do not resist, let yourself be guided. *Uno due tre . . . uno due tre . . . uno due tre.* In America, the rule is to follow the rules and leave nothing to instinct. The matchmaking business is one of the most lucrative industries in the United States. This humiliating tradition of matchmaking, far from having died in America, has taken on a new lease on life thanks to modern technology. The love market here is a market no more nor less than Wall Street is—with its speculators, precise calculations, give-and-take assessments, negotiations, and surprise gains but also colossal losses. And the primary motivation adduced by young people to seek their soul mates through newspapers, the internet, or singles' clubs is simply lack of time. Some pay astronomical sums to bypass those means and use directly the old-style matchmaker. Personally, I have heard of matchmakers, *shadchanim, sensali, marieuses,* and *Heiratsvermittler* only from Victorian novels, from the gossips of housemaids from tiny remote villages, or from Sholem Alejchem's stories. The temptation to hum is irresistible . . .

*Matchmaker, matchmaker, make me a match.*

*Find me a find, catch me a catch . . .*

In a sense, America is like a village in Podolia, with the innocence and unshakable optimism of *Fiddler on the Roof.* In the small and backward country I hail from, the gratification of sensual needs is left to personal initiative: in America, beacon of modernity, if you don't get a pimp, you don't fuck. My sexual life will take a hit. This was unexpected.

I am not proud of our reputation as a hypersexed country. But at the opposite extreme lies a cold America where masses of young, beautiful, vibrant people don't know how to flirt: here they drink. Their potion against inhibition. America sells itself as a country of born winners: I gather that to win one has to strategize everything, even, and perhaps more so, love as well.

My initiation into the dating ritual had gone poorly—not exactly for me, as much as for my date. It all started with the usual zealous neighbors. It is a custom in America that if a new person comes to live in the house next to yours, you bring them sweets, flowers, or other propitiatory objects as a sign of peace offering and welcome, just like Pocahontas to the European intruders. I suspect this is a polite way to pry and to check who the newcomers are—foreigners? Vulgar rednecks who will depreciate the value of your house with their pickup trucks, their animated barbecues and beer cans on the porch, or worse, Black? I too receive this sweet "welcome treatment" (in which I don't read any of the profiling signs I just mentioned . . . but I am too new here to know) and I am thrilled.

I meet the family down the street with whom I fall in love. They are two Brooklyn writers relocated to Boston to raise their children in this safer and more refined environment. Their lifestyle is way too alternative even for the 1990s—a prerogative, I suppose, of their being outlandishly rich. They have done away with TVs and other technological distractions at home; they use the car only for long-distance needs, otherwise they stick to bicycles; they borrow books from the public library; and needless to say, their two children are brilliant, with all the moral values in the right place. They seem cut out of an advertising billboard: beautiful, young, healthy, with their large Second

Empire house surrounded by leafy trees. Every time I see them darting on their bikes, with books in their baskets, their organic clothes, and the thinness of those who eat well and measuredly, the world seems a better place. *Will I ever have this kind of serenity? A house, someone inside it who loves me, the certainty that something is really mine, stable, and no one will pull the rug from under my feet all of a sudden? I run after dreams that are unreachable or that turn into nightmares: where is the finish line? Why does it move farther each time I feel I am so close? I seem to be entitled only to horizons, never destinations.* My neighbors still maintain all their contacts in New York and, at hearing of my love for the city, they offer to share them with me. They ask for my phone number and, if I do not mind, they will pass it along to some people they know over there and whom they think I'll like to meet . . . people who could be an optimal way for me to slowly integrate myself into New York—their words. This is life: one miracle at a time.

A guy by the name of Richard calls me from Brooklyn. He got my number from the neighbors, the billboard family. He, too, like them, is a writer. We begin to talk regularly on the phone in the evenings. We talk of tons of things, *simpatico.* It's clear that Richard is older than I . . . considerably older than I. There's no lack of hilarious stories of maniac ex-wives, roach infestations in his Brooklyn home, homicidal literary agents, and a thousand anecdotes about the events that marked the history of New York before I was even born. Richard insists that I have to go visit him: "Come!" he enthuses. "You're not far!" "Come!" "Just a day or two!" "Come!" I go.

It will be the first time I see New York again after the week with Brett & Galina just over a year ago.

It's almost my birthday. What more suitable gift for my 26th? *Non rompere, e vai.* (It's a no-brainer.) I trust Richard's motives: his friendship is transparent. He often refers to his age as if it were the safest shield against any threat of sinful conduct. He jokingly refers to imagined admirers I surely must have at Brandeis, and he often teases, "Come have lunch with me, before someone steals you away and you won't have time for friends anymore!" (*I did tell him about Yonah, though . . . didn't I?*) He is trying to make me see that my impossible dream of living in New York—of which I evidently speak more than I realize—is in truth quite doable. He helps me see things for what they are; he must have guessed that I need a good nudge. The nudge of a good friend.

Like the seasoned juggler that I am, I'll throw one more ball in the air. I'll handle it. What's the choice here: a regular weekend in Boston or an extraordinary one in New York? Whose opinion should I seek? (If you do not ask, they cannot stop you.) I want to go so badly. Two nights, one full day. I tell Yonah, bursting with happiness. I wish he had offered we see *our* New York together before any other friend took the lead. Too late. (He doesn't offer, I don't ask.) Too bad.

I get a car ride from Shira (she's in one of my classes and we are pretty close) who is going to visit her family in Baltimore. Since New York is on the way, she'll drop me off in Manhattan and I'll take a Greyhound bus back— my old acquaintance.

I organize this trip to a tee. Brett & Galina would be proud this time: I consult various books at the library and discover a youth hostel on West 103rd Street and Amsterdam Avenue, with rooms at a bargain price. At first, I was going to check myself into a hotel, but I didn't know how to choose the right one and for fear of ending up in the wrong kind of establishment (I'm thinking criminality, prostitution, and drugs all wrapped together and delivered to my room at 2 AM), I decided for a youth hostel. (Young foreign tourists— what's the worst that can happen?) And in an attempt to shed the Princess and embrace this new, "adaptable Me," I book a shared room. (*Note to self: Pack the sleeping bag, the one you wisely stuffed in your suitcase when you left Rome.*) Tomorrow I will wake up in New York!

And so it is. I wake up. I am here. I can't wait to be outside.

I exit into the street, the autumn sun is very warm. I already know what to do . . . Walk one block west, take Broadway, and head south . . . toward the Statue of Liberty. I remember everything.

This time, however, there will not be time to walk the whole length of the island: I have to meet Richard, who told me on the phone before I left that he has planned a couple of activities for our day together. On a piece of paper, which I apprehensively clench for fear of losing it, I wrote: "42nd Street. Intersection—Fifth Avenue. Staircase. Lions."

Maybe I should have taken the subway, because the walk starts to make me sweat, and I'll arrive with makeup running down my cheeks, my hair stuck to my forehead, and with a limp because my nonwalking shoes are cutting into my Achilles tendon. (*Note to self: buy sneakers as soon as you return to Boston.*)

I reach the designated point. This building is beautiful. Now I understand what Richard meant by "in front of the lions." (I had not bothered to ask, and only later it had dawned on me that I might never find a place whose very definition I had totally misunderstood.) The New York Public Library, protected by these two big kitties (named Patience and Fortitude by Mayor LaGuardia) who slyly watch over the thousands of people passing by. The Beaux-Arts style building is almost disproportionate. People go up and down the stone steps, inside and out, in endless streams. Some just sit there to play guitar, to sleep, to eat a sandwich or wait for a friend. I see large posters announcing public lectures to be held here, in the elegant rooms with hundreds of seats, and frescoed ceilings painted in bright colors, magnificent crystal chandeliers, large windows. In *Ghostbusters,* the first ghost appears in the New York Public Library. It is here that Audrey Hepburn, gorgeous in her fine woolen cardigan, large sunglasses, and hair gathered in a bun, reads all she can about Latin American culture in preparation for the unlikely marriage with Brazilian millionaire José da Silva Pereira in *Breakfast at Tiffany,* which could only be born out of the imagination of another New York adoptive son, Truman Capote.

Is that him? Dark green corduroy trousers, so worn out that the characteristic tufts are flattened and the channels evened out. A sweater that must have seen better days. A classic Brooklynite (as per stereotypes in books and films): tons of money in the bank and a lousy wardrobe. A puff of black hair wrapped around half of his skull perimeter—the lower half. Thin in the way of people who do not practice a sport. Tall as me. Of course, it's him: here is Richard! In seeing me, he lights up with enthusiasm. Too much enthusiasm.

For the second time, here I am, feeling perfectly at home in this place. It can't be a coincidence. I can't be wrong. My heart swells. I breathe better. I see the future, I walk facing it, chin up, big smile! I turn from *australopithecus* into *homo erectus!* (For *sapiens,* I'm afraid, we'll need to wait.) I didn't tell Brett & Galina, nor my parents, that I was coming here. I wanted to handle this decision and this moment on my own. I wanted to feel the effect of being in

New York without chains, without other people's opinions making me doubt my own. I wanted to be here "as if," well, as if I were from here, as if I had always belonged nowhere else but here.

I catch the Greyhound bus back to Boston, full of very different thoughts than the last time I was on this same trip. On the one hand, I feel a latent frustration at having to return to Boston, which, despite Yonah, hasn't grown on me. But on the other hand, I know that this is only the beginning of a much grander adventure. As Richard says, Boston is a stone's throw from New York. And as Galina says, Boston is a "foot in the door" (of America). The other foot, however, will move to New York, this I swear on my future grave.

The Greyhound bus goes too fast. I wish it were headed to Alaska to give me enough time to revisit in every detail, as it deserves, my day with Richard yesterday. My first birthday in America, my first birthday in New York City. Serendipity's, Central Park, the Dakota, the spiraling Guggenheim, the lions of the Public Library . . . and these scenes, as if from *Hannah and Her Sisters,* were only a prelude to a climax, an apogee, a zenith of joy which I could never have foretold.

Richard, on top of taking me out for the most exquisite lunch at Serendipity's, the greatest café I've ever seen, had also made arrangements for the evening "to celebrate your upcoming 26th birthday in style," he had said. How much more happiness could I soak in? I was already saturated, satiated, overdosed on bliss. I was expecting and would have been delighted with an anonymous but formidable Indian restaurant, or perhaps Italian in my honor, or even a cheerful Mexican where the mariachis deafen the public and the enchiladas are stuffed cannelloni the size of small howitzers smothered in an ocean of salsa, guacamole, and sour cream. I did not expect the Carlyle Hotel. Instead, I received the Carlyle Hotel.

Richard cleaned up nicely. I reckon that meeting me in person must have provided essential cues for his own next appearance.

Mentally, I retrace our walk down Madison Avenue at night. The doormen, in wrinkleless liveries, who guard the gates of luxurious buildings—images from Edith Wharton's novels. The Carlyle Hotel. The Carlyle . . . such enchanting halls, walls covered in murals reminiscent of the jazz age,

Prohibition, the Great Depression, corrupt police, gambling (on everything: from oil markets to horse races), prostitution (less and less hidden), and the era too of great poverty for millions of immigrants on the Lower East Side who were fighting tooth and nail to drag themselves from the southernmost tip of the island (which meant pain, hunger, humiliation, mass cohabitation, nonexistent hygienic conditions) to the "upper" sides of Manhattan: Upper East Side (for the real winners of the money race), Upper West Side (for everybody else) . . . upward toward wealth, pursuing the dream of conquering a seat at the table with the Rockefellers of this world. The original Art Deco of the Carlyle is exquisite. All American presidents spent a night here, from Harry Truman to Bill Clinton; J. F. Kennedy owned an apartment on the thirty-fourth floor. This place heard historical performances by George Feyer, Elaine Stritch, and generation after generation of famous artists. Our table is small and intimate, with plenty of space around it, an excellent view of the surroundings (it is full of people), and just the perfect amount of light. I hope that if it exists, Heaven will look like the Carlyle. I time traveled back into the 1920s and I am in no rush to return to the future right now. I order *risotto al tartufo*. I never make the mistake of eating Italian food outside of Italy, but tonight my intuition tells me that I can trust the chef here. My intuition rewards me: the scent of truffles pervades my nostrils, while my tongue sweats with pleasure at the contact with the creamy and aromatic taste of the risotto.

I notice that Richard is endeavoring to communicate something without words: he looks at me and slightly throws his chin forward in the direction he wants me to turn. My neck has not yet rotated the 45 degrees it takes to fully turn toward a small stage by us, that a clarinet begins to play a lively Dixieland tune and I simultaneously lock eyes with Woody Allen. Woody fucking Allen! Woody Allen, who returns my gaze, nods a polite hello, smiles at me with his eyes. Woody Allen playing the clarinet thirty-nine inches from my nose.

I feel my eyes burning, my cheeks flushed with emotion as I play over and over again the film of these events in my mind, while the bus takes me back to Boston. I must be happy, and grateful, to be in Boston, to know Yonah. To desire more is hubris. Woody Allen, his band and his freckled skin! The Carlyle . . . Serendipity's . . . Richard's worn-out corduroy . . . the lamp posts in Central Park . . . St. Louis Blues . . . hot dogs . . . truffles . . . Gershwin . . . Woody Allen . . . Central Park . . . Woody Allen . . . Serendipity's . . .

My throat tightens. It makes no sense that I'm going back to Boston! At age twenty-six, with clear ideas about who and where I should be, I am instead following a path that is not mine. Perhaps the real hubris is this. I have to recalibrate my aim. I have to get back at the helm. I have to get a green card.

This, with Richard, was not a casual appointment between future eternal friends. It was a date, and I did not understand it. Or even if I had guessed it, I would not have expected that dates here lead either to the altar or to an irreversible goodbye, with no middle ground. I will not find him when I call tomorrow. And he will not answer the next day either. Not even my emails will reach him. I will never hear from Richard again. He has plenty of friends already; he did not need another one, and he certainly did not need me. He needed love. Too bad. I need New York and a green card.

Back in Boston, it is Thanksgiving time. My first. I spend it with Yonah. Every new American embraces this holiday more than any other with commitment and devotion: a true test of patriotic loyalty. I suspect that given the choice "People, just one holiday this year: Thanksgiving or Christmas?" a unanimous quorum of Americans would choose Thanksgiving.

What more perfect place for my first Thanksgiving in America than New England, I realize. It is 1996, the coldest winter on record in a century. We are under four feet of snow. We drive (thank God!) to the house of Yonah's friend, Arielle, opera singer and synagogue cantor-in-training. She lives in Brookline. Brookline is like Brooklyn: all brownstones on four or five levels, antique reddish bricks, front stoops, large bay windows, on tree-lined avenues, elegant but not as exalted as a Parisian boulevard or Park Avenue, much cozier and more welcoming. Arielle's house is warm, comfortable, it smells good: I have no idea what to expect, and it makes me anxious to be formally introduced to Yonah's closest group of friends. I find it hard to make out most of the foods that overwhelm tables, countertops and credenzas between the living room and the kitchen. The atmosphere is extremely convivial. Some here are musicians, others writers and artists, many are graduate students like us. It also comes up that until a few months ago, Arielle was Yonah's fiancée, but she broke off the engagement. (The person who takes great care in bringing me up to speed on the details is Jennifer, a recent divorcée, mother of one, and with her eyes fastened on Yonah.) I did not know anything about all this until now and the turkey is about to be served. I go with the flow.

The libations at Arielle's are worthy of a royal feast: everybody contributed, according to the custom of potluck, another American invention I will refuse to adopt. *Who on earth demands guests bring the dinner they are invited to? It's the most undignified idea I ever heard.* Guests were asked to bring a dish in keeping as much as possible with the Thanksgiving tradition . . . albeit the kosher factor puts faithfulness under great restraints. Turkey is kosher—well, at least since American Jews declared it so—but rodents are not. So corn, which today is featured on our table in mouthwatering cobs, was used by the indigenous tribes of Massachusetts not on its own but always mixed with beans to obtain a *succotash,* which in turn was kneaded with squirrel meat. *Forget about historical faithfulness!*

Then something shocking happens. The lady of the house raises a glass of red wine, and everybody puts down their utensils and poises themselves for listening with great attentiveness. *To what?* I put down knife and fork, pat my mouth clean and observe. Arielle is actually thanks-giving. Literally.

"I give thanks . . ."

I eject an ironic snort, preparing for a punchline to follow.

"for the health . . ."

This is no joke! She means it: "and the love of my family; my new job; and for the good fortune of being able to do what I love most, every day. Above all, I give thanks for the wonderful friends I see around me" (a murmur rises from the touched audience) "and whom I love as a family. Without you my life would not be the same." I feel tears surging . . . tears of embarrassment at my earlier dispraising reaction, at my unwarranted prejudgments. On the one hand, sentimentality turns my stomach. But these words are felt. I have to block out for a moment everything I always thought, believed, or took for granted—and which is predetermined by the specific stimuli of *my* personal environment, *my* circumstances. It is high time I open my mind's door to the possibility of conceiving the world in brand new ways. Who knows that I won't discover the secret of a happy life—like Arielle! Arielle: so happy, with a giant and luminous presence, the voice of Cecilia Bartoli and likewise raven black hair. Serene, harmonious. The way the people around this table are expressing their mutual feelings is almost religious, like a prayer that fails to mention God. Yes, the exercise is so corny. But so what? My friends and I, in Italy, hug a lot, we tell each other "I love you" a thousand times, we are so physical with each other (we even kiss on the mouth sometimes . . . and parents certainly do with children), and yet a thanks-giving speech would be unthinkable. In this changed scenario, however, people completely identical to those I left behind (by age, profession, social affiliation, intellectual sophistication) do something utterly different, unanticipated. The host makes speeches. Big bloody deal! No reason to mock. Only an imbecile would mock on such a moment. And that's precisely what I had started to do. I am an imbecile! From now on, it'll be different. I'm a changed person! I deeply commit now to what is happening. Go America!

"I thank you . . ." starts Yonah who sits on Arielle's right.

Holy cowboy! Everyone gets a turn? It is not just the lady of the house who gives speeches! The renewed goodwill toward my American experience swiftly withers and dies. My old me appears unchanged. I am so distressed by the thought of having to give a sappy little speech soon that I pay no attention to what Yonah is saying. Except that, at a certain point, the murmur from the touched listeners seems to float in my direction. If he just proffered loving words for me, I missed them. I crack a frozen smile and wipe my sweltering forehead. My clothes stick to my chair like glue. Ineluctably, my turn arrives.

"Thank you. . . ." I swallow, I look at the greasy mash potatoes and the two pieces of yam stranded on the plate, the undercooked Brussel sprouts, the cranberry sauce expanded into a vermillion pond, and finally my mind clears up: "I thank Arielle, Yonah, and all of you for letting me into your home . . . your lives. For making me feel welcome"—never been an orator in my life! Where am *I* coming from?—"I give thanks for being here with you on my first Thanksgiving, and for being in America . . . Thanks for the wonderful foods you have prepared . . . with some practice, by this time next year, you'll see me spread cranberry sauce even on my morning toast"—they laugh. They must have gathered that this type of thing is not exactly second nature to me. More than one hand reaches out to touch my arm, to affectionately pat my shoulder, and Yonah smiles encouragingly from where he sits. It's true, I am in America . . . and in the frenzy of the last three and a half months, I had not let myself fully realize it.

We eat so much that at some point, instead of putting two fingers down our throat as the ancient Romans did to make room for desserts, we decide to take a walk around the block. It's a magical evening: we sat down around 4 PM—in America, dinner parties start at what we'd call late lunch in Italy; we walk under the stars because, being the end of November, darkness has long fallen. The street lamplights illuminate the snow; we're not the only ones on the street; others have had the same idea. We greet each other, among strangers. The neighborhood is beautiful under the snow at this hour: I think that if I had to live in Boston, I would take a house here in Brookline. But this is a spurious idea: I don't "have to" live in Boston, because as soon as possible I'll make my way to New York. The Carlyle . . . Serendipity's . . . lamp posts in Central Park . . . St. Louis Blues . . . Woody Allen . . . me.

Yonah drives me home and we continue to talk. We spend our first night together. It's the coldest night on record.

The relationship with Yonah is blooming. After Thanksgiving and my birthday, we also celebrated Christmas together in the manner of American Jews: ignoring it.

In Italy, all holidays come in pairs: Natale (Christmas) and Santo Stefano (the day after Natale), Pasqua (Easter) and Pasquetta (the day after Pasqua), and two Carnival days (fat Thursday and Tuesday). Only la Befana (January 6) is all alone on the calendar and nonexistent in America altogether. Americans apparently can take no more than one-day holidays. While others are busy doing with their families what I wholeheartedly hated doing with mine, I go out and watch a movie, shop, visit a museum . . . because everything is open and deliciously available (unlike in Italy which, between December 24 and January 7, is such an empty tundra that even Jews, bored stiff, start decorating trees).

Yonah is writing his dissertation. I admire him for the excellence he puts into what he does (serious) and who he is: (devoted) friend, (affectionate) son, (loyal) partner. In particular, Yonah has all the qualities of a born brother. That's why he is a magnet for women: he is a living Linus blanket. And he doesn't seem to ask anything else but wrapping someone in his warmth . . . or (but this is surely an irrational as much as incorrect impression of mine) wrapping any body in his warmth. Indiscriminately. Since I've been here, I've already met two ex-fiancées of his, a tide of female friends . . . but no male friend, now that I think about it. The only man was his father.

He and his father, Bob, who visits from the West Coast, invited me out for a brunch. We talked about politics and what is happening in the world: the repercussions of the disastrous Reagan years, Israel according to my personal experience, what the assassination of Yitzhak Rabin will mean for the country, and the elections rigged against Shimon Perez, genocide in Rwanda, international terrorism, the sarin attack in the Tokyo subway, the bomb at the World Trade Center, the other bomb at the Atlanta Olympics. Yonah must have taken after his mother because he looks nothing like Bob. His pianist brother does, judging from the photos. Bob is very masculine, he must have been a real catch when he was young, a hippy in Woodstock and a Freedom Fighter in the 1960s. Yonah is more "domestic," maternal, with a deceptively insecure air: the kind that would not dream of imposing his own opinion and sinking that of another, even when the other person is wrong. Father and son listened to me with great attention, as if I were a guest of honor. They were very courteous, friendly, and full of compliments and kind words. I sensed that Bob approved of his son's choice, and that this final judgment is what he was summoned for.

One evening, it is still so cold outside that we can't take off our coats even in the car, and the frost blinds the windows around us, we chat parked in front of my apartment on Orange Street. There is a lull in the conversation, a serene silence, before I open the door, say goodnight, and return to my attic. With the engine off, but the hands still on the steering wheel, a little tense, Yonah turns to me and says: "I love you. I want to be with you." *Do I hear synagogue bells?* "Let's live together. In the future, we could . . . maybe . . . if all goes well . . . we could get married." *If all goes well.* The silence is swelling with the untold. I do not move, I do not breathe. It is not a marriage proposal, but a cohabitation proposal. *Careful what you say, Fania! It's not the right time to make the wrong move.* Before I can put two words together, he continues: "I will wait here with you until you finish your PhD, then we can move to New York. I will work for both of us, and you can write, be whatever you want." He is not holding his finger in front of his face this time, he does not speak in short hiccups, he does not divert his gaze in ten different directions. He looks at me, scrutinizing my reaction, keeping both hands clasped on the steering wheel at an imaginary 10 and 2, while he recites in one breath a script, not improvised but rather rehearsed although deeply felt.

My eyes are hot with tears. They are not tears of joy but of despair. "New York." "My novels." "Me and Yonah." "Security." "Normalcy." The dream! No fears anymore. No running away anymore. New York. My art. New York. The Carlyle . . . Serendipity's . . . lamp posts in Central Park . . . Woody Allen . . . "If all goes well." And if it doesn't? And even if it goes well, it would still go bad because if an American does not marry me, my dreams and I will be shipped back to Italy, one way only. Everybody says so. Of course, it'd be un-romantic of me to point this out in such a lyrical moment.

I say yes. But I think he knows I have qualms.

In these months—or is it already years?—I lived a double life. One, of-ficial, open, public, as revealing as a window on a Dutch house; and another, dark, diabolical, secret. The shady one clings to me, and I do not know how to get rid of it. I tried once to mention it to Yonah, but either I did not explain the seriousness of the situation adequately enough, or he preferred to stay away from it and pretended not to understand. I cannot judge. My mental clarity is reduced to a tiny flicker of light, about to extinguish itself. I am drowning, I am sinking into quicksand . . . I had counted on getting myself out of it alone, but I was wrong: I am losing the battle.

I read somewhere that quicksand does not suck you down, as we imagine. It does nothing. The way to escape it is to float above it, stretch your body as one does when one floats belly-up in the sea, and roll yourself like a barrel on the surface until you reach dry land. This information is of no use to me, however, deep in the Boston snow, sinking. Factoids rarely are.

Yonah doesn't understand. The most amazing fairytale manifests itself before my eyes, and I sit still, mute. I cannot tell him that this is the most wonderful minute of my life. Neither can I tell him that right this second, we may not be alone, that no one is safe. I am dreadfully aware of the fact that behind every bush, parked at any street corner, watching behind every street café, hides a monster . . . about to call, about to whisper, about to chase me, about to catch me. It is not a metaphor. Nor a fantasy. I am talking about a monster in flesh and blood.

# PART 3

# The Storm

# 6

Again, I will take a step backward, back to the past. That's where everything always ends up anyhow.

The years between 1993 and 1996 are painful years. For a minute, I was Simone de Beauvoir . . . I was Virginia Woolf . . . Me, a new Mary Shelley . . . But after Janusz Budulec took my heart and my hopes (not to mention all my friends) away, all I am . . . is nothing. I am left with a stinky purulent wound that completely defines me. I cannot shake myself from the shock. A voice that I internalized a long time ago, when I was too small to refute it, emerges from the depth of my being, repeating a refrain I know all too well: "*Quanto sei cattiva!* And because you're so bad you'll always be alone, Fania!" It is my mother's voice. She even indicts my generosity as my flaw. Or otherwise put, she says that I buy people's love. True, I want so badly to be wanted. I want to scream my love to the world and, hopefully, the world will say "Me, too, Fania! Me too!"

In English, they make the distinction between being alone and lonely: in Italian, we don't. Same thing for the words liberty and freedom. Liberty is an inalienable right, freedom is not. I yearn to eradicate both solitudes and conquer both freedoms. I still nourish the dream of meeting the one great love, the heroic prince of my childhood fantasies, who will not go away but who will help *me* leave . . . someone to trust, someone who will not give me material or emotional things just to suddenly yank them back and leave me naked and exposed like a little worm in the middle of the road. Someone who doesn't hurt like my mother. When I was small, my mother used to pile presents on me, edging on the obscene, in fact, by the standards of the 1970s (not an overly opulent era)—then, without warning, she would donate all my toys to the children of friends and acquaintances, to the poor, to charity, to Biafra moppets, accusing me that "You did not play with them!" or "That child deserves them more than you." And so from one day to the next my rag doll disappeared, or a half-finished puzzle, a wooden Pinocchio puppet, my carnival dress, my white shoes with brown ribbons, two bicycles, a cork-shooting rifle, ping-pong *and* foosball tables, the Barbie house (a four-story mansion with indoor elevator), roller skates, easy-bake oven, clackers, projector, electric car racing tracks, and every piece of small jewelry bought *not* by her and therefore labeled by my mother: "too vulgar." I thought I had found safety in my Polish boyfriend. But, ironically, Budulec did exactly the same to me.

Thanks in part to my family's money, and my undivided support, Budulec and I had built a publishing house together; we had assembled an impressive entourage of friends and international contacts; we had big prospects. The first shock came when Budulec told me, out of the blue, as if it were a thing of no importance at all, that he was married. All that time I had been with him, another woman with a legal claim over my lover had been without him. I got over his marriage, or rather the fact that he had hidden it from me, once he produced the divorce papers. A few years into our official relationship, while I happened to be back in Rome for the summer exam session, without even a word of explanation, a letter, or a phone call, Budulec disappeared. Three months earlier, he had started a sentence with a smashing "Faniusha, one day we will marry." Three months later, he was gone. I looked for him everywhere . . . nothing. Anyone who had a phoneline in the house got a call from me, everybody else a letter. No one saw him. *Is he dead?* No. *So where is he?*

"I'm going to Warsaw to see what happened," I told my parents, willing to postpone my exams at university and catch the first available flight.

"Get a grip! You have no dignity! I'm ashamed of you," thundered my mother, disgusted by her daughter's weakness. "Let *him* come find you!" But he never came. No one helped me reach him. Even our closest friends covered his tracks. Worst of all, I believed them when they told me "I have no idea where he is." It was as if he had died. (*I should be that lucky!*) I mourned him the way I would have on his grave. Except that I did not have a grave to visit. Sadly, he was alive and exceptionally well. I came apart. I cried until I damaged my eyesight; my father caught me by the belt of my blue jeans, as I climbed over the balcony's wrought iron rail, just as I was ready to jump; my mother kept hissing "What did you do to him?"

Budulec, *rydaktor naczelny* (editor-in-chief, as he liked to repeat proudly) with an ego of steel, a heart of mud, and a soul of distilled alcohol, left me without a farewell, without giving me a chance to understand what went wrong, without giving me a chance to fix it. We didn't fight, we didn't grow apart, we didn't fall out of love. Well, *I* didn't.

There was academic research to be finished in Warsaw, but there was no Warsaw for me to go back to. My mother bellowed: "What happened to your honor! I'd rather die than stoop to beg for anybody's love or going back where I am not wanted. Do not give anyone the satisfaction of seeing you broken like this, a discarded second-hand thing!"

The people who orbited around the publishing house, like icy comets who would be lost without his magnetic attraction, stuck to his plane. There was no room left for me in that cosmos. Even the books we worked on together were purged of my shadow. Oscar Wilde's *De Profundis* and W. B. Yeats's Cuchulain cycle, still on the shelves of every Polish bookstore, bear the name of only one of the two translators who produced them, the name of the one of the two who didn't speak a word of English. I had to start all over again. Including rewriting from scratch my dissertation, because the old topic was too enmeshed with that lost world.

Occasional sexual partners, and I had hundreds, are a safer bet. Nothing is asked of or by one-night stands or married lovers like Gwidon Goldblatt, who wish to betray wives not divorce them. For me, there is great solace in such barren dealings.

Budulec had taken Warsaw away from me, so I took Krakow by storm. Nobody knew me in Krakow. I found accommodation in a small apartment at 28 Szeroka Street. The tiny place was nestled between an old synagogue and a lifeless Jewish museum, and just opposite two café-restaurants practically next door to each other, both named *Ariel*, but owned by two different men in mortal competition against one another. In one of the *Ariels* stuff happened; in the other, nothing ever happened. One always had people inside, in the other the chairs and tables only accumulated dust. I chose the lively one. I spent one unforgettable year there. I met musicians, photographers, painters, actors, playwrights, and poets. I grew strongly attached to the whole microscopic Jewish community, whose older members had vivid firsthand memories of the past horrors and shared them with me.

It was there, at the cool *Ariel* café, that I made friends with one of the loveliest people in the world, Helena Jakubowicz, and later with a Dostoevskian character, Misha Davidovič Popkin—a Russian escapee in his mid-twenties, who with immense difficulty dragged himself out of Moscow and was on a slow, daedal way to Texas. His first stop: Krakow. Emaciated, lanky, with a head of curly blond hair, and, judging by the uncanny resemblance, made of the same genetic fabric of a Danny Kaye, Misha was disarmingly naïf. He understood very little of the world. He knew nothing about Judaism, other than his being Jewish caused only troubles in his life.

Misha had an incurable handicap: his mother. She was hell-bent on stopping him from leaving Moscow without her. He had attempted several escapes from Russia, but his mother's meddling had ruined his plans and forced him to desist, to return home, to invent new strategies. He made it to Krakow with the excuse of a doctorate in computer science at the Jagiellonian University. (At the time I had not put two and two together: it hadn't occurred to me that these PhDs are the Mayflower of a new class of emigrants.) Misha needed time to figure out how to inch onward, westward . . . next step, Berlin, and from there, Houston. In Texas, he told us, he had a patroness who would help him. A lady of a certain age, widowed, extremely wealthy, who apparently wanted to subsidize Misha and facilitate his asylum in America. This piece of information had not helped soothe his mother's fears. He called her a few times a day every day (very difficult and expensive, and certainly not private—the KGB in Moscow liked to listen); he promised, he reassured, he cajoled . . . unlike the KGB, his mother didn't listen. Instead of leaving her son alone, she cried, worried him, and guilt tripped him. He swore that he wouldn't abandon her, that their separation would be only temporary, until he obtained the papers and saved enough money for her to join him.

One day, Ariel's doors swing open, we all lean over our table to see who decided to join us (since no one expects customers in this place, ever) and what do we see? Framed in the doorway stands a tiny woman in a Soviet-style trench coat tied at the waist with a belt, big mop of black hair, and a large suitcase. She scans the place, squinting her nervous eyes like a raccoon who just found the cheese cave open. We jump and turn to look at Misha who moans out loud, "*Oy, mahma, oy!*"—in those soft, tender Russian syllables. Against all dictates of common sense, his mother has come. And to make things worse, against his specific admonition, she brought with her suitcases upon suitcases full of jewels, silverware, precious rugs, art objects, and family heirlooms, which the patrol officers on the train have readily seized. By the time she arrives in Krakow, her eyes are inflamed from crying: she begged, pleaded with, and offered to bribe the guards at the border. But the guards did not need to be bribed with a *kezayit* when they could have the whole *matzah*. Instead of giving her an earful, Misha consoles her as best he can. We sit there, sip our coffees, and giggle at this weird plot unfolding before our eyes.

At some point, without ceremony, I was evicted from my apartment on Szeroka. It seemed that the landlady, a certain *pani* Zosia (Mrs. Sophia), discovered that she was renting her apartment to a "suspect" individual—that is, neither Polish nor Christian, in short not the kind of girl she wanted. What she wanted was a girl who paid four times as much rent and in dollars. At my refusal, *pani* Zosia kicked me out. I didn't know what to do in the short turn-around time I was given (a matter of hours, not weeks). But Helena offered me her late grandmother's apartment. It was huge, it was vacant, it was for free . . . it was perfect! It was not in the old ghetto, but in one of those classy fin de siècle buildings, Viennese style, on Królewska Boulevard.

I made a lovely new life for myself there. I had loads of new friends. A glorious roof over my head. My writing was flourishing again. But I was blinded by sorrow. A deep melancholia blanketed even the happiest experiences—and I had plenty in my last year in Poland, at the Jagiellonian University. The only clear thing to me was my pain. And the fear that more pain could be inflicted any time by whomever I allowed myself to trust and love. Yet, I longed for love so much.

If I wanted to avoid more deadly blows, I must have concluded, I had to remain a moving target. A sitting duck gets the bullet.

So I keep moving. I move to Israel. *A bullet would have been better.*

Twenty-four hours after my arrival at the *ulpan*-kibbutz, they throw a party for us, *olim chadashim* (new immigrants), to get to know one another and launch in style this new life we are about to start here, together. It's fun. I find myself talking to everyone (I may be the only one who has access to all the languages spoken here, except for Flemish), and I feel quite safe among these kind and friendly people. Among Jews. I realize it feels bloody great to be the majority for once.

I dance all evening with an American. He is a handsome guy, two years older than me, with an athletic built, very tall, straight shoulders as if he had forgotten to remove the coat hanger from his shirt, a nice smile, very white teeth, full lips, and hypnotic green eyes. I can see he likes me. *Maybe there's a little fling here waiting to happen,* I wonder, amused. Why not?

On balance, it's all very well: he's American! I had forgotten about America. I had forgotten about New York. He too is here in Israel to become a citizen, but he does not seem very convinced of this choice. He also has the insurmountable limitation of a chronic monolingualism: this guy will never learn Hebrew. Ever. He has no talent for languages, he's like one of those "typical" Americans about whom comedians (especially non-American ones) go to town. For him, only America exists. He has no interest in (or knowledge of) other places. His parents urged him to come here and make *alyah*, the "repatriation" to Israel to which every diasporic Jew is automatically entitled. It was a maneuver to get him out of their way, but above all, to get him out of trouble. Apparently, in New Jersey, where he comes from, things were not going too well for him, he tells me . . . serious, seething.

"Where is this New Jersey?" I ask, indifferent to his dramatic climax.

"It's the state that borders with New York." My ears perk up. He has my full attention now. I am unmoved by the *Familienroman* he intends to share but quite taken instead by this extremely attractive fact about him: New Jersey . . . a step away from Manhattan . . . America. I see some potential. Maybe he is not quite the prince of my dreams, as I cannot spot too many apparent qualities in this one that would qualify him as the hero I was hoping for. But wait: He has a sense of humor! Notwithstanding his quirky laughing without making sounds, which is a red flag, like a limp handshake. If he moved here, it must mean that he has some curiosity and a taste for adventure—even if one has to dig real deep to find any overt sign of it. I will dig, no problem.

On the contrary, I should have paid attention to the whole story of how he ended up here, instead of digressing and starting to build castles in the air about New York again. One night, the New Jersey police stopped him, made him blow into the breathalyzer, and found signs of alcohol. After spending the night in a cell, he was released to the care of his shocked parents, who, before the rumor spread through their private clubs and circles, offered a new future to their degenerate (or degenerative) son . . . shipping him, first class, one way, to Eretz Israel. The land of the forefathers. The favorite desert of the Great Tetragrammaton. People (like any other substance) should be released into the world with "Warnings," "Instructions," "Stop use and ask a specialist if . . . ," and "Side Effects" specified in a personal leaflet or inked on the underside of their right foot.

The American and me—I'll call him the Criminal—explore a relationship further. He is very attached to me. He is perhaps too attached to me. While I flutter my wings like a lively butterfly, insouciant, he stays calm, quiet, away from most people, firm on his good conduct, almost obsessed with the idea of behaving and demonstrating that he's marriage potential. Definitely too obsessed. Too bottled up.

I alternately like him a moment and dislike him the next, until gradually the dislikable moments tip the scale . . . heavily. If he had seemed an interesting mystery to decode at first, he soon reveals everything there is to know: a catastrophic and thorough shallowness. I notice the admiration with which he speaks of his father (at the limit of the pathological), and most of all I am annoyed by his aggressive competitiveness that seems to be his only way of relating to everyone and everything. When he can't compete in the first person, he does so in the third: "My father made his first million before he was thirty years old," he manages to declare contemptuously in response to someone's mentioning a brother or a relative who just switched jobs. Zero empathy, I conclude.

These traits of his character irritate and alarm me, but I want to see where they lead, how much they affect the entirety of the individual, on balance, before drastically cutting all bridges and declaring this chapter closed for good. At the beginning there are also nice moments, affectionate, enjoyable.

Error. The one between this stranger and me is a story chained to a time bomb that starts ticking already at the first kiss.

He hates being with others. I love company. He keeps his true personality for the private sphere, hidden from the world's eyes. I overshare and lean on group support. I pity the sad blighter: he is so out of place. No one takes to him. He broods and feels sorry for himself. He is gnawed by guilt: he is sorry that he failed at the banking job his father had forced on him back home and that he hated with a passion (*he* dreamed of being a baseball coach). He is sorry that he failed as a son, sorry that he drove inebriated, sorry that he has been a pretty mediocre student who will do nothing of his education, and o so sorry that he went to Florida for an ill-advised hair transplant of which he bears the brunt on part of his forehead (he's obsessed with his look and its defects). God sometimes gives us signs—a toupee, say, or a full mustache are usually very good ones. He tells us something. He tells us, "Run! This one was a mistake, my bad."

We, the Criminal and I, don't work out. A closer look immediately puts into focus certain sides of his personality that are highly disturbing. We begin to quarrel: primarily, because I tell him I do not want to see him anymore. We begin a sentimental yo-yo: break-up, reconciliation, break-up, reconciliation, break-up. The reconciliations are always linked to how well, each time he wants to win me back, he paints the picture of a future together grounded in security, happiness, serenity . . . not alone. Like Brett & Galina, like Budulec and his new blond girl, like Paul Newman and Joanne Woodward, Queen Victoria and Prince Albert, Jane Eyre and Rochester, Orpheus and Eurydice . . . *no, maybe not Orpheus and Eurydice.* It's Israel's fault that he is so unhappy (he claims). In America, everything would be different: "Believe me" (he swears).

Polonsky's phone call arrives. Without any regard for the feelings of the Criminal, I erupt in paroxysms of happiness and deliver my good news to the four winds: "Sorry, everyone, I'm going to America! I wish you all great things. Good luck!" *Pheeeew,* I escaped. Brandeis *is* a life saver!

When people ask me about America's first impact on me, I always rehash the fiction I know they expect: "Fantastic, all so beautiful, oh my God, how amazing!" I skimp on the truth. I omit that I arrive at Logan Airport, August 14, 1996, pass through customs, head to the beautiful glass doors that separate that no-man's land that is an airport from the everyman's land that is the real world, the doors slide open on both sides . . . and waiting for me, out there, tall, white smile, straight shoulders, I see the guy from the kibbutz. He followed me.

Facts have a genealogy often more complex than memory wishes to admit.

I knew he wanted to follow me, I was not unaware of it. I had discouraged him but with the tone of someone who subliminally suggests, "Convince me!" It's my fault.

I ask myself: is it better to face this adventure in such a huge and mysterious country alone, or to have a solid anchor on the spot to avoid drifting, a point of reference to turn to for support? If, as he claims, he wants to return to America to live with me in Boston, to help me, to make it easier for me—*me, who struggles all alone all the time*—perhaps this is the time to acquiesce. My fault.

When I had mentioned to the Criminal over the phone that the university was providing housing arrangements for the first few weeks (I read of their dormitory called The Castle, with breathtaking views of Boston at the horizon), he had made a great argument against the idea: No! It's a bad idea! I mean, he grew up in America, went to university as well, he must know better, I need to trust what I hear from those who know better. If *I* knew better . . . but I don't. The Criminal was hurt, hard to distinguish from angry in his case. "You do not trust me! You don't think my intentions with you are serious! You'll see if I'll take care of you . . . Tell them to go fuck themselves and their student housing! I'll handle that. I'll go to Boston, find a house that suits us [house, he says, not apartment] and by the time you get here, it'll all be ready, and I'll be waiting for you." *Che fortuna!* I had told myself. Lucky me! This is a dream I can fall for: I won't be alone; I will be a stranger in a strange land, but I will not have to decipher everything by myself; I will have the help of someone who can translate this new culture for me, who can teach me how to navigate these uncharted waters without shipwrecking at the first whiff of wind. I will be as safe as . . . Eurydice with Orpheus.

I did see those houses (though in passing) on the outskirts of Boston myself, when I first visited. Stuff from *Little Women, Gone with the Wind, To Kill a Mockingbird* . . . I saw those houses all my life in the movies, in my imagination: the immense kitchens with white cabinets, the romantic fireplaces, front porches and gardens on all sides, bay windows, and skylights, sunrooms and screened doors on the back. I will be like Glenn Close in *The Big Chill* when she sits on the terrace with her friend Margaret JoBeth Williams, a cup of tea in hand, the breeze caressing them . . . and oceans or woods, mountains or lakes at the horizon. Can this be possible? Can Fania be good enough that someone indeed wants her? Wants her *so* much? Then what my mother used to tell me wasn't true! I might have been a bit naughty, but not as bad as I was made to believe. Not so bad as not to deserve love. It was just something my mother said to "teach me." An orchestra explodes in me, Judy Garland's voice rises like a wave from low to high . . .

*Somewheeeeeee-re over the rainbow*

*Ti amo,* I love you, Criminal!!

I arrive at Logan Airport, I see him standing by the large motion-sensor sliding door, he leads me to a taxi (he can't get a car until they restore his driver's license), and we go to a small hotel. He's been back a while but has not found a house yet. Once we are in the hotel room, he lets me know that he'll head back to New Jersey tomorrow. His father, whom he idolizes with unresolved Oedipal intensity, told him "I love you" (*for the first time?*) over the phone and offered, "Come home!" Since he couldn't keep him in Israel, and the prodigal son is unexpectedly back in the fatherland, he wants to assign him to a branch of his bank (in New Jersey) where he can slowly get back on his feet and make money like daddy does (in New Jersey). In New Jersey. But I am in Massachusetts. And in a few hours, I'll be (to be more exact) under the bridges of Massachusetts: on the street. Naturally, I can't afford life in the hotel for long. I could have been at The Castle, and instead I have to thank God if I find as much as a stable. And again, I didn't pack a map of the city with me, so I do not even know where we are. But I know where I am not: I am not in the house of *Little Women* or *The Big Chill*; I will not drink coffee on my porch, with a sweeping vista of woods and oceans, and neighbors who pass by and wish me *"Buongiorno,* Miss Fania!"

The sun rises, and the Criminal is gone.

I begin a desperate race against time to find an accommodation in this university town, home of Boston University, Harvard University, MIT, University of Massachusetts, Boston College, Northeastern University, Tufts University, Berklee College of Music, Emerson College, Bentley University, Wellesley College, Lesley University, Simmons College, Boston Conservatory, Fisher College, and Brandeis University, where as early as June each available room is stormed by millions of students from all over the world. I arrive late and . . . what is in motorsports the opposite position of pole position? Shit position? There, in tears and stress-vomiting, I stand, behind everyone else.

I shut myself in a phone booth on the street and call my parents, trying to explain the inexplicable. The whole family springs into action: Operation Daughter-Abroad Rescue. (Not a new genre for them.) I give life to a new character in the Italian emigratory mythology: the counter-stereotype of *lo zio d'America* (the uncle who emigrated and made it rich in America and is now expected to help everybody back home). I, *la figlia d'America* (the daughter in America), must be saved embarrassingly often by those I haughtily left behind.

I lived in Rome, in a house of marble floors, antique furniture, precious canvases on the walls, comforts and leisure, a life run smoothly by people who take care of you, squads of efficient helpers, modern appliances and hot water springing magically out of the showerhead, and I moved to Boston (which is not New York) where all I have to my name are a few hand tailored shirts but not much else. This is how my American nightmare begins. Fania's *incubo americano.*

Surreal weeks and months follow. On the one hand, I try to heal the psychological shock I just suffered, and on the other, I try to sustain the fiction with the rest of the world that everything is well; my own personal fiction is that I can lead a parallel life in which everything runs as smoothly as in a Hollywood film, just the way I had originally scripted it. In my cheerful Neil Simon-like comedy, I make new friends (Yonah, the billboard family next door, Shira), I attend university courses, I have a great time at holiday parties and dinners with professors and peers: behind these people's backs, a Sophoclean tragedy unfolds and becomes more and more problematical.

I dare not confide in anyone. Only my parents know more or less what is happening to me. With them there is no risk of losing face.

Through a friend of hers in Rome, my mother manages to place me for a while with an elderly couple who live in Newton, a rather chic area, halfway between Boston and Waltham. The woman, Liliana, is Italian, of humble origins: from a poor family with an overabundance of children, she had been sent away to work as a cook for some rich people when she was still a young girl. Her salvation in disguise. She had learned to cook so well that she was offered a job at the Italian Embassy in Lebanon, which, wisely, she accepted. While working as a chef there, she learned to speak French and turned into a classy woman, with almost no traces left of her plebeian genesis. She also married in Beirut and had two children over there. She is beautiful and possesses an innate aristocratic grace. The man, Azad Sarafian, Lebanese Armenian, is a very skilled tailor, with a head of crazy hair like Einstein, a mustache like Saddam Hussein, the physique of Super Mario, and the typical crankiness of the Mediterranean soul. Always on the verge of getting angry. Generous to a fault. He sounds like he'd stab you if you don't eat to your bursting point, if you don't do as he advises, if you don't move in with them as a guest permanently, if you try to pay at a restaurant instead of letting him offer, if you as much as think of refusing his gift of a new bike, new mattress, a chair for your desk, and so on.

Their story has a sassy twist: and I wonder if it wasn't this excessive generosity that got Azad in trouble. Liliana, with her then husband and children, left Lebanon as refugees and went to Canada where her brother-in-law had already settled down with his own family and was willing to help them. Her brother-in-law was Azad. Azad and his wife took their relatives into their home: and then Azad took Liliana altogether, eloping to America and triggering a half-century-long family feud. Predictably, it wasn't a cordial separation for either couple. But the extraordinary thing is that our modern-day Mark Antony and Cleopatra spent the subsequent forty years of their lives in battle. Each doesn't trust the other and both are dedicated, heart and soul, to destroying each other. They are the less striking version of *The War of the Roses*.

And I find myself in their house playing the role of Marianne Sägebrecht, Michael Douglas and Kathleen Turner's governess in the film. Liliana's jealousy toward me makes my days a living hell: the more Azad unloads his generosity on me, the worse the situation with her becomes for both of us.

On top of the list of what constitutes her domestic drama—which includes the fact (1) that to punish her, Azad has never officially married her, (2) that she holds a secret job as caterer in order to set aside enough money to run away from him one day, (3) that she must prepare for him three meals a day, at strictly set hours, worthy of a pasha or otherwise "I'm in trouble," and (4) that Azad spies on all her phone calls and controls every step or breath she takes—well, all of the above aside, she ranks the biggest problem of her life not having a driver's license. She explains that in America you cannot survive without a driver's license. "Look at me!" She howls in anguish: "I am stuck!" I immediately look into how to get one. It is Azad himself who accompanies me to the driving test, in his huge Lincoln Coupé. It's a cinch. I do not know exactly what I need a driver's license for while I am here as a graduate student without a car for only a limited amount of time, but something, perhaps Liliana's howling, tells me that it's better to have one than be without it.

The Criminal reappears. Repentant. He shows up more and more often, unpredictably and uninvited, when I least expect him. Where I least expect him. His promises are even more tempting than before: more tempting as they now imply that I can leave the house of Azad and Liliana where I am about to get a colossal nervous collapse, because of their arguments, tensions, and jealousies of which I am the epicenter. The Criminal returns with moods and intentions I can't quite read. Azad and Liliana know why I ended up with them (my mom told everyone), but they do not know that the Criminal is back, prowling around his prey. I dare not confess it to them. Meanwhile I walk on eggshells, weighing my odds, trying to figure out what's better: the frying pan or the fire. I suspect he hides everywhere. I am besieged by loonies.

I find the attic for rent in Waltham. Azad resents me because I'm escaping his hospitality, an affront. Liliana resents me because she is accused by her husband of having made me feel unwelcome, because now she will be alone with him again, without a scapegoat, because she won't have me to practice Italian with, because she loses the only other woman around who reminds her of herself when she was young with the game of life still unplayed. The Criminal resents me . . . because he is the Criminal, that's all.

Azad, as a good Ottoman patriarch, insists on meeting Charles Fisher on Orange Street and letting him know that I have a family of sort here and therefore "Don't get strange ideas with her, treat her honorably!" Poor Azad, he's barking at the wrong tree.

The Criminal's apparitions, now that I am gaining a certain independence even from him, begin to be less peaceful, less promising. Unfortunately, he already knows where I live.

*Somewhere . . . over the rainbow . . .*

Liza Minelli, daughter of Judy Garland, Dorothy in *The Wizard of Oz*, married Jack Haley junior, son of Jack Haley senior who was the Tin Man in *The Wizard of Oz*. Some people's stories do have happy endings.

The Criminal now has a car and also a new job in New Jersey, courtesy of his father. He begins to call me, occasionally at first, constantly after a while: and those are good moments between us. He is a completely different person then. He jokes, he talks sensibly, he is interested in how I am doing, he asks me if I need favors or advice. Over the phone, he starts talking about the future. About "our" future, together. Over the phone I let him say whatever he wants; and I feel well-disposed, thanks to the geographical distance that helps a lot with the physical safety. He makes promises which would be great if they came from a sane and balanced person who could actually bring them to fruition: he sounds so sane and balanced over the phone. Promises which I'd like to believe because I am stubborn, because the alternative is too demoralizing, and because I absolutely need them. I let myself be attracted by the brightness (too intense, in fact) that his promises project like stage lights in a theater, which is otherwise totally dark: you need lights onstage! They animate the scene, lighten it up, make it real . . . the limelight reveals the plot toward which I extend and it places it within reach. I stretch out for it, but, abruptly, pain yanks the veil off the eyes of reality: the limelight is illusional, a flame for the moths. It is nothing but a mere lark mirror, a deceptive instrument to attract birds that like shining objects. In the darkness, you see the little light and think it's a safety exit, but in reality it is precisely beyond that luminous threshold that the realm of the discernable ends.

The Criminal appears and disappears. The Criminal hurts me when he appears. I go home to my attic and find him there, without warning. (*But Charlie does not see or hear him?*) After a few nice moments—I learned to be gentle, persuasive, deft like a lion tamer—the Criminal is invariably overcome by an uncontrollable rage that he vents against me and my few but dear possessions. Then he disappears and I can go back to pretending he was never there in the first place and return myself to the beautiful half of my double life.

I do not say anything to anyone. The Criminal is my dirty secret, one to be kept in the skeletons' closet. I'll handle the Criminal. I am smarter; above all, I am sane; and so I'll win this war, even if I'm losing all the battles. The Criminal is a sportsman, hence a competitive creature; his daily bread, since he was young, were sports and competition: "I always win," he assures me. Not necessarily thanks to his intelligence, but thanks to pure tactical strategy, I start to realize. In one of the "reappear" phases, that is, one of those periods when he comes back to hunt for me, and I, in order to catch my breath (fleeing all the time is exhausting!), let myself be "caught," he insists that I go meet his parents.

His family welcomes me with overacted enthusiasm. They are a cross between the Patimkins in *Goodbye Columbus* by Philip Roth and the protagonists of Irène Némirovsky's *David Golder*. The environment is pharaonic. From the magnifications of his son, I had pictured the father as a man not too dissimilar from Patrick Swayze, while instead I find myself shaking hands with Danny DeVito, who has to tilt his neck back to take a good look at me with his brown eyes unnaturally close to one another. He has an amused smile on his round face, between smug and sarcastic. A man who may want to wear little bells around his ankles to be tracked down as he walks in this house so much bigger than he. Both parents are bankers: the father knows how to make money, the mother knows all the rest. You could define her as a Yahoo, the frightening pseudo-equine race from Jonathan Swift's *Gulliver's Travels*, complete with all the required character frills—cunning, manipulative. She is the jailer (with a human face) of her two invertebrate males, an ally of her two daughters, and has specific plans in mind for them in the implementation of which no one better hinder her. The sisters are two beautiful girls, affable in that disinterested yet unfavorable way that only a thoroughbred American Princess can optimize.

His parents and siblings gather all the information they need, all the while trying to conceal that I am undergoing the Third Degree. The father wants to know about my future plans: the fact that I am studying for a PhD exerts a big dose of admiration—for Americans, educational qualifications are like nobility titles for us Europeans. To my surprise, they are particularly moved by my desire to live in New York and stay in America after the PhD.

"If possible," I say.

"It *is* possible!" says the mother without hesitation: "You must get your documents!"

"The documents?" asks the father, short of imagination. A conversation for four voices—like a dissonant mid-century concert—ensues. Son, daughters, and mother are all talking over each other about documents, about the labyrinthine immigration bureaucracy, about the green card . . . without me or the father having to put a single word of ours in. The green card project begins. The philanthropic and Samaritan aspirations of the women at the table troubles the father a little: the women sympathize, empathize, identify with me, and become more and more enthusiastic. The man is suspicious and a bit bored. They've embraced this new cause of theirs: but I no longer know for sure what they are thinking about. To lobby in Washington for a change in the immigration laws? Or the future of the Criminal? No matter, they are playing this hand of the game with all their cards on the table. They take me off guard. I relax, I open up. This is an atmosphere that I know well, because I too grew up at a table where everyone has something to say and does not accept to be left hanging without chiming in. I do not feel like an alien, but an appreciated guest, who is quickly gaining a place in the hearts of those who welcomed me. I look at the Criminal with a different eye: you do not really know a person until you place him within his total, original context.

I carry my dish to the kitchen, and I run into an African American woman, sitting in a corner, hands in her lap, who is quietly waiting. I jump a mile, and so does she. *Why would they force a woman to hide here in silence and isolation?* My first instinct is to ask her if she wouldn't want to join us, but the words catch in my throat. Something tells me that the lady of the house would kill me. I only manage a faint "Thanks" raising the dish in my hand, to indicate that if, as I suspect, she is the one who cooked the food we ate, it was all quite delicious and full of undeserved care and quality. But before I can put my syllables together, I hear the slightly hysterical voice of the lady of the house summoning me back to the table: "What are you doing?! Come here, please!" By then everything has been fully planned.

They talk about "serious intentions." They practically put my hand into his. I go with the flow. But I am as still as a statue not to rock the little boat I'm floating on. If I humor the Criminal without too much resistance, if I let myself be carried away for a while, like *dead* weight, say, then he won't even see it coming when one day I will beat it without leaving a trace. A little like Liliana, but with a driver's license.

But he's a better strategist than I: because where his mind ends, his muscles begin. Where the sentimental conquest fails, the tactics of bodily destruction take over.

Unlike in Israel, where the physical distance (or was it the holiness of the place?) had had a taming effect on him, and he was busy making amends for his faults, America infuses a new courage in the Criminal. Here, he plays on his homefield. Now that his father has forgiven him, rehabilitated him, and put him back on track (work, money, late grandma's apartment to his name to live in), he has raised his crest again, ready to enter his home arena in a match with an opponent who knows neither the field nor the rules of the game.

The Criminal appears in Boston unexpectedly, out of nowhere, and ends up making disconcerting scenes. More and more destabilizing for me. What of the marriage proposal? And the green card? And my entry into the benevolent bosom of his family? He is overtaken by sudden rages, which he conveys violently in ways that I thought possible only in sentimental B-movies—but even the soapiest telenovela at this point would *Fade, Black out, and Cut!* The camera instead keeps rolling in high definition through my life's next act.

So instead of jumping up and down with joy and rushing to pack when Yonah tells me "One day, if it all goes well," I sit on pins and needles. I wait for a more hands-on proposal, while part of my brain fixates on the possibility that someone is hiding in the shadows of the tree fronds, in the spaces between houses, inside a car with fogged-up windows. Behind every bush there hides the monster, at every step I hear the chains rattle . . . how do I tell Yonah that I am "possessed"? That I am not free, and I do not know how to free myself? And above all that informal cohabitation is not a winning proposal at the moment? My eyes tell him: "No, marry me, as soon as possible! . . . And while we are at it, let's also call the police!"—but not my lips. My lips remain sealed.

I am too ashamed to confess that I lied to him all these months. That I led a double life. That I prefer the one I have with him, but I do not know how to get rid of the other one. That I am making a mistake and need help, because I cannot trust my ability to pull myself out of this tangle. And most of all, that I need him to be a hero and rescue me.

In *The Purple Rose of Cairo*, Tom Baxter (a film character who leaps off the cinema screen in mid movie and wants to remain in the real world) sits in the car with Cecilia, a working-class woman whom he loves and whose husband is an abusive brute. Tom Baxter (Jeff Daniels) tells Cecilia (Mia Farrow): "If he hits you again, you tell me. I'd be forced to knock his teeth out." To which Cecilia says, "I don't think that'd be such a good idea. He's big." But (pay attention, because this is where the hero shows he is no everyman) Tom Baxter unfazed replies: "I'm sorry. It's written into my character, so I'd do it." *O if only our actions were dictated by good screenwriters!*

I venture a few words about what's going on behind the scenes; granted, in a tentative and inconclusive way. Yonah looks imperturbable: it's as if these fragments of information do not concern us. Or rather, as if he lowered a barrier to protect himself from them. It's as if he didn't hear my voice. "Did you hear me?" I would like to shake him. But, after all, it is better if he hasn't listened. I am ashamed before him. One who puts herself in a situation like this is not material for a Yonah.

I need time. First of all, I have some cleanup to do. Better to handle the mess with the Criminal in a hurry, on my own, without involving third parties, and then I will be free to explain to Yonah in detail what I cannot even explain to myself at present. And at that point, we will be able to pick up where we left off.

Rather than confessing the dimensions of the tragedy in full, in the end, I decide to cut loose the rope that ties me to Yonah. For now. Just for the time being. For a while, I will see him a bit less. *Machiavellian maneuvers. Ninja moves. Nifty manipulations. I'm good at this.* I end up not seeing Yonah anymore.

# 7

I keep losing weight, and I am always sleepy. I often fall asleep in the large lecture hall where Art Green holds his lessons on philosophy and Kabbalah to an audience of hundreds of students glued to his voice. I fall asleep when I go hear a guest speaker. I even fall asleep at the cinema. I feel hot and sweaty. My mother scolds me on the phone: "It's anxiety! You are always anxious! Take a sedative! *Cavolo,* calm down!"

I can't calm down. I am persecuted by the Criminal, who appears, destroys, goes away, and restarts the cycle after each pause. His rage now is due to the fact that I did not accept his marriage proposal: if instead I had accepted, had I said yes, *he* would calm down, he would be an angel, I would not have so many problems and . . . bruises. "Never again! Never, I swear it," he swears. Yonah who was so large in my existence has now shrunk, to a dot.

I can't wait for summer to arrive: the sun will help.

Everything went awry since the start of the year. For winter break, all students left en masse. Not me. I have decided not to go to Rome. Why should I? I came to *be in* America, to integrate myself fully into the flow of the local life, to have an authentic experience. Returning home for the holidays would be like admitting that "home" is actually elsewhere, not where you are, where you work and live, but where mom and dad are. What kind of independence would this be? My choice would only look like a whim, a form of academic tourism. I am different from the others! Let those Italians behave like . . . Italians, all the time. Run home to mom and dad, loving families, good foods, old friends . . . No sir, I am here: here with the Criminal who turns and changes like the weather, who demands a stable relationship (no matter how unstable he is from every standpoint); here in Waltham, a town already desolate all year round, but which, in the cheerful Christmas season, becomes so dreary that even the flies commit suicide and fall dead on the snow. I stay here, where the top of bon ton for people is to switch their usual t-shirts for a sweatshirt.

For my birthday at the end of November, my parents sent a hefty package with edible and wearable treasures. For New Year's Eve, my mother has envisioned me in a long, black, velvet dress, with an open décolleté, and the tiniest lace around the neckline. She sent it together with the whole matching trousseau: underwear, makeup, pantyhose, shoes options, *pochette,* and foulard. Things cooled down significantly since Yonah's proposal—upon which he hasn't returned. But he and I made plans to spend New Year's Eve together. I take it as a good sign. New Year's Eve is supposed to be fun: after the night's party, we plan on spending the first day of 1997 marathon-watching episodes of *Seinfeld,* reading the year's first edition of the *Boston Globe,* and eating pizza.

However, on December 31, at lunchtime, the Criminal shows up unannounced. It ends with me on the phone, unable to hold back the tears, telling Yonah that I won't be able to go through with our plans for the evening party, morning *Boston Globe,* and all that. He, with sweet discretion, accepts the situation without insistence, without further investigation . . . probably to respect my privacy. *I wish for a prince who does not believe you when you lie to him under duress, one who trusts his instincts which, at present, clearly suggest "The princess is in danger, I must save her!" And he comes and saves me. Prince Charming fights for you, he does not give you up, he insists until his love triumphs over all adversities.*

For now, the only one who insists, who does not give me up, even when explicitly and unambiguously rejected, is the Criminal. Who, when he senses that his love is not triumphing over the adversities he put in its way, pushes me down the stairs, sending me to the ER (*end of romance?*). At the ER, the Criminal insists on being in the room with me while the nurse takes her records and asks about the nature of the accident. So I give the nurse the oldest explanation in the world: I fell. *Felice 1997!*

Yonah smaller and smaller at the horizon.

Sooner or later the good season will come.

The sweating, sleepiness, and anxiety do not subside.

The Criminal, frightened by the hospital episode, doesn't manifest himself for a while.

I do not feel like doing anything. I am exhausted and dejected.

I take an appointment at the university students' clinic. The doctor looks at me and asks: "Have you noticed that big lump on your neck?" No, I reply. What lump? *Here it is, the evil disease I have been awaiting all my life, feared and awaited, awaited and feared . . . Cosmic irony at work. The hour that puts an end to all hours. Everything was for naught! Paris, London, Warsaw, Doctorate, Tel Aviv, surviving the bomb on the Jerusalem bus, writing (especially writing), love, hate! All was for naught!* She chuckles unaffected: "No need to undress: that lump is from your thyroid . . . I'll send you immediately to the hospital for a screening."

"Am I dying?" I ask.

"You're lucky!"

Right, then I *am* dying.

"You are in the perfect place for this! Here we have MGH [*My God in Heaven?*] which boasts the most cutting-edge Endocrinology Unit in the world. Even the Sheikhs come here to get treated," she says. I am glad for them. But this doesn't help with my own diagnosis and prognosis. I'm sure the Sheikh would be fine in *any* hospital . . . because it's not the hospital that makes the Sheikh, it's the Sheikh that makes the hospital. I doubt that the common patient receives the same treatment as those who come out of a black limousine, colorful turban, armed escort, a suitcase full of diamonds, and a pledge to the doctor for either a premium villa in Qatar or beheading by scimitar—depending on the surgery outcome.

The first thing that Dr. Gilbert Daniels at MGH asks me is "Have you suffered a big shock recently?" I blink at his words and fail to come up with an answer. He continues: "Hyperthyroidism is hereditary [*thank you, mom!*], but it could remain latent all your life . . . until a strong emotional trauma—like a loss in the family, or a divorce—can activate it because of the tremendous stress such events carry with them." *A psychopath who wants to marry me but who also wants me dead, and who haunts me for two years, would that count?* If I told him, I am sure the doctor would say, "Well, take a sedative, and stop seeing the psychopath." I limit myself to suggesting: "Perhaps, the move from Europe, the new life at the university . . . it's been a very difficult period." The doctor ventures a 360-degree diagnosis: "But you must be a ridiculously over-sensitive person then." *Would that be curable?* I don't think it's a compliment. Only a really weak person, I think the doctor is insinuating (well, stating, actually), would let such a change in her life affect her health to this point. In short, my condition could have been avoided. My fault.

I am in Boston, a three-hour drive from New York, and I have Graves Disease. My head automatically translates it into Italian: *malattia della tomba* (tombs disease). Which, when I think of it more calmly, may not refer to the destination this disease inevitably leads you to but rather to the Irishman who discovered it in 1835, Robert J. Graves. In Europe it is more commonly called Basedow Disease, named after the German scientist, A. Basedow, who cataloged it two years later. I do not know what is less ominous: a disease that takes its name from Doctor "Graves" or from a German doctor whose first name, usually only initialed, for good reason, was Adolph.

New personal discovery: the American hospital. A five-star hotel, in which you gladly live or die in lavish luxury.

Mass General Hospital and its Thyroid Unit should be included in every single tour guide in the world: in particular, there should be state-mandated expeditions for Italian visitors. My experience with hospitals is rather want-ing. The first occurred at the San Filippo Neri Hospital in Rome, where they misdiagnosed my abdominal cramps as peritonitis and then operated and in-fected the wound in a life-threatening way. I was twelve and the cramps were due to my first menstrual period: I ended up in surgery, recovering from an appendectomy and fighting back the rottenness on my belly while suffering the torments, and confusion, of my first female bleeding.

The second was a hospital in Krakow where I checked in because of in-tolerable spasms in the lower stomach. The X-rays (printed on a nineteenth-century daguerreotype slab) revealed a dark mass in the pelvic area. Thanks to Gwidon's intervention, the whole Italian diplomatic apparatus got into action, and *bibbidi-bobbidi-boo!*, I got out of there, back to Rome, in a private clinic this time—where it turned out that the dark mass in my guts were un-expelled feces. (I have always suffered from constipation . . . the doctors could have asked.) Constipation aside, my adventure in the Polish hospital is etched in my memory and bears a distinct smell of burnt cyanide-coffee. A *déjà-vu* straight out Bulgakov's *A Young Doctor's Notebook* with Gogolian overtones.

They were all so curious about me in that hospital: a nonbenevolent curiosity. There was something offensive about me . . . even intrusive. What was I, a foreigner who spoke perfect Polish and with money to be treated anywhere else, doing in that hospital? Unless I was a spy? Or a nutcase, hence to be feared just as much as a spy? I was quiet and reserved while also affable toward everyone . . . all qualities that rang suspicious in such a hellish environment: if in a place like this you preserve a sliver of the human spirit, it obviously means that you are an alien, a "sick" one, destined to perish. I remember a small room. My bed was against the wall. On another bed, there lay another woman, large, not old, with a very maternal air about her. There was something about this lady that suggested that her hospitalization was not going to be temporary. She looked like someone who came here never to leave. I did not ask for special treatment, and I did not receive any. Yet I had the impression that being treated on an equal footing was already a special treatment.

In the morning, we were awakened at half past five by the priest on his ward round. I nodded my good morning, but inside I was bracing myself for a confrontation.

"*Nie, dziękuję,*" I utter quietly. The priest, communion wafer in hand, stares at me without a word. He knows that an accusatory silence is more powerful than any vocal injunction to behave like good Christians: sooner or later, the Christian breaks. Less so the Jew.

"No, thanks," I persist unbendingly. Had I set fire to the priest in his black burqa with a flamethrower, the news couldn't have spread more quickly all over the hospital, and possibly would have had a lesser effect. "The new patient, the Italian one, refused the holy wafer." "The Italian refused the holy wafer and Jesus' blessing." "The Italian refused the holy wafer and . . . the Italian is not 'Italian'!" I couldn't be a greater disappointment for the Poles: how can one be so lucky to be born in Rome (Rome! Heart of Christianity! The seat of the Polish Pontiff) and yet have the brazenness, the impudence, the carelessness of . . . refusing to be Catholic.

I now imagine the whole sad scene: The priest hears that there is a woman from Rome in the Gynecology ward; he spends the night waking, praying to become worthy of the encounter; he carefully smooths his cassock in the morning and straightens the stole just so and rushes to the ward, hoping to bask, albeit indirectly, in the holy light of Karol Wojtyła's city, of St. Peter's princedom. Instead, the Italian waves her hand sheepishly and says: "No, thank you." He was a thin man, with a serious face, without a single smile for me. He aroused great fear in me. The following day, he ignores me completely. He doesn't even utter a generic "Good day" addressed to the room—to indicate "Hello to all of you dear women, in this valley of misery, good Christians or not"—as I would expect one of his colleagues in Italy to do, especially in Rome where priests tend to be mellower and have a decent sense of humor. Once ignored by the prelate, I am immediately seen under a terrible light by everyone.

At that point comes the call from my powerful friend at *Politicus,* Gwidon Goldblatt. In his native language, Polish, Gwidon delivers his message, flavoring it with that very special tone that only members from the same national tribe grasp in all its intimidating nuances: he tells them that an Italian has been admitted there, that the Italian consulate has been informed, and the government is getting ready to repatriate her. They better make sure nothing happens to her. His surname doesn't fool his *lantzmen:* he is also *not* on the priest's team. He is hated and feared in equal measure. What I didn't know at the time is that the Ur-call, the one that had mobilized Gwidon in the first place, had come from my mother, who, in a panic over knowing I was in a hospital in Krakow, had turned to Gwidon, asking him to intervene. She had come up with the perfect idea: my friend, my boss, and my secret lover of so many years. How she got his number is still a mystery to me. And if my mother knew whom to call, did she also know why? Why him. None of this was ever discussed.

I could be more grateful to Gwidon in retrospect, were it not for the fact that I owe my third hospital experience to him. Gwidon acted recklessly, and I was visited by catastrophe. "Oh come on! What do you think will happen? You don't get pregnant for doing it without a condom *one time!*" he derisively responded to my bewildered yelp, and the subsequent hysteria, upon realizing what he had just done. The amorous intercourse with him was so cursory, so precocious, and so imperceptible—because of size issues not worth further belittling here—that one never knew exactly where or what his pecker was doing. I had an abortion. The San Filippo Neri in 1995 was still the same indecent slaughterhouse I had known twelve years earlier. They did a terrible job of it, and I suffered greatly. Lifting my honor like a magic shield (as my mother would have liked), I had told Gwidon, "Don't worry, no need for you to accompany me." He should have refused my refusal, he should have insisted on coming, he should have taken responsibility. He didn't. I never slept with him again. He never assigned me another article to write.

Here I am now at MGH, where one thing is clear from the beginning: you can eat your lunch on the floor, lick off any drop of mayonnaise that should escape from your sandwich, and survive without undesired effects. It is a bit like being a character in one of those films where a person dies and awakens in Paradise without realizing it at first. Now I finally understand why in these films (American films, obviously) the protagonist flaunts that typically idiotic expression that says "where am I?" which makes no sense to an Italian. If, after an accident, an Italian came to and found herself in a clean place, without graffiti on the walls or vandalized latrines, she would immediately know that this is Heaven, not Italy. While it is clear that an American might actually think at first glance, "Oh, I must be at the hospital!"

MGH features clean, gigantic elevators, a striking lack of crowds. (In Italy, you'd have to zigzag your way through a sea of confused masses scattered in search of information, lost in corridors that have no signposts, endlessly queuing in front of abandoned service windows.) You don't sense the typical atmosphere full of panic and dejection you invariably encounter at the Spallanzani, San Filippo Neri, Sant'Andrea, Forlanini Hospitals. Here, it's like entering an office of a very rich firm: secretaries with manicured hands use high-tech machines to dig all necessary data about patients, and they file hard copies of your documents in folders, files and boxes perfectly organized by shape, color, and size. Once your information (especially race) is in the system, a whole different assembly line is set into motion: a nurse makes you sign the entry and release papers, one guides you to a second waiting room, where a third one weighs you, while a fourth takes your blood pressure and temperature. All this in decorated, clean rooms, which suggest serenity and well-being, echoed in the bright pictures of tens of magazines piled up here and there, and the reassuring sight of water dispensers with small glasses at every corner. After the examination, Doctor Daniels himself calls me at home to give me the results of the tests, and he tells me to go back to see him in three days. Three days. In Italy, it takes three days to get through to someone on the phone.

Like a contestant on a quiz show, or one of Portia's suitors in *The Merchant of Venice*, I receive three options: if I guess the correct one, I might live. (1) Surgical removal of the thyroid—dangerous for the vocal cords; (2) medications—effective immediately but uncertain in the long run; (3) radioactive iodine—two terrifying words, the most aggressive method. Doctor Daniels gives me a book to read on the subject. Only indication: I must decide quickly. "I give you three months at most," he says with a handshake. Three months of life! *If I have only three months of life left, the most effective of the methods offered will still only grant me one or two extra months at best?! But I want all my life, not just a piece of it!* "Three months, I mean, before you incur serious risks of cardiac arrest," specifies the doctor. The cardiac arrest was about to be induced by his hasty words "three months at most." I breathe again. I choose radioactive iodine.

The day of the procedure, I return to the hospital with a face fit for a funeral, my own . . . therefore particularly gloomy.

I am assisted from beginning to end by various professional staff members in white smocks. If they have a smock, it means that they know what they are doing. They don't give out smocks to people without some kind of medical degree, I presume. You cannot have a smock and not have the authority that comes with it. Their smiles are soothing: they know they are dealing with someone who can potentially lose it at any point, I think. Pearly smiles. Low voices. Clear eyes. Odorless breaths. They take all the precautions: they neither say too much nor too little. A fundamental art, so as to avoid lawsuits. They assign me to a little room, even though I am not technically admitted for a hospital sleepover: there is a cabinet where I must lock my belongings, a window with a view of the intensely blue Boston sky, a sofa, two armchairs, a coffee table, a TV set, a bed, a bathroom, two wardrobes, a colorful rug, and two types of lights: 100-watt incandescent for good news, 40-watt florescent for illness.

At the end of a long, immaculate corridor, I see a very tall door to the right, with a glass porthole on the upper third and a large red light affixed on the doorframe, like those used in radio stations or a Swiss bank. They lead me inside: it's a very small and dark space. Octagonal. It is a bare room, save for one single chair in the middle of it. It reminds me of a Beckett stage. *Enter doctor:* who, after the perfunctory greetings, embarks on an endless explanation, the gist of which is that I must be complicit with my own end. Come to think of it, Americans exclude beheading from their capital punishment methods: too fast, too sudden, and it catches the convict unprepared. They'd rather you fully understand what is happening to you. And while I think, *Why am I here?* my folks are sitting at the dinner table right now: night has fallen upon Rome, there are those who are preparing for an evening show at the Sistina Theater, others are about to catch a late meal at Insalata Ricca, and I am alone, without a soul outside waiting for me, at Mass General Hospital, taking care of a problem that I accepted as real as soon as it was presented to me, without asking further questions or a second opinion, at the mercy of a doctor who I believe is the best in the world . . . just because they told me he is. Too late.

He leaves the room through the same opening from which he came. This was just a preliminary chitchat. When he returns, he has changed into a space suit complete with a full helmet and gloves like huge oven mitts. Squinting, dazed, as if to steal the secret of a trick that I hadn't anticipated and that now feels pivotal to my survival, I follow every movement of his with growing concern. I am at the center of a masterful dramatic operetta in which I will be the only character absent from the stage at the end. Finally, I notice a small, tiny bottle in the middle of the doctor's right mitt. The glass bottle is black like ink.

Doctor Daniels dramatically places the potion next to me. The black bottle faces me with its single, universally readable sticker: the image of a skull with the two cross-sectional bones under the chin. Either Mass General is a pirate ship, or the medicine I'm about to take is fatal to humans. I'm waiting for the doctor to say something, but I do not hear his Darth Vader rattle from under the NASA armor. He moves slowly as if he were fighting the absence of gravity. Slowly he walks away from me and the radioactive ampoule. *Exit doctor.*

Once out of the room where he left me, Doctor Daniels opens a porthole in the middle of the door, looking his old self again, and acting as if he had just chanced into me at the Russian Tea Room on a Saturday afternoon: "Great! Now take the bottle . . . over there on the table . . . and drink the content." I manage to get out a whisper and ask why I have to drink something that he does not even dare touch. But the doctor shuts the window without answering. I am the type of convict who lowers his collar so as to inconvenience the executioner as little as possible.

When, many months later, my medical relationship with Doctor Daniels and MGH finally comes to an end, I read in the medical records they handed me on my way out, that "The patient talks about eating problems, and emotional troubles due to strong anxiety and extreme stressful situations." That "The patient moved a year ago from Italy; the change caused her stress." That "The patient does not seem to have suffered any other trauma or intense psychological shock." *They all always believe me.* Synthroid once a day for the rest of the patient's life.

A textbook case: Hyperthyroidism = a pill every morning. A very simple and reassuring equation. That's what I love about science: cause-effect-solution. For all other existential cases, though, I am in the dark, feeling my way around for a black bottle that clearly declares with a skull and two bones under it: "Here's death."

# 8

*Winter.* My friend Shira speaks of nothing but marriage. She doesn't have a boyfriend and I do not think she cares about love per se: but she really wants to have children, so she needs a husband—she herself puts it that pragmatically. We laugh about it together. I am even less romantic, I reassure her: I'd do without marriage quite well, were it not for that little issue of the green card . . . and I don't want children and hate those who do, which makes her think I am utterly insane.

Every now and then, her parents summon her back to Baltimore to introduce her to this or that son of their friends and acquaintances. Her father is in the laundry business, he owns a small store chain: her mother is a housewife. They sent Shira to Brandeis hoping she would meet a good Jewish boy here: a future doctor, a lawyer, a politician, a Wall Street broker, or (if all else fails) a dentist. Clearly this grandchildren idea is very dear to them as well. She is in no way a nerd: she is going through the motions for her master's degree, without enthusiasm, because she "must" and soon it'll be over. She is using graduate school to fill the days between undergraduate school and motherhood, in a suburb of Washington, DC, a short distance from her parents' house.

I introduce Yonah to her, but I don't tell her about the Criminal. Like everyone else, she too is bowled over by the sight of us together: "Such a perfect couple, you two!" So intellectually alike, with so much in common . . . a match made in heaven, they say. About 47 percent of marriages in America originate in the classroom: high school for working class folks, college classrooms for middle-class boys and girls, graduate lecture halls for upper class people. Therefore, statistics are on Shira's side. And therefore, it is absolutely normal that one day I show up on campus with an engagement ring. The women notice it immediately, and a chorus of "ooooooo!!!" "uuuuuuuu!!!" "awwwwwwwww!" raises to heaven indeed. Just the right culmination of such a beautiful love story!

Except that the ring did not come from Yonah. The Criminal put it on my finger. Nobody knows anything about the Criminal. I wish so much to lie. To say it is from Yonah instead. But this would be too big a lie, even for me. If I lie, it'll be like throwing downhill an innocuous snowball that in about two days would turn into the avalanche of Mount Huascarán proportions (*22,000 feet, 4,000 deaths*). We are, after all, on a small campus. Someone will soon meet Yonah in the history department (Polonsky himself, for example) and congratulate him, "Mazal tov! I heard the good news!" I can imagine Yonah squinting, as if trying to stare down an oncoming eighteen-wheeler, while mentally devising an escape exit not too demeaning for him, or perhaps for me.

*Somewhere . . . over the rainbow . . .*

My horizon seems to move farther away, and we know, where the rainbow ends there are the leprechauns jealously guarding their pots of gold. I am the exact opposite of Dorothy from *The Wizard of Oz* and her glittering red shoes. I have a profound aversion to any kind of red garment: when I was little, my mother used to read me the fairy tale of the child who dies a horrendous death in her red shoes, forged by the devil. The little girl, who loved to dance, wanted a pair of red shoes and for her birthday the shoemaker makes them for her. She is so happy. But as soon as she slips into her glittering new shoes, her feet begin to move, she starts dancing despite herself and cannot stop. She dances and dances, whirls and pirouettes, at the tempo of speeding music, without stopping, no matter how much she cries and prays. Exhausted and terrified, she returns to the shoemaker and begs him to chop her feet off with his ax. Moral of this story? Little girls should not ask for anything. Their every desire, even the most innocuous (like a pair of shoes or dancing) is a sinful vanity that offends God, the Kings, the fathers, the husbands, the human race. The girls who deserve to live are those like Dorothy, who just wants to go back to her house, to Aunt Em and Uncle Henry, in Redneckland, Kansas: and therefore she is rewarded. Maybe that's why, regardless of the famous soundtrack, I always hated the movie *The Wizard of Oz*.

I am more suited as "little lamb lost in the wood" from *Someone to Watch Over Me* by George and Ira Gershwin—not that I'm proud of it, but it fits me like a kid glove:

*I'm a little lamb who's lost in the wood*
*I know I could . . . could always be good*
*To one who'll watch over me*

But who will watch over me? And how long have I got as the lamb? I hum this song and in my imagination, I see myself with that "someone who'll watch over me" walking hand in hand on the tree-lined avenues of New York, snow stuck to our boots, the warm lamplights through Central Park, the smell of the woodburning fireplaces, Broadway . . . The Carlyle, the Public Library lions, Serendipity's, me.

But it is the Criminal who, as good as a lamb these days, has proposed marriage. I held back at first, for as long as I could: I kept refusing for months. Until I said yes. I put the ring on. *It's just a ring, for God's sake! It can be removed just as quickly as it was put on, any time.*

I don't know if Yonah understands that the reason I am making myself as invisible as possible to him is that I am ashamed of my mistakes. I hope he doesn't think that I am expecting him to contend for the prize of my hand. *What a prize!* Perhaps, as my mother would declare, the Criminal deserves to have *me* . . . an apt punishment for someone like him. On the other hand, "Poor Yonah!" she would say. Because my mother adds the honorary title "poor" before the name of every boy with whom I've had a relationship. There was "poor Janusz" before Yonah, as well as "poor Brett." (Yes, Brett still qualified despite the inconsequence of our short *affaire de coeur*.)

Yonah has detached himself from me. I wonder if when he looks at me, he still feels a small pang inside. But with courage, he took the right path, he chose the only thing that made sense, he looked after his own good, protected himself. Who could blame him? Poor Yonah.

The clock ticks. At the end of graduate school, they will ship me back to Italy, not New York: End of the American experience, kiss your dreams goodbye, *finito, basta, ciao ciao* . . .

In an emptiness that kept on widening, my fantasies made new room for the Criminal. He pounced on the chance. I would have preferred to keep this thing secret from Yonah, but he found out anyway.

*Spring*. It's the end of my first academic year in America. May 1997. Students and teachers disperse for the three-month summer break. Americans go home. Italians rush to Italy. I remain, a bit like a suitcase forgotten at the station. It takes me less than two days, though, to figure out how to spend my break: I'll go to New York . . . *obviously*.

I get a room at the youth hostel, buy the newspaper before unpacking my toothbrush, and head outside in search of the ideal post where to spend the next few hours, reading the real estate section and learning everything about the rental market. I sit at the University Place Diner, steps away from Union Square, a cheese Danish, endless coffee refills. I start going through the lists of apartments available. There is a telephone booth right at the corner of the street. Although I have enough coins in my pocket to cover all the calls to all the dozens of listings I collected, I go in order of importance and at the end of the day I spend only 25 cents. I made only one single phone call in all. One guy, Matthew, advertised a studio apartment in the Village for $500 a month. No point in looking any further: I won the real-estate equivalent of the Lotto! "When can we meet?" he asks. "Even now," I offer with my newly found go-getter spirit—a spirit I had forgotten I had. I don't even go see the place: we meet at a café of his choice, introduce each other, have a coffee (I pay), and before the sun goes down over Manhattan, me and the guy shake hands and seal the agreement. The apartment is mine: 237 Sullivan Street, Greenwich Village. Zip code: 10012 . . . *One zero zero twelve*. That 1 that signals to the world: I am in New York!

I look at the piece of paper on which I wrote it: I examine it, I contemplate it, I adore it. 10012—Manhattan zip code. Sullivan Street. 10012. NY, NY. I rewrite it several times on a scrap of paper to practice the happiness I derive from it. I've already paid Matthew first and last month rent: I'll go to Boston to pick up my stuff tomorrow, and the next time I'm back, I'm back to live in Greenwich Village . . . *will it be a one-way trip? I'll think about it later.*

As soon as I set foot back in Waltham, I hear that the Criminal, whom I haven't talked to since a really bad row, is on my trail. He has been looking for me, sniffed every clue, left no stone unturned . . . unfortunately to the point of calling even Polonsky. I grab everything I can carry myself (and fit in the Greyhound storage compartment) and leave.

Matthew, young and fun, is waiting for me at the place to show me in and hand me the keys. There is no Criminal, no Brandeis, no sexual intimidations from the perv at *Politicus*. . . there is nothing else right now, but my first home in New York . . . New York, New York 10012. I feel with all my senses, with every molecule of my body, with the mind but also with all other perceptive or receptive channels whose existence I ignored so far, that my life is about to start again, that I am in exactly the right place at the right time: that this *is me,* and there is no other me outside this one here . . . the one who is climbing the two flights of stairs, in an anonymous building on a street in the middle of the universe. I feel like Connor MacLeod, the Highlander, when he kills Kurgan the penultimate immortal. It wouldn't surprise me if the overwhelming energy emanating from me right now escaped all of a sudden and blew the city's manholes, toppled over the fire hydrants, and smashed the buildings' windows within ten miles. I am in New York. I live in *Noyorc!*

The first night, I sleep on the floor, because Matthew asked to stay one more day: he takes the sofa. The sofa is the only piece of furniture in the studio apartment, which is endowed with a single window overlooking Sullivan Street and through which the neon light of a bar sign infuses the whole space all night long. At night I could hear the deafening noise of the passersby, sober, drunk, happy, sad . . . and the chitchats of the pushers parked on their two unstable feet downstairs in front of our door. I can't understand how an architect came out with such a flat. The only explanation I have is that the owner of this building must have erected walls here and there in order to subdivide the space and get more "apartments" to rent out. Not unlike what the Soviets used to do to provide a home for every citizen: but that system was meant to help the population, this is to screw it. Behind the entrance door there is a small cubicle that functions as the bathroom (hyperbolic word in this case): that is, a toilet, a sink, and the shower head attached to a wall without cabin or a curtain. No kitchen. No kitchen sink.

But Sullivan is practically *Barefoot in the Park,* and despite the fact that I got a far worse deal than Jane Fonda and Robert Redford in the film, the true bohemian potential of this arrangement does not escape me in the least. I have never felt such complete happiness before. Rightly in English they call the realization of oneself or of one's dream "fulfillment" . . . a satisfaction that fills you up to burst, a fullness that can't be contained by our limited physical casing. *Realizzazione* in Italian does not even begin to express the same overpowering concept.

And as if all this were not enough to fill the rest of my days with ecstatic giddiness, I also get a chance to meet Alexander Stille, Ugo Stille's son. I go visit him in his exquisite apartment on the Upper West Side. He has a job for me, or rather a collaboration: he would like me to help compile his famous father's papers and organize them in a volume we will publish together. When he opened the door, my heart skipped a beat. *New York New York 10012 and a job.* I already can't remember the name of the street in Waltham where I was living until yesterday. I don't want to finish the PhD.

Matthew does not leave the apartment or the couch. Not on the second day; not ever. On the third day, though, he brings us a friend. Now we are three in the apartment on Sullivan, no shower curtain, no kitchen sink.

The girlfriend who was supposed to pick him up from New Jersey is procrastinating. So Matthew is hanging about. One morning, we sit around aimlessly (I wouldn't be that aimless if he weren't here), me on the floor, he on the couch, with two cups of coffee I got us from the Deli at the corner. *Me, in Greenwich Village, going downstairs in my flipflops to get a cup of coffee at the corner! It's all so New York City!* Matthew is cleaning his hunting knife and nonchalantly asks:

"Has it ever occurred to you that I could chop you up and nobody would ever find out?"

*The answer is "Yes, it occurred to me, way before I knew you had a hunting knife."* . . . "Sorry, darn thing, I forgot the newspaper!" I say instead. "Let me go downstairs grab one. I'll be right back."

I do rush to the corner store, this time devoid of any "Greenwich Village cool girl" frivolity in me and purchase an international calling card. I lift the half-burned receiver of a filthy payphone and call mom and dad. Me in hysterics; them as well.

Within two hours, Salvatore makes his grand entrance, in his luxury Cadillac. He loads me and my stuff and brings us to Pelham Parkway, in the Bronx. Salvatore is a cousin of my mother's childhood friend; he immigrated here in the 1950s and is now retired.

But I had a taste of the seductive apple.

I've been too close to the heart of my dream to let go of it now. I am in the Bronx, the Bronx is between Waltham (200 miles) and New Jersey (9 miles). Which one is closer to my ultimate goal? Which of the two is the most likely to bring me where I need to be, which is *right here*, where I already am?

The Criminal had insisted that I go spend the summer with him in New Jersey. (This was the reason for our latest row.) Now he's willing "to talk," to discuss (our? my? other?) options—"To meet you half way, I promise." In other words, alternative options to my going back to Waltham for next semester, and the next one, and the one after that. Imposing on Salvatore for too long is out of the question. Whom am I kidding? The marriage proposal is still valid, an option on the table, the joker in Joker's hand . . . Let's try to make this plan work: a plan that, at the moment, seems the one to bring me closer to my end, direct if not ideal . . . either way, literal.

Before moving in with the Criminal, I decide to take a quick trip to Rome. Since I have re-accepted his marriage proposal, I can't hide it from my family anymore. The Criminal is extraordinarily subdued; he is cheerful, optimistic, he even exhibits a sense of humor I had forgotten he had; he is more affable, adventurous, and his will to reformulate a career path for himself, without his father's oppressive interference, seems revamped. The Criminal's family is in raptures. They want me to join them so that they can start planning the wedding. His sisters offer me their friendship, and they make me feel I've already become one of them. His parents wrote a letter to mine: they paid a translator to make sure the message would go through loud and clear. The message was, reduced to its essence, that my mother's only daughter (her absolute and indivisible possession) will be safe with them and their son, loved and taken care of as if born out of their own loins and womb, one of their own lineage. (An argument that, I am sure, will have the opposite of the desired effect on my jealous, controlling, and wrathful mother.)

It may be because it's finally *primavera,* springtime, the season of life and renewals, but I sense so much joy in the air. Shira has returned home to her parents. I have no idea where Yonah is. My friends in Rome ask me to come see them again and tell them about life in America. *"I do," says the bride. "I will," think I and fly to Rome.*

There is only one thing to do: "Cancel the place on Orange Street for now. Then, in September we'll see," orders the Criminal with reassuring impartiality.

The Criminal discusses his plans for our future in a more rational way. He always wins (he warned me many times): and these well-studied moves, the perfectly strategized steps, the outmaneuvering of all enemies are leading him unhindered toward the finish line. He's ecstatic. Someone here is in total denial. Me? I try to be honest with myself. But being honest with oneself doesn't necessarily entail that one can't also be a tad selective and, above all, partial. Something is off—a little inner voice tells me—but then again, I also think that I'd be very happy if all goes well. I want with every fiber of my soul for things to go well.

I know I have a blindfold tied over my eyes, I know that I am about to enter a tunnel that I am digging myself, like a mole: like the mole I have the foresight to groove different paths out, my hidden corridors branch in all directions so that, in case of flight, I can take refuge in the depths of any of them. In fact, I end up never sticking my nose out of my hideout again. And to think that only 20 centimeters above my head the rest of the world lives on, immersed in light; there everything is clear, there people like Yonah, Shira, Brett & Galina, with heads held high, their integrity unsullied, walk with secure steps, honest, serene.

There are good hours and bad hours: during the bad hours, I devise plots to get rid of the Criminal and to make him pay—because getting rid of him is not as satisfying as the incommensurable pleasure of destroying him, *smerdarlo* (of exposing) him publicly, of wiping my feet on him like the human *shmata* that he is. During the good hours, I forget my anger, I forget my revenge fantasies, I reproach myself for not appreciating how good I have it . . . obviously. Others would jump up and down, others would behave, others would consider his love a blessing. Poor Criminal.

Is the attraction that bonds me to the Criminal due to a subconscious awareness that the Criminal won't give up on me, that he won't leave me? He is not leaving me alone . . . which is still a form of "not leaving."

This attachment (codependence, I hear the nudniks correct me) feeds off the lymph of my abandonment syndrome. That's how my mother calls it . . . which is ironic, since she is the source of this syndrome. Until 1978, my life as a child was almost a bliss (almost, not completely, but what is). I'll do the math again: mother, father, two sets of uncles and aunts (Adriano and Fabiola, Sergio and Adriana), two sets of cousins (in coeval pairs of sisters: Ambra and Chicca, Sandra and Claudia); and *dulcis in fundo*, one (maternal) grandmother, grandma Binde, who lived in our house. Although I was an only child, Ambra and Chicca stayed with us all the time and therefore I grew up with them like sisters. My father, mother, and *nonna* (grandma) Binde lived for us, we were the center of their attention and adoration. We girls had a great time. We couldn't be happier. At the dinner table it was a bedlam: we all talked together, laughed, gossiped, and commented on the news or other life events. It was an absolute matriarchate, in which my father's voice was drowned by the needs and demands of all the women around him. He wouldn't have wanted it any other way. His love for us was boundless.

I remember our black-and-white TV set, with its bulky on/off knob: in our family parlance we used to say that the TV had to "warm up." "Warm up the TV, the evening news is about to begin!" That's because it took an eternity for the image to come up on the screen. Italy had only one State-owned TV channel. So, if people were watching TV, they were all watching the same thing. A national experience. We didn't know anything else, hence we were all perfectly happy with this arrangement. There was a Saturday night show that entertained the whole country with its musical guests, dance numbers, and hilarious comedic sketches. My cousin, Chicca, and I performed our own dancing and singing bit every time, as soon as the soundtrack began with the opening titles. We had no bedtime and no censorship in my family. (In those days, there was very little risk to expose a child to something pornographic or particularly vulgar. TV programs underwent a pre-screening and were ridiculously censored by State and Church before they were allowed into people's homes.)

My grandmother was constantly thinking up dishes to entice me to eat: I was an extraordinarily picky eater, and she feared I'd die of starvation. (They had all lived through the war and what they got out of it was an indomitable terror of starvation and cold weather!—something we children could not begin to appreciate in its full tragic extent.) The only way to make me eat (*really stuff myself*) was to cover everything under a blanket of melted cheese: *mozzarella in carrozza, supplì, fiori di zucca fritti*, pizza, lasagna. And one of these cheesy things was invariably served for the Saturday feast.

During the week, I walked to school alone with Chicca, two years older than me, who held my hand tightly all the way to the school door. On the way out, we would find our grandmother, planted in the courtyard, waiting for us: she would walk us back home, scrub us squeaky clean, and feed us while telling us the most entertaining fables I ever heard. Some were actual folktales from another era (completely inappropriate, scary, politically incorrect, but oh-so delicious) and many she simply made up on the spot. I've never found these stories anywhere. They got lost with those lunchtimes, in the sundrenched kitchen, where I sat with my fat Persian cat, on my lap, my cousin always near me, listening to *nonna* Binde's wonderful stories.

One summer day in 1978, my mother and I ran into some neighbor on the street who stopped us for a brief chat:

"Mom won't make it to the end of the year. She has at most a couple of months," I hear my mother tell the lady.

It's my first encounter with death. Before then, death was just a concept related mostly to cowboy movies, in which the bad guys are shot and fall on the ground or tumble, still on top of their horses, into the canyons (but "They get up again, don't worry, the horses are not really dead," the adults promise me). Yet I instantly get the picture. The exchange was crystal clear. Realizing the lady's shock at my shock, my mother swivels around to face me and adds, "Well, you're big now,"—I am eight—"You are old enough to understand these things: *Nonna* is dying. But she does not know it, and you . . . you cannot tell her! You can't say a word about this, are we clear? It's a secret, and woe unto you if you tell her." *Woe unto me? And what worse woe could I get than losing my grandmother?* I obey.

But from that moment on, my days will be a nightmare. Send in the neuroses! Grandma is bedridden: now that my eyes are open, I recognize that she's wasting away, that she has become so thin. She has cancer: thyroid. I am around her all the time. She holds my little hands, she speaks to me, she is happy that I don't leave her for a moment. When I think she has dozed off, I hide at the foot of her bed, and I offer desperate prayers to the Lord. I have never seen anybody pray in my family. My family and religion are like oil and water. Zia Fabiola is too Voltairean for silly superstitions of this sort; my mother is too shrewd and, in her own way, too feminist to bow to the sovereignty of any Father; as for the men, I don't think they have the right to ideas or beliefs of their own in this family. And in any case, they, being the oldest, had the hardest childhoods of all, and I think that the illusion of a God evaporated for them a long time ago . . . I want to say, about 1941? I join my hands (even I know that this is the proper posture), and I start *shokeling* madly, back and forth, with eyes squeezed shut to the point that when I reopen them I'm blind for a few seconds . . . and I beg, entreat, bargain with Who's listening: "Don't let her die! Don't let her die! Don't let her die!" And, "Take me and let *nonna* live." Don't let her die! Don't let her die! Don't let her die! Don't let her die! It's more an enchantment than a prayer, my first face to face with the occult. . . . My first neurotic episode? Anything will do. My grandmother dies all the same. In November.

I am left all alone. My aunt takes her daughters back. My parents keep their work schedule. I have no one left around me. *Alone and lonely . . . if only Italian had both words!* This is when my mother has the idea to move me to a different elementary school, so that I lose also Laura, my only friend. Laura is so lucky because she is the only daughter of two absent parents, who replaced themselves with a full-time governess. This elderly lady, in her impeccable clothes, gloves, and hat, follows Laura everywhere. She walks two steps behind the girl and never leaves her. Laura and I adore each other. But we will never see each other again.

I do not want to be alone, I *cannot* be alone. (One more thing Yonah and I have in common.) Perhaps it is also for this reason that when the Criminal tells me "We will always be together" I ignore the adage *"meglio soli che male accompagnati"* (better alone than in poor company) so dear to my mother. I accept. Because as the American adage goes instead, beggars can't be choosers.

It looks as if my "Yes" has fixed everything, all is back to normal, every problem has dissipated. The Criminal's family pulls me into its caring embrace, like a daughter. I am surrounded by love and support. I'm not alone.

*Summer.* The wedding invitations have been selected. The date has been set and so has the place. The rabbi has already instructed us on the details for the ceremony, which will take place in New Jersey, in the presence of a couple of hundred guests: the entire social circle of the Criminal's parents, and the guests from Italy who will be sumptuously settled in a private residence. My friend Marco Cassini will be my witness for the civil license: they all found it very strange here that the bride chose a male friend and refuses (*categorically*) to have bridesmaids.

The part that amazes me most is the cake selection. I had to scroll through pages and pages of photographs of architecturally stunning cakes, and I was made to taste loads of samples, without as much as a drop of coffee to flush them down. In a glycemic coma, I decide on a multi-layered sugar monument, with white icing, and a cascade of edible flowers dropping from one story to the next. It will all look so tacky! But as my mother would superiorly say: "Gauche by the chic is posh."

I still have some commuting to do between New Jersey and Boston to take the rest of my stuff. There are those who congratulate me and those who look at me with a question mark in their eyes. But I am never alone on these short journeys; there is always the Criminal with me, tall, smiling, charming . . . and no one has the opportunity, or the courage, to offer a more honest comment. Along the highway that leads to Boston, I always notice the exit signs for SALEM. The word creeps me out. Every time. "It is a big tourist attraction," the Criminal explains. Maybe so, but it's no attraction to me. Even just seeing the giant letterings on the road sign makes me uncomfortable. It's like driving through Austria and suddenly seeing the directions for MAUTHAUSEN. Certain places should change their names after history has forever associated them with irreparable atrocities.

All my friends from all over Europe bought tickets to fly here and so did my few living relatives. I have an unshakable confidence that the positive energy surrounding me at the moment will channel only good fortune into my life. It's a good omen.

For now, we live in the apartment of the Criminal's paternal grandmother, who died recently. His parents gave this place to him when he returned from Israel . . . not to have him in their home all the time, I suppose. They live in one of the wealthiest counties in in the United States; the Criminal and I, instead, are in the small town of Paterson, one of the most dangerous slums in the United States.

It is time to address the invitations—operation to be done strictly by hand, as per tradition. (*So I am told. I am learning so much about American ways these days.*) We need three tables we don't have in the apartment to accommodate the outer envelopes, unsealed inner envelopes, invitation cards, reception cards, response cards and response cards' self-addressed envelopes. In Italy, wedding invitations are done quite differently: the groom and bride, separately, with their respective parents pay a visit to the people they intend to invite and bring along a *bonbonnière,* a decorative box of bonbons personalized for the occasion. Those who live out of town will simply get a phone call and the small souvenir box later when they show up at the ceremony.

I will never make it alone! I'd better begin. I write: "Mrs. and Mr. Horowitz" . . . and this, suddenly, turns the Criminal into a beast.

If a husband (we'll call him Samuel) is a judge and his wife (say, Rebecca) is nobody, they *must* be addressed as "Mr. and Mrs. Samuel Horowitz." That is, a wife loses her identity, first name and surname. (*How don't I know that?! I haven't learned enough!*) I can't think of a country in the world that would do this to a woman. And for the most prestigious guests, those whose title I cannot, *I must not!* omit, the Criminal instructs me to write: "The Honorable and Mrs. Samuel Horowitz." Well, come on, I do not think anyone will be affronted if I write "Mrs. and Mr. Horowitz"! I insist. I should not insist, I should not offer my ideas when they are not requested, I should not highlight my foreignness in everything I do or don't do, I know nothing and I should shut the fuck up. A scene ensues. The scene turns into a commotion. This time more vigorous than usual: it could be that the peace of the last few weeks have rewound the Criminal like a coil, to a spasm. Like a spring that has made a thousand turns on its axis, ever tighter and tighter. Meanwhile, I have nowhere to hide. He unleashes a blind, abiotic violence. Non-negotiable. I run away from the apartment wearing one single shoe because, in the haste, I lost the other one, and from a pay phone I dial 911. A policeman asks: "Miss, are you married to this guy?"–I tell him I'm not. "If you were married, we could do something," he dispassionately says. "But since it's not your case, all the better. Don't marry him. If you were my daughter, I would tell you to leave the guy." That's all.

The fact that the policeman's answer is completely against the law does not cross the antechamber of my mind. On the other hand, as the Criminal would say, *what do I know?*

I grab what I can and run back to Boston. I fold the wedding dress into a box, an antique piece from the *Priscilla of Boston,* and . . . that's about it.

*Fall.* I start again to search for a place to live. The Criminal starts chasing me again, repentant. A phrase echoes incessantly in my head, "If you were married, we could do something."

After several disastrous attempts, I eventually find another attic, this time in a colossal house, at 2 Raeburn Terrace, in Newton. It is the home of an old couple, Camilla and Modestino Criscitiello, who in lieu of rent would like me to converse with them in Italian; they'd love to learn the language. Modestino was born in international waters on a ship headed to Ellis Island where his parents were emigrating, poor and hopeless, from Naples. Camilla, on the other hand, is old stock, she fits the bill of the perfect genteel New England lady. They have been married for an eternity, and through the entire duration of their blissful love story, she has never called him by his given name: instead, she calls him Chris. Was the name Modestino too hard to say, or too ethnic? Was she embarrassed of the "mixed" marriage that his name announced? *Maybe in our first language lesson, I'll teach her how to say it correctly.* Modestino studied and became a cardiologist at Harvard. A gentle, delicate soul who, like so many scientists, has a weakness for fine arts, classical music, and foreign languages. Camilla, a homemaker, is an unstoppable woman, who doesn't take No for an answer. She raised many sons and daughters; she volunteers her time at Planned Parenthood, at the local library, and human and animal shelters; she is an eco-activist and recycles everything, greeting cards included.

Americans have an obsession with greeting cards: they send cards for every occasion. Greetings for the holidays, greetings to the newlyweds, condolences, happy birthdays, happy anniversaries, Happy Thanksgivings, and, of course, thank you cards after having been at someone's house for dinner or for having received a present from someone. In Italy, we say *Grazie* on our way out the door and that's it. No day-after phone calls, no card either. Our friends believe us. They take our first *Grazie* seriously.

Camilla has devised a way to save money and not to contribute to the destruction of the planet by reusing the part of a card that hasn't been written upon. Let's face it, we all write on just one of the two inside faces of a card: either on the blank one or on the one with the card message. So generally, one of the two remains unused: and *that's* where Camilla has found an opening to wedge in her acumen and revolutionize a nationally sanctioned genre. With a big pair of tailoring scissors, she patiently cuts the cards in half and keeps the side on which she'll write her own wishes to family and friends, and whenever possible, she'll deliver them in person to avoid postage and indiscriminate pollution. Camilla does not tolerate waste.

They are both birdwatchers. Such a non-Italian word! The first time I heard the word I couldn't make out what it meant. They do have a porch, but I never saw them sitting there staring at what passes by in the skies. Then, one day, while starting my breakfast, I hear them come back from an inhumanely early outing, dressed in the queerest outfits and glowing with glee. They spotted something through the binoculars still hanging from their necks. What? I didn't understand. But they had had a blast.

My second Thanksgiving in America will be in their home. Camilla and Modestino keep young by surrounding themselves with lively, cheerful, interesting people, mostly students. They even adopted an adult gentleman, a blind African man, whom they are now sponsoring for a green card, and they are helping him become independent, study, and build a career. (Damn, luck *is* blind!) At their Thanksgiving a large number of foreigners, from all over the world, contribute, in line with Camilla's order, with dishes typical of their countries of origin. Thus, Camilla exemplarily avoids enriching the capitalist system by spending an exorbitant amount of money to feed so many guests: the burden is equally redistributed upon all.

Camilla's and Modestino's house will remain the standard against which I measure any other house that I will ever see, rent, buy, or dream of. A huge red building, on three floors, full of hidden corners, niches, double entrances to each room, wide wooden floorboards and stairs, pantries, a cellar so cold that they can keep their cakes and eggs there, and, of course, a habitable attic under the roof on the fourth level with a microscopic bath (all for me), illuminated by natural light coming from a skylight. It is a private apartment, within their sumptuous palace. Since the kitchen is in common, I will almost completely stop eating so as not to disturb them. But this does not ruin my experience at all. I could not ask for more. My two roommates love erudition and encourage me to finish graduate school at Brandeis. At the end of this academic year, I will finally qualify for a master's degree. Then, another three years (*three years away from New York*) to complete the PhD. My stomach turns at the thought.

Almost all my possessions are lost in New Jersey. In fleeing, I took what I could drag in my carry-on: I do not know why, but I also grabbed, in the confusion of the moment, the two silver *kiddush* cups we received as a gift from some Honorable Judge and Decoration Wife. Now I use one to hold my water for the night on the bedside table. On the way to Port Authority from New Jersey, I stopped at an unsightly jewelry store and sold them my engagement ring. They gave me 50 dollars for it. The Criminal must have spent thousands: I didn't bargain for sure. With that I bought myself a slice of pizza and a one-way ticket to Boston.

These months are calm and joyful. Thanks to Camilla and Modestino, I also get myself a car. In this last year—not a stable year however one looks at it—I walked myself to death, miles and miles, under all weather conditions. With great tact, Camilla and Modestino, on whom the spartan life I lead has not gone undetected (too spartan even for Camilla, and that says it all), sit me down at their kitchen table and begin: "Listen, there's a friend of ours who lives on Cape Cod and who recently lost his wife. Now, he finds himself with an extra car he doesn't know what to do with. It is old but it has very few miles on because they used it only to go shopping. We thought you might be interested . . . he wants $500 for it." It sounds stupid to buy a car in a country where, after all (if I read the signals from the universe correctly), I'm just passing through . . . A car seems such a permanent step, like taking on a cat or a dog. What if (the image of the Criminal surfaces) I suddenly have to beat a swift retreat to Rome? It's not like I could take the car back by plane! On the other hand, I think of my feet, crippled by blisters. As I am weighing all these considerations, Camilla nudges me, without looking as if she were forcing my hand: "We believe that you cannot do without it," she presses on. Even Modestino, who is always reluctant to meddle in the business of others, ventures a "If you had to leave, you could either sell it, or donate it. What would you have lost? Only $500." Invariably, they make more sense than I do. They tell me that it is a Ford Taurus station wagon and I have no idea what form or shape that signifies. Is it a Monte Carlo rally car, or one of those minivans as in *Eight Is Enough?* Before I can ask further questions, Camilla, who until now has suppressed her decisive and authoritarian mother-bear side, becomes impatient and declares: "We already took an appointment for you on Sunday. We'll drive you to Cape Cod and get the car."

My new car is huge. Burgundy, like my old beloved shoes. The color on the hood is faded because it was corroded by the brackish island air. The trunk is a marvel: with the backseats folded frontward, it can hold practically everything I'll ever own here. The front plate of my Ford Taurus station wagon says: Cape Cod Symphony, and below, A Sound Experience (with a treble clef in place of the *s*). The man selling it to me for a song is the retired conductor of the Cape Cod Symphony.

I leave Cape Cod behind, following Modestino and Camilla, who lead me home in their car, and as we near the exit I read the road signs: 95 North/ Boston—95 South/New York. For a split second I fight the urge to jerk the steering wheel left and head south. But I can't turn left while Camilla and Modestino are turning right, northbound, because it would give them a terrible scare . . . and then there is Brandeis (*cazzo!*). Nonetheless, I make a mental note: "95 South = New York." Shuddering at those sinister signs announcing the exit for Salem, I proceed to Raeburn Terrace, Newton, Massachusetts.

I fall in love with my beautiful second-hand car. Perhaps it's an acquired trait of our species to deeply bond with whatever allows us to move (from Santoni shoes to a Ferrari). Surely, in primordial times, the Bronze Age man loved his stone wheel and spent time cleaning, smoothing it, getting mad if his kids touched it. And before that, the Australopithecus probably spent a fortune for the tablets that he tied to his feet to better slide on the winter snow or for the hollow tree trunk in which he sailed.

When I register my car at the local DMV, I receive the plates: 600 EJW. I wish Yonah were here, we'd laugh ourselves silly. It looks like the word "JEW" typed by a dyslexic bureaucrat. I must remember to show it to him when he comes back.

*Winter.* The Criminal does not show up for the rest of the school year. I no longer have parallel lives. The two collided, pulverized each other, and now I walk on a single lane, visible to all those who care to watch. I have no more secrets to hide. Everyone knows what happened last summer. I have received only empathic reactions, sincere expressions of support and encouragement . . . and infinite pity (the most hurtful of sentiments). Except for this one message from Keith Botsford. Saul Bellow introduced us almost a year ago, and we stayed in touch. But I am wary now of old mentors, of over-sixty gurus who offer to take me under their sticky wing. So despite his kindness and friendly disposition, despite his overt outreach to pull me into his starlit entourage of Nobel-winning names, I make myself rather scarce. I try so hard not to give the wrong impression; not to send a signal that may be misinterpreted. Another one of my NO that is received as a YES. I haven't escaped Gwidon Goldblatt and Inferno to come here and fall through Alice's looking glass, again. Because of this evasive behavior, Keith nicknamed me *Primula Rossa* (Scarlet Pimpernel)—he speaks a bit of Italian, like Bellow.

Keith insists I go see him and I do, but I stay only a couple of hours and do not accept as much as glass of water from him. He is curious: he asks a lot of questions, and I outline for him my situation, among other reasons, because I find narratives to be pleasantly purgative. Talking does a lot of good to the speaker.

From: "r@bu.edu" "Keith Botsford" 8-OCT-1997 04:38 :26.92

Dear Pimpernel:

Some things became obvious during your brief stay. Most obvious is an instability which I think you should look after, and quickly; it makes all aspects of your "work" seem highly doubtful. I would say, were I in a harsh mood (which I am not, having returned from six pleasant Roman days), that you like to use and be used. I need not point out the dangers of this. At some point it is going to be very necessary to grow up and confront your own problems, and for this, I now think, you need help: not from friends and "friends," but from a professional.

Saul has been having a bad type [*sic*] with an arhythmia [*sic*] of the heart. You are not going to see him in the near future.

Thank you very much for the name of the man in Paris. I will refer the library to him.

I am back, but very busy for the next few days.

"My work"? What work is he talking about? "I" used "him"?

Of course, I will never respond to either this or any other communication from Botsford. *Remove yourself immediately, Fania! Lick your wounds in the closet, wipe the tears, and forget this ever happened.* But what just happened exactly? *The only thing that matters is that you gave him the contact of that librarian in Paris he asked you for when he knew you were going there for a week . . . that you were of service . . . that you have no debt with this man.* What just happened?

I wish to die. If circumstances allowed, I would apply to a different university, change my name, switch to a third continent, start all over.

Yonah writes from time to time. Shira is busy dating to the bitter end. Brett & Galina ask me for news day in, day out. Galina's messages indicate frustration at my idiocy. I am particularly ashamed before Brett & Galina: their pity humiliates me beyond measure, they behave like true and loyal friends, wise and infallible, and I wish I had never met them now. I find myself reading and rereading, almost ritualistically, the letters Galina sends hoping to learn something, to latch onto a word that'll save my life, a lifeboat from wisdom. (*But there's no saving the Titanic.*)

I make two new friends, Italo and Ludimilla, from Riccione, Italy, who got married just before leaving for Brandeis where Italo came to do a PhD in scientific matters. Ludimilla, who otherwise had no reason whatsoever (or interest) in leaving home, came with him. They were in fact Camilla's and Modestino's tenants before me. I met them *after* the "bad stuff." Strong, decisive, generous, and enormously simpatico, it is Ludimilla who arranges for Camilla to take me on. She is hilarious, brilliant. They are both wonderful and I imagine them together forever: I imagine them with two children, a perfect house, maybe a cat or a dog, and aunt Fania who plays her loving role in the background at every birthday, carnival, 4th of July barbecue, Thanksgivings and so on. The evenings I spend together with them help restore my sanity and give me strength. I don't hang out with anyone else. With nobody who met me *before* last summer. I focus on my studies. I hide as much as I can. I avoid people. I chew, swallow, ruminate the sense of loneliness and defeat. I get used to Camilla and her micro-managerial streak.

The circle of my loneliness swells. At least, I get some satisfaction and happiness from teaching: I must admit that it is quite enjoyable to play "Professor Chips." 1998 is around the corner.

*Spring.* This past February, Yonah successfully defended his thesis. I was there: to my surprise, he invited me too. It was very exciting to see him in action, lecturing about World War II and presenting the results of his research in the Polish and German archives. (*That's where he was for months!*) Polonsky was about to burst from pride. His pupil: a real winning horse. Now he's left with me . . . but I am not panning out as Polonsky expected. Yonah speaks well of me to him, professors Jonathan Sarna, Art Green, Ben Ravid, the secretaries, the other students all speak well of me to him: but Polonsky has his suspicions. He might be giving me up for lost. He'll have to start looking elsewhere for new recruits. The more I feel guilty, the more I shrink inside and out; the more I shrink, the more his self-fulfilling prophecy proves right. I am so ashamed of myself. Polonsky must have understood that I am the sole cause of all my evils. All of them must see this. Yonah in the first place. Maybe I disgust him too a little. Perhaps both Yonah and Polonsky were disappointed to find out that I am not the brilliant woman the world thought I was. Better concentrate on the PhD. I still have a few years of hard work here at Brandeis, while Yonah can now throw himself headlong into the future. *Who knows if he still imagines it with me sometimes?*

For the time being, Yonah is headed to an *ulpan* in Israel, a school specialized in crash courses in Hebrew language. Who knows if he started applying for jobs too? If so, he hasn't told me. Well, we talk so little at this point. Practically never.

The academic world can blow you in any direction, like a hurricane: when a university offers you a job, you go, without even consulting the map or dragging your feet. The competition is fierce, the positions are limited, as academia remains one of the most prestigious professions. Personally, I do not understand a damn thing about how the academic career works. I'm not interested in the PhD; I am not interested in becoming a professor. It was an excuse to go to New York, to be happy and become a great writer there . . . instead I am actually doing a PhD, I stopped writing, I'm in Boston, and I am miserable: I'll never live up to a Yonah or a Galina, I hate archives; I hate research; I hate what happens at the end of years spent in the archives . . . you stand in front of a firing squad of international academics who will scrutinize every affirmation of yours with a magnifying glass, to catch you in an error, to kick you out if you missed something, if you overlooked a fragment of papyrus that four thousand years ago ended up by mistake under some pharaoh's sarcophagus and of which no one never heard until the day *after* your book on that pharaoh is published. And you'll be publicly chastised, your career is over, because, alas, your book does not mention the blasted scrap of papyrus . . . with pharaoh's maid's shopping list for the day. I prefer journalism, I prefer to be an opinionist—I prefer to make up my own truths.

Yonah was OK with me not becoming a professor. I long for osmosing with Yonah into a better, more grounded self. But besides my blocking shame, there's reality to reckon with: that boat has long since sailed away.

Not to dawdle in Schadenfreude, but the rest of the nation too is going through a rough patch. America is in the grip of a scabrous scandal: the

Lewinsky case. Every year there's a new infamy: last summer, it was Lady D.'s death, this year the luckless presidential blow job. *Wait, I thought that in America men do not exploit their position of power in exchange for sexual favors from subordinates. I was so sure of it! The films . . . the news . . . Were we lied to?* They talk of nothing else. A blue dress, with an infamous spot. There's something nauseating about this story.

Feminists are silent; they can't find their voice to defend Monica Lewinsky. (I wish I could tell her: "I know exactly how it happened, I've been there, sister," or more usefully "Just don't say a word, no one will care!") Women all over the world rallied tearfully around the memory of the princess who, with her lover, met her tragic end in Paris . . . Nobody rallies around Lewinsky: too Jewish, too zaftig, not regal enough—neither by blood nor by looks. Even those she thought were her friends are betraying her. I was wrong: apparently, a president in America *can* afford to cross the threshold of decency and law and go unpunished. Worse still: instead of openly siding with the victim, she's become the pinnacle of public derision, the butt of all jokes of an entire nation. Destroying Lewinski is like shooting fish in a barrel. When she was born, her father Bernie lovingly exclaimed "my little *farfel*" (noodle in Yiddish): she was a 7.5-pound baby. Now they are feeding his *farfel* to the sharks. Who knows if her being chubby, not as anorexic as Lady D., and not as Christian, doesn't play against her in the public perception. Clinton, on his end, seems to have established a pattern: he keeps his distance from fire, but never far enough not to get slightly burned. *Peccatus interruptus.* He smoked a joint but "didn't inhale," he does his intern but without full penetration . . . he just dips in a bit.

It both touches me and terrifies me to see this girl publicly reviled. She has no one on her side. I do not know how she doesn't commit suicide. Maybe she's too stupid to fathom the possibility, maybe she doesn't grasp the extent of the shame befallen her. Or maybe she has some strength *I* can't fathom. Let this be a lesson to all girls who—when they end up simhasana, svanasana, or shavasana under their bosses' desks—go around spilling the beans. You swallow the beans! Disgusting things are kept to oneself. Unjust things as well. Shameful things are not to be revealed. Because you can never be sure that you are not partly in the wrong, can you? And the smallest amount of wrong can invalidate any part of merit . . . no matter how hugely "right" you are. (*I do well not to breathe a word about Gwidon, and that other tosser at Politicus.*)

Since he's in Israel, Yonah will not attend his graduation ceremony in May. But I do. I am also graduating this year: on the way to completing the PhD, I have fulfilled the requirements for the Master's, and I want to mark the occasion. Although I am not supposed to (after all I'm enrolled for the full doctorate), I ask for the MA diploma first . . . a teaser, if you will.

Yonah calls me up from Israel to congratulate me and chat about my preparations for the ceremony. But this is small talk: the really pressing issue, he can't wait to share, regards *his* news. He met "someone." This, in Yonah's vocabulary, can only mean a marriage-bound relationship. He wants to thank me because I made this thing possible. "I was thinking of you, and I remembered your descriptions of the Italian Jewish neighborhood in Jerusalem . . . so I went there"—*so he was thinking of me? Missing me? So much so that he went to find traces of me in the old pinkish stones of the holy city's roads . . .* He rang at the Italian Cultural Center, and a girl, of the right age, answered the door. That was enough: she opened, he went in. He knocked, she turned the knob. "*Congratulazioni!*" I say with an enthusiastic sisterly tone. Luckily, he doesn't see the expression on my face, which is not at all that of an enthusiastic sister. I add phrases of circumstance—"*I am so happy for you!*"—all recited so perfectly, with such falsity, that even I end up wondering whether all there ever was between us was in fact just a friendship and that only in my romantic delirium I saw it as something else.

The commencement is a state affair. I would not miss it for anything in the world. I am disappointed to find out that one must pay for the toga. At least they give me free tickets to invite whoever I want—otherwise, the event tickets are really expensive. My mother says no: they don't want to come. I offer my tickets to Camilla and Modestino.

I remember the day of my thesis defense at La Sapienza, in 1995. My family was present and after, we regaled ourselves with cappuccino and *maritozzi con la panna* at a café in Viale Mazzini. It was a beautiful day. My parents also organized a proper dinner party at home, for family and friends, and we had *torta mimosa* and champagne. Food is my father's answer to all existential modalities: Eat if there is a misfortune (it'll help). Eat if you're happy (to celebrate). Eat if you're sick (it'll restore your health). My father, in wartime, knew hunger (*"quella vera!"* he says raising his tone of voice, putting both cupped hands in front of his face) . . . and hasn't made up for it yet. Were it up to him, on top of the splendid libations, he would have ordered a fireworks show over Rome . . . but mom's good taste didn't allow it.

On the contrary, in America, they don't recoil from a spectacle: fireworks, bands, cheerleaders and all. It's the opposite of an *affaire privée:* the celebration for a diploma (from nursery to graduate school) is perhaps the closest thing to the ancient Roman *ludi,* lavish public games, that still exists today. It is a self-congratulatory pantomime of Olympic proportions. It is no coincidence that these ceremonies take place in stadiums, in large arenas, in Colosseums. They represent a metaphorical pat the nation gives itself on the back: they symbolize the success of the American system, the success of teachers, the success of students, but more than anything else, the show exists to flatter the parents' Ego. It is like saying: Well done, you are a good parent, you are beyond reproach! You who paid $150,000 to give an education to your son, who now, thanks to us, is equipped to conquer the world and make more money than you did before him and your father before you. Your trust in us was well placed!

The university diploma is like a magic wand that spreads shining dust on the life of the graduate: with it you become special. This, it must be kept in mind, has no relation with any concrete body of knowledge: that people with a BA know less than a ninth grader in Italy is no crucial point. With the diploma you will have access to a career that is above average: you will become rich, you will become a true American. The fact, however, is that if this was still true to some extent in the 1960s, nowadays such a myth is like the light we still see in the night sky from stars that died millions of years ago. Nowadays everyone has a BA: and if everyone has a BA, a BA is worth nothing. If everyone is special, nobody is.

The tremendous draw of the graduation ceremony is that it gives each party involved (from the individual student to the honorary speaker, to the university president, to mum and dad) the opportunity to feel at the center of the universe: the feeling of omnipotence is the core of American ambition. Hearing one's name announced, getting on that stage, grabbing the rolled-up diploma tied with its red ribbon, wearing one's Alma Mater gown, listening to the motivational speeches of famous people and shaking their hands as an equal . . . American omnipotence.

In place of my family, Camilla and Modestino accompany me. But there are also three guests, out of program, who have come to celebrate me on this happy day: the Criminal, the Criminal-father, and the Criminal-mother.

According to tradition, parents bring their kids out for a sumptuous meal after the ceremony. The Criminal-family insists on bringing me out for a celebratory lunch, because they think of me as "a daughter" . . . "maybe a future daughter?"—one of them trickily submits. They made reservations (already). I smile candidly on the outside, terrified on the inside. Are they serious? But why did they show up? And what will Modestino and Camilla think of me now? It took them nine months to get me back on track, to nurture my healing, to put me through the Criscitiello emotional detoxification program. The Criminal sits docilely with eyes brimming with love and promises of great changes to come, new beginnings, happy tomorrows . . . to which (*see?*) his parents are his witnesses. Yes, they are serious. I remember the words of the 911 policeman in NJ: "If you were married, we could do something . . . But since it's not your case . . ." What if I called his bluff? If it works, everyone's happy; if it doesn't work, 911 won't ignore my call . . . A win-win situation.

The life package the Criminal dangles in front of my eyes, like an alluring sack of carrots, is replete with job options, location varieties, all sorts of goodies . . . and no stick. Just carrots. We'll both live in New Jersey (almost Manhattan), in a house (not the old, moldy apartment of his grandmother, *may she rest and so on*), together . . . always. Forever. Till death do us part. (Death? OK . . . almost in Manhattan, though.)

If I give him what he wants, if I behave, if I am good, he will calm down and who knows that it won't all end in a beautiful fairy tale. At least for a while. All I need is time. I have tumbled into an abyss the moment I stepped out of Logan Airport almost two years ago and everything I've seen, done, heard has happened to and rolled off me in the course of that endless fall through a bottomless chasm. I will not be able to pull myself back together until I stop the free fall.

I can't take Boston, the edge of Boston, and even life with Camilla and

Modestino anymore. With them, I am a twenty-eight-year-old stuck in the role of a fourteen-year-old pleasing a loving, decisive, authoritarian mother and a very sweet, weak father . . . *sounds familiar?* This was not in my plans when I got a ticket to America. None of the things that happened to me so far were in my plans. I got the master's degree, but I do not have the stamina to carry on through the final phase. I need a break. And without objections, Brandeis's administration authorizes me to take a leave of absence: I can simply suspend the membership (as in the gym) for one academic year, after which I am allowed to return and pick up where I left off.

*Summer.* The wedding this time takes place at the town hall of Paterson, New Jersey. End of August. In the presence of a justice of the peace, Criminal-father, Criminal-mother, and the two Criminal-sisters. I did not bother to tell anyone in Italy, except my parents who couldn't care less about being there. The Criminal-son and I take a taxi to the town hall from the apartment where we live. *Is it true, as they say, that it is bad luck to see the bride on the wedding day?*

I bought my dress in Manhattan this time around: I had the perfect *Sex and the City* day there. I went to a random hairdresser on the Upper East Side and as soon as I announced "I'm getting married tomorrow" the beauty salon went into hysterics, and everybody jovially helped with getting me the right look for the part. I entered the salon with long hair, well below my shoulders, and came out with the same pixie-cut Gwyneth Paltrow vaunts in *Sliding Doors.* I got a manicure and a pedicure. And the dress, from a small boutique in the West Village, is a masterpiece: an ankles-long two-layer cream camisole, softly hanging from two thin shoulder straps. Simplicity incarnate on my skeletal body. (*Right, I appear to have lost some weight.*)

The Criminal wanted to drive there, but I insisted we should take a taxi today at least. The journey is very short. Through the dirty cab windows, Paterson parades before my eyes. Clusters of men gathered on this or that sidewalk, goalless, under the sun. Boys pacing, slowly, back and forth . . . to kill time. Groups of Muslims gathering in front of a friend's small shop. Not even stray dogs wonder about Paterson. Long out-of-business stores with lowered shutters smeared with graffiti from ten years ago; burned garbage cans;

windowless empty buildings. Paterson, New Jersey: its crime rate is higher than Chicago, New York, and Los Angeles combined. It was a very rich industrial center once, entirely set up by Italians, Irish, and Jews. It is located on a natural promontory along the Hudson River: therefore, it served as a port for the ships carrying silks from China. Paterson was full of factories that processed the goods arriving by boat from abroad and turned them around to be sold all over the nation. One of the richest industrialists in the textile field, Catholina Lambert, emigrated from the English Yorkshire without a penny and became a silk trade magnate here: his castle, built in 1891 on the Aquackanonk cliff, still dominates the highest point of the city. There is also a gigantic synagogue in the heart of Paterson, built entirely by Italian masons, one of the most beautiful I've ever seen, able to accommodate thousands of worshippers.

Then nylon was invented. The silk trade died. And with it, Paterson. Irish, Jews, and Italians packed their bags and left the city, taking with them their talents and desire to work hard. The vacated space was filled in by African Americans, who, in times of such economic crisis for the town, had no chance to prosper. In the 1970s and 1980s, years of fierce social uprisings, crime fermented as the infection on an open and undisinfected sore. The absolute police corruption—one of the few things that Hollywood did not invent—and the rotten moral fabric of the politicians and the judiciary system supporting them, juxtaposed to the poverty of the most oppressed ethnic groups, along with almost complete unemployment, had the effect of a lit match thrown into a petrol barrel. The spark to which we owe the detonation was the 1966 case of a black boxer, accused of committing a triple murder in a pub in Paterson, on an evening when the poor guy was not even in the State of New Jersey. He was accused by one of the surviving victims who had been literally punched blind by the robber. Neither the exclusively white eyewitnesses nor the all-white jury helped the black sportsman's case. He was Rubin Carter, known by the nickname Hurricane. In 1976, Bob Dylan dedicated one of his finest songs to this disgraceful case of blatant injustice.

"*In Paterson that's the way things go*" says Dylan's song. The Criminal is very proud of this musical cameo.

The Criminal's grandmother continued to live in what are today's Projects even after everyone had given up on the town and despite the irrevocable depression. He and I are the only Jewish people in Paterson. Every now and then, if you look outside the kitchen window, you see an old woman, with her walker, drag herself slowly from one side to the other of the cement courtyard that connects tens of high-rise buildings and where all the trees are dead. At the end of the morning, if you look out again, she has hardly covered two quarters of the courtyard. Her tiny presence drowns imperceptibly under the loud music, the bestial fights among adults, the cries of poorly kept children.

Today even African Americans have been partly pushed outside of Paterson by the new immigrant currents: first by the Jamaicans, then the Trinidadians, and lastly by an enormous wave of Arabs. The imposing synagogue of Italian style is now surrounded by halal shops and stores for cigarettes, batteries, newspapers in English, Arabic, and Spanish, and colorful rugs for the Muslim prayers.

We'll have no honeymoon. For two reasons: one, because the Criminal is stingy to a paroxysm, and two, because next week I start a new job and there is no time for frivolous trips. The day after the wedding, however, the Criminal feels obliged to do something special and takes me to the famous Jersey shore. I have never seen such a crowd on such a small strip of sand. Each family group has its own boombox and personal soundtrack. There are flies everywhere attracted by the endless banquet of delicacies piled under tents and umbrellas, on chairs, and inside huge plastic basins. If Bo Derek came out of the waters right now, with her sexy braids and the golden bathing suit from *10,* they would force a roast chicken thigh into her mouth and urgently call the ANOREXIA INTERVENTION toll-free number and have her committed to a clinic.

I learn the word "boardwalk" the hard way, that is, being on it. It's crammed with people who walk back and forth, each time grabbing different food from one of the eateries along the way. They eat, drink, run, roll on skates and skateboards. But above all, they eat, eat, *eeeeeat!* And suck liquids through 8-inch-long straws. Hot dogs, ice cream, pizza, fried chicken, Tex-Mex, tandoori, fries, candy, cotton candy, and rivers of Coca Cola to stay hydrated. (*Hydration: very important to Americans.*) I dare not jump into the ocean: even if I could punch my way through the barrier of human lard that separates me from the water, I would not be able to swim. This is no Sardinia. This is no Mediterranean. The ocean is inhospitable. One step away from the shore, you stop touching the seafloor under your feet, the waves suck you away with a force unknown to our sea. It scares me terribly. I love swimming so much: I always excelled in diving from any height, but I feel dizzy just looking at this endless watery expanse, furious, violent, so alien. And speaking of fury, out of the waters comes the Criminal, newlywed, rehabilitated man, fellow traveler (metaphorically, of course, because I doubt we'll ever go on trips). He wanted to take a dip—he can't resist an athletic performance. His shoulders so straight. His physique so fit. I immediately notice the detail. It is easy to see something missing from a man in trunks: the bare man is there, the wedding ring is not. He realizes it too. It must have slipped off into the water.

The Criminal is livid with rage. End of the honeymoon. It is rare for honey to go bad, but if it did, it would taste just like this moonless day. We return to his apartment. Day One.

I start working for Radio Italia, a radio station that transmits from Fort Lee, a point on a map, not a real town, on the other side of Manhattan, just by the George Washington Bridge. Going to work, I see the shining west flank of Manhattan along the Hudson River, and the glorious bridge, all cables and honking cars . . . it takes your breath away. But I turn, each time, just a second before the road continues into the City . . . because Fort Lee is in New Jersey, not in New York. The view of the skyline seems to mock me, to mock my dreams . . . or perhaps it's there to keep them in front of my eyes so that I can keep my love alive, so that I don't forget our perennial "date." It says, "Don't be late! I'm waiting for you."

Silvio Berlusconi's brother invested some money into Radio Italia, named after the country, where he has no intention of returning because he is wanted by the Italian authorities for a number of financial and miscellaneous crimes. We are four broadcasters: I (news), Luisa (music), Fiorenzo (news), and Giacomo (sports). Fiorenzo, the oldest, is an elegant gentleman, in the style of Nathan Lane, originally from Tuscany. He's a closeted gay man in an ocean of uncloseted homophobia, who lives alone in a tiny apartment on the Upper East Side, and confesses to the urgency of procuring himself a façade-wife who will give him the green card, as his status here is in serious danger. Like many foreigners of a higher league (that is, those who can afford it), he has been going in and out of the country every three months in order to comply with his tourist visa requirements: but sooner or later the farce will have to stop, and he risks being arrested, deported, and, worst of all, having to live in glorious, refined, lavish, enviable Florence, where homosexuality is as tolerated as in Saudi Arabia or Iran.

Luisa is happily married to an Indian man: they had a traditional wedding in Mumbai and are perfectly happy. He is an American citizen, so she's OK. Giacomo grew up here and his Italian, with the lowliest Calabrese accent, makes us peal with laughter. He speaks a funny form of southern dialect no one understands (well, none of us, university-degreed bourgeois assholes from the north), while to the first- and second-generation immigrants listening to our programs from New Jersey, his dissonant speech of jumbled words glued together by an a-syntactical structure is music to their ears. In a segment in which the microphones are open for requests from the public, a man asks me, "*But you, Signorina, non italiana?*" He doubts I am Italian. I see Luisa, on the other side of a glass separating our studios, mute her microphone and bend over, holding her ribcage. "Yes, I was born and raised in Rome," I answer with my Alberto Lupo diction, the Italian equivalent of Lawrence Olivier. "*Ma no! Ma what Rome! You sound foreignera!*" insists the guy, whom I eventually succeed in distracting from his *idée fixe* and have him tell us a bit about his story: the same as always, the same as all immigrant stories . . . they seem made with a cookie-cutter except that instead of chocolate dough they are shaped out of sheer crap. Southern Italy; poverty; a boat to New York; success as builder; wife from "his parts;" children from "these parts" who live very close by; from nothing to "*tutto questo!*" all this.

I immediately sent my retainer to an immigration lawyer to start the green card application procedure.

That's it. I am happy. I immerse myself in this really fun job, and additionally I start collaborating as a reporter with an Italian-language newspaper distributed all over the TriState area called *America Oggi*. My days are busy: the parts that are not busy, those with the Criminal, will pass really fast. I won't even notice. Like certain gasses in nature, it'll be invisible, odorless, colorless, and hopefully painless. All I need is for things to flow like this, undisturbed and steady, for exactly two years. I need two years to regain my footing, to lay the foundation of a solid ground on which to securely walk, advance, and, if needed, run; I need time to learn to navigate the changed reality, to get the green card, to clear my mind, and then we'll see. I owe this satisfied bliss to my friend Francesca, who offered me both jobs. Francesca ended up in America in tow with her boyfriend, Cesare, who was admitted to New York University for a PhD in Political Science. They both speak with very strong *erre francese* (i.e., the letter *r* pronounced with a gurgling retroflex flap rather than the fricative trill Italian requires), which heralds their Milanese derivation from two miles away. They are the Italian equivalent of Brett & Galina—but without the over-honeyed self-complacency. The rationality they apply to life draws around them an aura of safety, frankness, clarity, and logic. Luck gives birth to fortune. Only more serenity can come from serenity.

Fourth day. Even before I leave to go to work—my news segment is at 7 AM, so I have a really early wakeup call each morning—the Criminal seems to be itching for a fight. I sense a tension in the air: it does not presage anything good. I quickly shut the door behind me.

Fifth day. Upon returning home from the radio station, I find a letter addressed to me. The envelope is pearly, of smooth *papier velouté,* so precious at the touch. I open it. The honor of my presence is kindly requested at the wedding of Yonah Hausmann and Adina Semania, to be held in Turin, on the day such & such, of the year such & such, in the presence of the couple's joyous parents, family and friends. RSVP.

Sixth day. The Criminal starts a new job in another branch of his father's bank. It's a higher rank, with more responsibilities. He is eager to make a good impression on his coworkers who understandably look at him as you look at one who's placed above you through nepotism. But inside, he's in turmoil: a flaming anger is eating him from within, he has already started admitting this much . . . anger at having gone back exactly to where he had escaped, anger at his parents' relentless hold on his future, anger at the death of his dream career. He wanted to be a baseball coach, and instead he sits behind a desk, to please daddy, to play daddy's role. The air turns electric. The apartment seems to be filling, little by little, with an invisible noxious gas.

Let's see. (*Whistle whistle . . .*)

I need two years. Time to get back on my feet and then start again. And in two years I'll have a green card. The last two years exploded like dynamite: the blast caused tons of dirt, dust, debris of all kinds to rise in the air . . . I need time, time for this fog to settle and for complete visibility to return.

Seventh . . . Eighth . . . *Escalation* . . .

Ninth day. After three explosive days, the volcano of repressed fury erupts. It's pointless to hope I can put a lid on it. Lapilli and lava will leave nothing standing in their way.

Point is, my job at the radio makes him real unhappy. Too many friends (me), too much social life (me), and it's too much for some (him). Am I getting away from him? He rhetorically wonders. "And once you get the green card, what, you're free to go?" In an attempt to make me jealous (*he's gotta be kidding*), the Criminal speaks of a new female colleague with qualities different from mine which are very much to his liking. (*Good god, let it be so! Go and be happy!*) My pacific (yet deeply felt) indifference to his clumsy provocation shakes the Criminal to the core. All I need is a couple of years, even merely one year and a half will suffice, just give me twelve months, please . . . Two years, a year and a half, a bit of time, the green card . . .

There's no time. "There is no more time" must have been the last sentence of every single inhabitant of Pompeii, I bet you.

The memory of the O.J. case fleetingly passes through my head. I keep forgetting that one of the reasons why it's unwise to quarrel with athletes is that they sometimes feature the two most frightful characteristics wrapped in one: stupidity and physical strength.

I can't decide whether this sadist intentionally brings me *only* to the threshold of the underworld, or whether he is too much of a loser to succeed in properly killing me, but either way, this is what happens to me for the subsequent forty-eight hours:

(1) He hangs me by the legs out of the fifth-floor window, and he threatens to let go of me. I am hanging so low, that my dangling arms almost reach

the window of the apartment below. That wouldn't be bad, actually: because maybe that way I could make eye contact with the family on the fourth floor, probably sitting at the dinner table at this time, who could not avoid coming to my rescue, since, apparently, my desperate cries (*Help me! Someone call the police! Please, help me!*) do not seem to move anyone to action. While I hang in the darkness, the terrifying thought that my screams may annoy our neighbors, and that therefore everyone at this point may hope the Criminal will let go of me, makes me giggle through the tears. Gallows humor, I suppose. My giggles infuriate the Criminal who transitions from this simple threat to execution.

(2) I am barbarically raped.

(3) I get crushed between the steel front door and the wall behind it, like a fly trapped in the folds of a concertina. Open close open close . . . I tried to run, but the key lock, chain lock, swing lock sliding bolt, dead bolt (it's Paterson, NJ, one can't be too careful) were too much. The Criminal was there *presto,* not out of chivalry to open the door for me but to slam it to my face, my face stuck behind it. O doorways! ("*Doorways, it seems, are where the truth is told,*" said Alan Alda in his commencement speech for his daughter in 1980.) The truth is that the creature trapped between wall and door gets smashed—depending on body types—nose first, then shoulder blades, the fingers (imprudently launched forward to stop the impact), and last the ribs.

(4) He throws me down the stairs. I land between floors, he springs forth and kicks me down the next flight of stairs. Five floors, two sets of stairs each floor, all the way down—"You want to leave? There, I'll help you leave, go!" Heck, he knows how to kick a ball. (*Note to self: Rent only ground floor apartments from now on.*)

Other approaches that he thinks worth trying involve (A) frying my face on the incandescent stove's burners, (B) locking me in a closet the whole night through, (C) bouncing me against the walls every time I pass by, (D) smashing waffles, smothered in maple syrup, on my face—one wouldn't think so, but hot maple syrup really burns one's eyes and does a good job of blocking your nostrils like wax.

Black out.

In the hospital, when I come to, a Pakistani doctor tells me, with an expression of pure disgust toward me (I do not blame him), "You'll be all right" (very strong *r*). The nurse runs after him and whispers something in his ears. The doctor chases her away with an irritated gesture of his hairy hand as if the lady were a mosquito. But the mosquito, true to its nature, does not relent. The nurse comes directly to me: "If you tell me what happened, I am obliged by law to call the police." *And the doctor is not?* I get it: the doctor, educated in America (*ah, these PhDs!*), graduate of one of the universities of this great cradle of progress, has assimilated what was useful (a few scientific notions) and said screw you to any mental progress. For him, even in America, even with a fat bank account, even with children born here, and neighbors who welcomed him with baskets of muffins for the love of multi-ethnicity, a woman will always be less than a flea-infested bitch.

"You do not have to tell me the details. You just need to nod. I ask you a question, and you don't have to say anything . . . just move your head," the nurse continues slowly, motherly, but firmly. "Was it your husband?" Ah, I remember the policeman's words, "If you were married, we could help . . ." I nod. The police arrive. They stand tall, strutting, in their tight dark blue uniforms, the sparkly badges in which I'm reflected like a mirror . . . I avoid looking, though, because something tells me, if I interpret correctly the expression on the face of the only policewoman among them, that this is not my finest hour.

They mention a complaint and a "restraining order": I know the word restrain and I know the word order . . . but I don't get what a restraining order is. My impeccably good English leads everyone to assume that I understand the context in which the language is spoken: but I don't, the two things are completely separate. Knowing a bunch of verbs and words does not mean knowing the culture or the cultural rules in which a language moves as confident as a snake, not in a straight line, but with sinuous, jerky, mimetic moves, sometimes visible and sometimes not. If I ask and they think I'm dumb, I might lose points with them . . . points the Criminal might gain. *Fania, concentrate!* Restraining means "that which restraints," order is . . . *oh c'mon!* Pretty self-evident. The image of Hannibal Lecter in *The Silence of the Lambs* forms in my parietal lobe: Anthony Hopkins tied to a bed, with a straitjacket, and a muzzle. It seems a bit too much. A formal complaint will suffice.

Discharged from the hospital, I return to the late grandmother's apartment. I have all the time necessary to make sense of the situation, gather my thoughts and my things, and depart for safer (and completely undisclosed) shores as soon as possible. The Criminal is in prison. This apartment which I hated from the first moment I was introduced into it, with its old people's smell, old-fashioned carpet (in depressing mauve), claustrophobic, without balconies, without views, with low-ceilings, and a kitchen that makes you want to eat out every day . . . suddenly, this same place, without the Criminal, seems to me almost cute. Despite the spots of my blood scattered all over. All I need is a couple of hours to recover, pack, drink a nice cup of coffee, and I'll be fine. Someone knocks on the door. It is not the kind of knock which asks to be let in, but the kind which indicates that this door is about to be opened whether you want it or not.

Enter a policeman, the doorman, and the Criminal.

The policeman has a document in his hands and presently he readies himself to assume the posture of *praecō,* the public announcers of ancient Rome. But he stops in his tracks for a moment, looks at me, and with sudden clarity he takes in the situation. He feels cheated: he had come to evict the troublesome (and perhaps a bit crazy) wife of this distinguished young man and found himself facing a different truth, hard to ignore. He glances at the Criminal whom he now sees under a different light. If looks could incinerate . . . but the Criminal does not possess a soul on which the righteous policeman's eyes can have any effect, so the man in uniform can't but carry on with the procedure. Work is work. Duties must be upheld. And evening is near: his wife and family must be waiting for him at home.

I am reminded of the final scene in Molière's *Tartuffe,* when Monsieur Loyal shows up to destroy that fool of Orgon and take everything away from him:

Now, please, Sir, let us have no friction.
This is nothing more than notification,

An order to evict both you and yours,
Put your furniture out and lock the doors

"By order of the judge Such & Such . . ." the policeman begins to read out loud, with little conviction. This is not a comedy, and no *deus ex machina* intervenes to save the good and punish the bad. The Criminal issued a restraining order *against me*.

I, due to wounds in the abdomen and ribs, talk with difficulty, being unable to take in too much air at a time, but I try nonetheless to explain to the gentleman that it's me the offended party. "See?" I point to the arm immobilized in the blue sling. "They asked *me* to do a restraining order at the hospital, but I, to be kind"—I look at the Criminal at this point to send him an implicit message, "*Got it? I could have hurt you, but I chose not to*"—"I said it wasn't necessary." The policeman with a regretful expression says: "Too bad, my colleagues should have told you that by law anyone can request a restraining order against someone else, it is up to the judge to decide whether to grant it or not . . . So, whether you're his victim or not, this doesn't prevent your husband from filing it against you." (He throws another incinerating look toward the Criminal who stands beside him with a smug expression that says "I always win.") *No, your colleagues at the hospital did not explain this to me. I assure you. Had I been made aware of this legal detail, I wouldn't have hesitated a moment to put my signature on his death sentence.* Yes, I wish death on this distinguished young man from such a good family that bailed him out of jail before I could make myself a cup of coffee.

I'm on the street in a matter of minutes. I took only a few things with me, as in my state, it's not like I could carry much anyway: some clothes, some randomly chosen books, the violin, my passport, the invitation to Yonah's wedding.

I am in my Ford Taurus station wagon (*A Sound Experience*), I turn on the ignition, and I let myself be driven as if I were not at the wheel, and I can devote myself entirely to sobbing. The state of shock makes me immortal, I think. I am enveloped in pain. I think I am about to get on the George Washington Bridge . . . I recline my seat, lying practically horizontal, and close my eyes. I hardly touch the steering wheel and let the car lead me wherever it wants. I wait for the sound of metal crumpling, for the impact with the river waters below. This time, I won't resist what needs to happen.

I wanted two years, but all I got was ten lousy days.

*Fall.*

# PART 4

# The Island

# 9

I'm in front of a building door. I take a deep breath, but it comes out in broken spasms through my sore ribcage. I hesitate, I savor this moment. I give a tight squeeze to the keys I hold in my hand. I notice my reflection in the glass of the door. A frightened little bird with a mop of short yellow hair on her head. No Gwyneth Paltrow: rather, I look more like Tweety Bird if Sylvester the Cat had ever had a chance to catch her. I enter the building at 254 Seaman Avenue, Apt. E 1, New York, NY 10034. Home.

I'm in New York again. New York, New York.

*Oh, it's a long, long while from May to December*, sings Sarah Vaughan, whose immortal voice is infused with the melancholy of clock ticking. *And the autumn weather turns the leaves to flame. One hasn't got time for the waiting game*, Kurt Weil's lyrics remind me.

Surprisingly, I did not drive off the George Washington Bridge. My Ford Taurus station wagon delivered me safe and sound (*A Sound Experience*) to Salvatore's doorstep in the Bronx.

I made it safely. The spell is broken. I am overcome by a very deep, abnormal lethargy.

The plan is to hide at Salvatore's for a while and, in the meantime, do all I can to get back in the saddle: I need a home, a job, a green card, and a contingent of lawyers.

My friend Francesca assigns me articles to write for the cultural section she manages at *America Oggi*. I do not know if *America Oggi* really needs my pieces or if they are an excuse Francesca conjectures to keep me alive. She asks me to write a piece on Little Italy in the Bronx . . . or, as Salvatore calls it, Littelittalì. Unlike its homonym on the Lower East Side, the Bronx's Italian village is still authentic and busy. The place is a godforsaken ghetto. Since the grimmest gang violence appears to Francesca as the least of my problems, she has no qualms sending *me* for a reconnaissance to Littelittalì.

And thus, on East 187th, I come across a shop called *La Casa della Mozzarella*. There's a giant bear of a man in the store's back room, bending over two barrels brimming with milk: he dips his huge right arm, naked and hairy, inside the liquid up to his armpit, and using it like a paddle he gently stirs the white potion. He dips in further, down enough to grab something at the bottom of the barrel from where he pulls out a long rope of elastic filaments, like interlaced rubber bands. He breaks a little piece, makes a knot of it, and hands it to me. Caught between revulsion and lust, with my lip upturned like a flehmening horse, I take it in. It's warm and rubbery, and it sends an electric discharge from my tongue to my ears: a pleasure so intense that it reconnects me with a vitality in my body I had shut down, reminding me that I am alive, that apart from the chaotic darkness in my mind, the rest of me is alive, in its place, and eating the best mozzarella in the world. I love the Bronx. Once again, the Bronx delivered.

Throughout my stay with Salvatore, I can't stop going back, over and over, to the hirsute giant at *La Casa della Mozzarella*. I sit in my car, and without fork or knife, without plates or wipes, not to mention oil, salt, or pepper, I chew, chew, cry and insatiably chew.

Is this what the bottom feels like? I finally reached it, after a two-year headlong plummet. I no longer have a sense of myself. It is as if I have lost my own image. I cannot rebuild it mentally. I try the mirror, but it doesn't help. I feel split into two: between what I believe I have always been and the wretched one I have become. The two me's don't clot, they simply coexist. The one with university degrees, a couple of Nobel Prize-winning friends, the Eurochic wardrobe and Eurocentric attitude. The one with the bruises, the sling from shoulder to arm, the dark sunglasses to hide the purple circles around the eyes . . . who, at the first kindness from a cashier or a perfect stranger in the subway, begins to sob. This one is white trash. I, reduced to white trash. I ask everyone, implicitly and explicitly, for help. I have no dignity left. People withdraw, I can't blame them. I represent something no one wants to become, so everyone must pretend that I don't exist: one oughtn't open the door to that which shouldn't be admitted, otherwise we'd all go insane. It's only natural. The hidden face of the Moon is not *the* Moon.

Salvatore looks at me frowningly. He wants to believe I did something wrong. But he leaves on the table fragrant loaves of freshly baked bread for me and a bottle of thick green oil he buys from a neighbor who grows and presses the olives in his Bronx backyard. It's his way of loving. I'm grateful.

Salvatore prides himself on speaking several languages. He never heard me speak English and assumes that I do not know it and that I'm a bit thick, because when he speaks, whether in Italian or English, I can't understand that jumbled of mispronounced words and make him repeat things ten times. This authorizes him to scold and lecture me, warning me that if I don't learn fast I'll sink here. I am not American material. I haven't had an opportunity to tell him anything about me, about my "beckcrount," as he says. He wishes to scare some sense into me, but instead he amuses me when he talks, so insecure in his own mouth, that he's forced to raise his voice and sounds permanently in a state of rage: "Parka el carro qua!" he yells, or "Sendi un parcel to casa!" in a mystifying mixture of English, Spanish, and Italian. He explains to me, "I waz uh brickoliere". Only from the context, from his gesticulation, and after several days of cohabitation, I understand that "brickoliere" is his way of saying bricklayer, making up the word by adding the traditional Italian ending for nouns referring to professions, "-iere," to the English word brick. He gets cross with me for not understanding right away that by brickoliere he means *muratore.* He laid bricks. Tons of them. Including those of the house where we live on Yates Avenue. He worked like a mule, Salvatore: it's written on his face, on his excoriated hands, on his lean body typical of those who are a bundle of twitchy nerves and muscles incapable of keeping still. Brick upon brick, he made his small American fortune, which allowed him to keep his wife at home (his proud way of saying that she didn't need to work) and send all the children to university. He arrived from Italy in the 1950s, via Canada, where he claims to have learned French. "Palampaquay" (Pelham Parkway) was a totally Italian neighborhood when Salvatore installed himself here: where the Italians ended, the Orthodox Jews began—the more worldly Jews instead went to Manhattan and Park Slope. But his neighborhood's morphology has changed, and these two communities are now reduced to a handful of old-timers, surrounded by other ethnic groups with which they persevere in not getting along.

Salvatore walks me a few steps down the street to show me concretely the invisible border that demarcates the territory between this or that group: his house is sandwiched between the "Jewdas" on one side and the "Blex" on the other, he explains. Among Italian immigrants, there is no greater tragedy than that of a son or daughter who marries into a non-Italian family: but if this *has* to happen, at least let it be with anybody but a Blec . . . because the "Blex" (plural of Blec, Bronx-Italian for Black, in Salvatore's rendition) are "*no buono,*" he says shaking his head. A mixed marriage tainted his own house too: but fortunately his daughter married a Jewda. And even if they are as strange as Martians, at least the Jewdas are family-oriented, they do not get in trouble, they make money (here Salvatore needs only make the international sign of rubbing thumb, index, and middle finger together), and they are not "Blex."

All the "Palampaquay" Italians call the Jews Jewdas. I am not sure how they spell it, but it is clearly inspired by the name of the famous traitor who got Jesus in trouble and every Jew a bad rap in perpetuity: Giuda, or in English Judas. In the small villages these immigrants hail from, there were no Jews, they had never seen one before coming to America, and therefore they had never had to learn the term in Italian—*ebreo.* When they arrived and met for the first time these mythological creatures whose name, they now learned in English, is Jew (pronounced like the Italian word for "down," *giù*), they must have scratched their heads: "How are we going to say it in Italian?" Knowledge generates conundrums. It must have come like a stroke of genius: Jew . . . Giuda . . . Jewda, that's it! To be clear: the fact that these illiterate masses ignored the Italian word for "Jew" doesn't mean they ignored the *ebreo*'s guilts and flaws. Antisemitism has never needed Jews to exist.

Salvatore, who knows how much I love pizza, especially from the Bronx, brings me to a small joint on Morris Park Avenue, where the pizza is so damn good that I can't stop shoving one slice after another into my mouth, as he looks on with an amused grin while the oily juices make a mess of my hands and face. I don't believe Salvatore when he tells me that each Wednesday, a policeman enters the place around noon, takes a large pizza with a bribe taped on the bottom of the cardboard box, and leaves. So we go on a Wednesday and sit strategically in a corner: midday comes, policeman enters, pizza man hands over the boxed pizza with the "extra dough," policeman exits. All the customers pretend not to have seen but exchange ironic looks. I guess my palms weren't the only ones greased that day.

Morris Park Avenue is lined with small cafés where characters out of *The Godfather* sip coffee, smoke their lungs away, and gossip about what goes on in the neighborhood: *Nothing buono.* But most of the area is a desolate land, blighted, with basketball courts where no one plays, treeless sidewalks along which rare groups of kids float silently, having nowhere else to go. Here various gangs thrive, and sometimes from this or that alley gunshots are fired, and if you are not careful where you walk, you can accidentally get killed. Taking a walk or a ride at night around here is out of the question.

I would not preclude that one day a stray bullet will hit me: in fact I practically expect it. Or is it that I wish it a little? Among the absolute worst things that can happen to a foreigner abroad are getting sick and dealing with the law. I've tried both. The former was once resolved with a laxative and a radioactive drink. As for the latter, I'm not sure how or if it'll be resolved. Maybe a stray bullet will keep me from having to deal with it. My inclination would be to die of a gunshot in a hospital bed, preferably in Manhattan, twenty times rather than find myself fighting with a judicial system I do not know, all alone among bloodthirsty enemies.

I am between a rock and a hard place: because of the legal case against the Criminal (countered with a case he filed against me), I cannot leave the United States. But I cannot survive in the United States without the green card that allows me to work. I cannot stay and I cannot go.

I discover that all the beautiful things Galina explained to me a while back about pro bono lawyers and legal safety nets, or the tight network that exists to help, support, and catch the victims in midair as they come down like sacks of potatoes thrown into the abyss by their violent husbands . . . that none of this applies to my case. Fania: Out.

Hidden in the former bedroom of one of Salvatore's children, I sift through the yellow pages under "Legal"—Legal Aid, Pro Bono, Pro Bono

Pro All, Safe Horizon, Family Sanctuary, NoDomesticViolence, StopAbuse, Women Safety, Women's Portal, Save the Mothers, Mother Courage, Mother Theresa . . . I find pages and pages of ads that promise free, disinterested, non-for-profit help for battered women—new word: I look it up.

From the Merriam-Webster Dictionary, we learn that:

Batter (verb), to beat with successive blows so as to bruise, shatter, or demolish

Batter (noun), a mixture consisting chiefly of flour, egg, and milk or water and being thin enough to pour or drop from a spoon

Battered woman *ergo* can be understood as a woman beaten up by someone as well as prepped for the frying pan. Makes sense. I feel like both.

Ring. Ring. Ring. The notepad on my lap is filled with notes, scribbled everywhere, disorderly, like abstract Dadaist paintings: half pieces of information, names I didn't quite catch, acronyms I never heard of, and new phone numbers they advise me to try, toll-free numbers, 800-numbers, hot lines, cold lines. . . . But the problem can be reduced to a rather elementary axiom: there are plenty of help lines, but the help lines are not there to help me.

"Would you say you belong to the Afro-American minority?" Hmm, no.

"Is your ethnicity Puerto Rican, Dominican, or Hispanic of another kind?" Hmm, no.

"Of native-American protected genus?" Maybe? Sorry, joke.

"Do you have any children?" No.

"Your bank account is solid zero?" God forbid!

"Do you have American citizenship?" No.

"Do you have a valid visa . . ." Yes! I have it! I got it! F1 Visa, still valid. "Ah, pity . . . if you were illegal you'd be better off."

"Can you read and write?" "Not an orphan?" "Do you use fork and knife? . . . Too bad, you are entitled to zip."

Lesson # 1: The middle of the way is no way. Being in the middle is the worst position to be had. The only two categories that will survive the civil apocalypse to which we are inescapably headed will be those on the top—with their inexhaustible resources, with a monopoly over all alternative plans, from B to Z—and those on the bottom—who have absolutely nothing and therefore have absolutely nothing to lose. To those in the middle, the supreme élites will not stretch out so much as a saving finger, while the first-rate have-nots will have the sandwiched-class for breakfast.

If I were not me, mine would be an adequately pitiful case: but since I am who I am, no aid is foreseeable. I don't fit within any of the required parameters. Mindful of what the New Jersey policeman told me, I venture to report, "But I married him! We're married . . ." "It doesn't matter!" everyone confirms, "It makes no difference!" If I could manage to make myself more miserable, I'd be fine. Or I could pay a private lawyer $375 an hour—the current rate for unimpressive lawyers in 1998 (those who send you to jail and take bribes from your enemy). Or I could choose not to fight at all: anyhow, I've already lost. The divorce is the easy part. I can forget about any kind of compensation, restitution of personal property, not to mention alimony (ten days of marriage do not even give me the right to take back what was mine from his apartment).

In my desperate search for legal help, I talk to dozens and dozens of people on the phone, and some of them mention the same person to me: Father Kelly, a priest who is not listed in any telephone directory. No one can give me a specific address for him, and most don't know how to track him down at all; indeed, many know of his legendary existence but not much else; in the end, however, I get a single clue I cling to for dear life . . . the name of a church, Saint Brigid. So I set off on an interminable journey: Brooklyn bound.

Monsignor James Kelly, the undisputed ruler of Saint Brigid Church, is a priest from Limerick and an immigration lawyer: tall, big-bellied, with a thundering voice and a few graying strands of hair, pomaded to one side, theatrical movements, and a passion for illegal Cuban cigars and whiskey. It is not his Christian impiety, though, that landed him on the radar of FBI, INS, and CIA (and possibly the Interpol), but his involvement with the IRA. Father Kelly studied law and became a paladin of the Northern Irish cause, helping many anti-British separatists get documents to escape to America when enemy fire reached too close to their arses. He is an enthusiast of codicils, petitions, recourses, and appeals; he uses every trick to win against the system and advocates the cause of the disinherited of whom (*just look around!*) there is no shortage in the neighborhood where his church is located. And these days, his needy flock is mainly composed of Latin Americans, especially *los ecuatorianos*. So much so that Father Kelly now delivers his Sunday sermons in Spanish. But when he started out as a priest, he trained in Rome and now he is excited to speak Italian again with me. However, he looks at me from his unusual height with a scrutinizing eye: does he like the rareness? or the risk? *Who is this girl?* I hear him think. *This is a new typology.* I still hear him think. *A Jewish girl at the Church door? Oh, the irresistible irony!* I still hear him. (*Please, shut up and help!* I yell back in my head.)

Saint Brigid's church and legal office are like an ant colony. They are teeming with people who seem to be employed, and very busy, in all sorts of capacities: custodians, assistants, managers, facility watchers, ushers, chamberlains, secretaries, surveyors, repairmen, painters, cleaners, cooks, gardeners, carvers, organ tuners, masters of the tv antennas, clockwinders, astronomers. Father Kelly looks at me and explains with a grin: "In America, an employer can decide to sponsor you for the green card by giving you a job, so I do. I hire!" When all lines have been filled and Saint Brigid is left with no legitimate task that wouldn't raise the INS' suspicions, Father Kelly knows at which door to knock to collect an old debt and forces his Irish pals to hire the neediest cases. Many of the people I see here come from desperate situations: out of loyalty, they hang out at St. Brigid helping Father Kelly in whatever way they can and forming a safety fortress around him. Father Kelly is the first real Robin Hood I have ever met in my life.

Among his faithful, Father Kelly can count Pablito, a helper more or less my age. When he was seventeen, Pablito and his brother Esteban walked on foot from Quito, Ecuador, to Brooklyn. But on the way, in Colombia, the revolutionaries kidnapped them, beat them up, chained them to the toilets of a public bathroom in the middle of a jungle, before realizing that these two boys (by then starved half to death) were no means to a ransom. As the world goes, henchmen are not known for resolving such mistakes with a laugh and an apology: they usually kill their victims and dispose of the bodies. Pablito and Esteban could hear them discuss, heatedly, on the other side of the thin wall that separated the women's toilets in which they were imprisoned from the men's toilets where the gang members held a meeting about how to get rid of these two mistakes. One of the captors got the better of the others, and the brothers were freed. Thanks to this act of mercy, I meet Pablito.

Father Kelly has big dreams for him. He has taken him under his wing and wants him to be his successor—not as priest, but as lawyer. The old Irishman is teaching his dedicated apprentice the ins and outs of the trade, instilling a knowledge different from what one finds in books, the kind of practicum law schools have no courses for.

Pablito's and his brother's case was solved straightforwardly by Father Kelly: political refugees. But me? I represent a completely different challenge. Father Kelly is galvanized. "Pablito!" He bellows from his baritone diaphragm. Pablito, like a caricature of the over-obsequious Mr. Heep from Dickens's *David Copperfield*, rushes in, rubbing his neat hands together, and takes orders on how to deal with my case. "This [an index finger points straight at me] is exactly what we were talking about! *Es el VAWA!*" Vawa? I am cut off from their conversation, as if I were not in this big dark wood paneled room with stained glass windows, books and crosses everywhere. "*Es perfecto!*" Father Kelly enthuses, "*Sabes que haser. Ocupate de ella!*" Pablito nods: let's hope he really understood. In any event, I'm already a step forward from those pointless phone calls made from a corner of Salvatore's house in the Bronx, my SOS launched into an unresponsive void. Even if it turns out that Father Kelly can't do anything to help, I'd rather stretch out here, on this bench in the hallway that still smells like the tree it came from, and never move again, become an invisible worker ant, around Father Kelly's robe. Here, at least, there is a bit of peace.

I am about to open the faucets of a desperate sob when, indifferent to my pathos, Pablito and Father Kelly excitedly begin to explain about a bill Senator Joe Biden (*one of monsignor's Irish chaps?*) put forth in 1994 and that was recently signed into law by President Bill Clinton. The bill, called Violence Against Women Act (*vah-wah!*), is meant to protect victims of domestic abuse, women and children: prompting the senator to act is the vertiginous increase in domestic abuse cases as well as "sex slaves" cases in America. These victims do not go to the police to report the violence for fear of being arrested, imprisoned or, worse, repatriated (their brothers and fathers may not have compassion once they find them back, and "spoiled," on the threshold of their houses). So Clinton, who wishes to get back in women's good graces, has turned Biden's bill into law and decreed that if an American citizen is caught abusing a foreign woman, his victim has a right to justice, compensation, protection, and above all a green card—which after five years is converted into citizenship. The law is very new and has not yet been tested. *Enter Fania.*

Father Kelly, all fired up, lights a beautiful new cigar to celebrate the occasion. "You could be the first case to test this new law in the whole nation," he gushes. *Lucky me.*

I don't think Salvatore loves hearing about these developments. Salvatore lives alone and drinks heavily in the evening. But when he is sober in the morning, he tells me that nothing will come out of this, that it is my fault that I took the rotten guy: "Women are good only at ruining you!" he screams crossly. He sees me as the embodiment of all that is wrong with my gender.

Salvatore drinks to forget having been left by his wife. He can't get over the fact that his sons plotted behind his back to take their mother away from him. As they escorted her out, Salvatore started destroying stuff to stop her from taking anything away. Now the house is a disaster, and he refuses to buy new furniture to replace what he smashed to smithereens. It seems that he was beating his wife, not too much—he defends himself—just a little. *Just enough.*

This information and his violent tantrums keep me on tenterhooks, make me puke often and nearly pee myself when he barks too close to my face. I am on pins and needles. I see the potential in Salvatore of raising a hand against me for a slap or a little push. . .just a little. Meanwhile, these days he drinks more than usual because he senses that I "too" am plotting to get away from him and he was so enjoying my company.

I discreetly continue my search for an apartment with renewed zeal.

I sell the wedding ring so as not to set eye on it ever again, not even by mistake. I see signs everywhere in Manhattan announcing, "We Buy Gold." There are many such places, and I don't care which one is better: "We buy Gold" and I sell it, so I choose at random. They are such ugly dumps: decayed, stinky, full of old rubbish and filthy. It was in a place exactly like this that a year ago I sold the engagement ring. What are these "stores"? Just like the other time, they give me very little for my ring: same amount, in fact, $50. Liberty is priceless, so I accept; I throw the receipt in the first garbage bin at

the corner, because I don't want anything, not even a piece of paper, to connect me to that object, and I spend the money immediately.

Since the Criminal has wiped my New Jersey bank account clean, and
we feared that the Criminal Family with their banking connections could
intercept any further financial transactions of mine, my parents decided to
bring the money themselves. When I pick them up at JFK, I immediately
spot them, plump and happy as always, nicely put together, distinguished,
pulling elegantly several suitcases and tons of bags with gifts. They look decidedly on vacation. They scan the crowds in search of their daughter in that
disorientated expression we all bear when we land in a foreign country, and
we are dazed by the alien context: their eyes reach me almost simultaneously.
My father stops dead, pulls out of his coat pocket the white cotton mono-
grammed handkerchief I know so well and turns away, so as to hide the tears.
Something about my appearance has caused a shock somehow.

Despite the tragic reason for their visit, my mother insists on seeing New
York thoroughly. She has to miss nothing of the tourist experience. Given
their utter dependence on me, I must guide them, explain, translate, take
the right bills out of their wallet and hand them to the cashiers, swipe their
MetroCards through the subway gate machines, help them buy presents to
take back home and so on, which brings me away from the urgent demands
of my legal, illegal, judicial, real estate, medical, business, or work-related affairs. But my mother doesn't see this as a problem. I am required to chaperone
them, take pictures, be happy that they are here: "You don't love us! If we are
such a bother, we won't come anymore!" *I wish.* I unceremoniously put them
back on a plane the first time my mother dares a "poor Criminal." I meant to
kill her; sending them away is a kindness on my part. The last thing I remember is my father, at JFK airport, pressing one last exhortation: "Eat!"

The same day they leave, I rush to meet Larry Horst, a man who rents a
flat in the Inwood neighborhood.

I have already visited so many apartments everywhere. Almost all unaf-
fordable. But for those I could afford and that were habitable, I was unable to
get a lease, who in the hell knows why. This latest apartment seems perfect.
Empty, newly restored, waxed and polished parquet, freshly repainted, one
bedroom, one large living room, eat-in kitchen, two corridors, one bathroom,

a dozen windows, $700 a month, rent stabilized. Larry Horst informs me that he is the owner of the whole blasted building! I have not met any of the owners of the establishments I previewed so far. There was always a realtor or a "super" to meet me. The super is the building's factotum, I learn: the manual administrator in place of the owner. If you break something, it's the super who fixes it or breaks it further, depending on whether you get a smart one or not. The super hands you your keys when you move in and keeps a copy for himself. *So you can find him in your apartment any time?* He doesn't always live in the same building, but he is there every day, an omnipresent figure that keeps an eye on you and, more importantly, keeps an eye on your neighbors and the company they keep. Faced with the hypothetical injunction of choosing a friend, one single friend for life, in New York, I highly recommend choosing your building's super.

Larry Horst's property is one of those humongous apartment buildings erected before the war for the proletarian masses in the least affluent areas of the city. After the tour of the place, Larry insists that we sit in his car and talk. My mind goes to Gwidon, to Inferno, to other men their age who can't refrain from the urge to put their hands all over you. I mentally throw together some statistical odds on the assault risk I'm facing (*I'd say a 79 percent chance? 85 percent if I take off my jacket?*) and on the outcome (*o percent chance I will denounce this guy, no matter what he does to me. Because no one would believe me at this point, they'll think I am a paranoid bitch who goes around destroying men's lives, and my whole case against the Criminal will be dismissed*). I sit in the car with Larry.

I don't understand why one can't simply put a signature on a piece of paper somewhere, shake hands, exchange keys, and say good-bye. I don't know why we need this interlude in the car. He certainly seems interested in having me as a tenant, something tells him he can trust me. He explains that he owns tens of buildings like this one all over town, and the kind of tenants he gets often don't pay in time or at all ("they" make a mess; "they" are a mess) but I, with my flair of czarina fallen on hard times, my clean-girl looks—in a word, albeit hidden between the lines, White—I inspire trust, he says. OK. I tell him how happy I am to meet with him, how much I loved the apartment he showed me. I am fine with the price, I will pay punctually, I'll be a stellar tenant. We stay in the car. We are not concluding. We sit, the windows gradually fog over, the negotiations aren't sealed. I reassure him that I will be very careful, and I will not damage anything. Anything! Ever! I will pay, really! (*Note to self: Always have a job before promising punctual payments of any kind.*) Nothing. Until Larry breaks the silence, a bit exasperated: "Look, it works like this: you give me $700 cash, under the table, *get it?* just between the two of us, and the apartment is yours." *La mazzetta*, of course! A perquisite, a bribe, a buyoff . . . that's what he was waiting for! That's what I was supposed to offer to all the middlemen, intermediaries, intercessors, patented gangsters, who had shown me the other places! That's why they had not rented them to me. They wanted to take a cut.

I consider this extra $700 the fair price for this private lesson on how to get by in this place, or an activation fee for my membership in the New York Lowlife Club. Had Larry not put his cards on the table, I would have never gotten my apartment on Seaman Avenue. Nor any other.

Ludimilla is the first to call on me in my new apartment. Apartment E1. As soon as she hears the sanitized recap of my misadventures, she arrives from Boston in her new blue Beetle, latest model: a French mime's type of car, with that preposterous flower-vase Volkswagen has glued on every dashboard. Ludimilla has just bought this car even though she'll soon leave the United States for good. I wasn't there for her while her private drama was unfolding. In fact, I knew nothing about it until now. Out of the blue, Italo showed up after school in their precious little abode in Boston and declared to his dumbfounded wife: "I do not feel like it anymore." Just like that. As if their marriage were a day at the mall one could tire of or the wrong dessert ordered fecklessly after a big meal.

"Well, a Swedish graduate student is involved," she explains. My jaw drops. "I was brought here practically against my will and now what? I'm going back home. I hate America." She does not cry though. She looks radiant, put together as beautifully as ever, her shiny black hair with red highlights, her impertinent smile. I admire her for not seeming to be fazed at all by all this. She is here in New York with me, sitting on my newly waxed parquet at Seaman Avenue, and we laugh uproariously. I am stunned. She has the situation totally under control. Even though she and Italo are Italian citizens, on student visas, and did not marry in America, she has managed to find a way to get a divorce here, in three months rather than the half a dozen years or more it would take her in Italy. I admire her strength and clear-headedness, the kind I've seen in Galina, Francesca, and Camilla.

I do not breathe a word about the Criminal.

Ludimilla brought me some gifts: two terracotta mugs with frosted interior finish in blue; a 12-piece set of forks, spoons, and knives; one teapot. I order us some food, and we eat together on the floor of my empty apartment. When the sky grows dark, Ludimilla grabs her Italian coat, tightens the belt around her wasp-waist, wraps me in her arms (*and I breathe in her sexy perfume*), and leaves me. I wave bye-bye with my hand, tears wetting my cheeks, as she whizzes away in her fragrant Beetle along Seaman Avenue. I reenter the building, I tremble a little, I immediately put on the kettle for some tea. It's the last time, I know it, that I will see my friend. This tea set will help me remember her.

I still have Francesca and Cesare. One day, they come to drag me to IKEA. "Drag" because the only IKEA that has finally opened in the Tristate area is in New Jersey. I can't see or hear anything, my senses shut down under the weight of unmanageable fear, I do not participate in the conversations in the car, and if it were not for my motion sickness I would lie down on the backseat with my coat bandaged around my head. I am in the grip of terror: if I run into the Criminal, I'm done for. Francesca and Cesare literally flank me like bodyguards: they understand my state of mind, but they don't give up. I need furniture, and I need someone to help me load the stuff and take it home. In short, I need them, and they won't take NO for an answer. Once back, we spend hours assembling the Benno, screwing together the enormous Groland, and hanging the Grundtal, three Enudden, two Ekby Håll, and one Bygel on the kitchen walls (*Note to self: To really prepare to face life, get an electric drill.*)

Francesca, whose favorite pastime is studying the IKEA catalog thoroughly, knows all the unpronounceable names of stuff and when she talks in her funny patterns, with her strong retroflex "r's," I practically split my sides with laughter. "Look Cesare, this Anneberg sofa is really cool! Right, Cesare? We too should get a Anneberg *sofa* or, look, a Nartorp. *Perchè no!* Why don't we, Cesare?" She's like a character from a Natalia Ginzburg's novel.

All I can think of is: I will never set foot in New Jersey again.

I don't get why everyone insists I eat. One morning, as I take a shower, I pay some attention to my body for the first time in months. That is, to what remains of it. I see two ill-defined breasts hanging floppily from my chest like empty latex gloves. The pelvic bones protrude outward. There is nothing left of me. I have literally no flesh on me. As soon as I finish washing, now hyper aware of the limp creases of skin under my fingers, I take the yellow phone directory and order an extra-large, extra-cheese pizza from the Bronx.

My apartment building is at the northernmost tip of Manhattan, just a bridge away from the Bronx. I have been here before. The coincidence hasn't escaped me. Parallel to Seaman Avenue, there stretches Park Terrace West, and at number 83, apartment 2B, there still live, as they always have, Brett & Galina. The day Larry Horst called to show me the place, I had no idea where I was headed. But as soon as I put my nose out of the subway station (①—207 Street), the flashback hit me. Now it's time I tell Brett & Galina about this new development. They don't know I live a block away from them. I wonder how they will take it. Only a few years ago this would have been a source of surprise, jubilation, and a perfect excuse for a house-warming party. But today my penchant for celebrations has vanished: the only celebration I wish for involves me as the only guest, sitting cross-legged on my shiny parquet, nibbling pizza. Today I am not even sure that the best part of living on Seaman Avenue is being around the corner from Brett & Galina. On the contrary, it is perhaps its only tender spot. Today the idea of meeting them again means subjecting myself to compassionate and moralistic glances, never again on a par with them. But I must inform them. Brett & Galina had really tried to help me: it's not they who failed, it's me. I must live with the consequences.

As always, they one-up me. They offset my schmaltzy announcement (*Guess what? I moved here! Yes, "here" as in just around the corner from you guys!*) with news of their own that leaves *me* grasping for air: "Guess who came to live upstairs?" asks Galina and pauses for effect. My automatic thought, even if without an ounce of logic, is "The Criminal!" I do not say it because, objectively, I know it can't be, but I still feel the grip of panic clutching my chest, freezing my heart. Paving the way for a plot twist worthy of Steven King, Galina lets an interminable time pass, before she finally says: "Yonah . . . Yonah Hausmann. Our same building, apt. 1E." We all ended up a few meters away from each other. In New York, New York.

My blood flows down to my feet, leaving my brain dry and blank.

Yonah got a job at Yeshiva University. This explains the Hebrew crash course in Jerusalem: a requirement for his tenure-track position. Yonah hadn't told me. Academic job openings are advertised in early autumn. This means Yonah must have applied in September 1997. A year ago! It also means he found out he had been hired while he was still in Boston, probably around January 1998 . . . hired in New York, in the heart of Washington Heights. In the very heart of our dreams. The background of so many stories by I. B. Singer and Bernard Malamud. Galina knew it. Adina, a perfect stranger, whose claim to happiness resides in her having opened a door in Jerusalem, knew it. *I* didn't.

Brett & Galina organize a small do. They, Yonah, and I together for the first time. His fiancée, Adina, is still in Italy, getting ready to move here, but she is dragging on the preparations as long as possible, because she is really not thrilled about New York. She hates it, I hear. Brett & Galina's studio hasn't gotten any bigger with the years, so there's no room for a proper crowd for a party: it's only the four of us and we do spend a pleasant couple of hours during which I stay as quiet as it is proper to do. I interact in the friendliest manner I can manage, but without the old panache. In English they say "the elephant in the room"—well, everyone pretends not to notice the elephant in the studio apartment. More than in a scene from *The Big Chill,* I feel at the center of *Babette's Feast*—minus the feast.

Yonah needs a favor. In order to issue him a marriage license, the Italian government requires foreign spouses to show up at the consulate with two or more witnesses who act as guarantors: that is, the Italian government ascertains that Yonah is a good man before handing over in marriage one of its daughters.

Galina and I are asked to play witness: I, in a main role, as I know Yonah better than anybody, and most important because I am Italian. I can't refuse (*can I?*).

Galina, Brett, Yonah, and I make a date to go together to the Italian Consulate on Fifth Avenue. I have become one of those model exes from a sarcastic comedy who, without rancor or jealousy, behaves like a true friend, pretends that the past never happened, with the aplomb and aristocratic dispassion of one who is above vulgar fripperies such as feelings. As we sit in the yellow taxi, talking animatedly, on our way to the consulate, I realize the humor in the situation: here I am, with two of my ex fiancés, one of whom I have already "donated" to my best friend, and the other one whom I am expediting to the wedding canopy, so to speak.

They let us all in together. We are led into a large office room, full of papers piled everywhere. Yonah, Galina, and I are sitting in one row in front of the consul's desk, while Brett makes himself scarce in the background. Galina and I answer every question with the typical overdone zeal of those who are afraid of being caught lying. Where a simple "yes" or "no" would suffice, we add excess embroideries to the fabric of our responses. I think we are all nervous. Personally, I am as comfortable with bureaucracy as I'd be with pustules all over my body, so in such situations all my mind can focus on is a way of escaping this office. One never knows how quickly a banal administrative process can turn into arrest, imprisonment, and torture. We sing Yonah's praises with gusto and, with perfect poker face, we affirm that we know everything about him and that on the basis of this profound intimacy we can attest, under oath, that we have no reason to believe that anything in his past (*an open book*) would make him less than ideal for this Italian girl (*who is not even here, with him, and who demands they get married in Turin instead of New York City*). This last part about Turin and the future bride, whom none of us has ever met, we don't say, though. Indeed, what we say implies that we know her well. We are ready to sign off for Yonah. And we actually do sign an official statement.

The bureaucrat is about to walk to a different room in order to photocopy the documents at hand, when Yonah raises his index finger in that same pose I remember from the first day we met, he winces and ventures, keeping that forefinger before his nose and mouth.

"Let's say, for the sake of hypothesis, that the statement I gave you about not having been married before was not true . . ."

Pause. Galina and I throw a furtive look at each other, suspenseful, ripe with questions, but we both sit stiffly as if struck by sudden paralysis. I barely move my eyeballs, oscillating my gaze from Yonah to the consul, from the consul to Galina, from Yonah to Brett, who in the meantime has taken three steps backward, crayfish-like, flattening himself against the farthest wall. "*Spergiuro.*" Perjury. The bureaucrat, who has seated himself again, says cold and blasé: "It would be a real problem." Arms folded on the desk, he leans forward and stares at Yonah giving him time to reflect on what to do.

Yonah nods his head pensively, as if to approve a philosophical idea he hears for the first time, then he slips his right hand into the inside pocket of his coat and pulls out a bundle of folded papers. He hands them to the consul with a whispered "Here." Clearly, the consul appears to know Yonah better than any of us: my reaction would have been to laugh, to mistake Yonah's question for a joke, and keep going to the copy machine; instead, this guy immediately caught his drift. Something bureaucracy is great at: lacking a sense of humor.

This time the consul walks to the other room to make copies of these new pieces of evidence, while Yonah fills out anew the generic forms, this time placing an X in the little box under "Previous marriages." From the threshold, the consul turns again, this time engulfing Galina and me in a single incendiary glance, and asks: "Did you two know about this?" Neither of us emits a sound. I mimic "No" with stunted but quick rotations of my head, as if my skull were about to unhinge from my neck. When the consul is out of the room, Galina and I remain silent, but from the wall behind us Brett's sardonic voice reaches us: "Well well, Yonah . . . please tell!" We get a case of the giggles. Until Galina recovers her cool and raises the question, "Now will they arrest us for false testimony?" *God, that's all I need!* "If so," I say instead, "we will demand to be locked up in a prison in Rome."

Once we leave, Brett & Galina grill him, leaving him no time to conjure up new lies and semi-truths. A bit blurredly, Yonah explains that during his years in Poland, he had married a girl, out of sheer friendship, because she needed a green card in order to move to America. *So Yonah was not new to the American immigration astringencies . . . why didn't he try to unchoke me?*

I had not felt so close to Galina in years. For a couple of hours my friend and I are "me and my friend" again, like once before. I stop focusing on Yonah; I prefer to look at and up to women with real balls.

While we walk toward the subway, chatting and laughing, it becomes very clear to me that I will not return to Brandeis to finish my PhD at the end of this leave. It is the easiest decision of the last two years.

I will have to overcome my embarrassment and write a proper letter of explanation and apology to Polonsky, to Ben Ravid (for whom I worked as teaching assistant), and Alan Mintz (the literary virtuoso who had so intimidated me during my first introductory visit and who turned out to be a nice man and a great scholar to learn from).

My only hope is that a master's degree will suffice to get me a job. I start answering the job announcements in the Sunday *New York Times,* at full blast.

*Dear Mr.—— [Blank],*

*I am very glad to introduce myself by means of my curriculum vitae and the following letter.*

*Blah blah blah . . . blah blah, blah: blah. . . .*

*I consider myself lucky for the unconditional freedom I possess over my time, which I can easily make available for extra work whenever it becomes indispensable to be there.*

*Blah blah blah . . . blah blah, blah: blah. . . . However, a personal meeting with you blah blah blah . . . blah blah, blah: blah. . . . I am eager to explore this possibility together.*

What am I saying?! Frig it, I need this, and I'll declare myself "Your humblest subject" if I have to. This is no time for smugness. *You don't want to upset Larry Horst's stereotypes on who pays rent and who defaults!*

Letter upon letter, customized to suit job calls for Interpreter at the United Nations, Editor for any magazine that needs one (from gardening to antique musical instruments), Italian Language Teacher, Photographer, Costume Designer, Storyteller, Caregiver for the Blind, Dog -Sitter, Plant-Sitter,

House-Sitter . . . hundreds of letters dropped in the blue mailbox at the corner of Seaman and West 215th, every week.

Once I even answered an advertisement for an "underwriter" thinking that that meant a lower level ("under") author ("writer") who works for a high-level creator ("upperwriter"?). I thought: A kind of apprenticeship for starting journalists? In any case, without looking it up in a dictionary, I applied. The position was advertised every day, many times a day, on WNYC, the local public radio (*acronyms for radio stations as well?! That's taking the piss!*). I wrote to Mr. Vincent Gardino one of my staple self-selling letters, with hyper tinseled expressions (my English vocabulary is still so poor that, for lack of new terms, I must overdo the few I know), such as "I am a wordsmith," and "I exude professionality and determination." Americans usually respond even to those who they do not intend to hire: they thank you for your interest, apologize for not being able to accept your candidacy, compliment you for the exceptional gifts you have, and wish you good luck in your search for employment. Gardino never bothered. I must have made quite an "impression": probably they framed and hung my letter on the WNYC's bulletin board as the office joke and are still laughing themselves silly at it every day. How was I to know what an underwriter is?!

*I love keeping informed about all current events: Blah blah blah . . . blah blah, blah: blah. . . . Most of all, Blah blah blah . . . blah blah, blah: blah. . . .*

Idiot.

But a desperate idiot at that.

I kept on working, irregularly, for Radio Italia, in Fort Lee, but the station is just about to shut down. It can't survive the legal battles its owners, the Berlusconi brothers, are undergoing back home. Whatever façade it was supposed to keep up, it came down like a sandcastle in the rain. Thus, my only stream of income has gone dry . . . a travesty that comes, however, with the positive perk of not having to cross the George Washington Bridge into New Jersey again.

The radio station pays us in dollars but the *Italian way*—that is, with "informal," untraceable checks handed out in person by a guy who shows up at the offices in his limousine every couple of weeks. I am officially undocumented, and Fiorenzo has offered to charge the station for the hours I put in, collect my paychecks, and then give me the money at the end of the month. *He's a good friend. Lucky me.* As soon as they make it official that there is no need for anybody to show up at work one day, I go see Fiorenzo to collect my meagre salary. He has elegantly stored the money in an envelope— *I appreciate that*—which he hands me saying: "Look, I have deducted taxes [*but we do not pay taxes on this because it figures as salary earned in Italy, off Uncle Sam's jurisdiction*], expenses for gas, and the George Washington Bridge toll." Fiorenzo knows how much I need this money. The expenses he talks about were for *his* going to work, not mine. Italians don't carpool. But the Clementi tribe never quibbles about money matters: it's vulgar. Better to die than to elbow one's way to the trough. I thank him profusely—because the stronger the shock, the less rational the reaction—and leave.

On the way home, I walk slowly along Isham Street: I feel as if my feet are slowed down by the heaviness in my heart, which crushes my whole body. I walk holding the envelope in two hands; whatever is left from Fiorenzo's theft is utterly repugnant to me now. It won't suffice for one month rent. Despite what I promised Larry Horst.

It's a beautiful sunny day, and all of nature has come alive in Isham Park. A day that, were it not for this blow, would seem full of beauty and positive omens in the air. But for me parks spell a different inspiration: I do not pass by one without thinking "What liberation to hang by a rope from a strong tree!" Not only is today no exception, but today this thought is more vivid than usual.

I reach my building. With automatic, depressed moves, I extract the post from my mailbox. I notice an envelope of unusual size with the unmistakable typographic characters of high-rank bureaucracy. I pull it out of the bunch, like an unlucky gambler at the card table gradually spreads his hand before he folds. I see the INS logo stamped on the upper left corner. Right on the spot, I open it: The US Government just delivered the green card to me. . . it just delivered *me*.

# 10

One of my favorite games as a child was pick-up sticks, which in our home we called *bastoncini cinesi*. *Bastoncini cinesi* works like this: First there is chaos—the sticks fall tinkling on the ground, rolling, bouncing off each other, heaping, overlapping; then there follows a moment of stasis—for as messy as they look, at this moment the sticks have found a fixed collocation, a new formation of their own, there is calm and a lingering promise; but permanence is an illusion, and this phase is followed by the battle between the player's vibrant hand and the rigor of the inanimate . . . now the responsibility of not throwing the sticks back into chaos lies upon the player, not on chance.

My life at present corresponds to Phase 2 in the pick-up sticks game: however chaotically, the sticks have stopped rolling, bouncing, heaping, hitting the ground hard, they have "shaped" into something concrete, if not permanent, at least with a promise of steadiness: and now it is a question of dexterity, watchfulness, and courage to move the right ones in the right way.

I hop in the car and drive to Queens for my first job interview. It is far away, no public transportation reaches that far. I arrive at a horrid building, a hollow block of cement in the middle of nowhere, surrounded by nothing, topped by a tin roof. I let myself in: What a mess! Scenes from *All the President's Men*—with more faces like Dustin Hoffman than Robert Redford. When someone finally notices me, I am rushed to the Managing Editor's office, Tamara Hartman. She is a young woman, just a year or two older than me, without makeup, long brown hair kept in a ponytail by a rubber band (obviously grabbed out of a desk drawer); she has an open, honest face. I brought my dossier containing all the articles I published in the last ten years for *Politicus, Tygodnik Literacki, L'Unità, Il Manifesto,* and *America Oggi.* Chuffing hell: not a single publication in English! I did translate some of the articles, though. I didn't sleep for nights. All I have is dogged determination. Hartman's office walls are plastered with clippings, leaflets, calendars, photographs, maps of the Tristate region, her industrial metal desk is heaped with papers, three phones, felt-tip pens, and whiteouts everywhere, and take-out boxes from who knows when. She invites me to sit on the short side of her rectangular desk, so that we are at an angle from each other, with nothing between us, physically close, with our knees almost touching. I introduce myself and put forth the best-selling pitch I know how, with the greed that only the most desperate fools show.

"My father," Hartman begins, dreamily, "was a penniless kid when he said 'The hell with everything,' left Ireland and came to America." She points a finger toward a beautiful plaque hanging on the wall which had escaped me because of the stuff half covering it: it bears the name of her father and a presidential recognition for his work as a reporter. Now I also distinguish more photos of him around, some with his daughter who followed in his footsteps (same bright eyes, same sincere expression). He died recently: she must have loved him a lot. "He always talked about all the hardships immigrants face in a new place, and that, were it not for those rare people who gave him a chance, he would have never made it."

*Me, emigrant? Her great-grandfather must've known the Great Potato Famine of 1845, but I ate roasted chestnuts by the Trevi Fountain and cheesy supplì at Franchi's every Saturday afternoon. I see in my mind the young Hartman senior, tweed flat cap, the collar of his jacket turned up to shield his bony face; and me, on a luxury TWA flight, wrapped in my wool full-length Max Mara coat. Emigrant, me? No! Rather a cosmopolitan émigrée. . .I'm Gertrude Stein, not Tevye the dairyman! And yet . . . and yet, I need this job as much as Hartman senior and thousands of others who arrived here with hardly one shoe per foot (and not by Valentino) before me . . . How am I different?*

Every nerve on my face, neck, and body is stretched like a violin string, concentrating on every nuance in Tamara Hartman's voice and expression. However, her words are like running water; I listen to them but I don't quite hear them; they are remote, they are smothered by the vortex of anxiety, fear, and suspense that are in permanent session in my head.

"So I want to give you a chance," says she.

I can't talk. I'm choked with emotions.

The job is mine! Reporter for the Queens Tribune. $16,000 a year, no expense reimbursements.

Like a zombie on steroids, I walk back to the car, sit in it quietly and begin to shake spasmodically before bursting into tears. It's not the *New York Times* . . . technically speaking it's not even New York because Queens is another world, but it is Tamara Hartman: Tamara Hartman who looked at me with those honest brown eyes of hers and accepted me, shook my hand, and said "You start Monday." I shudder as if I had been electroshocked. I can't tell where the pain ends and a new happiness begins. All my feelings surface mingled together. "Cry, Fania, it'll do you good"—my mother would say, with her appreciation for catharsis . . . and honor suicide.

"*Autumn in New York . . . Why does it seem so inviting?*" asks Billie Holiday, and I can answer that.

Whoever invented the phrase "time flies" did not live through 1998. Not only does this year never end, but it continues to accumulate plot twists, new contortions, new visions, new versions, and increasingly different, incongruous, surprising adventures. Ten months ago I was in Boston, seven months ago I was posing, smilingly, between Camilla and Modestino for my graduation photo, six months ago I left Raeburn Terrace, three months ago I got married, three months ago I was almost murdered, three months ago I escaped, three months ago I was eating mozzarella with my hands in "Palampaquay" while hiding in my car and crying my eyes out, two months ago I was looking everywhere for a place to live: I was fleshy, I was all bones, I was on the street, I was in an apartment with a freshly polished parquet, I was in a three-story house, I was in an attic, I was at university, I was out of university, I was alone, I had company, I was alone, I was loved, I was alone, I was hated, I hated, I took decisions, I was wrong, I did the right thing, I had bad luck, I was lucky, I lost everything, I had a friend to hug me, I worked illegally, I installed an IKEA Benno, I received a green card, I became a full-time reporter in New York.

The year in New York is divided as follows: spring = purgatory, summer = hell, autumn = paradise, winter = the season that makes you miss hell.

From October 1 to December 22 there is no place more romantic in the world.

*Autumn in New York. . . . glittering crowds, and shimmering clouds, they're making me feel I'm home.* The holiday season begins, and I am in the right place. Finally. The days get shorter, Halloween and Thanksgiving turn the world into hues of orange, black, and yellow, like the maple trees, aflame with colors that seem capable of emitting light; the few bluebirds left in the city snatch some grass from Central Park to weave their nests. There is a mass urge to walk, shop, party, change wardrobes, try out all the restaurants, find new hangouts, have a drink with friends, get carried away by a date, see every film, listen to every jazz concert, or laugh at the Stand-Up Comedy Club. They are all outside, overtaken by this euphoria, and I too rush to join them. I haven't gotten anybody to laugh or eat with, but I satisfy myself by watching them be happy and fantasize about a day when I'll be part of a group of new friends, a new blank page to be written with people from a future who know nothing about what I was reduced to only a few months ago. I hold dearly to the small bouquet of New York memories I already have: I continually retrace the steps taken with Richard, with Brett, with Galina. Everything is where I left it: the Carlyle, Serendipity's, Central Park (West and East), Bergdorf, Chelsea Peers, the Cloisters, the stinking poop of pigeons kneaded in horse excrements at Columbus Circle, the New York Public Library. To these I add a few discoveries of my own: Zabar's, The Strand's bookstore, and Pommes Frites. Now that the weather is much cooler, homeless people in Tribeca begin to fight over the manhole grates along the sidewalks (their winter beds) out of which constantly flows the boiling steam of the underground power plants (their only blanket). Anorexic models wrapped in Oscar de la Renta pass by, sprinkling around the magic powder of their infatuating beauty. Make up your mind, in New York: either look up, or look down . . . the view changes enormously. This is Gotham, the Empire City.

'Tis the season to be jolly—as the famous Christmas carol says, *tralalalala lallallalà*. But I hate Christmas carols, it must be said. New York has nothing to do with Christmas or its churchy tunes. On some sections of Broadway, on the Upper West Side, shop owners who understand their city well play through loudspeakers that reach the street the notes of *Santa Claus Is Coming to Town,* or *White Christmas* sung by Bing Crosby (from the homonymous film that made me fall in love with Danny Kaye as a child), but also Nat King Cole's *Christmas Song.* I begin to sing around October *"Chestnuuuuuuts roasting on an open fire"* in the shower, cooking, shaving, making my bed . . . and I don't stop until February.

The fact that these classics have the word Christmas or Santa in their lyrics add very little religiosity to the songs. *Santa Claus Is Coming to Town* has as much to do with faith in Jesus Christ as did Eddie Cantor who sang it in 1934. These songs were not meant to send people to church—all the more so because they were composed by Jewish musicians for the most part. Rather, they tried to offer through their melodies an atmosphere of joy and hope in a world that was increasingly devoid of it. I have no illusions that these are songs from better times. On the contrary, it is precisely because the times were not better that artists had to counterbalance them with something that would raise people's morale, that would make everyday life more tolerable. These songwriters identified with the American Dream that they themselves helped create.

The great wave of immigration, with its highest surge from 1881 onward, had the effect of an antidote injected in the isolationist, nativist, racist veins of America. The minority subverted the majority: they came by the millions to Ellis Island, with a very clear idea of the kind of country in which they wanted to live, or see their children live in, and they did not let themselves be discouraged by the fact that such country wasn't here (yet). They modified what they found and shaped it in the likeness of their desires. They were not going to accept another "No" from life. "Wide Awake!" was the slogan of the nativists, horrified at the sight of the massive invasion of Irish people in the middle of the nineteenth century. Then they were horrified at the sight of the Jews, the Chinese, the Italians, the Greeks. Horrified by the Blacks who did not come by choice. Horrified by the Natives, who were always here. They were comforted only by their ferocious repulsion toward the "others" of all kinds. They heroicized the newborn Ku Klux Klan. (Of all the absurd acronyms I'm imbibing here, this is the one I like best because it's as ill-sounding as the "organization" it shrinks into a pathetic stammer: *KayKayKay* . . . Robert Musil would have loved it too, I suspect.)

The new and most revolutionary means of mass communication ever invented, the cinema, opened boundless horizons to the propagation of the SOS that the "real America" had to urgently communicate to its native sons: American identity was in danger, it had to be saved at all costs. The WASPs maintained an absolute control over the nascent cinematographic corporations, of course. The time came for the masses to find someone who made movies *for*, not *against* them. A couple of enterprising immigrants tried to break through the cinema world, sensing its boundless potential, but they hit the glass ceiling. However, these greenhorns had not traipsed over half of Europe on foot and escaped the clutches of tsars, popes, Cossacks, and Bolsheviks to take a "NO" from the D. W. Griffiths of America lying down. And so, Adolph Zukor, Carl Laemmle, Harry Cohn, Louis B. Mayer, William Fox, and the brothers Jack and Harry Warner went west, far from the old stock, away from the shores of the Mayflower, into an almost biblical desert, where they would institute a new Promised Land, with its laws, its parameters, and, this time, without borders (but with powerful pharaohs in charge): California, Hollywood . . . *Cut!*

Now the Lower East Side fishmongers, the *briccolieri* from the Bronx, New Jersey, or Chicago, the Midtown's dressmakers as well as the Baltimore's seamstresses, could spend their hard-earned quarter dollar to enjoy the (made up) portrait of a society as they would have liked it . . . as they had dreamed it would be. A world in which the little ones beat the big guys, in which love and hard work conquer everything, where nobody asks you about your religion or pedigree, where class (and even racial) mixing is a goal to strive for and where talent, humor, and above all heroism define what kind of human being you are.

Zukor's sons and grandchildren had no idea that they were Jews, because the famous patriarch had omitted briefing them on it. Samuel Goldwyn (or Shmuel Gelbfish to his *mamelah*) discarded his first wife Blanche Lasky (Jewish like him) and married the ultra WASP Frances Howard with whom he felt more at ease entering that same high society he had fashioned for the new American (Jew). In Beverly Hills, in the home of Louis B. Mayer, born in Minsk during the pogroms of the 1880s, Christmas was celebrated with memorable exuberance: Mayer claimed not to know his birthday and therefore adopted, rather tellingly, the Fourth of July as the day to celebrate it. The *new* America was forged by the fire of these men's imagination. The *real* America ended up identifying itself with this fanciful invention: it *hollywoodicized* itself. Setting aside objective reality, America created an image of itself based on the projections on the silver screen of these newcomers' dreams and desires. The moguls, their producers, screenwriters, actors (with mimetically anglicized names and looks) knew what they were talking about when they talked to America through their films.

*Puttin 'on the Ritz, Top Hat, White Tie and Tails, Cheek to Cheek,* as well as the holiest Christmas carol of all, *White Christmas,* were composed by Irving Berlin. Born in poverty, in Russia, son of a synagogue singer, it is to Berlin that America also owes its unofficial anthem, *God Bless America.* Eisenhower gave him a gold medal for it.

In addition to popular music, New York also identifies with the fullness and orchestral complexity of the avant-garde compositions of the sons of Moishe and Roza Gershowitz, Israel and Jacob. Moishe escaped forced conscription into the tsar's army (magnanimously reduced from twenty-five to fifteen years at some point) and, as a cobbler, managed to build a humble prosperity for his young family in Brooklyn where their first two sons were born. In order to facilitate the linguistic and cultural assimilation into the New World, he changed everybody's name: he took Morris for himself, Rose for his wife, Ira and George for the kids . . . and Gershwin for the whole family.

I speak of New York as if it were all Jewish, I know: but basically *it is,* just as Lenny Bruce said when he joked that in New York everyone is Jewish, even those who are not, while outside of New York no one can be a Jew, even those who are.

Is this true, though? Like all countries, this nation too is built on myths. Those early American Jews subconsciously knew that they did not belong fully, they stuck out like a single polka-dot on a wedding dress. Outsiders everywhere, they were particularly out of their element in a nation whose national archetype was the independent and solitary (not to mention healthy) cowboy, in the empty prairies of the West. An inconceivable ideal for a Jew:

dependent on his community and perfectly at ease in the civilized society of ideas and discourse (the more the merrier), never solitary (in groups of three, one argues better), and certainly always a little worried about his health (one hardly enjoys death more than life). And thus, through a literal masquerade, the Jew, who longed to be part of "team America," satirized himself and his klutzy inadequacy . . . he wasn't (unlike Griffith and his peers) trying to degrade or mortify those who, like him, had been so hated and denied access to their America. It was also a way to laugh white-American mythology into oblivion. When Mickey Katz takes on *Home on the Range,* the anthem of cowboys and Western pioneers, he revolutionizes, through parody, the idea that a nation, especially *his* America, must stick to a homogeneous ethnic face. The "home on the range" can be home to everyone.

> *Oh give me a home*
> *Where the buffalo roam*
> *And the deer and the antelope play*
> *Where seldom is heard*
> *A discouraging word*
> *And the skies are not cloudy all day . . .*

or with it a Yiddish spin:

> *Oy gib mir a haym*
> *Mit to vaybele shayn*
> *Ver der shepsn und of tsigelakh*
> *loyfen*
> *Oy gib mir a hoys*
> *Mit gisinten cowboys*
> *Und a couple hundert kettle tsu*
> *farkeyfen . . .*
> *(Oh give me a home*
> *With a beautiful little wife*
> *Where the sheep and the goats*
> *run around*
> *Oh give me a house*

*With healthy cowboys*
*And a couple of hundred cattle*
*to sell . . . )*

New York is my home on the range. And I invent it a little too, hoping that my version will make room for me.

Autumn blows in an air of love, of mountain hikes, of board game matches in uptown apartments with friends. I see them, I hear them, I have the impression of knowing exactly what each of the 10,000,000 passersby here is thinking or about to do. I can't be *with* them, but I am *of* them, I too am part of this landscape. I don't want to go back. Most important, I get it only now, Italy wouldn't want *me*—it's not even my choice, actually.

Monday. 7:30 AM sharp, I enter the Queens Tribune building. *Thanks to these daybreak commutes, I'll dodge the agony of alternate parking. Everything's coming up roses.* The office has an open floorplan where all reporters work together at their desks scattered without symmetry throughout the room. They have already arranged a desk for me. So I didn't dream it. It wasn't a film I scripted in my head. This is actually happening.

They endow me with a hygienically suspect phone and basic office supplies (chewed-on pencils, missing the lead, which I will touch only with my gloves on, pretending to be cold). Over the weekend I wisely invested a considerable sum in a professional tape recorder: trusting one's linguistic skills is good, not trusting them is better. When I interview people, I'll both take notes and record them. Apart from the editor-in-chief, all the reporters are boys and girls my age among whom it is easy to distinguish, at a glance, those who have majestic ambitions and those who will grow old at these desks. We all have our stories, our personal baggage that—like a tide brings flotsam to the shore—beached us here, *in culo alla luna,* if by *luna* we mean Queens. But we don't talk about it: the whole day is taken by telling the stories of others (the Julliard student who leaves the Stradivarius in the taxi and the cab driver who brings it back to her; Mayor Giuliani, who wants to clean up the Projects and institute zero-tolerance against crime; the wedding dressmaker who reveals all the secrets of her art), and therefore nobody has the strength or egotism at the end of the day to put themselves at the center of attention. In my case, I don't really see the advantage of poisoning the atmosphere with my banal drama.

I don't let on what is truly going on inside me. No one guesses. I have continuous panic attacks. Riding the subway train is a real effort . . . too claustrophobic, too many stairs to trip on. I immediately burst into tears as soon as I hear police sirens going off somewhere. My first thought is "They are coming to take me!" (Normal people don't even realize how many sirens ring at once in New York City at any given minute of the day.) My fears have complete control over me. I live in the absolute certainty that, secretly, livid with rage and rancor, the Criminal is plotting my final destruction, the last iniquity. I imagine him staging an intrusion into his apartment, causing himself a couple of injuries, and then declaring to the police that his ex showed up at night and attacked him, and based on that, a judge will issue an arrest warrant against me. I await any moment for the authorities' fist to bang on my door. *Ennwhypeedee,* handcuffs, electric chair.

My colleagues at the Queens Tribune like me. Tamara Hartman has made it her mission to keep me under her protective wing. The editor-in-chief is very happy with my work and the good-humored punctuality with which I show up at the office every morning and the fact that I never complain about my assignments. Self-cleansing starts here. I don't expect to degrease the tarry residue of my past by pouring it on other people, so I do not talk of my situation with a soul. I refuse to turn into a pathetic case, the victim with her "special status" pinned like a badge on her chest—like a pass for the disabled that gives you the right to privileged parking but also to an ill-concealed antipathy by all those who have to drive around the block four times to find a place. I'd rather do without people's pity and antipathy, if I can.

Collaterally, I am also developing an unusual kindness toward my fellow humans which I would never have suspected I possessed: it is not true kindness—I still don't volunteer anywhere, I don't take care of orphans, I have no missionary inclinations—but rather a form of subservient servility, dictated above all by the terror that someone may accuse me of "bad character."

"Good character," I discover, is an official term in America: it is used in court; the police use it; one has to prove "good character" to apply for certain jobs or to be accepted as tenant in a high-end building. It is attestable:

perhaps the closest thing in Italian would be *buona condotta* (with that gourmet prison aftertaste to it), except that the English language uses the word "character" instead of conduct, which speaks volumes about where the stress falls: that is, not on whether someone has broken the law (implicit in the Italian expression) but much more broadly on a person's general everyday behavior. If it turns out, say, that you are someone who does not wait for the old lady to make it to the elevator in which you are impatiently standing and push your floor button to get yourself where you are headed before you are too old to remember, well, that's "bad character." If a neighbor accuses you of mixing your recyclables with your trash or catches you just as you drop that one candy wrapper in the street: "bad character." If you can't find someone to write you a letter of recommendation to prove your "good character," that's "bad character," too. My reaction to this is to be good, very good, ridiculously good to everyone. So that the Criminal may find no one to drag to court to testify against me. I live in fear of his retaliation. My path is laid with crystal, sooner or later I'll put my foot on the wrong vein and it'll crack and I will fall down into a dark and deep gorge from where no Father Kelly, no Tamara Hartman, can pull me out.

The weeks pass. The police haven't handcuffed me yet.

My days are on loan. More than a coherent life, mine seems to be a concatenation of disconnected days threaded like beads along a string: at some point the piece of string may just end, or the beads may break, or a little undoable knot will bring everything to a halt. No matter, one bead at a time is the only way to proceed.

On Sundays, cross-legged on the comfy sofa in front of my large windows, I leaf through the pages of the *New York Times*. I don't need much. What I have is all I ever wanted. Here I am. A cup of coffee and the certainty that all I have to do is step outside and all of Manhattan will expand before me. I walk tirelessly, in total anonymity, from one park to the next, from one riverfront to the opposite one, over bridges, along infinite windy avenues, with no particular destination.

I need a new job, though. The outgoing money is about to surpass the incoming money. According to my calculations, it should take about three months. What I make—$16,000 a year, minus taxes, toll charges and gasoline (which costs 80 cents a gallon)—is a subsidy, not a salary, in New York. However, for three months, five days a week, ten hours a day, I have been placing my byline, black on white, at the top of interviews, book reviews, restaurant reviews, film reviews, political reportages, cultural reportages, analyses of social interest, exposés, and obituaries. There is no section of the newspaper to which I have not contributed.

Advantages of being a reporter in New York: (1) Being a reporter in New York; (2) getting to know every corner of Queens and Manhattan as my father knows Trastevere and Rome; (3) getting to know every piece of dirt about famous people (there is no political or cultural figure whose private affairs don't get scrutinized and ridiculed in the editorial office, and there's no limit to how deeply they allow reporters to dig into them . . . down to the most sordid depths)—which helps, by the way, put one's own life and errors into perspective, but also to take a crash course on who-is-who in the local and socio-political history; (4) food reviews! The sweetest perk, hands down, is being paid to eat out for free—from the most obscene little tavern (where they make their best effort not to poison you) to the highest end restaurant (where, until you marry the dentist of your dreams, you couldn't otherwise afford to go).

The most sensational meal of my life so far was put on my plate by the San Domenico, on Central Park South. A colleague had been assigned the review but brought me along because it is more elegant to dine in company and because he would look less blatantly like a reviewer this way. No doubt, they already knew the reason for our visit, and it is possible that this influenced the particular care with which they prepared the eleven or so dishes that we felt obliged to order. The goat cheese pie with hot plums and truffles got me off with pleasure. My colleague embroidered a lyrical review . . . in part to account, in the eyes of the editor-in-chief, for the $1,400 our supreme meal cost the paper.

New York has not always been the eating capital of America: at the beginning of the nineteenth century, New York had only a few taverns and some lunch canteens for the lower classes who could not afford the luxury of taking a break from work to go home to eat in the middle of the day. But the cultism of foreign cuisine finally took hold thanks to the initiative of European chefs (like the Delmonico brothers) who tried their luck overseas, and once they fired their ovens in America and began to *flambé, piqué, béchamellé* real food, they could not be snubbed for long. Philip Hone, who for a short time was also mayor of the city, went down in history as one of its most famous epicureans. He was to be seen galloping along Broadway every day, almost two centuries ago, always in the company of friends, frequenting all sorts of establishments to keep up with the latest fads and gossip. He was a well-known figure in all of Manhattan's eateries. With a critical tone, he notes in his diary in 1830:

> Saturday, December 18.—Moore, Giraud, and I went yesterday to dine at Delmonico's, a French *restaurateur,* in William street, which I had heard was upon the Parisian plan, and very good. We satisfied our curiosity, but not our appetites; and I think are prepared, when our opinions are asked, to say with the Irishman who used lamp-oil with his salad instead of olive-oil, that if it were not for the name of the thing he had as lief eat butter.

Butter had low-class connotations. But one should never explain a joke, even a bad one.

The two brothers Pietro and Giovanni Delmonico, Italians from the Swiss Canton Ticino (who mysteriously spoke only French), had been pioneers of the restaurant business in the New World, breaching the hardy wall of conservative resistance that was bound to crumble under the weight of their sauce béarnaise. In fact, within the next fifteen years, New York began its insatiable climb as the most opulent and hungriest (literally and metaphorically) city in the world. And while, despite numerous ups and downs and ownership transitions, Delmonico still exists, who has ever heard of that dandy Philip Hone?

Economic benefits of being a reporter in New York: zero.

We also worked on Christmas Eve. And it looked like a movie scene: there was Ira Cohen, tireless photographer of the Queens Tribune; the editor-in-chief; the editorial staff (minus the secretaries); and, while the snow piled up outside, we toasted in good cheer. Tamara Hartman gave everyone a small gift. I received a brooch fashioned in the shape of tiny glass jar. I am not sure if I am supposed to put an actual little flower in it or not, but for reasons that have nothing to do with the intrinsic, extrinsic, or aesthetic value of the object, it touched me to my core. I wore it right away, on my favorite sweater which I had on that day (bought at J. PETERMAN on East 42nd Street, this sweater consists of a thick piece of blue wool that buttons to the side like a bathrobe and occasionally I still wonder whether it was supposed to be a vintage maternity smock). It is eccentric and it goes swimmingly with my glass brooch.

> Dear Mr. Drew:
>
> I am very glad to introduce myself by means of my curriculum vitae and the following letter.
>
> . . . .
>
> My experience as a Reporter for the Queens Tribune has taught me . . . As the numerous articles I published demonstrate . . .

Yes! Now my letters say something! Let the climb begin.

Mr. Drew hires me. The new job is in Manhattan—a considerable improvement. I am hired as associate editor at *Town & Village*. I share a very small office with Mark Marlin. There is no one else. Not even a secretary to split in half. Just the two of us (me in charge) putting forth, including manual composition, each edition of the paper. This new experience will teach me a lot. And probably it'll get me to know this guy pretty well. Marlin is a man about fifty years of age. I sense that he regrets not having met me randomly in a pub, one night, while drinking, rather than in the formal work environment that forces him not to risk his livelihood by a false move. I find him a dash revolting. And he sets my nerves on edge. Sometimes I detect some of the Criminal's features on other people (*not everyone—I am not paranoid*): and like an electric shock this realization paralyzes me on the spot. OK, maybe I'm getting paranoid, and yet this insight is never wrong. For example, Marlin tells me that he was left by his wife: he expounds on the incident by adding that she accused him of domestic violence; he embellishes with information about his getting drunk sometimes. . . in the past; he also says that he is very angry with life and with women in particular. *Trembling. Sweating . . . I pretend absolute impassivity.*

Meanwhile I learn. I learn more. My hypervigilant antennae are up, attuning to everything that goes on: because I know absolutely nothing of what goes on. I don't know dummy, cutline, jump line, roll-end, color key, cold type (well, not in publishing anyway), and I understand folio only because I know Latin! Marlin says a new word and I feign comprehension and then wait for a hint from the universe or its lowest denominator, Marlin, as to what it means. I trust my adrenal medulla to overinfuse me with so much epinephrine and norepinephrine that I won't bleed or feel pain if stabbed ten times. I learn all the technical typographic terms, how to manually set type and design all pages, what those abstruse drawings that have no connection with either text or advertising are called (they are called dingbats); I learn to write by very short phrases, to make no mistakes, to catch all typos, to express myself concisely and without an error; I know how to get to anyone by phone, there is no ivory tower that I can't penetrate, there is no skid row that I don't dare explore. But above all I learn "their" ways! The Americans' way to say stuff, the way to do stuff, the way to dress in order to endure an endless workday, ways to order take-out from the office, ways to hail a cab, ways to be in the elevator, on the bus, at the edge of the road in order to beat everyone else to it when the pedestrian light turns green. I embody them. I pass to perfection.

This job doesn't pay anything either, but now I am in the heart of Manhattan—however invisible—and in the paper's personnel box, I appear as Associate Editor. Phenomenal.

For *TOWN & VILLAGE* I get to interview Malcolm: a thoroughbred pug, who lives at the National Arts Club in Gramercy Park. Malcolm, torpid and obese, speaks through the intercession of the club president, Olden James, who washes, feeds, dresses, and cares for him every day, who brings Malcom to play, to poop, and who gently installs him on his throne to rest during the dead hours: the throne is a huge red velvet chair, with a gilded wooden structure, an antique arrived here from some European court. Malcolm was inherited, along with a collection of porcelain pug figurines and a generous donation to the National Arts Club (the first to have admitted women as members) by his owner Sylvia Sidney, the *grande dame* of the stage and screen of the 1920s and 1930s. Sidney had made the club her home in the last years of her life. James deposits next to Malcom one of Sidney's shoes: "It [the shoe] still smells of Sylvia," James explains in a stage whisper so as not to be heard by Malcolm.

By the fourth week at *Town & Village,* I begin to dissect the *New York Times* job ads again. During my lunch break, instead of eating, I go to job interviews. I am astonished by the number of interviews I am called for. I am not super desperate so I can take my time. Meanwhile, I get to know the city in an intimate, deep way, both its geography and its internal mechanisms or dynamics. I discover, for example, that those horrible goldsmiths that had surprised me so much when I sold them the engagement and wedding rings, those with the characteristic "We Buy Gold" signs all over Manhattan, are *not* jewelers at all. Which explains the absence of jewelry in them. They were pawnshops—which in turn explains the moneylending vibe when they bought my gold at usury rates. So the receipts I threw into the trash were not receipts but redemption tickets.

Yonah got married. I did not go to the wedding. First of all, with the ongoing lawsuit, I could not leave the United States, legally speaking. And not to put a fine point on it, I did not want to. I had the temerity however to add yet another blunder to the already long list of "False Steps with Yonah" that will make me look the other way or hide every time I bump into him: that is, I did not even RSVP. (*France should forbid Americans to use the expression.*) I simply ignored the invitation. (*They must have had hundreds of guests: they must have counted the yeses without keeping tabs on the noes. Unless they expected a gift anyway? What could I have bought for a ducal wedding!? I am in the wrong.*) For the honeymoon they stayed in the bride's family's second home in Jerusalem to properly sanctify the union: if I had to guess, Yonah would have preferred to wake up on that first holy morning in Coronado Beach. Eventually, unable to postpone any longer, the bride let herself be taken to New York. For the time being, they are still living around the corner, in the two-bedroom apartment Yonah found for them in the same building as Brett & Galina, at 1E of 83 Park Terrace West. I imagine that Adina will want to move as soon as possible. Let's call it a hunch. As soon as the first child arrives, the excuse will be born to look for a more suitable place. *Tick tock, tick tock . . .* my guess is that a first-born is already *in ovo.*

As for the offense against etiquette I committed, I am happy to report that at least Yonah seems to have forgiven me for it, on the off chance he noticed the absence of my RSVP in the first place. One Saturday, I run into him on his morning jog around the neighborhood. He is on Seaman Avenue all sweaty and out of breath and asks me for asylum. I blink a few times before he begins to laugh. He needs a place to stay for a few hours, he explains. "I can't go back home, because I forgot my keys, and Adina doesn't answer the intercom." It's Saturday, God rested on the seventh day and did not answer the intercom, and neither does Yonah's wife. Adina adheres to the Levitical rules with unexceptionable devotion. I invite him for non-kosher coffee upstairs.

Nothing has changed between us, the way we talk, and the way he looks at me. But I behave as if the past were not there. And basically it isn't. The past is a state of mind: in fact, it doesn't exist except in its psychic reverberations . . . like, my fear of falling down the stairs, for example. That's how my past stays with me.

The truth is probably more banal and less flattering: I was attracted to Yonah, but the passion is gone, vanished, I choked it under a wet cloth like one extinguishes a small fire before it gets out of control. It is the mind that wants to curl up on his lap, be pampered. The body does not want any part of it. As they say here, I missed that boat: this awareness causes a sort of numbness in me, of hibernation of all my senses toward him. Without having to put it into words, we are still very close, yet a void has opened up in me, a hole that is not for Yonah to fill. The music, the movies, the books, the common interests, the obsession with New York, with Woody Allen's films, the sarcastic criticism, the love of Judaism, atheism, humor, socialism, anti-obscurantism, anti-conformism—that's all still there. We'll always have all that. *So much indeed: but no chestnuts.*

Objectively, at present, the chestnuts are roasting on Adina's open fire. I am not the type to break a family . . . if anything I set people up together. I remain the spinstery "aunt" of other people's children, *la femme fatale*, Countess Olenska in a world of Newland Archers, as in Wharton's *The Age of Innocence.* The woman everyone craves but no one, in the end, dares take. I came to America as a Countess Olenska but it would seem that I'm rather at risk of becoming Lilly Bart, from *The House of Mirth,* only with little mirth and definitely no house.

I don't even ask Yonah if he has changed his mind about having children. (Had we worked out, he would've had to get a vasectomy.) I have studied couples, from my solitary corner, for a long time: theirs falls under the "Classic" rubric. Adina may have fooled around, but no one before Yonah has forded the hymen. She is of marriage and childbearing stock. The official news will arrive any moment now: "We are going to have a baby"—and so the congratulations, the greeting cards, the gifts, the baby shower . . . which, like a Super-G medalist, I will sidestep one after the other. Without as much as an RSVP.

I ring Adina up a few times, because Yonah explicitly asked me to. He told me that Adina feels lost without anyone here. Yonah believes her, I do not. But anyway, for his sake, and because I *too* need friends, I leave a few chirpy telephone messages in Italian, letting her know that I am, sincerely, at her disposal. She never calls back. She has no intention to get to know me, no interest in making friends with me. It seemed tactless to ask Yonah if he told her "something" about our Bostonian parenthesis, or if, as usual, Brett did the honors of chronicling the *gesta Faniae* (Fania's epic deeds). It seemed more tactful to assume that everybody minded their own business. But judging by the allergic reaction Adina has to me, elegance *n'oblige pas* around here. She can't wait to take Yonah elsewhere. Tick tock, tick tock.

New millennium, new life: the first baby Hausmann is born, and the happy parents leave Inwood on the quiet. Bye bye, Yonah.

Meanwhile, one letter after another ("*Dear Mr. X/Y/Z, allow me to introduce myself. . .*"), I hop from one job to a better one. From miserable salaries to less scanty ones. No millions in sight. Nor millionaires. But I make a good living. I go out on a couple of dates—procured by merciful acquaintances—but they never develop into anything. In fact, after a first meeting, I never get a second date. Maybe I am not giving myself fully. I go meet these men without much enthusiasm and always return home alone. I make only a few Italian friends and fewer still American ones. With the exception of Francesca and Cesare, all expats are like little critters, with sharp teeth, frightened, trembling, in constant fight or flight mode, ready to bite whoever comes too close to the lair we managed to dig here. We all have, it takes me years to understand this, something in common. Although we would never admit it. I realize that those who came before me will not help me: they have secrets they'll never share. On the contrary, they will do everything in their power to give me false versions of their stories, of what brought them here; they do so to protect themselves and to confound the enemy, to sink the others and to elevate themselves, but perhaps also from a sense of fear and shame.

Take the case of Lana, whom I met in the Village, the summer when I briefly lived on Sullivan Street. She hung out at an Italian bar downstairs from Matthew's apartment, called Valdino. I was often there, chatting with the Italian owners, baristas, and patrons. The Criminal was breathing down my neck, and I was desperate to find out what options I had in order to stay in New York, disengage from Brandeis, without having to rely on him, or any other man, possibly avoiding death and suicide as alternatives. I was visibly vulnerable, both inside and out, and I made no secret of it with Lana.

"Lana, how did you get the papers to stay in America, how did you do it?"

She replied with her brutal Milanese accent (with a piercingly retroflex *r*) and an arrogant smirk: "I don't know . . . what can I tell you? It was supposed to be a short vacation. *Sono venuta per sette giorni, e sono rimasta sette anni.*" "I came for seven days but ended up staying for seven years." I heard her repeat this sentence several times. I tried to extract from Lana, like a good tooth that resists the forceps, the truth, the details, some useful specifics: "I came for seven days but ended up staying for seven years" is all I ever got from her. I used to feel an infinite admiration for these types of people who insouciantly, without baggage, simply lived life as it should be lived: weaving desires together into a glorious tapestry of only happy experiences. No drama, no trauma, no tragedy, no sordid entanglements in illogical, dangerous, and above all discreditable situations as I had woven.

Later, by pure chance, the editor of one of the magazines for which I end up working as a freelancer in my spare time, and who, like all rich New Yorkers, has a passion for Italy and its language, tells me that my job had once been held by another Italian woman, from Milan. No other than Lana. "Did she ever tell you about the time when she ended up in jail and I had to bail her out?" The lady indiscreetly tells me with a mischievous twinkle in her eyes. It appears that some untoward action had landed Lana in jail. And once under the radar of the American justice system, it was discovered that Lana had overstayed the three months allowed under the tourist visa. The INS caught her and deported her to Italy, critically smearing her criminal record. Unperturbed by the seriousness of her predicament, Lana had returned and gotten married within a few weeks to a very old gentleman, sidestepping the former legal difficulties. As far as I know, she is still in New York but possibly flagged in the records of the State Department, Immigration, CIA, Treasury, Cultural Heritage, Office of Hygiene, Parks and Recreation, Motorways and Public Bridges. The "I came for seven days but ended up staying for seven years" legend did not account for the days spent in prison, crying, calling all her contacts to beg them to bail her out, procure her just the right lawyer and just the right husband as speedily as possible.

Father Kelly wins. I have a green card now. Thanks to him and Bill Clinton, I start working jobs of all kinds, in search of an ideal niche for me. I am told that it is a mistake to fill out one's curriculum with too many positions because this indicates that, as an employee, one is a flight risk, someone a company can't invest in with confidence. I'll fudge my CV then. Whatever it takes.

I become Managing Editor of the *Journal of Dermatopathology,* founded by an eminent scientist, Dr. A. B. Ackerman, who also invented dermatopathology. He is very famous all over the world. I believe, deep in his heart, he aspires to the Nobel Prize. Ackerman's laboratories are situated in an elegant downtown block: a few floors are dedicated to research, and one floor, on which I work all alone, to his publishing enterprise. I am in charge of the quarterly magazine *Ardor Scribendi* and the publication and distribution of feuilletons and advertising materials. I last exactly one month there. The crisis hits within the first few days, that is, as soon as I receive the package of photographs to illustrate the next edition of the magazine. Devastated skin samples, purulent warts, cancers and tumors bursting into deep craters on the epidermis, inside which there is only one truth to be observed: death. I begin to obsessively check myself in the bathroom mirror at the office or at home. I wait for the moment when, while giving me instructions for our week's work plans, Ackerman will stop in mid-sentence and say: "Fania, did you notice changes in that mole on your left shoulder blade?" and he'll scribble anxiously a name and a telephone number on a piece of paper and say, "Here, call him right away, he's a friend of mine. Go to him today and have yourself examined. There is no time to lose!" On the subway, I look around and I see the sad and grim humanity that surrounds me reduced to a gigantic, threatening malignant tumefaction.

I have nightmares at night, every morning shower is a moment of recognition . . . a face to face between me and a tomorrow that may not be there: I examine, I measure every freckle, I compare, I scan my dermal horizon for a last laugh from the universe at my expense. I quit the job.

I get a tip for a new gig from an Italian woman, Daria Zillo, for whom I freelance at Berlitz. She has a full-time managerial position and every time she commissions a job to me, she takes a plump cut for herself off-the-books. Daria is an extremely heavy woman, full of energy and cunning, and a skilled social climber, with a fabulous atavistic brute force. She was born to survive and thrive. She married an American man and, according to rumors from fellow freelancers (exploited like me and therefore perhaps unfair judges of her character), she sent him to jail with the help of an unscrupulous lawyer with whom she had a tryst (his wife and children notwithstanding) while being his client. Out of all this came a zero-balance legal bill and a flat on East 23rd Street. She is marked by a healthy sense of self, incarnated in an insatiable sexual appetite. "I am beautiful, rich, independent," she says without irony: "All men here go crazy for me!" She is almost hysterical (not in a ha ha sense). If there is money to be made with Italian language in New York (translations, private classes, dubbing control), Daria is there . . . and leaves no crumbs for anybody else. She is infamous among her employees. She takes advantage of them and spits them out like cherry pits.

So I am taken positively aback when she directs me to her friend David, also known, she explains, as *il manzo* ("the Beef"). He is from Rome too and his nickname refers to his gigantic size. He is a huge piece of meat, I guess, and not particularly toned either . . . but also in the sense of tender and sympathetic. Son of an American Jewish father and Italian mother, David is the opposite of Daria, because unlike her he has nothing to fear, he need not keep the bone between his teeth, under the table, growling at the puppies in his own litter with distrust; David "belongs," he fits in this world, he is not a poseur nor a passing fake. English is his mother tongue, and so is his funny Roman accent in Italian. David is the real thing. I am fine with *il manzo*, I really like him. I feel we understand each other. What I do not understand is how a smart and seemingly perfectly adjusted guy like him can stand a job like his.

In a skyscraper on the West side of Columbus Circle, there is a famous law firm dealing with international cases on behalf of huge corporations such as Sony, Microsoft, Nike, Coca Cola. They have offices with 365-degree windows, lush leather couches, secretaries who look like Playboy Bunnies, bottles of champagne cooling in stainless steel refrigerators; in the employees' coffee stations, there are only first rate DeLonghi espresso machines, liqueurs to "reinforce" the espressos, and all kinds of delicacies brought fresh twice a day from a catering service on the company's payroll (not from a roach-infested Deli on Broadway). And then, there is David, who heads the "Patents" department which is located in the basement of the building. "Basement" doesn't quite apply here, because this skyscraper occupied entirely by this firm has several layers of basements: of all the basements available to the building, we are on the very last. The elevator goes down, down, down, until it tests the geophysical limits of oxygen permeation. And to reiterate that the weight of the whole building is on our shoulders, this floor-cellar has very low ceilings, which forces *il manzo* to walk hunched over, in a protracted bow.

There is only one door to our space, and David's office is in an area separated from the team by a glass screen, like a recording room, from which he sees us and we see him, bent over his desk, placid, always ready to smile. Our computers have huge monitors that emit intolerable heat gusts. Ninety percent of my colleagues have rotten teeth, greasy hair, and this or that kind of handicap: from nervous tics to lameness, from obesity to extreme emaciation due to drug abuse or alcoholism. There are some who hold the record of having worked with *il manzo* for fourteen years. Few, of course, but they give one pause.

We sit together, in this sort of large classroom, and books in hand, we scour the stratosphere in search of the planet's worst delinquents, scammers, and Panurges. The books they give us contain all the logos and trademarks of the companies under contract with the lawyers on the upper floors—those with views on the Hudson and champagne in the refrigerators—and through the internet, we search the world for someone, say, a merchant in a remote country, who may have appropriated for his shop an insignia dear instead to Coca Cola, Puma, or Ferrari. Any detail, the vaguest similarity, a color scheme will suffice. We do not care if he did it knowingly or by mistake. Like hawks, from the upper floors the lawyers of our company will swoop down on him, be it in Calcutta or Ngoura, in Nong Kiaow or La Azulita, they will close his business, crush every resistance, get the better of any local court, shatter the hopes of these worms, send the lawbreakers to jail, put them before the choice of either selling their underage daughters to the prostitution racket or begging on the street for the rest of their insignificant lives.

I am careful not to find a single match or even the slightest infringement. After a week, I resign. In fact, I don't even officially notify them. One day I simply don't show up. And no one notices.

# 11

New York, the city that never sleeps. New York, the cultural capital of America. New York, where there's always something to do—if you can afford it. Not only financially but physically: after eight or nine hours at the office and the commute in the suffocating subway full of tuned-out people (undone, dissatisfied, hopeless), after walking back home carrying heavy bags on exhausted swollen legs . . . if after all this, you have the strength to jump in the shower, dress up, put your best face on, and return to the street, to the subway already filled by the latest shift of office workers (undone, dissatisfied, hopeless) to reach Carnegie Hall, the Angelika, a Broadway theater, a Soho restaurant, where to drop half of your monthly salary . . . well, if you do, then you deserve to make it in this town. You should be on the 7 o'clock news! Personally, I listen to more classical music at home than at Lincoln Center where I have a membership but no intention of dragging myself under these conditions . . . and unaccompanied.

But today it's a nice sunny Tuesday, a glorious September day, and I oughtn't give in to these depressing considerations: I should shake off anxieties and fears, look far into the horizon (*well, if only there weren't buildings and cement everywhere*), and see a bright tomorrow, consider blonder highlights for my long hair, make friends, get laid. Instead, I am dissipating positive energy on the commute to work today, like all other days, by paying attention to the desolate human panorama around me. The "No one cares in New York" is a myth (*like "The City that never sleeps": it does*). Of course, everybody notices everything! (*Of course, everybody wants it quiet and calls the Police if you are noisy. Only the abused and exploited are up nonstop to serve the abusers and exploiters of this capitalist society of big-hearted liberals.*) No one can do anything about what they see.

It's not the capacity to look that has disappeared, but the human ability and everyone's freedom to turn the mere bodily function of "looking" into a productive action upon reality, that is, actively engaging in reality's transformation. Why look if not in order to either appreciate or change what we see? Looking for the sake of looking, as an end in itself, is debilitating in a place like New York: here people hold their heads down, their gazes lowered to stare on the ground, or behind rumpled newspapers, or shut behind dark sunglasses even when there's no sun shining anywhere. For the act of looking to make sense, I should be free to say, "Excuse me, Miss, you may want to be a better mother for that toddler of yours, who is currently on all fours by a giant pool of someone else's vomit." Or: "Sir . . . sorry, Señor, yes, Usted sitting with your *culo* extended over two seats and your bag occupying a third so as not to allow others to sit, would you mind not eating pistachios and spitting the shells on the ground in this rush-hour train full of people?" From the most refined to the plainest person, from the best educated to the illiterate, no one puts the hand before his or her mouth while yawning: and being the exhausting city that it is, everyone yawns in New York, even while they chew. Man-spreading, the obscenest of modern postures, is the body language equivalent of spitting on someone's face: it expresses utter unmitigable contempt for one's fellow human being.

Of particular ethnographic interest is the local custom of spitting: in the last two years I have noticed an increase in this habit which has by now become perfectly integrated into the New York way of life: spit on the open ground, on the street, on stairs, on the bus, in the subway, and in the subway train, everywhere. I quickly conclude that people here spit more to spite those around than because of a bronchopneumopathy pandemic. And the stink! The nauseating stench that we all pretend not to smell.

I do a Cirque du Soleil balancing act to avoid touching anything in the train: once we get to Times Square, it will be the human tide itself that lifts me up and carries me out. This is the first place I saw in New York when Brett brought me here directly from JFK, but it has lost the charm of that day. I wander, like a soul lost by mistake in hell (*I wasn't prepared for hell*), along corridors, tunnels, escalators as high as ziggurats which lead to more corridors, other gray underpasses, more nauseating stench, all the way to the next train, the crosstown shuttle. The buzz of those who don't stop talking on the phone, the smell of those who don't wash, the shoves of those who run faster than me, or who push me with the excuse of running but who do it, really, just for the satisfaction of bruising an anonymous fool like me who won't react to any insult. *Calm, calm, keep calm.*

*Pwahhh,* I'm out! Finally, the sun, the air!

An air full of dust, smog, hair detached from the heads of human beings that trundle everywhere like tumbleweeds in the steppes of Wyoming. Out. *Think positive, Faniusha. Stay calm.* It's a phenomenal day, fresh like iced lemon, bright, autumn is coming, the best season is about to begin; in two and a half months, there'll be Carnegie Deli cheesecake for my birthday; in a few weeks the stores will start playing Irving Berlin's songs; I will go back to humming "Chestnuts roasting on an open fire . . . la la lala . . . Eskimos . . . la la lala . . ." all day; then the snow; then the scent of the woodburning fireplaces. The days will shorten; there will be dinners with friends that maybe I too will have by then; long coats and warm scarves; Central Park lamplights; a new feel-good romcom; Milli the cat in bed sleeping on my belly (*that's right, I rescued a little kitten . . . no, scratch that: a little kitten rescued me—and now we are inseparable*); General Tsao tofu and broccoli with brown sauce in front of the TV; roasted chestnuts (*no, actually, that's not happening: 100 years ago some virulent pathogenic molds killed all the chestnut trees; the worst ecological disaster since the Ice Age for North America and me*). Maybe I'll dye my hair red, like maple leaves. Like Rita Hayworth. A September morning like this can only herald the coming of a more bearable time (weather-wise) and a more joyful time (mood-wise). The cool and blue sky are already restoring my good humor. My subway panic gradually dissipates. I think of people who may be planning a fabulous weekend at the Hamptons, or perhaps in Mexico. (*When will I too have a house like the one in* The Big Chill *and a family like the one in* Hannah and Her Sisters?) This is still the city of and for the rich. If being rich is great everywhere, it is particularly great in New York City.

I walk toward the office building, down Third Avenue, breathing deeply to relax and to recoup a happy smile. I look up toward the gorgeous azure sky.

I see something: some patented idiot of a pilot, who probably received from the control tower at JFK the order to do a little taxiing in the air because of aviation traffic, must have had the brilliant idea of showing off from up close the city to his passengers onboard . . . the flight with a million-dollar view. Will the passengers give him an ovation for the treat? I've never seen anything like this. I almost get run over by a car for keeping my nose in the air: the plane flies so low that the shadows of the passengers' heads are clearly visible through the portholes of the cabin. New York, city of extravagance and endless bullshit.

Elevators. First "Good morning!" exchanged with more enthusiasm than the heart would truthfully afford. It is Tuesday, therefore we are beyond the limit within which one is allowed to ask, as if we cared, "Did you have a good weekend?" just to fill in the void of the journey all the way up to the tenth, twentieth, millionth floor. So nobody says anything. We look at ourselves up-side-down, reflected in the ceiling mirror of the elevator cabin. We watch the numbers light up as the floors fly by, as if the life of each trapped employee in here depended on the whims (quite predictable, as whims go) of the switch-board. I plump down, already as tired as if it were 5 PM, on my aerodynamic desk chair. Luckily, they will leave me alone for most of the day.

Miriam (*I can never remember what she is in charge of*) rushes by my door, frantic, with distorted facial features: I am about to open my mouth in a wide and rather insincere "Hellooooo!" But the expression she is wearing stops me dead. She speaks before I can say anything: "Hurry! Everybody is in the hall-way. We are under attack!" I blink. I cock my head forward as if I were hard of hearing and wanted to have a chance to catch some remote sounds again. She can see that I did not understand and repeats, almost shouting "America is under attack. New York has been attacked!" and disappears from sight in that way hummingbirds do. A moment there, *bzzzzzzz*, and a moment later, *bzppp*, they are gone.

I remain seated: the sense of hearing intensified abnormally, but I hear nothing. It's as if I were underwater. I remain seated because I no longer have legs. The euphemistic "to be paralyzed by fear" takes on a new meaning in this very literal moment. I cannot move. I will not move. I see a couple of colleagues sliding by the door of my office, as if on wings, they don't notice me or maybe they don't care about me being here. Their eyes popping out of their heads, their strides inhuman, their faces as long as Greek tragic masks, unrecognizable.

Mom, dad. I am not sure how my left arm moved to reach the phone receiver and brought it to my ear. No dial tone. I close my eyes. I wait for a *boooom!* I guess it's just a matter of seconds. The war today is no longer played with cavalry, we are in the atomic era. Will it make any noise? Will it be a very strong hot gust? If so, if I'm lucky, I will not even feel it coming. Nobody will hear anything. Mom, dad. They must be terrified. Perhaps, though, they are not even *there* anymore. If enemies have made it to America, who knows what's already become of Italy. Or Israel. Oh, God, Israel must be gone! I hope Israel had time to shoot at least one or two missiles of its own . . . to disappear with a kick and a loud scream this time around and not a hopeless moan.

Come, gusts of fire, come! Hurry up!

When is the *boooom!?* I open my eyes. No one runs down the corridor anymore, where is everyone? They did not come to call me twice. I am inessential. Except for mom and dad. At the thought of them, panic resurges. *Keep breathing. Hang in there.* How much time has passed? What time is it? Minutes? Days? My legs are coming back to life. One step at a time, I hobble out and eventually find the full staff, dozens of people, speechless, standing in front of the TV screen that usually serves to keep secretaries and visitors company in the entrance parlor. How scary when adults stand still without saying anything. I join them. What death are we all going to die, I want to know. The blast must be imminent. We are on an island. There's nowhere to run to.

On the TV screen I see the World Trade Center. Only the World Trade Center. I do not see Washington, DC, looking like 1945 Dresden, I do not see fighter bombers flattening American cities. I see only the World Trade Center. Who is attacking us? And with what means? What chances do we have? I look furiously at Miriam: *what the fuck were you screaming before!* But my mouth forgot how to talk. I focus, I look more closely. One of the twin towers has a hole on one side and is on fire. They replay something extraordinary: an airplane . . . a tower . . . an airplane . . . in the tower . . . flames. . . people. At least, I think those are people. They rain down. Pablito. His jaunty face pops up in the middle of my consciousness. Pablito had to go to the immigration office to file some documents for me and other clients of Father Kelly this morning. Those offices are right by the Twin Towers.

I cut through a thick crowd of colleagues and strangers, like a shark through a school of sardines. Our building is occupied by military forces . . . American ones. It is classified as "high risk" because we are very close to the United Nations and because we house here the World Jewish Congress and our (Jewish) publishing company. I take the stairs. The street on which I emerge is empty. I start running. I run. I run in my inappropriate shoes. I run and the cool weather of a few minutes ago turns to heat. I run through Third Avenue, turn on 42nd Street, then down 42nd Street until I make a left on Sixth Avenue. I keep running down Sixth Avenue and, suddenly, I realize that I am actually not alone. The city is as full as ever, nothing has changed, everyone has come in like any other day, to their workstations, to do what they've been doing for ten, twenty, thirty years. They are all here. But they are like apparitions. They are still mannequins. An array of statuettes.

9:59. There are no radio transmissions or telephone lines in operation. There is only a large crowd and a great silence. Nobody talks, no one honks, taxi drivers have opened the doors of their yellow cabs and are standing beside their cars watching the horizon ahead. Pedestrians—like extras without a line in a movie—stand still watching the horizon ahead. The traffic lights switch from green to yellow to red to green with a quiet click. I never heard them click before. The traffic is completely blocked, no, worse, it's petrified. I look ahead too. I look in the direction where they are all looking . . . south. There Sixth Avenue ends in a cloud of smoke. No, not even smoke, it's a black grayish screen, it's a scenic backdrop that hides the familiar view of the World Trade Center at the horizon, at the end of the Grand Canyon, as they call this huge boulevard often whipped by winds blowing from the ocean at a hundred knots. I run. I do not know why. I run because I want to exhaust myself physically. Because exhaustion is better than bottled energy. There is no more Pablito. *Get ready, Fania. Pablito is gone. Tomorrow the real pain. Tomorrow we cry. Now we run. Tomorrow the phone call to Ecuador to tell his parents that Pablito is no longer. His mom can stay at my place. And is mine alive? Is Italy still there? And Israel? What will Father Kelly do?*

People jump. People are jumping out of the building. Tell them not to jump!!! Don't jump!!! No! No! Black clouds. 10:28. Pieces of metal plunge into the air. The catastrophe is peaceful. Like a cardboard box compressed under a steamroller. Everything crumbles. People break like things. They plunge into the air, head down, feet up, no resistance, only the force of gravity. Force. Gravity. What gravity, on this September day.

Pablito is alive. He is here, in front of me, and he confirms it. He was on the ① train when all hell broke loose on the surface, and he got stuck for hours in the subway tunnel, one stop from the Twin Towers. The passengers had no idea of what was happening. The unspeakable could have happened, but it did not happen, not for them. Apart from this, there is nothing else to say. We don't say anything else. I feel as if we, New Yorkers, will never say much about this day again. There is no need; words among witnesses of the same disaster are superfluous. Let the others, those from the outside, start the media bullshitathon. We instead stand in line, patiently, every day to give blood for survivors who are never found. Liters and liters of blood, and no one to infuse it into.

I feel as if I were wearing, upon my body, like a palpable piece of covering, the effect, or impression, of every second of last Tuesday 9/11. 911 a new emergency number. From my senseless run all the way down to Tribeca to the walk back home up to Columbus Circle. I must have caught the only train still in circulation at the Columbus station. We were no more than four people in my car, maybe ten in the whole Ⓐ train. Our faces were human again: we looked at each other, we held each other's gaze, without embarrassment or awkwardness. I would recognize those four passengers anywhere. We smiled painful, real smiles. No tears. Tears belong to a different stage of suffering. Tears are for opposite extremes: either for beginnings or for the endings. We cry when we categorically reject what is coming or what has just passed: which is, either when we face the unknown or when we have seen everything there was to see. Tears are an emotional battle cry that announces the war. In the middle of the battle, however, one has no recourse to them.

Death is there to remind us that no one is essential to life. In a country obsessed with *hic et nunc* like America (anchored in positivism, archenemy of negative thinking), this tragedy gets overwhelmingly amplified. Americans are constitutionally unable to sympathize with the dead. They see in death a mirror of the triumph of life. What for me is the existential tragedy par excellence (death), for them is an exhilarating cause of rejoicing and believing more strongly in their God. This is why they like funerals and they turn them into a celebration of those who remain rather than of those who (probably not too optimistically, I imagine) depart. At funerals, Americans sing, play videos of the dead's life, eat in great abundance, and make speeches which invariably have a humorous twist in order to entertain the audience. It's the most ancient rhetorical *pas de deux:* always draw out a good laugh before you stroke the sentimental chords that bring the audience to tears . . . largely tears of emotion for the presenter's oratory talent, not necessarily for the dear departed. There's no business, like show business! And business or not, in America everything is a show. The life of the dead is depicted in lavish hues of heroism, predominantly rose colored. In the old world, birth and death are still moments under the strict control of the spiritual authorities who guarantee that the stress fall on the meaning of existence *in toto* and *not* of the single individual. But in America, where the individual is deified, funerals are monuments to the individual's greatness, and divine inscrutability is neither challenged nor questioned (neither feared nor understood). In God We Trust, the banknotes here say. Yet when it comes to organizing the last earthly party, God is totally set aside, and they overfocus on the human being, in an almost Dionysian and profane way.

Going forward, 9/11 (with the profile of the Twin Towers almost mystically reflected in the number 11) will trigger a heroic feast of colossal proportions. For years, I'm sure, what will remain of this tragedy are going to be either its "Heroes" or its "Anti-heroes," with very little in between, the fewer complications the better. And to the anti-heroes, George W. Bush and Dick Cheney, today's Pinocchio and Mangiafuoco, wasted no time in declaring war to the bitter end. Good luck with that.

Days with nothing to do. Needless to turn on the television, read the newspapers, listen to the radio. There is nothing to know.

Where the towers stood, the mayor had the city place two beams of light that illuminate the night and are visible in the distance from every borough.

The first time I see a plane that looks as if it flies through them, I almost scream . . . and only thus the power of this acute symbology hits me: two towers of light that we can't but see, that can't be taken down and that stand for what is no longer there. They talk about holding an international architecture competition to find the most suitable memorial: but there is no need for one. New York already has come up with the most suitable monument. I hope they never turn off these beams of light: I hope they do not erect any monuments in that place.

No one expected an ideological massacre on this scale. Or at least not in New York, the city that luxuriates in its uplifting stories about how successful it was in absorbing so much diversity, in welcoming people from all over the world, and in making friends of everyone—people who back home would be mortal enemies—turning a chaotic mass into a safe community. We don't even have the word "community" in Italian in the English sense of the term: for us *comunità* is the rehabilitation center for drug addicts. (*With the only exception, now that I think of it, of the* comunità ebraica, *Jewish community. Why?*) Seriously. We just don't use the word "community" to describe ourselves as citizens . . . *obviously* because we are not one. Here community refers to the set of citizens joined by their free choice to respect the rules, help each other when needed, in dignity and decency and not because of some political, regional, or family gonfalon they pledged fealty to. All concepts extraneous to the Mediterranean basin.

For the collective good of the community in America, you collect your dog's poop from the sidewalk; you don't steal the Halloween or Christmas decorations, because they are there for the enjoyment of the community; you don't park your cars over the public flowerbeds, on top of the disabled access ramps, on the tramway tracks—because parking within the predefined lines keeps the streets in order and traffic under control and makes the day more livable for the whole community. Even New York City, the great, the strong, the ruthless, the fierce, the tireless, the unstoppable, the cruel New York City has its community, its civic sense. Or it would be a circle in Hades. It would be Brasilia (or Naples) and not the Big Apple. And New York's proudest badge of honor is that its community is a melting pot of faces of all colors and all beliefs, with a curiosity for each other and respect for the mutual right to be what you want. The famous phrase by Voltaire, *Je ne suis pas d'accord yada yada yada* but I'll fight for your right to say it anyway, died in Europe with him, but it was successfully transplanted in America, in the fertile soil of Monticello—the farm-mansion of Jefferson, the farmer, the illuminist, the founder of the University of Virginia, the signer of the Declaration of Independence, and, alas, the owner of slaves—and has become the motto if not of all of America, certainly of New York. Only desert theocrats could not understand this.

Worst, what happened here is not the result of a miscomprehension from people from far away who buried their hearts in the sand and came to kill: what hurts is that those outsiders were helped by "insiders," by brethren who lived here for years, who for years worked as newsagents in Manhattan, in our melting pot. Think of the merry "Good morning!" they wished to and received from secretaries, mothers, businessmen, nannies, bums, students, children, lovers, porters, dentists, Muslims like themselves, Jews (often with a masochistic love for the Other), Christians (often with a sadistic love for the Other), the guy pissed off with the world, the one in a good mood because he is about to have a son, the one in a bad mood because his wife left him . . . How many times, in giving the change to their customers, they have touched the palm of a black, white, yellow, red, olive, blue, purple, rainbow hand . . . or shared subway seats, received a favor from a neighbor, a gift from an acquaintance, a special holiday tip from a regular in the area, help from a policeman who kept an eye on their news stall and their safety? Why didn't they pick up the phone, call their friend in Saudi Arabia and tell him: "No, wait! Look, these are people like us! I work here every day, they are not bad . . . A little loose in the moral department, granted, of easy virtue, sure. I have that gay neighbor who shaves his body and, dressed only in a scanty kimono, sits on the fire-escape stairs and sings opera! *Heeheehee* . . . OK, I digress. But as a whole they do not hate us. On the contrary—they love to march in solidarity with everyone! Come visit! I'll show you . . . It's just people, people like us. And their pizza is great." But they didn't make this phone call. They didn't want to see; they refused to understand.

A piece of the towers' metal pierced through the windows of my friends Erez and Stephanie's Tribeca loft. Emma, Francesca and Cesare's two-year-old daughter, developed a sudden respiratory problem: they suspect a lung tumor.

Everybody's life is crumbling down. Truth is, however, that my personal reality goes far more swimmingly than the national one. In the less obvious, most unexpected moment, my healing begins. This fledgling autumn finds me in tip-top shape. I am not insensitive to the unfairness of this fact. The life of thousands of people collapsed, mine is coming together. The air is toxic. I finally breathe.

Since they closed all offices for a few days, I take long walks through Central Park: some people have picnics, unleashed Labradors chase tennis balls, the neglected grass has time to grow and it is green and fluffy. There are no crowds of tourists at Strawberry Field. A few street musicians play at Columbus Circle and their notes in the quiet air can be heard far, all the way to the Friedsam Carousel; I walk down Poets' Alley where there's practically nobody, so strange for a sunny September day and no humidity. It gets dark earlier. It is beautiful.

I read the dedications on the park benches: "For Carlito Who Loved Sitting—1947–1997" "To book lovers: Amanda Jonas, Pat Klingestein, Dinny Morse, Laura Strauss, Lee Strong, Susan Zeckendorf." "In Loving Memory: Your Mother—1995–2000." I love the "Adopt a bench!" campaign the city started in 1986 for fundraising purposes. Some benches are dedicated to famous philanthropists, others to anonymous parents, friends, and children; some spent money to dedicate a bench in Central Park to Central Park itself and still others to commemorate their dog who loved, just as much as I, to walk around here every day. I wish for my bench to say one day, "To FKC: Who truly loved only NYC and her cat" (accompanied by the date of birth and death, which I hope will be cabalistically significant).

After more than two weeks of numb stupefaction—aside from the frenzy of journalists and commentators, empty puppets more than ever, manipulated by a not-so invisible hand up their arses—real people pick up their lives where they left them only a few days ago.

My life is ready for a turnaround, though. I won't have to answer job ads any longer, because I am not looking for a job. I'm going back to university. I was admitted to the PhD program at the City University of New York

Graduate Center. I'm in. That is, I'm back . . . to square one, to the starting point, like in *il Gioco dell'Oca.* Or better still, Monopoly, the most American game of all.

I deliberately set in motions the gears of change last spring (spring 2001, before the Twin Towers, before the end of our world). It was time. I felt ready. First the application to graduate school and then, in May, I started looking for a new apartment. This time I wanted to buy it, make an investment, take root so deeply that even a tornado can't blow me away. I felt it was time to change. Seaman Avenue had run its course. The nine-to-five editorial job had run its course. Adventitiously, I happened to go to the Graduate Center for a lecture one afternoon, and during the posttalk cocktail, I struck a pleasant conversation with the chair of the Comparative Literature Department who invited me to apply. Now that was an interesting proposition! Made all the sweeter by the good man's offer to let me start taking a few courses immediately "Just to try it out . . . as auditor"—but "if you join us, we'll count those for credits, of course." (*Of course. Naturally. This is America! Land of pitfalls, but oh-so-many opportunities as well!*) The graduate courses are all in the afternoons, because in New York students work hard to pay rent and the university adapts to accommodate them. I think back to the very first description on record in the English language of New York by Daniel Denton, who wrote in 1670:

> That I may say, and say truly, that if there be any terrestrial happiness to be had by people of all ranks, especially of an inferior rank, it must certainly be here: here any one may furnish himself with land, and live rent-free, yea, with such a quantity of land, that he may weary himself with walking over his fields of Corn . . . That I must needs say, that if there be any terrestrial *Canaan,* 'tis surely here, where the Land floweth with milk and honey.

Today, New York is the city with the highest rents in the world, a density per square meter that defies the laws of physics, and people of lower rank eat harmful corn genetically modified by those of higher rank who, in the name of God Money, enjoy annihilating them . . . precisely as happened to the Canaanites.

I am managing editor at the Union of American Hebrew Congregations Press. (*OK, UAHC Press—even I see the point of an acronym here.*) Its office building is just a few blocks away from the Graduate Center, which occupies an impressive block at the corner of Fifth Avenue and East 34th Street—originally house of B. Altman & Co. Department Store, designed by Trowbridge & Livingston. As soon as I leave the office at 5 PM, I walk to my classes. I shake with excitement. My days make sense again, finally. I am not sure from where I am drawing this euphoria, but I want to hug people, shout my joy at the top of my lungs, throw off my clothes, and join the Naked Cowboy in Times Square. I have strength to sell. I feel brave. I feel I could defend the oppressed and punch on the nose anybody who deserves it.

I also feel a bit disloyal in showing up at the office now, as if nothing were the matter, knowing full well in my heart that I am about to dump them come spring 2002. I still give my best to the projects I direct, I do my duty well, but my heart is elsewhere. The heart beats for tomorrow. In the office, I use their Xerox to photocopy the books I need for my courses, I may "borrow" a notepad or two, a couple of paperclips, pushpins, pencils, bulldog clips, erasers, folders, and, well, of course the computer to surf the internet, take appointments, stay informed about the world outside UAHC Press, and at lunch time, I run to see apartments for sale. My life is hanging at the edge of a new dream of happiness . . . this time hinging on three easy things: Milli the cat, a house of my own, and a PhD.

I gain weight and look healthy again. Milli too, who was scrawny and malnourished when she came to live with me, has grown a funny fluffy belly and proper permanent teeth, and she doesn't fit anymore inside a 32-ounce yogurt cup as she used to.

These days, we are also under the constant bombardment of horror stories from 9/11 . . . and as a corollary, gossip, whispers, half-mouthed lies begin circulating. The nonsense becomes louder every day. *The Mossad was behind it. The Israelis knew about the attacks. The American Jews, who were supposed to die en masse in the Towers—since they control the world's economy from there—were instead spared because,* obviously, *their "cousins" tipped them off in time.* We have a mentally retarded president, and behind him, a brilliant master puppeteer in Dick Cheney. The worst possible combination: it's like living the sequel of *Doctor Strangelove.* I am considering pitching a few opinion pieces and interviews to the Italian newspapers—news from someone who lives here and understands what's going on, unlike the clueless minions sent from Italy to take a look for two days and who return home with some preposterous conclusions.

The universe is finally tuned in to me.

From out of nowhere, from that dead emptiness that is the past, I get a phone call from my former boss from *Politicus*: Gwidon Goldblatt. Gwidon is in New York. They sent *him* for a year to take charge of their foreign bureau here. Life's script rewrites itself!

The search for a new apartment goes quite differently this time. I distinctly remember all my blunders from September 1998. Were it not for Larry Horst who opened my eyes to the inner workings of the New York real estate life, I would have ended up dead under a bridge, or in Rome richly pampered by my parents which, to me, would've been a different form of death.

I aim for a studio—Italian word, pronounced differently in English, signifying something different too. Let's go check out what New Yorkers mean by "studio." Got it: single window overlooking the cement of the opposite building, with fetid moldy staircases, no elevator. Interior design: no kitchen, only an open cooking-eating area which overflows into the all-in-one living-room/drawing-room/bedroom/office-space/work-place and, at will, suicide-room when you can no longer take the claustrophobia, the noise, the stench, and the neon lights from the street that turn your 9-square-meters studio fluorescent all night long. Starting price $450,000.

After two solid months of investigations, I don't abandon the idea, but I stop believing in it and therefore I am free to have fun: I go see every single apartment available in Manhattan. If someone advertises on the Thursday and Sunday *New York Times* real-estate section, I call and show up. Wherever there is an open house, there I am too. Above all, I make sure to get into all luxury apartments. *Perchè no!* I know my Italian clothes give the right (false) impression. No one will kick me out if I look the part. It takes me a while before I realize that it's not a matter of looks, real millionaires never show up—well dressed or not—they simply send a delegate to choose for them. The "open house" for high-end homes awaits you with a small banquet of refreshments, which sometimes includes champagne. Those for lower end homes, starting anyhow at a hefty half a million dollars, leave you instead with a bitter taste in your mouth. No need for stale muffins.

Problem is, salmon-crème canapés notwithstanding, the apartments I visit do not steal my heart. They are mostly modern, anonymous, without even an architectural frill one could fall in love with, an aesthetic fetish that could make a place worthy of the $10,000,000 one pays for it.

Of course, I'd have better luck if I hired a real estate agent: but the fee the intermediary charges seems impractical. Rumor has it that without an agent, you do not sell or buy, rent out or rent in. In a position of total disadvantage, again, but this time with amused awareness of it, I don't quite give up.

By the end of August, I decide to give it one last big push before putting this silly project to rest. One last Sunday marathon! My real estate aspirations may be defeated, but I get to step inside practically every single building in Manhattan. It's a consolation of sort. I know this town, and myself, like no one else.

I draw up a roadmap for the day: I will start with the geographically farthest ones, the Soho-Tribeca area, and will walk my way up the island all the way to the last one in Morningside, a neighborhood south of Harlem I don't know at all.

After about a dozen apartments, and miles under the sun, I am on the brink of capitulation. It's exhausting and a tad demoralizing. It's also unhealthy as the thermal shock between the 110 degrees on the street and the interiors AC'ed at a glacial 60 is pushing my lungs to the brink of a collapse. I am a bit sad, because I know that this is it for me and my shot at owning a place here. I'll look at the Morningside place, though, before I call it quits, mainly for two reasons: one, that at least I'll get to visit a new neighborhood and two, that the ad was so weird and noncredible that I feel I need to call their bluff. By now I know that "cozy" is code language for miniscule; "quiet neighborhood" means "you are 3 hours away from everything;" "beautiful French doors" means that they subdivided this tiny dump into two sections, raising a bogus wall, that will give you the impression of multiple (two!) compartments, when in fact the real space is so small that a traditional door would have had no room to swing open. The announcement promises: Two bedrooms, 1 bathroom, kitchen, well lit, private basement storage, laundry, easy access to all subway lines and busses: $160,000. "Shameless liars!" I am going there to scream to their face. Or more likely, once I find myself in what is certain to be a decrepit pigpen at the boarder of the infamous Harlem ghetto, I'll all but squeal a "Hello" and beat it as fast as I can. Let me put it this way: I have not seen Harlem yet . . . let's add this to the list of experiences. *Perchè no!* 1264 Amsterdam Avenue, here I come.

I find myself in front of a brick building, on a very wide road that slopes steeply: Can it be this one? I check the piece of paper in my hand with the list of addresses I covered today: all of them, except this one, are struck through. The street is very clean and extraordinarily quiet considering that it runs parallel to Broadway, a block away. There are restaurants in place of 99¢ stores—indicative of the types of customers in the area. It's Sunday afternoon, so there's no traffic, I can even hear the birds chirp, and the terrible heat of the morning has been replaced by a pleasant breeze that has blown away the stagnant humidity. The building door is smaller than at Seaman, much more elegant, less proletarian than where I live now. There are the classic three stoops to reach it and the intercom is in gilded brass with old-fashioned buttons. I'm buzzed in and, unlike the other low-end buildings where the smell of spicy foods mixed with that of the moldy carpets in the hall choke you out of your senses, here I am enfolded in a puff of soapy freshness, minty, deliciously sterilized. The floors are of shiny marble in impeccable conditions and extend from the door to the staircases continuing through each step all the way to the sixth floor. No elevator. However, climbing the stairs in these conditions is not bad, not bad at all. The more I climb, the more my curious outrage (from reading the deceitful announcement) turns into curious delight. This is different. I find the red door to 5D ajar. I let myself in. I step inside and I know I arrived. I am home.

I move from one room to another, fearing that what I am seeing is the result of the dehydration and sunstroke from this morning's marathon. No, no mistake, this *is* the correct address. Yet the announcement didn't do justice to reality . . . so then, the price must have been a typo. Seven hundred square feet, windows on all available walls, two small bedrooms (not the optical-illusion type, real ones), exposed bricks in every room, restored wooden floors, very high ceilings, and noise-wise you can hear a fly sneeze because the apartment looks over the back of the building, not over Amsterdam Avenue and it is magically quiet. The real estate agent on location checks me out but says nothing. She is beadily studying my reaction. Maybe she doesn't intend to help because an apartment at this price is a waste of time for her. Or maybe she has already seen a thousand faces like mine—light up with interest—but leading to no final handshake.

For a moment I visualize Larry Horst's thumb and index fingers rub each other "If you help me, I'll help you," the local real-estate password. As I'm considering all this, the agent hasn't made a move toward me. She stands like an old codfish-stick in a corner of the living room: not crunchy. It's up to me to make a move then. "Ok, I'll buy it," I say. Without bargaining, pausing, pondering, sleeping over it. I'll buy it, I tell her. The enigmatic woman reaches into some fold in her body and pulls out a calling card and hands it to me. Why should I call and talk to her on the phone, when we are here face to face and can talk about it *now*, sign papers, agree on a deal? Perhaps another potential buyer is already in the picture and the "real" negotiations will be all held behind the scenes, pegging the competitors blindly against each other? Intuitively, I feel that the only other customer I saw here a moment ago will make an offer as well: it is apparent that that gorgeous African American woman was unmarried, up and coming in a good career, very respectable, someone everybody will want in their co-op, and totally local . . . that is, she knows exactly the magic number that will get her this place. Bing bang boom! That one doesn't make mistakes. I feel a flash of panic, the urgency is too great. I would like to say to the realtor, "Lock this house, do not let anyone in, I'll take it! I will!" But instead I run home . . . literally, I run. I do not care that it's Sunday, I call the number anyway, and if I get an answering machine, at least my message will be heard first thing tomorrow morning.

I dial the number and the apartment owner picks up. I'm startled. Taken aback. I stammer as I am afraid I misunderstood. Owners, no matter owners of what, are practically Fantômas, Bilbo Baggins, Griffin—invisible and often criminal. There is no longer any relationship in America between a buyer and those who make money on the purchase. From a hamburger to a $30,000,000 villa, the potential buyer no longer deals directly with the person who owns what's being sold. There are always intermediaries who, having no power, when things go sour, can always deploy the answer that puts an end to all questions: "It's not my fault. I'm only doing my job." *Famous opening line of all genocides.* This is the case with telephone companies, television companies, insurance companies, and even medical clinics where you reach an answering service, a secretary, or a dead patient before you reach your doctor.

From his voice I understand that I am speaking to a guy my age. He tells me that the lady who gave me his number is in fact a real estate agent but also a friend who was doing him a favor while he is abroad. He is a highly motivated seller (the co-op board doesn't allow him to sublet) because he has decided to settle permanently in Israel, where he recently met a girl, whom he's now about to marry.

I have one card, and one card only to play at this point: the truth.

I share my personal story with him, my life on the kibbutz, the M.A. at Brandeis, my parents' keychain with the JFK effigy, my grandfather's death from starvation during the war in front of his small son (my dad), my own father's hunger during the war, my mother's memory of the American and British soldiers liberating Europe, my childhood bank account that my uncle and aunt opened for me so that one day I could go to New York, and all the rest. Everything. Yes, everything I am so careful not to tell anyone else, I tell this perfect stranger. I wish him my best, and I am genuinely moved at the thought of the happiness awaiting him and his fiancée. I tell him that I envy him a little. I tell him, "Mazal tov!" He tells me, "I want you to have my apartment."

Little Emma, Francesca's and Cesare's daughter, does not have a tumor. At the Philadelphia pediatric hospital, where they urgently took her, they discovered that the black spot on her lung was a sticky piece of cookie. Erez and Stephanie, unharmed by the 9/11 flying debris, leave their Tribeca loft behind and move to Lucca, in the heavenly region of Tuscany, where they intend to spend the next two years, after which que será, será. What will be, will be wonderful. We are all fine.

Move-in day: November 1, 2001. 7:30, the buzzer rings at 254 Seaman Avenue. A minute later, six Israelis penetrate E1. Muscular, handsome, healthy, out of a

Bolshevik propaganda poster from the 1930s, they grab everything in less than two hours and deposit it, in perfect conditions, at my destination. My things have filled two lorries. Without sweating or panting, these supermen carry everything on their shoulders up to the fifth floor. They leave, and I drive back to Seaman Avenue to collect Milli and bring her to her new home.

One in the tight embrace of the other—Milli's nails digging into my left shoulder—we take a brief tour of what is now our old house: I leave to Larry Horst the IKEA wall units; there's also a handmade bookcase that Pablito permanently grafted to the structure of the building (*we forgot to ask Horst for permission*) and that will have to stay (*it'll increase the value of the apartment, I tell myself*); and a little bit of lint at the corners behind the doors. Now that the place is empty, the echo of my steps on the floor comes alive again, just like the first day. I hear the *tantantantantantan* drumming inside the heater syphons. It's a wonderful sunny day but the low temperature foretells the climax of autumn: the best of seasons finally unfolds. "Thank you," I say to nothing and no one in particular . . . to *this*. As soon as I put Milli in the car, she punishes me by peeing in her carrier and staring at me grouchily for the remainder of the short trip.

"What on earth was I thinking?" A diabolical voice slowly begins to whisper in my head as I drive away from Inwood. "What the hell did I do? *I bought an apartment in New York!* And now what? What if something goes wrong? And if I can't pay the monthly payments? And what if it was a mistake? What if, as soon as I'm there, I discover the most horrible flaws? Pierced pipes, parasitic infestations, a rapist-murderer next door, a gang of armed brutes coming to redeem monthly payments (nonbank related), asbestos in the walls that (good-case scenario) will cause asphyxiation and they'll find me and Milli lying in the corridor, foaming at the mouth, lifeless or (worst-case scenario) will cause a tumor of the pleura?" I comfort Milli: "Millina, everything will be all right! Let's bathe now!" She looks at me askance, as she hates water. She is probably considering letting in intruders to murder me.

I see the cat's whiskers and her pink nose react favorably to the beauty of the place. We are both very quiet, and we are no longer scared.

# PART 5

# Éclair

# 12

Morningside Heights is the district that surrounds Columbia University, from West 110th to 125th Streets, between Morningside Drive and Riverside Park. Basically, Morningside Heights has only two main arteries, Broadway and Amsterdam Avenue, and some side streets or tucked-away alleys. Surrounded by universities, bookstores (nonexistent in Inwood), elegant restaurants (nonexistent in Inwood), French cafés (non-existent in . . . well, I made my point), Tapas Bars every two steps—no McDonalds here—there are students everywhere and from all over the world: they go to Columbia, Barnard College, the Jewish Theological Seminary (with which I share the block and where, coincidentally, Professor Alan Mintz has moved from Brandeis), and City College.

There are buses every minute running up and down Broadway and Amsterdam, there is the ① train in front of Columbia, and on West 125th one of the main subway hubs gives me access to the Ⓐ, Ⓑ, Ⓒ, and Ⓓ lines. There are mom & pop stores that never close, 365 days a year, twenty-four hours a day. And here is also the diner where I had breakfast six years ago served by "Laverne," which means that I am also in the same neighborhood as the Youth Hostel on West 103rd and Amsterdam, coordinates that meant nothing to me at the time but today spell HOME. I am on West 122nd and Amsterdam and I can walk everywhere, without fearing anything, surrounded not by murderers —as New York is often portrayed in films—but by young people, artists, students, aging intellectuals, fledgling families, professionals, professors, musicians . . . people, people, people! Among whom I immerse myself, I mix, I melt. On Amsterdam and West 112th Street I discover Saint John the Divine, a cathedral where every autumn there takes place the blessing of the animals, by which I don't mean mere cats and dogs but also pythons, llamas, iguanas, giraffes, and birds illegally imported from God (apropos) knows where. (*If not God, at least the priest should call the police and punish the eco-tragic contraband.*) I make a mental note to go see it next year. "Next year" has such a nice sound to it. Next year I will be at 1264 Amsterdam Avenue. Next year I'll be where I am right now. This is where I will be found by 2002; it will be for 2002 to come to me, and no longer me running pursued by a ticking clock, pursuing shifting horizons, skidding on a slippery ground.

Every Wednesday evening and Saturday morning I go to a gym on West 103rd Street and Broadway where Michelle, a California yogi, gently opens for me a portal into a spiritual world that I had never contemplated before. It was not easy to find this place. The inspiration came from Ruta, my then boss at a place called Planet Leap (another one of my just-to-pay-the-rent jobs), who swore by her yoga—although she had to give it up when they fired her at work. The day after Planet Leap unceremoniously removed her, I resigned too and chose her friendship over my salary.

I tested several yoga centers. None worked for me. I discover that these centers and all gyms in New York are practically dating pools rather than exercise courts. Women and men who frequent these establishments are without exception gorgeous and perfectly sculpted; there's nothing the gym could improve. I suspect they expect much more than to simply tone their muscles here. I get a feeling that they don't come to the gym to become more attractive but rather *because* they are *that* attractive. From the first moment, I feel I don't belong: when I enter, I hear the heads turn on marbled necks to check the latest arrival; their eyes take me in and immediately spit me out like a bad olive. And then there is the price obstacle: $200 registration fee, a modicum of $175 a month (for the commonest places). There is a gym in Tribeca that is famous for its $5,000 monthly membership.

Nonetheless, I take advantage of the one-time trial classes at various gyms to test my affinity for yoga. At one, I noticed the euphoria of the members, who were visibly excited and chatted in high-pitched tones like children about to get the biggest birthday cake of their life. They arranged their mats as close as possible to the teacher's platform, they adjusted their costumes while admiring themselves in the wall mirrors, hair up, hair down, scarves artfully wrapped around the waist, bandanas around the ankles, very sexy. I understood the reason for so much studied preparation only when the Israeli yogi, of paralyzing beauty, finally entered the room. My first instinct was to grab the towel—I had not yet bought a mat (which marked me as a barbarian in everyone's eyes)—and run away. But I would have had to barrel through at least a hundred extra-firm bodies standing between me and the door. At some point in the lesson, the teacher chose me to demonstrate the Chair Pose. He got behind me, stuck himself to me like two slices of pullman bread, and asked me to bend my knees, as if to sit on him while, awkwardly, standing, thus becoming a human chair. My moaning was almost audible, but it was lost in the heavy breathing of the other students, women and men, who had been paying $300 a month for years and never been invited by the yogi to sit on his rock-hard thighs (so close to every other hard part of him). Holy son of Abraham! I ended up not signing up at that place either.

On the way home one day, I looked up distractedly at some big corner building on Broadway and noticed a gym on the second floor: its windows were plastered with posters that announced in big cheap lettering: SPECIALS! I went in to inquire: "Of course we offer yoga classes!" the cheerful, unpretentious girl at the reception reassures me. It is a huge exercise studio. I look around and see only women. And they are not that gorgeous looking. They are NORMAL! The place is open seven days a week, the membership offers unlimited equipment use and access to all group classes. Cost: $5 one-time registration, $19.99 monthly fee. My impression of this place shows in the giant grin on my face in the photo the receptionist takes right there and then for my new ID.

This gym for women only has branches all over New York. This chain bears the name of its founder, Lucille Roberts, a fanatic of diets and fitness, a Jew from Tajikistan who fled with her family from under Khrushchev and landed on Ellis Island in the 1950s. She became very rich, building her empire on the American fantasy of becoming skinny. Yet her gyms are not for the élite: they are only for women who cannot afford $300 a month to walk on a treadmill, who are also the women who most need to be on a treadmill.

Because the great American paradox, as far as I can tell, is that this is the only country in the world where poverty is measured in obesity: the poor here are all fat, and the rich filiform.

This is because the poor have access only to the worst foods—foods that block the arteries, full of harmful fats devoid of nutrients. While a loaf of bread, two fresh tomatoes and a hundred grams of brie cost you $15 at Zabar's, a "Family Meal" from McDonald that feeds you and your five children is $2. Half a gallon of organic milk: $3.50. Two liters of Coca Cola: 99¢.

Although I had failed to notice, I now realize that shops with human-grade food were not to be found in Inwood anywhere. The closest thing to a home-made meal was pizza and Chinese (which is really all Milli and I ever cared for). This is because Inwood is an extension of that part of Harlem where white ends and off white begins. So I start paying attention, in my tireless wanderings on foot, to the distribution of stores on the island: from 125th Street upward, there is hardly a bookstore—and none of the ubiquitous Barnes & Noble and their parasite, Starbucks, that, with general disapproval, have colonized every single block of New York City. From Harlem upward, no Pain Quotidien, no Westside Market, no Chelsea Market. From Harlem downward, you have to put some real effort into finding a McDonald, a Burger King, or a KFC (*if you are into that type of thing, which you are* not *if you are from below-Harlem*). From Harlem to Inwood, you find nothing but McDonalds, Burger Kings, and KFCs. In New York, a city so in love with its diverse, liberal, inclusive legend, only Lucille Roberts thought of satisfying the impelling demand of those who don't have the power to ask: she gave a gymnasium to those who need it most.

In 1995, the tycoonness beat all the other bidders and bought one of Manhattan's most desirable mansions, at a price rumored to be scandalous. Something tells me that the price raised shocked eyebrows not so much for its actual exorbitance as for the fact that it was afforded by this vulgar arrivée. At number 4 on East 80th Street, her palace is known by the name of its original owner, Frank Woolworth (whose niece married Cary Grant), and thanks to Lucille Roberts and the restorations and renovations she conducted, the building has been brought back to its original French neo-renaissance splendor. Villa Woolworth, which amounted to 19,000 square feet, measures now

20,000: seven floors, ten bedrooms, three kitchens, eleven and a half baths. This woman is a giant. Perhaps with the excuse of an interview, I will be able to meet her and become her friend.

At Lucille Roberts's there's no firm, horny *mossadnik,* but Michelle, a Californian Black woman, muscular, energetic, toned on every inch of her extreme rotundity and as flexible as a bamboo, her skin shiny with sweat, fusilli hair pulled back by a simple blue bandana with white polka dots. She bends, fluctuates, and pretzels and in a sweet voice tells us to believe in ourselves, speaks to us of our inner beauty, reminds us that we are not here to judge or compete, that with each inhalation and exhalation a new life, a new hope, a new light shall pervade us and it will last us until next class when we'll reinforce its vigor one more time. We are many, maybe thirty or forty: old, pendulous, young, scraggy, obese, dwarfish, overly tall, gay, single, angry, happy, dumb, on drugs, illness survivors, aspiring writers, frustrated secretaries, frigid wives, oversexed teenagers, public system students, public system teachers, divorcés, unmarried mothers, battered mothers, liberated mothers . . . a true-to-life sampler of reality. Except for the blessed absence of men: there's no man here to trigger the ancestral competition over the primary reproductive source. No man to condition women into acting differently among themselves. I too lean forward, crook my toes, corkscrew my spine, and smile with relief all the way back home. I walk home after yoga with a new lightness in my step, enjoying the sight of the sky, of people shopping or strolling around, the colorful Fresh Market's fruits displayed on the sidewalk mixed with bouquets of flowers, Columbia University students gathered for brunch, used-books street vendors, cops on a break who eat a large slice of pizza at Koronet. I can't resist Koronet and its greasy triangles of delight! I know, I know . . . the yogi told us to love our bodies and feed it nourishing healthy foods, no dairy (*she must be vegan*), no sugars (*she must be joking*) . . . but I can't resist, those cheesy slices call me from behind the glass display, it's practically self-abuse to deny myself and Milli! Milli, the true New Yorker in the family, loves pizza and broccoli with brown sauce.

After my Saturday yoga session, I feel full of energy, as if illuminated from within by an ultramundane fluorescence. In short, I feel I'm hot and special.

I put on my grungy blue jeans, cowboy boots, white shirt, and leather jacket, throw my Nikon camera across my neck, and with the coolest "reporter look" (*the look does half the work, sometimes*), I go out. I'm headed to Brooklyn. I decided to write a piece about a fledgling literary movement. It's born from the imagination of someone called Dave Eggers, who created a magazine full of peculiar collages, comics, fictional pieces by the most relevant intellectuals of the day after tomorrow. It is stuff for connoisseurs (because it is rare and hard to find), by the rich (because it costs an arm and a leg), and for a few elects (because it is purposely made inaccessible to most people), even though its declared intentions are inclusive, postmodern, anti-establishment. Now that Gwidon is here in New York and has gotten in touch with me, I don't want to miss the chance to start working with Italy again; to put my feet back in that door, but on equal terms now, with a different strength and authority. *Now* that I know what I'm doing, I will make my comeback with the agency of one who learned to say "NO" and make herself heard. *Now* I'm ready! I take the initiative to prepare this piece: when I see Gwidon, I will bring it to him as a tribute to our realliance, and he'll love it. Today I am an American journalist! I surpassed the teacher. Now I know how to write a compelling story; I am the goddess of editorials that hold the reader captive to the last word. And by the way, they need me! Because, at *Politicus*, they will never get any news worth printing if they keep sending those young scribblers (with their retroflex *r*'s) who live in posh places, who dress-speak-eat-taste-think only Italian. The true story can only be told by an insider like myself.

Despite my feelings of pride, joy, and hope still lingering after my yoga session at Lucille Roberts', I must admit I have a bit of anxiety as well. I haven't been in Brooklyn since Father Kelly's days. I am venturing out of Manhattan. I never leave the island. Bad memories elbow each other to reemerge into my conscious, and I try and fail to ignore them. I taste again in my mouth the bitter reminders they bring of the desolation, the loss of everything, the constant terror of making more fatal mistakes, of ending up dead in the street, or living under a bridge, in a lunatic institution, with dirty nails bitten to the quick, a drunkard, a druggie, a prostitute. What if Father Kelly had lost the case instead? What if the Criminal had had me arrested? What if I had never found a job? While these unbound thoughts unleash a rodeo of fears in my mind, the realization that pushes me to a panic is that my house is currently far away, in Manhattan, that I left Milli alone, and if I don't return who will take care of her? Who would know that I disappeared? Who would look for me? This stupid article was my initiative, so nobody knows where (or why) I ended up today. Who will know whom to call to give the sad news?

I shake my head like a wet dog. Maybe I should buy myself a metal name tag like the Marines in Vietnam with all identifying data recorded on it. *What's going on with me?* "Brightness! Endless possibilities! There is only peace around me . . ." I try to call to mind Michelle's yoga-infused voice in the failing attempt to calm myself. The Ⓕ train gradually empties out of people, only burly dudes remain aboard, lying along three seats, and a few boys with hoods pulled down to their chins . . . discarded newspaper pages on the ground, the train's windows blackened by time and paint sprays. Signs of spit everywhere. The rich people who live in Park Slope (*Gentrification Central*) where I'm heading obviously take other means of transportation because I can't spot a single sophisticated, "alternative" hipster around. They must all be in gyms doing yoga with the fuckable *mossadniks*. Finally my stop: 7th Avenue. Hm, it's nice here.

McSweeney's shop is horrendous. A narrow dark room in the middle of a long block, two people can move uneasily inside, three would perish: the shelves are cluttered with faux-old trinkets, ampoules of homunculi, embalmed heads of extinct rodents with, understandably, malevolent frowns. It looks like a full-scale reproduction of a lithograph by Ferrante Imperato, or a period film set that intends to recreate the London atmospheres of Dr. Jekyll & Mr. Hyde. But without London around to lend it the required authenticity, McSweeney's endeavor misfires: Park Slope is cheerful, optimistic, quintessentially American, and poorly dressed. It's not bourgeois, it's rich middle class. It's not Oscar Wilde material, it's Johnny Appleseed's land. McSweeney appears to have missed the not-so subtle demarcation—as wide as the Rio Grande—between *retro-chic* and *avant-merde*. It's the first true day of spring; there is a wonderful breeze outside blowing from every corner which makes one's mood dance. It's dreadful being in here. I take a couple of quick and un-inspired pictures and step out before I die of anguish in this cubbyhole, with its postironic attendant, dressed from head to toe in vintage clothes made of coarse wool that must inflame his skin like a cilice, the expression of studied intolerance . . . the epitome of the Death of Humor.

There is a small jazz group playing just by the shop's door—no way the contrabass could have fitted inside. They are supposed to entertain the audiences that don't seem to be flocking into McSweeney's. I carelessly pace back and forth along the block waiting for something to happen, for something worth photographing. I knew there would be a "concert," but I certainly did not expect it to be *this,* or to start randomly and unannounced on the sidewalk, before even a single bystander arrived. I have already had it with McSweeney and its ornamental caginess, and I see at the block's corner a far more unaffected café from which emanates a tempting smell of croissants. "Chez Isabelle" reads the sign. There is no one at the tables, neither inside nor outside, except for a solitary gentleman with the proverbial mad-scientist hair and wearing flipflops, who's looking at me. I feel an urge to point my Nikon at him and take a picture.

"Are you a photographer?"

"Journalist . . . more or less."

"Aha, we," he says with the innuendo of someone who is addressing a peer, a member of his own clan and blood (his accent is even funnier than mine)—"*we* know beautiful music." He shakes his left thumb in the direction of the McSweeney's band concluding, without lowering his voice, "Not this stuff!" His own pointed critique makes him chuckle.

I ask: "What do you mean by 'we'?"

"*We* . . . we Europeans!" His voice going up an octave on "Europeans," which makes me instinctively stand straight, bring my left hand to my heart and gurgle out Beethoven's *Eroica*. I must have come across, obviously, as a proud co-continental. I should explain where I come from, but I'll let him suffer the uncertainty a bit longer:

"Where do you think I'm from?"

"Why, England, of course!" He is very certain of his assertions. His eyes are green and decidedly smart, not exactly friendly but perfectly sarcastic. He extends his right hand before I can disabuse him of his impression.

"I am Philippe."

I am standing while he is still seated: I tower over him, with a certain self-importance, a position of strength. "Fania." Pause. He gapes for a moment, in disbelief and there is a sudden recognition of the truth: "*Italiana!*" He smiles a full smile. "Italiana!" he repeats, not disappointed at all. "I love Italia!" *Oh, I see, he's French.* "Well," the Frenchman continues, "then I can really say *chez nous* the least of the street musicians could do better." His eloquent thumb shoots again with more vibrancy at the poor sods making noise outside the door of the Victorian cyberpunk neogothic memorabilia shop . . . McSweeney's cabinet of curiosities, Brooklyn's Wunderkammer.

I remind him that if there is one thing Americans have a talent for, it *is* music and street entertainment. The French thumb returns with an air of disgust to point to the musicians, "Not these here!" I wonder why he is having breakfast at Chez Isabelle at 3 PM. I ask him what he does: "I am a musician," he answers raising his bushy eyebrows as if it needn't be said. "And a producer . . . R & B." He asks for my number. In America, men know to give their number to the woman who will be free to make the first move and get in touch, rather than putting her in the unpleasant and potentially dangerous position of being harassed by a semi-stranger. Philippe instead doesn't care for new-century formalities and takes my number.

I return home with a far more positive impression of this Philippe than of McSweeney's band.

On the Ⓕ train, on the way back, I start to write my piece for Gwidon in my head. I already know how I will title it: "La Fama del Mistero: Il (semplice) caso (letterario) McSweeney's" ("Fame and Mystery: The [simple] McSweeney's [literary] case") to satirize the postmodern bracketing. It will begin: "Crisis or no crisis, one thing America will never lack: an army of writers, young and old, famous or starving in anonymity, ready to publish whatever sells, whose password is 'being there, being there, being there.' Visibility in America, and especially in this omnivorous cult-maker that is New York, means everything." My description will include the following: "Aesthetically the opposite of the image we have of the penniless avant-garde, McSweeney's is a tiny booklet (sometimes a box of unbound pages), extremely elegant, and insanely expensive for those who produce it and those who buy it." Then: "McSweeney's is elitist. It's irreverent. It's the father of the new fashionable *démodé* trend. And it is the latest brilliant, if a little disturbing, gimmick by Dave Eggers, one of the creators of the now-defunct *Might,* the satirical magazine from San Francisco." The adrenaline flood, building up since this morning, is about to collapse: the reckless trip to Brooklyn, the new things I saw, the Philippe-guy who found me attractive, the thought of throwing myself into writing, which has always brought me happiness and pride and loads of money . . . I'm exhilarated. What a New York day! Let's not forget that writing short pieces every week for *Politicus* could mean my freedom to dedicate myself full time to the PhD. No other jobs would be necessary.

After their sustained surge, dopamine and serotonin begin a dizzying spiral descent. I want to walk around Manhattan until sunset and then go home, take a bath, and watch a good movie on TV. In my own clean (*I hired a maid*), cozy home. Me and Milli in our apartment, *chez nous.*

I have my job, my graduate courses, my own apartment in New York City, my cat, an unlisted phone number, an international restraining order against we-know-who; I am surrounded by things that I chose, that I created myself: I have certainties now. I just need all this to stay put, to not disappear or be taken away from me. I am recovering. When dark thoughts overtake me, I find the panacea in walking through Central Park, cheese shopping at Zabar's, eating Dobos Torte at the Hungarian Café, or tuning in to WNYC's Jonathan Schwartz's Saturday night radio show of old American standards. I'm a bit lonely. But that's no matter, is it? Who isn't lonely?

A week ago, I even dyed my hair for the first time in my life: now I am autumnal red. I barely recognized myself in the mirror when after three hours of dozing off on the hairdresser's chair, in Greenwich Village, I opened my eyes. Amir, the Israeli coiffeur, who doesn't speak a word of English and is also a bit dim, was very pleased with the results. Poor Amir: he has no hope in the world of getting a green card. Gay marriage being illegal, he has that route precluded to him. He lives in fear of deportation, and in a low and tremulous voice asked me for clues on how to get a green card, and how I did it. "Well,

I got it through the graduate program at Brandeis," I lied with impassive nonchalance. *I came for seven days and ended up staying for seven years.*

I like it when the sun illuminates the apartment, beaming through every window. I set the table with cheese, olives, and bread and tune in to Jonathan Schwartz for a four-hour marathon of Sinatra, Bennet, Fitzgerald, Pizzarelli and a few contemporary good ones. The phone rings.

On the other side of the receiver, I perceive a festive air: young voices, talking in the background and singing. A beautiful male voice finally addresses me: "Do you want to have children?" I gasp, wince, search for words. "Ciaò," he says in Italian, stressing the wrong syllable like only French people can. "It's Philippe, we met yesterday at Chez Isabelle . . . You want to have children?" What kind of question is this? I never did and never will want to be a mother. It's not that I hate children per se, but that I despise the people who want them. *Although, a tad contradictorily, I wouldn't mind if someone loved me so much and thought me the ideal mother for his offspring. I would still say Bugger off!, but I would like to be seen that way by the right one.* "No," I say and regret it immediately because it makes me sound ugly, degenerate, and because I don't know what answer he's looking for and I really want to give him the right answer, not the undiluted truth I just blurted out.

He says "Excellent!" and asks me out for a drink.

Philippe's English is perfect: with idioms, syntax, slang, current jargons all in the right place and a vast vocabulary . . . but all slightly coated in a French accent. This is because despite being born in Louisville, Kentucky, to a Canadian father who always lived in the US, his mother, Micheline Chabbat, is Parisian, and after divorcing her philandering husband, when her son was three years old, she took him to France to be brought up by her mother in a civilized place. After high school, Philippe joined his father in Los Angeles for about ten years, then returned to Paris for another ten, and now he is again phasing through the "American decade," which he is spending in Brooklyn this time around. He quickly reveals his age too and I wonder if he is trying to deliver all the bad news upfront to give me an out. He is thirteen years older than me. But for the quickie I have in mind, I wouldn't care if he had been born before or after the Great War.

I'm excited about the idea of this date. It will be necessary to shave thoroughly. Especially there where no man has roamed in years. I am by nature so hairy that if I don't keep it under control my hair would stick out of my pants and start grafting to the next person's leg like an invasive vine. I want so much to look cool for this bloke. I check the latest arrivals from Rome. (My parents haven't stopped overnighting me parcels, at regular three-month intervals.) In addition to clothes, shoes, underwear, *collants,* invaluable pieces of jewelry, and money, these parcels bring me food of all kinds, especially cheese, *pizza bianca* from the downstairs bakery, roasted chestnuts, Danesi coffee beans, and basil seeds to be planted in terracotta pots on the fire escape. Problem is, there is very little to buy in Manhattan. Even the Italian stylists who have branches here send to America what they think can be appreciated by local customers, that is, what Italians discard. As far as clothing goes, in the Anglo-Saxon world (especially in England, I should add), men are lucky. Women are not. American women appear to stick to two basic options: skirts and dresses above the knee (but never mini, God forbid!) for formal, informal, and who-cares events; and for all-eyes-are-on-you occasions, they invariably clad themselves like Deborah Kerr when she dances with Yul Brynner in *The King and I* . . . unfailingly bare shouldered. In sum, the choice here is always between Jackie O. or a puffy meringue.

I choose a white shirt made by our family tailor in Rome and a pair of studiedly torn jeans. I don't even own a skirt. I've given up for good pantyhose and pushup bras. I've opted out of perfume forever. I wear knee-high boots, like the dominatrix I'll never be. I go for a full Brazilian. Maybe I'll buy into vegetarianism. Maybe I'll start drinking a glass of red wine (though sulfates give me urinary tract infections). Maybe I'll smoke a joint every now and then. I never drank, smoked, used needles, used public toilets, or as much as sat down on a sidewalk. A bit of excess will do me good (if by "excess" we mean a bit of nail polish and maybe—maybe—going out without a hat).

Philippe invited me to join him in a club where a French friend of his is playing in the East Village. Philippe is late. It's cold and damp out, and the moisture in the air is devolumizing my hair. I had ironed it, extensively, with a giant electric tool bought for the occasion, but it is starting to dangerously fizz up again on the back while sagging in the front under the effect of the drizzling rain. Another drop of rain and the black mascara will reach my chin. Maybe I should leave. The alley is dark, and I am self-conscious standing here all alone while groups of friends and couples enter the club together. There he is! *Was that him?* I saw a figure of a man appearing out of nowhere, in such haste that the tail of his long coat flapped in the air as if he were on horseback. How tall! I did not remember him so tall . . . obviously because he remained seated throughout our chat by Chez Isabelle.

It's him. I jump over to the opposite sidewalk like a cat pounces on a bird. I gently touch his shoulder—I tremble a bit, it might not be him, and if it's him I'd tremble all the same. He swivels around and with a big smile of relief tells me he's glad I didn't leave. He apologizes for the lateness. I'm really happy to be here with Philippe. I feel that Philippe will always be a bit late, however.

We make out on a long sofa in the club, like two teenagers. A perfect kisser. In fact, the best kisser in personal memory. He invites me to a recording session at his house. I'll see him again on Saturday.

I discovered several things about Philippe that did not trigger any kind of alarm. For example, he is very straightforward: not so much incapable as much as unwilling to lie. He doesn't like it and doesn't do it. That easy. Life's too short, and he, at forty-five, has no time to waste. He was never married and never even got close to it, mostly because he doesn't appreciate the genre in the first place. I surmise that his parents' unfriendly divorce gave form to a natural reluctance to the concept of bourgeois family, sanctioned by a meaningless piece of paper and children. Philippe is imposing: his height and features bear traces of the Franco-Saxon DNA from the promiscuous times of Louis VII of France and Henry II of England, his leonine head, thick and disheveled eyebrows, straight shoulders, thin legs, and hirsute masculine arms. Only when he allows himself to laugh out loud can one see the upper and lower dental crowding typical of the British conformation, but, lucky for him, the Gallic sarcasm calls for ironic chortles rather than the coarse open-mouthed roars unsuited to less than ideal dentitions (and unlike me, whose tiniest smile stretches my face to a spasm between my overly pronounced cheekbones, showing everything down to the last molar).

At one point, Philippe pulls a device out of his coat pocket, brings it to his mouth, fires a puff from it and inhales deeply. He seems to suffer from acute asthma and is particularly allergic to cats.

He speaks with tender affection of *mémé,* his grandmother, who brought him up, feeding him tasty buttery foods. And his cousin, François, an only child like him, also brought up by the same *mémé,* to whom he is terribly attached. François is the son of Micheline's sister, who died very young. "Franc is an alcoholic" Philippe says without judgment, as a pure and simple piece of information that causes him much pain: "He goes in and out of useless rehabs in the south of France." He must be a very loyal person, this Philippe. I haven't heard a single snarky comment about those he loves. He speaks with disdain of his father, Gene; I don't suppose he likes him, but he admires him for his success as a writer and music journalist and for the jet-set life he lived during the debauched postwar years. The old man has been a lyricist for Sinatra and Bennett and the discoverer of Bossa Nova. The fact that he discovered it during a visit in Brazil on the trail of one of his exotic lovers at the time (while Micheline nursed their first child, alone and disgusted by the ugliness of Kentucky) will not formally make it into any of Gene's official biographies.

Philippe seems to look at me with interest, as if he awaited all my Italianness to flow out of me and into him at any moment . . . like a juice he can squeeze out of an orange and enjoy to the last drop. *Fat chance of that!* I have little Italianness in me. It never served me well. Philippe says, "*Parle-moi en italien.*" I do it and I realize that Philippe's Italian is nonexistent. But neither is he vexed by this: he is convinced that by osmosis, and with time, he will speak it as well as I. *With time? Have we got time?*

Philippe has always played the piano. It must have been the only concession by Micheline to her musical husband: knowing he had a father immersed in the world of American music, Philippe must have chosen this path to feel closer to that sensational, invisible man. Modestly he identifies as a piano player. In fact, he studied both jazz and classical music. But the concert career wasn't for him, and I can see that this is the secret thorn in Philippe's big heart.

We have a great night. We say goodbye with the arrangement of seeing each other again by week's end, in Park Slope. (*Oh no, the Ⓕ train again!*) On the way back, as always when I want to prolong a good day or the feeling that there are still endless possibilities open for me, when I want to chat with New York and tell it about my feelings, I get off on 110th Street and walk a few extra blocks along Broadway, among so many other *flâneurs,* and watch people (*people like me!*) still sitting in coffee shops, restaurants, and diners for a bite and a chat at 2 AM. The city that never sleeps.

Not ten minutes pass from the moment I set foot into his house (360 14th Street, Brooklyn, NY 11215, a crumbly brownstone), we end up horizontal on his sofa bed—already unfolded, or perhaps still unfolded from the previous night (a "No-no!" in my personal decalogue). I have an experience out of a romance novel. Philippe puts a graceful, respectful, yet decisive and virile calm in his love-making that seems to give a whole new meaning to the oldest act in the world. It's the first time I am having sex in years. Perhaps it's the first time ever. The foreplay is revolutionary. The coition is epic. Its effect on me is not electric, as they say, but volcanic: it is not a lightning current which shocks but lasts a moment, but rather it is like a slow lava, which takes unexpected paths and maintains its intensity from beginning to end, incorporating, burning, and at the same time fertilizing everything it comes in contact with.

I know practically nothing of love in America. My main sources of information on the subject remain films and situation comedies. The latter especially always imply that new lovers never sleep together all night through at first: it seems to be a national taboo. It is certainly not a problem in Europe: if one has the space available, it seems only obvious that the person you are having sex with (even if it is a touch-and-go type of situation) stays until the next day. It's a courtesy! This is not taken, as it is in America, as an implicit marriage vow. In America love is like figure skating: each step is studiously preconfigured—no improvisations allowed, and always surrounded by frost.

After doing it a second time, at which point it gets dark outside, I wonder if I should get up and leave. I begin to calculate: Philippe is American (*I probably best go*) but was brought up in Paris (*perhaps not as carnal as Naples, but neither as paranoidly defensive as Los Angeles*). While I weigh my bets, Philippe sleeps quietly: he naked, me naked. He puts his arm around my torso, as if to hold me and stop me in case I wished to get up and get away. It's decided.

I am cold, but I dare not say it or move. I would like to sleep too, but I can't. Inside, I'm in turmoil. I listen to the muffled and sparse noises from the street. People walking, a couple of cars, probably cabs driving people home after a party. It is very calm here. I hear the radiator hum and begin its classic hammering on the iron, followed by something like a locomotive hiss, and finally the intense heat spreads through the air. My naked body stops shivering. From the next room, the recording devices emit a bluish light that breaks through what would otherwise be almost complete darkness. I imagine the singers with whom Philippe works standing by those microphones, beating the rhythm with one foot and snapping their fingers, while the lyricists correct a rhyme or revise a text on the fly, with other people just lounging around to have fun, improvise catchy melodies, perhaps crowding this very sofa bed. (*Eww, better not think about that.*) My eyelids are heavy and I know slumber is finally hanging from them; but before giving in, I take a last look around: very big, half-burnt candles on the mantelpiece, an upright piano against the most beautiful wall, an antique armchair that invites a reader to lose himself on it but on which, at present, there's a pile of coats, shirts, music sheets, magazines, books, and clumped Kleenexes.

I am already asleep, but not so deeply as not to notice that Philippe is pulling a bed sheet and covering me with it. A bed sheet against my nakedness in the New York winter frost is not much, but I immediately feel an intense warmth envelop me, the body of Philippe very close to mine, a new sense of joy. I clearly feel that at this moment, through this embrace in my sleep, this gesture of tenderness, this imperturbable nocturnal silence, I am part of the world of the living. Of that world that for decades I have watched from afar, behind a soundproof glass, unbreakable. A great sense of peace, of gratitude, makes me fall asleep.

I wake up when he does because my sleep is very light, like that of a fugitive. Perhaps also because I've been nervously aware that I didn't take out my contact lenses and if I fell asleep too deeply they could have moved off and gotten stuck somewhere behind my eyeballs, sucked into my brain, and I was dreading the humiliation of having to run to the hospital, of bothering my lover on top of losing my eyesight. First thing I notice is that his arm is still woven around mine. He spooned me all night long, never left my body. I notice his strong skin covered with blond hair against my arm punctuated by freckles. I gradually turn around before he comes to entirely, and what I see leaves me baffled. There's a sock lying across his face, a cotton sock to shield his eyes from the light . . . there is also a pillow held between his legs as if his knees were forbidden to touch each other and a heap of cushions supporting his back—including the one that was supposed to be under my head. I don't know how to hold back the laughter that rises from my belly; this ridiculous view has freed my happiness from the humid and inhospitable jails of sadness in which it was stored. I laugh to tears now. Maybe I slept only a few minutes, I can't tell, but I feel as refreshed as if I had been out a week, like Orlando, the character of Virginia Woolf's homonymous novel. I loved *Orlando* the first time I read it! I'll have to tell Philippe, who loves books, and maybe we'll read it together one day if he'd like to. If he'd like to see me again.

We dress and slowly, chatting all along, we walk to Chez Isabelle for breakfast. There is Isabelle herself today, who immediately notices us. She pretends to be happy, but it's clear that she is a little piqued. She speaks to Philippe with great familiarity, puckering her French lips in the shape of a hen's ass every time she pronounces those perfect *ou*'s and *ü*s. He responds with measured distance, but with a naturalness that makes me understand that it is Isabelle who is playing a part—the part of a woman closer to Philippe than she will ever be—while he is implicitly telling the truth through his body language. Isabelle is beaten. She gives us two buttery croissants and two cups of coffee, and we bring everything outside, to a table on the sidewalk. It is as if time stood still: we have nothing else to do, we're neither in a hurry nor its opposite, whatever that is . . . there is only this moment and nothing to worry about. I don't think I've ever been so serene and present—not even at yoga, where we are told "Stay in the moment!" a hundred times but not how to do it. I physically feel the weight of Isabelle's eyes piercing at my nape while she stares at us from behind the counter. I was alone the day I met Philippe at this same corner, and now I am with him, neither alone nor lonely.

How long will it last? Will there be a second time? Is it only a temporary courtesy, a short miracle, which has already run its course like all miracles? I am fine in this picture, I fit impeccably: I cannot say it out loud, but does Philippe see it too, how well I fit here? I am careful not to reveal my story to Philippe. The hell with the past. I swing around to look at Isabelle still standing behind the glass: I am scared to think that this encounter was an isolated parenthesis. It'll be up to Philippe: If he decides we'll see each other again, we will, otherwise this croissant from Isabelle *chez-elle* will remain as unique and isolated as I am (*chez moi*).

Philippe does not seem to worry about the present *or* the future. He is extremely relaxed in his skin, emanates an L.A. 1960s vibe. He has a mastery over himself that makes me feel like both a woman and a child at the same time. We go home to make love again. Philippe plays the piano and I turn the score pages. The light through the old windows begins to turn golden, it is already almost sunset. I have to go home, wash, check on Milli, metabolize the events and feelings of the last twenty-four hours, prepare for tomorrow's workday. (*The sheer thought of that kills the smile on my face; the nine-to-five routine is so disheartening.*)

The subway journey gives me time to reflect. The Sunday crowd is pleas- anter than the weekday one. Perhaps because I feel closer to these strangers now, we have something in common, me and them, now. Now I am like them, I too am part of the world of the living, not just of the vegetative. I am beautiful, I radiate a light that is both animal and sexy. I notice eyes looking at me, friendly smiles, chivalrous gestures along with the traditional attitudes of indifference that never fail but that today I have the benevolence to interpret not as hate against me but mere distraction. I'm so comfortable in this city. I open my apartment door, carrying sushi and a tub of strawberry Häagen- Dazs, and I am greeted by the smell of me, of my things, of my peaceful life, the joyful Milli that slowly, not to give me too much satisfaction at once, gets off the sofa, bows, stretches, and finally rubs herself against my ankles sniff- ing, I'm sure, the smell of my night with Philippe. She is sniffing Philippe for the first time. The phone rings, and it is him, wanting to make sure I got home without problems. If there existed an antonym for "problem" in the dictionary, this would be the time to use it, because I don't think I have been as problem-free as today since November 1978.

A new week begins but this morning my commute to work is not as cum- bersome as usual: I don't care how long it takes, I don't care that the train is full, I don't care about what they'll assign me at the office, and I won't care to execute it less than perfectly because I have other things on my mind, more appreciable, more nutritious for the soul and the imagination. I let myself be swayed by the rhythmic movement of the subway, and I think that we will see each other, Philippe and I, on Friday. (He informed me of it as if it were a routine I must get used to and can take for granted.) If this is the case, then I'll soon invite him over to have dinner at my place. The idea of cooking for him spooks me a little: I'm competing against his *mémé*. He is going to pick me up at work for my lunch break today: my office is by Murray Hill, the area between East 29th and 40th, which is jokingly known as Curry Hill, because of its Asiatic ethnic profile. Indeed, it abounds with Indo-Pakistani restaurants and take-out joints whose flavors pour out onto the streets from morning to evening, and it's as if the air of the whole neighborhood were made of cumin. I already anticipate that we'll get something to go and enjoy it on one of the benches overlooking the East River. Someone is gently brushing my arm, as if to wake me up, to call me to attention. I shake out of my reverie, refocus on reality, and find myself face to face with Yonah.

Yonah.

Yonah smiling at me.

As soon as he realizes that I have finally put him into focus, he gives me, with affectionate impetus, a warm hug. We hug each other and like newborn mice squeal happily: how arbitrary to meet like this on a train! The other passengers look at us, intrigued. Every private event becomes public in this city and, bored with the daily doldrums, commuters always welcome the opportunity to witness an unusual scene, especially about other people's business aired live before their eyes. If only they knew how special this scene is! But from where they stand, they can't tell, and they lose interest, they return to their books, their 25-cent newspapers, they reposition the headphones to cover their ears or they keep staring, semi-comatosely, at the nothingness rushing by at high speed outside the train's window.

We bring each other up to speed, as fast as we can, we tell, we ask. It feels as if we haven't seen each other for a week, rather than for years. Here we are. Yonah and me in New York. I find him well, he finds me well. His hair, already inclined to gray six years ago, has now taken on a more distinguished elegance, gentlemanlike, less like a college kid, than when we first met, although he kept that unique resemblance to Alec Baldwin mixed with Cary Grant accentuated today by aging. I wonder what he sees reflected in me. It's a bit like bringing to a close a circle that we began tracing more than half a decade ago. I came to New York without him; and now, without owing him a thing, I've built my own path here. I even have my own apartment. Of course, I tell him about that. At least that can help give an impression of success, finally. To someone who's known me only since 1996, like he has, my life must appear as a braid of flopped strands, an inexhaustible chain of failures. I wish so much to give him a better impression. We have not lost the habit, nor the rhythm, of speaking simultaneously, yet without missing anything the other says. I weave one sentence after another, afraid that if I stop tears may start rolling down my face.

> Me: "On Amsterdam and 122nd. Right behind the Jewish Theologi-
> cal Seminary, yes. I'll start adjuncting this fall. City College. I know!
> Around the corner from Yeshiva, your kingdom! Do you know the
> Hungarian Café? . . . Who knows how many times we passed each
> other there then?"
> He: "Congratulations! I am still at Yeshiva, and I am up for promotion.
> Yes, tenure. I know the Hungarian Café! It's the greatest place! I'm
> often there."

With the corner of the eye, I notice looks of renewed curiosity all around us. In my opinion we emanate an air of romantic complicity that does not escape the alert observer. It may also be because we are speaking in rather loud voices to get the better of the public announcers, the screeching of wheels on the train tracks, and the uninterrupted miscellaneous background noises.

"I enrolled at the Graduate Center to finish the PhD," I say.

"I live in Washington Heights, you know, we are very close!" he says.

"I am sorry we haven't spoken in so long," I say.

"Adina and I are separated," he says.

They split up.

They have a young son, Frederic. (*Mazal tov!*)

"It's my fault, Adina has always been against my friends . . ." he says.

"Aww," I say.

Some passengers take a half step forward to get closer and not miss anything of this conversation that begins to reveal juicy plot twists. I mean, it doesn't take superhuman brilliance, if one paid attention so far, to stitch together the pieces of this story. It's definitely getting interesting.

"Are you seeing someone?" *No, please don't ask!! Not so point-blank! Shiiiit.* "No," I lie. My pitch way too high. I am back to lying to Yonah. Yonah and the truth permanently travel on separate train tracks, they never arrive at the same time. Here we go again. I look outside, I must get off: we reached Grand Central Station 42nd Street. He must get off too. So I pretend it's not my stop. *Lies, lies, lies.* I will backtrack by foot, not a problem, I'll definitely need the walk. I feel the grip of his goodbye hug extend that extra moment it takes to demarcate the abyssal difference between a hug among friends and a hug among two people who still love each other. My heart sinks. My blood boils as it rushes to recondite organs I have no use for. 212–662–4641. I scribble down my phone number, and he his, we'll talk, we'll meet soon, for now we wave bye-bye through the train door that slides closed, I see him standing on the quay still looking in my direction, with his hands in his coat pockets, and a sweet smile spread through every millimeter of his face.

Of all days! I repeat incredulously. Of all days! "*I met my old lover on the street last night, she seemed so glad to see me, I just smiled. . .*" *There's a Paul Simon's song for every occasion in life.* I notice the passengers who were eavesdropping on our conversation a moment ago are now putting the pieces of an intriguing love puzzle together at last, they study my reaction attentively: I smile to them with a look of understanding as if they were extras I hired to fake a crowded train and who played their part successfully in getting Yonah into my trap. But there was no trap. It was a fortuitous moment. I am the one who fell in a trap, if anything. But what could I tell him? "Yes, I have a boyfriend . . . since yesterday. I am seeing this Philippe bloke." My story with Philippe is too fresh, I do not know where it will land: how can I foreclose the possibility of a meeting with Yonah in the name of a virtually nonexistent relationship with someone met seven days ago, with whom I only slept one night. I have to stall. I need a strategy to slow down the course of the events and give myself time to figure out in which lifeboat to jump.

"*Still crazy, after all these years.*"

# 13

With Philippe, things proceed swimmingly. Every so often I get a call from Yonah inviting me to do something together: I stall, I play for time. "A Viennese coffee at the Hungarian place on Amsterdam and 111th, as we had said?" I'm dying to say yes, but I find an excuse to avoid it, until the invitations decrease, and I pretend not to notice. He is separated from Adina. He is single. I am almost single. And we're both in the same city, a stone's throw away from one another again, only sixty-two blocks, same West side. (*I like to be in America! pa pa pa pa pa pa pa paaam Everything free in Americaaa!*) We could finally have *our* West Side Story.

A few years have gone by, and fate offers us, with an apology, and on a silver plate, a second chance, this time less complicated than the previous one: "An offer he can't refuse," says Don Corleone. An offer we can't refuse. Except I'm not exactly single, and I can't make up my mind about becoming so for Yonah. He is on the threshold of his way out of his love story, I am on the threshold of my way into mine. And now he is a father. One doesn't interfere with this stuff. Not me. And if Philippe is the right one? On whom do I place my chips? On whom to bet? I seem to be constantly at a crossroads. There's no driving forward if the way is but a jumble of bifurcations . . . and no road signs.

Philippe is not connected to any nefarious past. He is a clean page, an elegant, tall "page" with green eyes and the prospect of musical evenings with the New York rhythm & blues jet set, trips to Acapulco, cocktails in Tribeca lofts, a future held by manly arms covered with soft blond hair.

My life now has the rhythm of *Somebody Loves Me* played by the Erroll Garner Trio without any certainty that somebody does love me but with a strong hope that it is the case. Weekends with Philippe are idyllic. When we are together, a great sense of peace invades me. The days warm up and lengthen. We like to spend them in Central Park. Above all, we like to sit on a bench and watch the people who parade in front of us: our criticisms are fierce and hilarious.

As far as I am concerned, the fact that, for him, I accept to sit on a public bench is already a major breakthrough. The unknowing nose would confuse for smoked paprika what I clearly know to be the stale stench of a tramp's cloak. The benches reek of it. This is my thinking: a smell doesn't linger much, especially in the open, because the molecules it is made of are weightless, volatile thingies. So if the nauseating stench succeeds in sticking to a park bench (in a park, the epitome of open air), I wonder what other residues, heavier and more anchorable than air molecules, we are taking home on our clothes, in our pores, and inside our throat every time we part our lips. Such considerations leave Philippe cold. If I said this to Yonah, he would ask me to develop my theory on the subject more fully, and before I had finished he too would start to squirm on the bench, feel as uncomfortable as I, and before too late we would both jump up and leave in a state of disgust, incapable of ever touching another public bench. Philippe, instead, admits that I am right, scoffs and with aristocratic carelessness declares: "Enough paranoias, *la poupette!*" When he makes fun of me, he calls me *poupette* like his grandfather did his wife—which is both funny and so sweet. With his disheveled looks, yesterday's stubble (his 5 PM shadow at noon), clean clothes but put together messily, and inopportune flip-flops matched to a warm silk scarf, he cracks me up. If he thinks I will not get a bubonic infection from sitting on a public bench, maybe I will not actually get it. They are two perfect versions of the same wonderful thing, Philippe and Yonah. And I wish I could have both.

One evening, we are on the street, on our way back from a restaurant, Philippe intones a song:

*"It's very clear . . . "*

He begins. He looks into my eyes and then at a distant point on the road ahead of us. Every stride of his equals three of mine: I look like a raccoon running next to a giraffe. He continuous vibratingly:

*"Our love is here to stay*
*Not for a year, but forever and a day . . ."*

He sings it like Gene Kelly in *An American in Paris,* soft and languid. And I, a completely inverted image of Leslie Caron, I melt . . .

I don't say anything. My eyes burn as if the air were full of smoke. Philippe, wrapping an arm around my shoulders, bends slightly to reach my face, now red with ill-concealed elation, and says: "This is for you, *la poupette.*"

At home, in bed, with Milli still squatting at our feet, Philippe inhales two puffs from his asthma blower.

In May, I plan a trip to Mexico, to an island called Isla Mujeres. The expenses have been many in the last months, between the purchase of the apartment, the move, the renovations, and the furniture; by the end of spring, I will resign from my full-time job to become a full-time student, at which point I will no longer be able to count on a fixed and abundant income. A restorative journey, I feel, is called for. At the news, without batting an eyelash, Philippe reacts: "But I'm coming too!" He says this as if it is the most self-evident of facts. I sit back at my computer, log into Travelocity, and I buy him a ticket. Grandma Binde would have called this *"gli affari di Maria Calzetta,"* a rip-off. Not only do I not find the lover who buys me a ticket to a paradise island, but I must buy it for my lover. An obviously hereditary family defect. I come from a long genealogy of people who always pay, metaphorically and literally. The word "free" is not in my experiential vocabulary. I pay even when something is free for everyone else.

I never eat at free buffets, parties, or ceremonies where the libations are provided by the host. If I go to a potluck, I don't touch what other guests have brought—out of skepticism toward other people's hygienic standards—and neither what I myself contributed—for fear of acting cheaply and in bad taste. In the American office cosmos, they have a habit of offering their high-ranking employees huge quantities of bagels and various delicacies for breakfast during big meetings. I observed my colleagues gorge themselves, taking advantage of this opportunity for a free meal, and once the meeting ends bring piles of stuff, prudently covered under a paper towel, to their cubicles . . . and later on to share at home with their spouses and children. These, I always think, are the kind of people who, in a concentration camp, safe from arbitrary selections, will always survive. I am not in this league. I come from a family of born payers. *Zio* Adriano is always the first to put hand to his wallet. My parents always host people at their home, but I have never seen them pass the threshold of other people's houses, not since I can remember. They have instilled in me a sense of hospitality in line with Homeric culture. We invite. We pay tickets for events we won't go to. If they ask us for 5, we give 7, so as not to give the wrong impression ("wrong" meaning miserly). If someone takes something from us, we look the other way to keep our dignity before the collapse of the other's. We insist on trusting those who betray us, because the alternative, to admit that we don't know how to choose whom to surround ourselves with, is too intolerable. On the whole, we are a family of adorable losers.

I make reservations for a hotel at random. The island is so tiny that I doubt the range between good and bad can be that vast. It is the first time in my life that I will go on vacation, a proper vacation (like the commonest tourists do), with a . . . a . . . date? partner? boyfriend? Never mind the title. Butterflies flutter in my pretzeled stomach like when a rollercoaster speeds downward, into the abyss. I am so scared of messing up the plans, of giving Philippe a poor impression of me, and of making mistakes in general. He who, as a young man with his father, frequented the most famous names from the jazz and blues scenes, in places like Copacabana Beach, Miami, and Los Angeles. Oscar Peterson held him on his knees. He sat on the stool of some fancy music studio while Sinatra recorded *Just in Time* or *Corcovado* with Jobim, translated into English by his dad, Gene. Philippe knows all about cocktails and does not need to use too many words to make a good impression, because in his presence you immediately sense that he knows what he's talking about when he speaks as well as when he is silent. Those thirteen years of difference between us, and two continents, make *all* the difference.

For the first time in my life, I am going to fly with someone on the plane with me. I cry of happiness, as I swallow two Dramamines, rest my head on his lap, and sleep until we reach Cancun.

I pay because Philippe is penniless. And I must say that the class with which he admits it does not offend me at all. On the other hand, I am doing very well financially, and why shouldn't I take care of us? In my constant quest for the ideal life, a quest for which I shattered some serious world records in failure, perhaps this is what I failed to grasp: that I subconsciously hold my independence dearer than the subjugation to a Prince Charming. My liberty defines me. Once you accept as little as one candy, you enter the status of debtor and take on the severe duty of gratitude. *What haven't I done to show gratitude!* When we run into a *clochard* on the street, Philippe imperatively says: "*Poupette,* give me five dollars." He, who doesn't have five dollars to his name, always uses my money to give alms to the poor. (Those other poor.) As I giggle inside and imagine the witty jokes my dad and uncle would make about us being a family of fools (always taken for a ride by whoever comes around), I happily reach for the purse in my handbag.

We have our fixed points: Café Minerva in Greenwich Village, a favorite of Philippe's; my favorite winter hangout is Café Lalo on West 83rd. The cinema we go to weekly is the Angelika (when he chooses) or the Lincoln Cinema (when I choose). At the concerts at Lincoln Center, where it finally makes sense to pay the prohibitive annual membership, we become uncontrollably emotional: each *chord,* each *phrasing,* each *bar* from Mendelssohn, Brahms, or Tchaikovsky invades and breaks something inside of us, and we abandon ourselves to sobs, positively shocking those around us. I believe that in terms of aesthetic sensibility, we are twin souls. Like a magic trick, the music draws out of our innermost chambers all sets of extraordinary images that surge into our brains. What one sees while listening to music is very personal and unique to each individual: but Philippe and I share a sentiment, a transport, a link with this music that clearly possesses a psychological as well as physiological power over us. It reaches us, it ensnares our viscera, it forces us to face that which, during the prosaic everyday moments, we pretend doesn't exist, which is a sense of the sublime to which we can expose ourselves only marginally and briefly, lest we die: because such magnificence, far beyond mere beauty, is too painful to tolerate. Its immensity crushes our smallness. The sublime is terrifying, as Kant correctly argued in the *Critique of Pure Reason;* in its presence, the mind experiences true agony when it's confronted by something it can't even begin to contemplate. The failure to express this enormous, overwhelming feeling is frightful, but, simultaneously, satisfying and rewarding in that it causes boundless exhalated pleasure. *Verweile doch, du bist so schön*–Goethe's Faust tells Mephistopheles, his life's stopwatch. The only way to keep forever that alchemical, perfect moment, is to freeze life right when it happens. *So schön . . .* so beautiful!

Philippe and I zigzag through miles of clothing racks, rooms, and salons at Bergdorf Goodman's. A few steps from it we enter the majestic Plaza Hotel. If I could, I would live at the Plaza, one of the most enchanting places in the city. I look with a bored expression at the jewelry display, with the phony ennui of the upper class that I know so well. I adore the tearoom on the Plaza's ground floor, with its Beaux-Arts décor, small round tables, antique chairs, and the huge crystal chandeliers. If I lived at the Plaza, I would have tea here every afternoon and I wouldn't need to bother to order because all staff members would know my preferences and jump into action as soon as I open the door of the Lady Mendl suite, where I'd reside, like Marlene Dietrich before me. On the other hand, leaving the house, if my house were indeed the Plaza Hotel, would be a real endurance test to the stomach because Central Park South is horse-carriage garage: the stench of horse manure mixed with rain water and the carcasses of pigeons is one of the most nauseating the city can offer—second only, but not by far, to the gangrenous smell on the subway trains. On the contrary, when I come out of the subway near home, the real one, I never smell anything bad. Downstairs from us, they are opening a nineteenth-century style café that features a pastiche of unmatching chairs and unmatching tables, not well lit but completely open over the sidewalk, like a theater stage, which produces plenty of natural sunlight to read by. So now, at most, I expect to get a faded aroma of organic sandwiches and pseudo-French pastries as I enter my building.

Yoga is about to end: exactly one year after I started, the guru, Michelle, has told us that she is going back to California where she got the job of her dreams. *Hollywood? Trainer for the stars? Actress?* She didn't specify. It is certainly a coincidence, but a year of Sun Salutation, Parivrtta Traikonasana spasms, and breathing through the Third Eye opened the cosmic gates of miracles. I hope the universe will not shut them down as Michelle departs.

I continue to work as a freelance translator and editor, and I also get a super fun job as language coach for the Metropolitan's opera singers. They need someone to correct their pronunciation in Italian, so that, in the name of the right note, the clarity of the utterance not be sacrificed. I'm their man! It pays exceedingly well and allows me to get a lot of free tickets for me and Philippe. I am forgetting sorrow. Pleasure finally outweighs it. I often formulate in my head a strange question whose power to calm me down resides in the simple posing it to myself (*the neuroses obviously are all steadily in place*): Who knows, will I be in a relationship with Philippe for three months? After the three-month mark, surprised that nothing horrible has happened and that Philippe and I are still together with the same joy and harmony that we experienced from the outset, I start again the neurotic mantra: Who knows, will I be in a relationship with Philippe for a year?" It becomes a magic formula, an apotropaic spell, a superstitious repetition that no longer leaves me.

Philippe is the idyllic alternative to the world I barely escaped. With Philippe, I am in New York, in total anonymity, and I don't have to answer to anyone. Anonymity is a form of self-protection to which, years ago, at the summit of my ambition, I had not given its proper importance. Years ago, I also believed in the good faith of those who make mistakes. Then I met with Gwidon Goldblatt again.

Gwidon arrived in New York following the 9/11 attack. His mission is to create an exclusive entourage of permanent collaborators who will cover the news from the States. Being that investigation is his thing, he located me. He asked me to pick him up at his apartment. ("*All within the norm! Don't fret! Just a quick bite, I'll show you my place and we'll go from there!*") I go brimming with enthusiasm, my heart bursting with the joy for an old friendship about to bloom again. I also brought my piece about McSweeney's. This is going to be awesome! A rotten history is going to be folded into a glorious future! I am so ready for this! I'll blow his mind. He'll be bowled over. On a nonpartisan playground, in New York not Rome, I can now fight and win the match on an equal footing. Now I hold all the right cards in my hand.

I haven't got time however to put any of my enviable professional qualities on the table. I hardly have time to cross the threshold to his apartment before he starts to grope me, patting me like a pear at the market, checking my ripeness with his lascivious, rosy little fingers . . . ten prehensile penises, circumcised to the quick. I wiggle out of his hands pretending he is tickling me. Giggling, I fake playfulness. With noble grace, I disabuse him of his expectations, and as if announcing happy news for which I expect to be congratulated, I inform him that I am now in a relationship: "I have a boyfriend!" And this is my last exchange with Gwidon. Italian people, if you heard of McSweeney's back home, it was certainly not under my signature. For the élite New York bureau, Gwidon will appoint a man: a young guy imported from Rome who, if told to find Times Square, risks falling into the Hudson River. I will never hear from Gwidon Goldblatt again. The disappointment lacerates me. For a minute, I think of death again, to erase the shame, to heal the hurt. But I resist the urge. I have my cat waiting for me, and a gorgeous Frenchman.

Michelle and yoga are gone, so it's up to me now to keep those cosmic doors, if not wide open, at least ajar. I'll deploy my body as a door stopper, if necessary. I'd rather be crushed between the doors of the cosmos than be pushed back into that dark and lonely place from where I escaped just in time before it completely erased me.

Our best hours are at the table, eating. On the couch, watching old movies. In bed, holding each other and contemplating the dream of the glorious future awaiting us, of the *château* that Philippe would like to buy us in France. I learn how to cook. I become braver at the stove: quiches, puddings, panna cotta have no secrets for me. Had it not been for Philippe, I would never have known what a salad tastes like. He teaches me to whisk the most delicious dressings, none of which includes the detested red vinegar, which, omnipresent at my mother's table, drowned all her salads rendering them inedible. And since there is no mischief that karma doesn't stick back in your ass at the right time, now I also bake bread—like Galina, whom I derided so much back when I wasn't her but wished to be. Now I am like Galina (the tiniest bit). I never fail to think of her and smile warmly every time I toss some yeast in the water and start my doughs. Now I am a dedicated vegetarian.

Philippe uncorks the wine, I plunge the pasta in the pot. Philippe makes coffee at the end of the meal and clears the table. I take care of the lighting in the room and make it cozy and soft. We sit on the sofa and each picks a section of the *New York Times*, we point out to each other the funniest cartoons in the *New Yorker* magazine. Philippe plays the piano, and I look outside the window. Philippe plays. We sing. Milli perches next to us. The wine becomes better and better as the evening rolls on. We go for a walk along Broadway . . . never mind the hour, at any time, the later the better. There is always an omelette to be had somewhere at 2 AM. When it is finally time to sleep, Milli nestles in the crook of my lap, and Philippe spoons me tightly (placing a *sockettina*, what he thinks is an Italian word, over his eyes). Philippe lives at 1264 Amsterdam Avenue, too, now. I've never known such love before.

We spend all Christmas breaks and New Year's Eves in Paris. Spring breaks in Rome. Summers in the Tropics. But *comme il faut*, we don't plan our journeys. We are not the type. We are the type who just get plane tickets. We don't research information about a place before we get there, we don't draw up itineraries, even when the right thing to do would be to (at a minimum) prepare and (at best) heed the tips from those who (with lots of time at their disposal, apparently) write trip advisories online and hardcopies for travelers like us . . . but not *like us*. I remember Brett & Galina, their impeccable travel strategies, the minimalist backpacks, the wisdom they apply to preparing themselves for every eventuality, the in-depth information they memorize—like a spy memorizes coded instructions—in order to avoid the surplus weight of the guidebook, and based upon which they are certain to do the right thing, in the right way, at the right time. Philippe and I come up with a zone or, when we are in a mood to be fussy, a country, and somehow we are there a couple of weeks later. The year we pick Costa Rica, we pack our swimwear, two beach towels, and a handful of novels. The only thing we heard about Costa Rica is that tourism there splits into two main options: Western coast, where all Americans go, because of its well-maintained resorts and beautiful golf courses; and the eastern coast, on the Caribbean side, where there is absolutely nothing. We go east.

We fly to San José and ask the taxi driver to bring us to any decent hotel by the bus station, because after a good night's sleep, we'll leave the capital the next morning and, passing through the jungle first, we'll head to the sea. The guy takes us to a relative of his, who runs an "establishment" that can't be called hotel by any stretch of the imagination. The place is filthy but, truth be said, within walking distance from the bus station. Philippe sleeps on a chair, draped with beach towels to avoid contact with it. I lie down on a tiny wood plank, on top of my suitcase . . . literally, like a curled-up kitty.

The taxi driver, who nosily inquires about our travel plans and is quite shocked to hear we have none, gives us friendly advice: *¡No se detengan en Limón!* He proudly boasts about the safety and low criminality rate in his country, so much so that Costa Rica doesn't have an army. (*See, no need to spend money for tourist guides at Barnes & Nobles.*) The only exception being, he insists: Limón. It is a very dangerous place, the Rotterdam of the Pacific. We ask him why and he describes the threat in three succinct words: "*Los negritos peligrosos*" . . . thrusting his chin forward as if to point to an imaginary group of them standing in front of the hood of his car, ready to attack at this precise moment. Latin America, he explains, is divided into three ethnic groups: Whites, Indios, and Blacks—in order of luck, I surmise. Three shades of color, unmixable (at least not without violence). Three steps of the societal ladder with unbridgeable gaps between one and the next. If the Indios are marginal—largely living in the forests, in the midst of a magnificent wildlife, or cultivating remote fields—Black people are outcasts. White people (those who own everything, who are a minority and yet whose control extends from politics to the economy, from plantations to industries, from the police forces to every single local administrative entity) unleash their hatred and dominance with particular brutality against the Blacks. For the Indios, this is still home: the villages in the forests are their ancestral places. But Black people lack this luxury, they were forcibly brought here as slaves, they were displaced, marginalized, driven by White delirium into a deep well of abjection where no light of hope ever penetrates. As we're being lectured on the evils of *los negritos peligrosos* by our cabdriver, Philippe and I exchange a look that says, "Should we tell him that we live practically in Harlem?" Instead, Philippe says: "I think we would like Limón."

A pullman takes us into the heart of the country: we see the jungle, we sleep on the elevations of majestic foggy mountains (foggy because of the active volcanoes all around), we are stunned by the intense luscious green (green like Philippe's eyes, I think to myself). The impenetrable vegetation, the natural spas of sulfurous waters, a pure oxygen our poor city lungs never breathed before. We sense that we are surrounded by animals we don't see: there is no human noise, only an incessant life buzz from below the ground, on top of the trees, among the dewy fronds, inside running streams, and the night is so dark that one walks through it literally as if blindfolded.

By the same local busses, we ride down the east coast where we are met by our version of paradise, almost intact. We ride as far as we can go. The coastal road dead-ends in Manzanillo. It *literally* ends: one moment you are on asphalt, a meter later on dirt. Not dirt road, just dirt. The local authorities must have run out of money, or permits, and one day the workers put down the hammers, hopped on the paver trucks, and headed back home. We are delivered on the last sliver of asphalt, the bus maneuvers its way around to face north again, we do the same and trace our route back to the nearest village: Punta Uva, just ten kilometers from the most populous and vital Puerto Viejo. We spend a whole week in bed. It rains the whole week. It doesn't just rain, it pours: an epochal tropical downpour, with raindrops so dense that you could soap and rinse your hair in it more thoroughly than in the shower at home. Hot rainwater, still smoking as it falls, it touches the ground and disappears without leaving a wet trace. And we fall asleep. We sleep solidly for seven days in a row. When we manage to keep our eyes open for a while, we read out loud to each other: I brought all my favorite Natalia Ginzburg books in Italian. Philippe brought Céline's *Voyage au bout de la nuit* and Aesop's *Fables* in French, which he performs in a masterful voice I can't get enough of, while outside the water continues to roar. One night our hut is visited by a bat. Another by a tarantula. If there are snakes, *and there are,* we are too tired to notice. On the first day, as soon as we landed in San José, my Epilady fell on the ground and refused to turn on again. Without further resistance, I'll let my bodily hair cover me entirely and hope to pass for a sloth.

Wearing mismatched parts of our pajamas, flip-flops, and unkempt hair, we venture outside and discover a few steps from our hut the remains of an old saloon. Water drips down on us from the huge leaves of plants we have no name for. There are some flowers that blossomed and look so animate that if they swallowed us whole it wouldn't surprise me. There is not a living soul around. We enter the abandoned bar and in an upstairs area we find a pool table. Philippe teaches me how to play, and it seems I have a natural talent for it. It's the most fun I've ever had. We look for bottles of whisky and pirate treasures in every cupboard, behind creaky doors, inside moldy wooden barrels . . . but everywhere is empty and suspiciously clean. Idly, with no care in the world, we walk back to our bed.

On the seventh day we both wake up completely refreshed. Detoxed from New York. We move to a different lodging more suited for tourist life. It is a set of bungalows owned by an unmarried woman who lives here with her only daughter and manages her properties all alone in the middle of nowhere. She took all her savings one day, brushed her blond hair, packed her passport, her child, and moved to the Caribbean. *Por qué no!* There is no moon more magnificent than here, they say. She started a good business for herself. The "apartments" are impeccable, well furnished, with all amenities and without unnecessary frills, and just steps from the immaculate beach. We rent two bicycles and, naively, get on the only road there is—the one they built along the coast, used by cars, buses, trucks, motorcycles, donkeys, horses, pedestrians, and animals tired of the jungle—and head for a romantic dinner in Puerto Viejo, which is a stone's throw from here . . . if a stone could land ten kilometers from the thrower. No matter, a bit of exercise will do us good, wake up our sleepy muscles and help us digest our meal.

We haven't thought this through, though. And as the sun goes down, we realize, candidly, only now, that there are no streetlights from Manzanillo to San José. (*Brett & Galina would have known that!*) We slow down our vivacious pedaling of a moment ago, pensive. Chivalrously, Philippe pushes ahead of me. Suddenly, from an undisclosed direction, a wild cry pierces the quiet air. At first, it sounds human but clearly flows instead out of the bowels of Hades. A roar that starts low, winding itself up into a frantic crescendo, without pausing for breath, louder and louder, a drumming growl that expands and expands until it reaches an angry, horrific note as terrifying as Chrissie's when she is dragged into the abyss by the shark in *Jaws*. We freeze up. Legs struggle to pedal, we carry on, but our necks lose control of our heads, as they turn, crazily, in all directions, scrutinizing the surroundings, looking for clues as to where the heck that came from and *what* was it? And then here it goes again . . . but this time it is nearer . . . *It* has quietly come closer. *It* begins as a desperate call and quickly morphs into a satanic grunt, Lucifer's last moan, a fierce shrill, an acoustic arrow bloodthirstily thrusted into the twilight, out of the jungle, in our direction. A third screech has already begun its ascent, from faint to murderous notes: we feel the lungs of this beast pump, bring air into the angry thunder that is about to be discharged, so clearly against us, so clearly close, little more than a leap from the road now. Philippe shouts something inarticulate and indecipherable in French while he skids around 180 degrees, spreading like jam half of his bike's tires on the asphalt, and while I am still trying to articulate a trembling "What?" I see him pass me by in the opposite direction and a moment later we are both speeding beside each other in the direction of our bungalow encampment. Still shaking, still incredulous and without any understanding of what we have just witnessed, we drop our bikes and go looking for the lady to report what happened. Perhaps she will have to call the authorities, perhaps we caught a jungle tribe in the act of sacrificing innocent humans to their idols. Not at all fazed the lady cuts short our incoherent recount: "*Alouatta*, the screaming monkey. Are you hungry?"

The screaming monkey, the world's least active primate, but with hyperdeveloped sense of territoriality . . . and also perhaps a sense of humor.

It is difficult to enjoy dinner, or "the good life," when the laziest scamp of the jungle has just made a monkey out of you. A bit crestfallen, we eat our dinner and go to bed. Tomorrow more beach, swimming, and tons of fresh papaya.

The mood is exceptionally good upon awakening. Everything is flooded with sunshine. We explore the neighborhood, we endlessly swim until our fingertips become all pruny from cooking in warm salty water, our books fill up with sand, the pages curled by the humidity, and the austere Gallimard editions take on a lived-in look. I am covered in freckles, my hair returns to its natural *frisé con brio* (away from Amir's stern irons). Philippe's skin turns golden, and he looks rejuvenated. *Las playas* are divinely empty. Small families of tourists appear now and then but only for a night or two. We stay indefinitely.

I fill up all the Moleskins with notes and narrative ideas. Philippe jots down new musical arrangements: he feels invigorated. On the one hand, we wouldn't mind remaining here in a permanent state of vacation; on the other, we can't wait to be home and implement our great new projects. Especially Philippe: his sixth sense tells him that his big break is about to happen. I am in seventh heaven for him. For us. We bring up New York a lot: Philippe spits poison on New York; I let him, since it does him good, it's cathartic. The subway, the dirt, the *clochards,* the impossible prices, the apartments like hamster cages, and the absence of "*Ça!*" he says with a theatrical gesture of his beautiful arms, long and strong, "This!" Meaning, the air, the calm, time for oneself, people who look you in the eye and smile, who don't perceive you purely as a competitor, who don't shove you aside to assert their aggression, who don't lie about things being "so easy, so cool!" so that you'll feel like the only loser in the world when you try and fail.

As far as New York is concerned, Philippe has clearly passed the tolerance threshold. The American phase is about to run its course. Philippe enjoys the sea and the sun: he enjoys in a visceral way all carnal, material pleasures. He loves wine, and he loves flavorful, rich dishes. He loves Italian clothes. He loves great music and has no patience for the merely good. And youth. He venerates youth and its Olympic beauty. He looks at girls and boys in their twenties and reveres their natural musculature, their agile sinuosity, the firmness of their skin, the power that derives from their utter unawareness of what it means to have one's ego crushed. Philippe bemoans being past his prime. His thirties, with their phantasmagorical promises that didn't pan out, are far behind. Problem is, these considerations make *me* feel old too, and I have to shake myself back into reality sometimes and remind myself that I am only thirty-three. *I* am the free-spirited youth Philippe chases after. He carries a heavy sadness inside, and a good dose of resentment, my Philippe: he is aware of his talent but is also impotent before a world that rewards age, not performance, the illusion, rather than truth, the virtual, not the real. He idealizes Europe: "*Ach! les belles lettres! Ach, chez nous!* What do New Yorkers understand of Stendhal or Brahms!" His is a sort of over-intellectualized Tourette's syndrome . . . and when he starts ranting, his criticisms grow so absurd (even for me) that at a certain point I invariably burst out laughing. I point out to him that he is a forty-six-year-old grumpy man, who looks like Mahler if Mahler went on a motorcycle without helmet . . . not a reassuring look for a believable satirist of contemporary mores and general vulgarity. He laughs and teases me but never ceases to put French language to the service of a good lashing of society, as God intended. *Who knows, will I be in a relationship with Philippe six years from now?*

Not far from our place, we find a restaurant with clean tables arranged under a glorious wooden pergola. This restaurant belongs to Dino and his family, who came to Costa Rica in the late 1980s from Trieste. Everything they prepare is made in their kitchen from scratch by his wife and one of their sons. The owner of a shoe company, Dino was extremely wealthy in Italy, but the unpleasant battles against the competitors and other business worries deteriorated his health, corroded and devoured him to such an extent that one day, in agreement with his wife, they liquidated all their assets and moved to Central America. The world is full of expats: how many are we, what stories are we hiding, what truths do we carry forward or bury behind? Dino was destined for success, whether in Trieste or Punta Uva. As soon as he hears that I am from Rome, he pulls me by the arm and practically drags me before his wife—*it feels like a war tribunal*—and commands: "*Romana* (Roman girl, meaning me), you tell her (pointing at his wordless wife): What kind of pasta do you use for the real *carbonara?* Spaghetti or rigatoni?" "Spaghetti," I answer without having to think about it; it's common knowledge. Dino fist-pumps the air. "Yes!" he exclaims mischievously staring at his wife with a wide grin, "Haven't I always told you?" I add for good measure, should a new fight arise when I am no longer around to help: "*Rigatoni all'amatriciana, spaghetti alla carbonara.*" General euphoria. Including from Philippe who anticipates, ecstatic, the deliciousness of what Dino will undoubtedly serve us. They do not charge us for our meal (or any meal at their place). And his wife's homemade *spaghetti burro and salvia* hold the memory of the most sublime dish I've ever had, and Dino and his family among the kindest, most cordial Italians I've ever known.

After food and a shower, we make love, an extraordinary experience that always floors me. We love each other so much, so healthily. I will never love like this again. I will never be able to be without my Philippe.

After months away, I am happy to be back in New York. Apart from my unresolved fear of flying, queuing for hours at JFK with thousands of people like boxed sardines in the Customs area, no smiles, no hands in front of incessant yawns, the suitcases violently thrown on the conveyor belt and you better not stand between a passenger and his upcoming suitcase, or he'll stampede over you without regrets; and finally, the yellow-cab driver. O unfriendliness incarnate! He hates you because you talk too much, he hates that you have luggage that you expect him to handle, he hates that you are there while he talks on the phone nonstop with God-knows-who in who knows what language, he hates the address you give him, and he hates whatever amount you'll tip him. Back in New York alright! But then you get on a first bridge, then another, and by the time you merge onto East 125th, you start breathing better. Sure, you anticipate the stench, the ugliness of the people on the street, a dejected humanity scattered on the ground like dirt, but there is also Milli, there is home, the warmth of my things, the familiarity of the stores I love, daily routines, and above all the feeling that I am in charge too, I am at the helm here. I am home. With its exhilarating beauty and degrading ugliness, Manhattan is the only thing I have, the only thing I want. I hear the music playing inside of me when I return to Manhattan. Philippe gradually stopped hearing the music, I think: it will be difficult for the record to play it again for him.

# 14

The rainy season starts once more, and with it the overheating radiators and the overpowering orange of Halloween and Thanksgiving. I have a new title: Adjunct Professor. I adjunct for the English Department of City College and a number of other higher-ed institutions on the island. I also keep freelancing for whoever needs me. In sum, I hold more than six jobs a week: money comes from every possible and imaginable source. Then there are the graduate courses I attend. I am surrounded by PhD students from all over the world, interesting, talented people: Anastassiya A., from Ukraine, who persists in this academic career, but who, in my opinion, would make a great rock star. Albert F., from Russia, an extraordinarily gifted painter, with an obscure side that I believe hides physical tragedies and psychological sorrows to which perhaps only his paintings can do justice. Beautiful, softspoken Veronika T., from Prague, whom I've grown especially fond of. I am friends with two Italian professors, openly gay . . . it is obvious why we are all here. We are all somewhat special people—all of us—who said NO! to something we didn't like, that bothered us deeply, but that we knew we couldn't challenge alone. None of us came here for lack of white bread.

We graduate students, as Athena's little soldiers, bring ideas, not war, to the undergraduates in our care—mostly children of poor families, often broken families, the first in their families to get a university degree, the first not to end up in jail, kids raised by mothers, grandmothers, aunts who help each other and take home every child in the *barrio* who needs a family. (Where there's food for nine, there's food for ten, we say in Rome.) I also teach children of parents so rich and with such impossible standards for them that if they get a

B they commit suicide, throwing themselves out the windows of their dorms or swallowing a bunch of medications so expensive that alone they could cover the costs of a week's meals in the home of the poor students who are proud when they earn a C. I teach at City College (once known as "the *shtetl* on the hill," because of its disproportionately Jewish student population, but now completely Afro-Hispanic-Asian), Fashion Institute of Technology, New York University, and Columbia. Yes, *that* Columbia, where Galina studied and where I had dreamed for a moment to find a future too.

The bulk of my riches, however, comes from the lessons I teach for Bespoke Education, founded by my friend, Tim Levine. At some point, he floated the idea of starting a private school which he defined as "boutique service" and asked me if I would be interested in teaching for him. Boutique, of course, means money. Boutique means *not* an education swamp to save the illiterate. Boutique means helping the idiotic children of the rich who can't afford the shame of a scholastically bankrupt offspring (*like himself, he says self-effacingly*). After all, as Tim points out, Manhattan has two things to offer that few other places in the world have: billionaires and the children of billionaires. Tim knows that I am a unique asset with my multilingualism in a city that longs to be cosmopolitan and where the élites pay handsomely for the illusion of learning a language just in time for their ten-day trip to the country in which it is spoken. My excellent English and my educational credentials will also allow me to offer repetitions in history and literature—nobody can object. Tim Levine's 2003 rates are $280 per hour, of which $175 goes to me. It's a no-brainer.

Thus begins my tutoring gig for the Bishops, diamond-level clients of Bespoke Education.

The Bishops live on Fifth Avenue, in one of the most exclusive buildings of an exclusive street. James Bishop is a very distinguished gentleman in his seventies: tall, thin, white-haired, the long equine face typical of the Mayflower breed. James (never abbreviated into a vulgar Jimmy) is quiet and reserved, and he probably grew up unaware of what "to make a scene" even meant. I imagine his parents downing their emotions with a gulp of whisky every night. As a young man, he was sent to Paris to study and to St. Moritz to ski every year until it was time to leave the nest, which in his case was the family plantation in Virginia, and go run an investment bank founded by his father and a Harvard mate of his. In short, the aristocracy of the Stock Exchange. Of him I only know the controlled "Hallo" when we pass one another in the corridor.

Next comes Debbie Bishop. Debbie is both half and twice the size of her husband. She is the real "story" here. A narrative, however, that must remain archived, keyed inside the secret recesses of beautiful antique cabinets. By hints and clues, I gathered that she is the daughter of a Slavic mother, who miraculously and singlehandedly survived the Tsar, Lenin, Stalin (Part 1), Hitler, and Stalin (Part 2). In her flight westward, at a certain juncture, she landed in Rome. In spite of the absolute secrecy surrounding this intriguing genealogy, Debbie is forced to reveal this particular datum because it explains her own otherwise incomprehensible bilingualism. Debbie's knowledge of Italian is not the kind you learn before vacationing in Bellagio for two weeks. Debbie was born in Rome, and I know that she still has several cousins over there. But how did it happen, if her mother was not from there? Who was her father then? And why is he absent from the next American chapter?

From Rome to America the step must have been easier than from Whereverstan to Italy. And as soon as the two women arrived at their destination in New York, the mother, clearly endowed with a survival spirit above the norm, made sure to make no mistakes in setting herself and her daughter up for the future. She married Jack Cassidy, the 1920s world heavyweight champion, famous under the nickname "Babe Whitie." There are black and white photographs throughout the Bishop's house that immortalize Debbie's mother standing ladylike, tiny, well put together, near the smiling boxing legend, Jack "Whitie" Cassidy, in a convertible, walking along the Thanksgiving Parade, or shaking hands with this New York City mayor or that president at the White House. I am fascinated. Once the near future was secured, the little lady with the stiff hairdo began to work on the remote future. It was imperative to find the right husband for Debbie, the second generation, better than just a beat-up boxer, an arrivé out of the Irish ghetto. Debbie wasn't young anymore, the clock was ticking. And then James Bishop crossed their path, after having divorced his first wife, a knockout Swedish model. Debbie and James have only one son, Kevin. And here I burst onto the stage.

Kevin, the sole heir to the Bishop–Cassidy fortune, is an asylum or reformatory case. Raised in the shadow of Debbie's super protective wing, by the time I meet him he has already developed a violent and unrestrainable matricidal hatred. In this luxury apartment on Fifth Avenue, there unfold scenes worthy of the darkest *cinéma vérité* of the 1960s. Seraphic, I sit at the big, lacquered table in the middle of the living room, with Kevin's books and notebooks in front of me, while various objects thrown at the wall by him fly hissing above my head. As little as a word from his mother, and as much as her entering into the room, sends her son into paroxysms of hysteria, and the thought that he could grab one of his father's shotguns and kill us all never leaves me. For Debbie, martyrdom is preferable however to showing up at a party or a presidential fundraiser and having to answer the question "So, where is Kevin at?" (Read: "What prestigious school can you boast for him?") with "My son won't hear of going to college." Unthinkable. Everything would be invalidated. Her mother's struggles to claw her way from the steppes of the East to the jungle of the Upper East Side would have been for naught. Any prospect for Kevin, who's otherwise a really sweet and generous kid, would fade away, not just workwise, but above all marriagewise. Never mind that he won't need a job, technically speaking. It is not enough to have money in America, one must reproduce it, grow it, and pretend to be interested in doing so. And the same goes for the lineage. One must leave all this money to someone after all. The yardstick of success: position and family. And what plutocrat would allow his daughter to get ten yards near a guy who hasn't attended Harvard, Princeton, Yale, or even Columbia or Brown, or at the very least University of Virginia?

There are three of us always with Kevin: me, Debbie, and Jenny the nanny. The nanny is a girl a few years older than I, expressly imported from England. When pregnant, Debbie, who would never trust any other local race, went to an employment agency in the UK, picked this girl, who left Liverpool without thinking twice, came to service at the Bishops and, twenty years later, is still in the Bishop household. She gave them her youth, her life, with a dedication, honesty, kindness, and loyalty beyond commendable. She could have gotten a green card and disappeared. But she didn't. She didn't get herself knocked up by the first repairman who came through the building. She didn't marry.

She gave no bad surprises. Jenny acted like a real Mary Poppins. And she is perhaps the only person to deserve and receive Kevin's love. Even Debbie loves her. Jenny says "Mr. and Mrs. Bishop" when she talks of her bosses in the third person with me. She is *that* loyal. Never a critical word, never an indiscretion comes out of her lips, even in the most frustrating moments. She must have seen an overabundance of people like me, coming and going (*some going faster than others*), and she must have learned that there's no trusting outsiders: if she intends to keep her position and power, to be this family's polar star, she cannot fall in the trap of getting cozy and indiscrete with the likes of me, putting everything at risk. She is not like me. Neither like the cook, nor like the cleaning lady. There is a hierarchy, and Jenny holds a modest but dignified position all by herself, on the top tier.

I make scads of money for Tim through my services at the Bishops. *I wonder if Debbie is aware of this. Perhaps I am one of those charitable acts of philanthropy for which New Yorkers are so famous. If so, she is the most elegant giver I'll ever know in my life.* I guaranteed Debbie my twenty-four/seven availability. There is no amount Debbie is not willing to pay. And pay she does, dearly, for all the private schools she moves Kevin from, until he makes it to the end of high school . . . and then university, God help us! Problem is, his mother is never going to let him get out of Manhattan. Kevin is the only New Yorker in the history of the local universe that at the age of eighteen has never set foot in a subway train: "Mom won't allow it," he says resentfully kicking the wall. It is only a matter of time before he finds the courage to productively rebel—not merely through kicks to the walls and the usual domiciliary Kristallnacht, but out there, in the world from which he has been kept away to an unhealthy extreme.

I sit at the big, lacquered table, a precious piece, in the living room, and I hear the hiss produced by the objects he furiously throws at Debbie fly over my head. It nearly makes me wet myself. I can feel my face flush. I gulp the saliva that suddenly my mouth produces by liters. I say nothing, lower my gaze, and wait for things to calm down. (*I worked so hard to forget a scene like this.*) I wait to be released, with a sunny and unaware "Go ahead, Fania, see you tomorrow." Kevin's livid rage brings me back in time, to sensations I had pushed and pushed against the bottom of my consciousness with the invisible piston of denial. As soon as I hear screaming, I shrink.

The doormen know by heart the traumatized expressions of those who leave the Bishops's house. Strangely Kevin, contrary to class decorum, loves to hang out with them. It is the only escape available to him: he slams the door, runs away (*but where to go?*) and doesn't make it past the threshold of the building. He just *can't*. Not allowed to him. Not ventured by him. And so he ends up hanging out with the Serbo-Croat doormen in the hall, huge guys in blue livery, with dark secrets behind those false smiles, full of hatred and contempt for this kid whose monthly allowance amounts to their country's annual gross deficit: this unknighted baronet who, innocent and therefore even more irritating, doesn't get it that it is out of place for him to be so familiar with them. For such transgressions, sooner or later, someone is slated to get the whip. And it's never the master's son. However, they do try to get in league with me, the Italian, mistaking me for a maid. (*I, who instead read through them like open books, who know their types so well . . . they have no idea how far they ought to keep from me! As far as from a UN Councilmember on war crimes.*)

As soon as I am dismissed, I run out of the building, jump to the other side of the street, enter Central Park, at 72nd Street, and breathe a sigh of relief. I focus on the treetops, the sky, the skyline, the Dakota towers, the cyclists, the joggers, the mothers with baby strollers, the homeless, the dogs chasing tennis balls. I am free, I repeat to myself, I am free. Free in New York. I am safe. I have my home to return to. I have Milli, I have Philippe, my books to read, my books to write, new dishes to cook, and dreams to reach. I don't recall the above-mentioned dreams any more at the moment, they have lost their contours, but they are stored somewhere, and soon, as soon as I stop, as soon as I catch my breath, as soon as I make enough money, I will recover them. I just have to put one foot in front of the other. *Uno due, uno due, forward . . .* Let the years pass, pretend not to see them fly away, and with a smile accept that this too is "life."

We all keep going, because we *are* New York and New York is unstoppable. Stronger, smarter, cooler than anyone else in the world.

And sicker, for that matter, but with fewer means to cure ourselves than anywhere else in the world. One of the disadvantages of not having a full-time job is that my health insurance disappeared with it too. To put it into perspective, let's say that if you break your arm (or someone breaks it, depending on the neighborhood you live in), without medical insurance, the cast costs $7,000 out of pocket . . . *your* pocket, if you even can afford a pocket. My therapy with radioactive iodine at Mass General Hospital cost Brandeis $150,000.

Not having medical insurance in America is not an option. Emergency rooms in all the big metropolises in the US are teeming with poor wretches who are not insured and therefore find help the only way they can: putting on the spot the hospital staff whose Hippocratic oath obligates them to provide assistance to everyone. (A doctor's office on the other hand has the capitalist right to slam the door in your face.) Of course, the hospital too will send a bill . . . and *that's* a pain from which no doctor can save you. It goes without saying that ER patients give false identity cards and fictitious addresses. Not me! Fania always pays . . . or she doesn't go to the doctor. Mom and dad send provisions of Synflex, Bactrim, Mercilon, Gyno-Canesten, iodine tincture, and Cruscasohn. Since Philippe moved back to America, he has lived without health coverage. And therefore, partly without health. In New York, health insurance is on everybody's mind and everyone talks about it all the time: a job is as meaningful as the benefits it provides. The first thing a person tells you about their job is: "They hired me at Blablah: with benefits!"—only then you can congratulate the lucky bastard. It's a constant nightmare. It may be due to the fact that this isn't exactly a healthy town *per se,* we are all keenly aware of our debt to Alexander Fleming and Madame Curie. Flying to Rome in the event one is stabbed in the subway, gets the avian flu, or takes three deep breaths in Times Square . . . is not practical.

I take things into my hands. I lost all my old illusions about who I really am: I thought of myself as an expatriate by choice (by choice and subversion), a sister of Gertrude Stein, a niece of Hemingway, a *doppel* of Samuel Beckett . . . and yet there is little difference between me and an unpedigreed migrant from "Outthereistan" or "Nowhereburg."

It is time I turn to the Russian underground coterie. Golda Silverman is my mole. Golda is Nathan and Jasmine's mother, my friends from the second floor at 1264 Amsterdam Avenue. We became friends as soon as I moved here: she knows that I (better than Nathan or Jasmine) understand her stories of Jewish Ukrainian exile, betrayed and deserted by her husband once they reached the Promised Land (Queens), and her great desire that their children have everything she could only dream of for herself. I often find her sitting at the café downstairs, and we have a cappuccino together, commenting on the American exoticness. She can't believe she's met an Italian woman in Morningside Heights who speaks Russian, who sings pre-war Ukrainian folk songs . . . and above all, who, with the kind of cards fate dealt me, has not bankrupt the casino yet! "You should be a star! What are you doing in this place?" she gestures wildly with both arms, being very literal and meaning this street corner, this small apartment, the man I'm with. I wish to answer "I lost it all once, and I don't deserve my place at the table anymore," but instead I laugh and assure her that I'm all right: "I'm not so special, Golda, believe me," I say, hiding how ashamed I feel.

Sunglasses and headscarf, like a British spy in a 1950s movie, I go meet Golda in (*where else?*) Brighton Beach, Coney Island. Finally someone shows me the famous Little Odessa! The childhood playground of Norman Mailer and Zero Mostel. The Native Americans named Coney Island "Earth without shadows" because it is exposed to the sun all day—but this was before the Horowitzes, the DeVitos, the MacKenzys of this world arrived and made it the capital of their business dealings . . . anything *but* in the open, if you get my drift.

We pay a visit to an office that looks quite legitimate with its honest windows overlooking the street. I pay a fee to the friendly secretary at the white modern desk. She enters a few pieces of information into her database, stamps a few pages of a thick file. I am insured.

At home, Philippe looks at me stunned when I hand him his new insurance card. Gynecologists, pulmonologists, ophthalmologists, endocrinologists, dermatologists, and above all, a psychoanalyst, are no longer off limit. (*Disappointing discovery: dentists and plastic surgeons are not covered by insurance. For those you need to marry well.*) Since I have no yoga classes to go to, the spirit has no one to turn to, so the mind decides to go fix itself elsewhere. I find myself the greatest shrink Manhattan can offer.

I am so proud of myself for getting us this far! Finally, I am getting the gist of how things work here. Various central pieces of the puzzle fall into place, interlock, become sharp, fit into a logical or totally illogical formation. Once Eliza Doolittle learns to speak and properly phonates *"The rain in Spain stays mainly in the plain!"* she won't go back to selling flowers at the market, and, vice versa, it is suicidal to think she could survive the slums while bringing three peas at a time to her fair lady's mouth on the back of a silver fork.

Now I am a local gangster, a clever street cat, a character from *The Lady and the Tramp,* who knows every corner of this city in depth. I have work aplenty, and I know where to get more if need be: I know where to go for a great hairdresser, the cheapest gym, the best pizza joint in town, and a first-rate supermarket almost everyone else ignores, Fairway on West 125th Street, a few steps from home. (*Dropping that mic!*) Every day is like the mechanism of a well-oiled Swiss watch. I'm back on my horse. Geronimo!

But Philippe wants to go back to Europe. He can't take it here anymore. *The clock gets jammed.*

The workweek is an exhausting roller-coaster, with its rapid highs and lows, tumultuous crescendos, deceitful *lentos* that hide treacherous upsurges, and, in reaction, our weekends become more and more Zen. The Lincoln Center membership lies unused; tickets bought well in advance for the French Film Festival, the Jewish Film Festival, the Italian Film Festival end up in the trash bin.

On Sundays, Philippe likes to spend hours at home browsing the internet for French villas and mansions for sale. We dream so intensely to buy one, we build our *châteaux* in the air with such enthusiasm and transport that in the end we are left with little energy for real life in a city that requires an overabundance of energy. Philippe has known a different America in his youth; closer to that of my dreams than to the reality in which we both live. He remembers well when Soho was the cheapest neighborhood in the city, where artists like him (today displaced in Brooklyn, trying to outrun its gentrification) could afford to live without starving, where your neighbor was someone like you, called Bob Dylan, Andy Warhol, or Allen Ginsberg. Around him, at Park Slope, there lives not the Keith Jarret of tomorrow but a little family of postironic hipsters, whose only creative act are their babies, which they showcase hanging from their chests (especially the fathers) lumped in $200 cotton slings, or pushed around in strollers that look like extraterrestrial pods and take the entire sidewalk, from within which the precious human germ looks at you with eyes without pathos through a plastic window, an impenetrable membrane between it and the outside world. In other words, people who make Philippe's studio rent skyrocket.

This is the New York wanted by Rudolph Giuliani. Rich and without crime, like Switzerland: and as sterile and pointless as Switzerland.

At least when Harlem was burning, Times Square a mere stage for low-class prostitution, and the Village a subversive den of bearded intellectuals, New York could still think, shake itself, act and above all re-act. Today, New York simply works. Work work work work. Because the credit cards have chained us: you must meet your credit card payments, your impossible rent, the stratospheric monthly bus and metro card fee. There are no strikes in New York. According to the news, there are no strikes anywhere in the United States. I see my City College students, submissive, downcast, silenced: the administration raises their tuition fees, and instead of setting fire to everything and walking out *en masse,* they take a fourth night job in some fast-food joint, exploited, badly paid—without benefits for themselves, their elders, or their children—or give up college. Allen Ginsberg started reading his poems in Union Square. Today authors and artists perform in exclusive circles, in the houses of cultural tycoons like themselves—open only to those who are already "inside." For the rest, there's only work. Only the overwhelming sadness of office, duty, "Do the right thing!" To become someone in America, I understand, skills are not the priority: Hemingway, if he came back to life, would be asked if he has an MFA before he even thinks of sending a piece to the New Yorker. The MFA, a degree in creative writing, a quintessential American invention. *Which part do they need to teach you? Writing? Or creativity?* Creativity too is reduced to part and parcel of this capitalist mechanism: like a can of beans, or any consumer product, intellectual genius is packaged, homologated, homogenized, strictly controlled, and sold. The denser the advertising, the higher the sales. The MFA Program doesn't so much teach how to become writers as much as how to become sellers.

Today, without the MA in journalism from Columbia University, no one is a journalist. The irony is that those who have been journalists for decades without ever having received a diploma in writing today teach courses in journalism and writing at Columbia University.

The bile-churning resentment against the state of affairs does not benefit Philippe's creative genius. The more he worries, the more I do. My fear for my future is stronger than my consciousness of the present. Although my future contains my beautiful Philippe who, once he's done spreading over everything and everyone his morbid criticism, gains back his natural, albeit contradictory, optimism and returns to hoping sincerely, acutely, convincingly, that the next record will be "the big break," that his next singer will be picked up by Sony, that between us and the *château* there is only a short overseas flight.

Yet when the song *Hold It, Don't Drop It* he produced for Jennifer Lopez's album *Brave* becomes a hit, the doors of the jet set remain shut to Philippe, and the long-awaited Emmy goes to someone else. Philippe throws in the towel.

The Swiss clock's mechanisms jam dead. The old Geronimo was drunk when he fell from his horse, and the little Apache hospital nearby didn't have the means to save him. So the man died. But not the myth.

My studies are going well. In a way, it would be easier if things went on like this, without coming to an end: I realize that with the thesis defense in sight, the end of graduate school inevitably will mean that I'll have to start making new plans. A chilling prospect. Fortunately, I do not have to dwell on it, masochistically, because there is Philippe: Philippe who is here to deal with the future together, like a couple. A love like this (like chickenpox) comes around only once in a lifetime: I am lucky to have caught it. I am not alone anymore, I will not end up in the street (even if in a shady recess of my subconscious this terror always persists), the police sirens whizzing down Amsterdam Avenue are never here for me, the Criminal hasn't looked for me (*or maybe it's that he hasn't found me*). We can roll on like this, there is no need to preplan the future, and it'd be a useless endeavor anyhow. *Der mensch tracht un Gott lacht,* says a Yiddish proverb. Man plans, God laughs. Which doesn't account for all the times we cry under God's plans.

My shrink, Dr. Laurie Weber, is enthusiastic about my progress. The only thing left to do, she insists, is to leave Philippe.

Debbie Bishop similarly says, "Philippe is such a nice man," which in her coded language translates into "I understand that at some point in your life a Philippe made sense, but now that he has done his part, give him up and get yourself a wisely chosen husband. I already made a list of eligible candidates. Tell me when you're ready, and we'll start." Yes, all of the above is conveyed in the phrase "such a nice man."

Even my dearest friends, Erez and Stephanie, have unspoken reservations. I remember them years ago, when we first met: they had just returned from their wedding in Venice, where they had flown relatives, friends, and a New York rabbi to get married in the most romantic place on earth. They love Italy! At the time they wanted to learn Italian and I had been recommended by Erez's brother, who along with his wife (daughter of a famous Israeli parliamentarian) was already hiring me for private language classes. Our friendship never died. I make them my *macedonia* and *tiramisù,* and they unfailingly shower me with a love and support I'll never be able to repay. Their money for my Italian lessons, punctually paid, on the nail, delivered in discreet thank-you cards, were my salvation. They knew it, I knew it, but it was never openly discussed. It was at their home that I spent my first Thanksgiving in New York, and it has remained a fixed tradition. After returning from the two years in Tuscany, after 9/11, they sold the grandiose loft in Tribeca and took up residence in a very elegant building a few steps away from me, on Riverside Drive. *How strange, such a huge city, and I always end up living around the corner from people I know.*

When they tell me I could "do better," I laugh it off. I know that they love me, and I appreciate their honesty. But I don't think anyone fully understands the situation. Yes, Philippe doesn't earn a penny, but *c'est Philippe!* It *is* Philippe: the embodiment of loyalty, the ablest lover in the world, a kind, brilliant soul. And a person is not the sum of his earnings, but of his character traits, his ethical and intellectual fiber, the power of his passion and *passion-alité.* At night we go to bed together, and in the morning, I wake up spooned against the body of this penniless musician, with a sock over his eyes, who gives me complete freedom to be and to love as I wish. "People don't belong to people," says Audrey Hepburn to George Peppard in *Breakfast at Tiffany's* when in the taxi he confesses to her, "I love you, you belong to me." But instead of throwing herself in his arms, like Lauren Bacall or Ingrid Bergman would with Humphrey Bogart, she turns away, contemptuously, and snappily responds, "No, people don't belong to people."

Tactfully, I advise Philippe to avoid his heavy anti-American rants when he's at work, or when we're with friends. Even if the environments in which he moves are progressive and informal, bystanders have antennas, people pay attention; not everyone appreciates French satire. Americans demand positiveness, they demand optimism, they refuse to awaken from the hypnotic slumber in which they are born, they demand upbeat attitudes—and he, who is a musician, should understand better than anyone else the type of rhythm that allows you to be invited to the dance here. He admits that I am right, but I doubt he can refrain. Molière would have been proud of him; Uncle Sam stabs him in the back. Above all, I shouldn't push: he doesn't tell me who I should be, and I have no right to tell him whom to be. With Philippe, my freedom is safe. Philippe respects our liberté: he doesn't colonize me, I don't colonize him. Despite our being together all the time—we play together, sing together, eat, laugh, dream together—our union does not require the leadership of either one, it has no center and no margins, it has all the rules in place but no regulator, it is perfect in its own liberating chaos.

# PART 6

# Autumn Leaves

# 15

*God Bless America!* I am summoned for the oath: I become an American citizen. In a huge New York State Courtroom, under the resplendent effigy of the 43rd President of the United States of America, George W. Bush, stands a crowd of all colors and creeds, veiled, short-sleeved, bald, bearded, tattooed, marked on the face with tribal cuts, young, ancient, illiterate, future Nobel awardees, assassins, saints, and heroes. In a loud voice, with the right hand on the heart, we all pledge our souls to the nation. Eyes well up, cheeks moisten. Mothers pick up their little ones to kiss them. Everybody celebrates. I give a congratulatory handshake to the man on my right and to the one on my left. I came to America alone and alone I celebrate this day today . . . and only I know whether it was worth it. I am alone, but not unique.

After a couple of days, I receive a new blue passport with a golden eagle that clenches, resolutely, a bundle of thirteen arrows and an olive branch. Prepared in war and peace, the motto reads.

I work too hard and run around like a blue-arsed fly all day long to have a real social life. In addition to my graduate classes and adjunct positions at three universities (from Harlem to Midtown, from dawn to late evening), I also have seven different freelance jobs spanning the entire week and the whole length of the island. They range from the hyper lucrative (the Bishops) to the rip-off (a young couple from Rome). With some funny, original, unusual variants in between.

I resumed teaching Italian privately, because it is always the best way to earn my loaf of bread and, if I were a cleverer person, also to build a network of connections that can come in handy one day. I hope that such day never comes though. As I still fear the next Keith Botsford who will accuse me of being a "user." *I'll make it on my own, thank you very much.*

When in the winter, I sit on the crosstown bus, cutting through Central Park along 79th Street, I derive a hedonistic pleasure from stealing what little glimpse can be stolen of the interiors from the luxurious homes along the route. There is an exact time for this crime of indiscretion: dusk, when it starts to get dark outside, and the maids turn on the lights inside and forget to draw the curtains closed. I happen to teach in one of these dream places: the mansion of Mary Benora. Mary is awesome. Long blond hair, so fine, practically a vision of pure glow from her contours to the depth of her voice. Wife of a billionaire, full-time philanthropist, with a helicopter parked on the terrace of their building on Central Park West where they live in a million-room apartment, with two children (slender, long blond hair, skins like fragile holy wafers), cooks, miscellaneous on-site staff, and of course the nanny (who dares not raise her tone of voice with the little ones, no matter what they do, no matter if she caught them torturing one of her own children. (*Her own children wait for her in an apartment as big as the little Benoras' toy closet.*) I will never meet the man of the house in person, but I reckon that in these types of families, fathers are evanescent figures, more simulacra than actual human footprint.

They open to me their homes, their sancta sanctorum, with civilized affability, dignity, and generosity. But to the American upper crusters, I remain a mysterious creature: I make them feel uncomfortable. Something tells them that I have more right to occupy their place than they, which generates awkwardness, uncertainty, and almost a sense of repugnance. I am not the servant from who knows where, over whom they imagine a superiority that may or may not be true: they know from "where" I come, because, unwisely perhaps, I make sure to remind them and because I embody my origins from appearance to behavior. Mary is a board member of the Metropolitan Museum: but I am the one who understands with every fiber of my being Vermeer's *Woman with a Lute*, Mary Cassatt's *The Cup of Tea* . . . I am Modigliani's Jeanne Hébuterne. They ask themselves suspiciously, "How come *someone like her* has to work to make a living? What's the catch? What am I missing?" If they were visiting my house in Rome, they'd find out; they sense it the way a crocodile perceives the inexperienced faun that has wandered too far from his mother to take a look at the watery swamp. They would be the ones to feel intimidated, bewildered: they would suddenly feel naked, barefoot like they were when they started the climb that eventually brought them all the way to the helicopter on the roof, their reaction would betray the onion sandwiches they had to swallow before they finally made it to caviar . . . which, in truth, they only pretend to appreciate.

All I ask is that they pay me what is due for my work. When the lessons are over, because the holidays arrive, or the enthusiasm runs dry, or they move on to a new hobby, I eclipse back into the void from whence I appeared, I delete their phone numbers, and I don't keep in touch, lest they think I am a leech, a slippery sycophant. *Fania, we don't lower ourselves to climb, my mother whispers in my ears.*

Friends like Erez and Stephany or Debbie understood this side of my personality. That's why I keep my relationship with them. They are like family to me at this point. I deeply love them.

When the rabbi of a Sephardic synagogue on the Upper West Side asks me to give private lessons in Jewish religious practices to an aspiring convert, I jump at the opportunity enthusiastically. It is a totally unusual and unexpected gig, but it is also up my alley and the coolest part, of course, is that the woman in question and her boyfriend are from Rome! They moved temporarily to New York to facilitate both conversion and childbirth. Yes, Juliette got distracted (*or was she clever?*) and got in trouble with Romeo, who probably would not have followed her until death had it not been for the unexpected new life she is carrying. What was Romeo to do? He got down on one knee, presented her with the most lavish diamond ring he dug out of the family heirloom coffers, and set his condition: Conversion. The ultimate proof of true love. But rightly presaging the thousand objections the Roman and Italian rabbinate will raise (*the Italian Jewish community is notoriously the most inhospitable* comunità *there is*), her Jewish Romeo resorted to "Plan B" . . . New York, that is. Everything is easier in New York, especially Judaism. Especially if you already have a small shop of Italian leather gloves and silk ties on Madison Avenue with a small apartment in the same building two floors up.

Problem is, Juliette, less cosmopolitan than one might have hoped for, does not know a word of English and this constitutes an obstacle to her conversion to Judaism: in what other language could she be taught by the rabbi, no matter for how short a period, how perfunctory the instructions, and how large a donation to his synagogue? With only three months left, there's no daylight to burn. I come into the picture.

This has got to be the most beautiful position yet in my career of "Voyeur Extraordinaire." This opportunity brings together some of the things I love most in the world: Rome and my language, Judaism, New York, and money. We are looking at three-hour sessions, three times a week. I will be the guide to this perplexed Juliette—kissed in the cradle by a lucky star—who is groping in the dark, can't quite understand what hit her, with her giant belly protruding forward like a human billboard announcing "*This* gives me the right to all of *it!*" She needs *me* to figure out Manhattan, *kashrut,* the English language, and the *Shemah Israel.* While Romeo is out keeping shop, busying himself to lay a solid, albeit perhaps not permanent, foundation for this new family, Juliette never leaves the apartment on Madison Avenue. She is always cooped up inside. She says she doesn't like it here, she doesn't care about anything the town has to offer, and she is fed up with this place. But whether she and the Montague bastard get enough fresh air is not my primary concern. My primary concern is that I already taught three classes, for a total of twelve hours, and haven't seeing a cent. I show up, a bit restless and my guard up, to a fourth lesson and when no pecuniary exchange takes place then either, I don't return.

According to the New York court district records, Romeo and Juliet make a habit of not paying those who work for them and of threatening their staff, intentionally selected among the foreign born (like their Filipina maid), to report them to the INS and have them deported if they complain about the missing salaries.

I throw myself heart and soul into a new project that is of enormous importance to me personally, but also to the universe of arts and cinema, of knowledge and global cross-cultural relations. My idea is up there with Brunelleschi's dome and Einstein's $E = mc^2$.

Here it is: A documentary film about the history of the Italian Jews, entitled *ITALKIM*. In English. For the transalpine public. I already have a kick-ass script and an accurate timeline: all I need is funds. And for the funds I need a trailer: everything depends, stringently, on the trailer. I have a script for that as well already. A humble budget will allow me to splice together enough clips to create the perfect visual teaser. (For the soundtrack I already secured the best music producer in the States: Philippe is all in.) For the clips, I need a professional camera and a $20,000 microphone. The interviewees are many and ecstatic; most important, some are still alive. I must hurry! Anyone I talk to about my idea ends up beaming with excitement and begs to be part of it. It's my stroke of genius. I have already bought the internet domain for the site and for the email extension to reflect they are mine: www.italkim .com, write to us at information@italkim.com.

I call Elie Wiesel. I have interviewed him in his Upper East Side office several times in the past, and I consider myself, if not a friend, certainly an acquaintance on good terms. I have his direct number, and the memory branded in my mind of all the stories he told me including the (apocryphal) one about his unshakeable friendship with Primo Levi, with whom, he claims, they were barrack neighbors at Auschwitz. The end of my trailer will be the voiceover of Elie Wiesel who recites in Italian—a language he is pleased to know fluently—*Shemà*, also known in English as *If This Is a Man,* the poem by Primo that opens the eponymous masterpiece *Se questo è un uomo.*

"No, I cannot do it," says old Eliezer, after I expound to him with eloquence and mastery all the splendid intricacies of my groundbreaking project, its historical value, its uniqueness, the genius of the never-done-before. *Do I hear Oscar bells?*

"The documentary is not about me."

I flinch.

Tenderly (*my voice trembles a little*) I remind him of his unshakeable friendship with Mr. Levi, he bragged so much about. I argue that he ought to do it in the name of his friendship with Levi who is no longer able to read his own verses, after having killed himself.

"But I can't because the documentary is not about me," repeats the old man. In fact, he repeats it three times.

First strike.

Second strike: my business partner disappears. Through an ad I placed somewhere, I found a woman documentarist from Brooklyn, Rosaria, who has all the necessary equipment I couldn't afford if I sold all my fertile eggs and throw into the deal a limb as well. She comes from an Italian family from the south of Italy (from the geographic south as well as from the social south . . . the lowest class imaginable), and she claims to feel a special connection to me as a woman and as an Italian artist working on something truly beautiful and meaningful. I can't pay her; but I offer her a partnership. We are in this together. In a moment of total hallucinogenic hysteria, however, Rosaria leaves New York, moves to Florida, and takes her equipment with her (fair enough) and all the footage of the interviews of local historians and experts shot together in the last three months (*is there any fairness in this world?*). She disappears without a word. I ask, I beg, I threaten a lawsuit . . . I give up. She never responds to a single message of mine. I dry my tears and start from the beginning.

Third strike: New strategy, new flop. In Rome I have a friend, Gianni Stonovič, who graduated in cinema studies and has been working since he was eighteen for RAI, the national public broadcasting company owned by the government. I ask him to help, he accepts. Philippe and I fly to Italy, where with a professional crew of cameramen and audio assistants that would put Spielberg to shame, I shoot hours of interviews with Lia Levi, Edith Bruck, the Chief Rabbi of the Jewish community of Rome Riccardo di Segni, Rome's Mayor Walter Veltroni. I have already lined up Clara Sereni, members of Primo Levi's family, Liliana Treves Alcalay, and Moni Ovadia next. Then we'll go to Israel, just a quick hour flight from Rome, for more key interviews. It's a smash! You can cut the enthusiasm with a knife! The people involved are moved to their core: finally, a chance to speak! This is an opportunity they never dreamed would come. And neither had I . . . until I dreamed it myself. For us all. And am now turning it into a reality.

The import of what we are doing does not elude Stonovič, who begins to visibly salivate. We catch Stonovič talking about *Italkim* as "his" project, "his" film." Philippe, who is always in tow, but less preoccupied than I with running the details of the on-site operation, follows better than I what is happening off set: he notices that, when he thinks he is not being observed, Stonovič gives his business card to the interviewees, takes them aside and whispers something about new arrangements, a slight change of plans. Philippe menacingly confronts him and tells him to drop whatever he is scheming or else he will smash his face. Philippe is the first person in my entire life to come to my defense this way. Poor timing though. Nothing can heal my sense of trust in those I enlist in my project. Not even Philippe's encouraging and chivalrous protection can mend my smashed resolve. I feel myself fade, evanesce, be erased like a chalk mark from a blackboard. We were right: Stonovič was pocketing my plans, counting on the fact that soon I would be going back to New York, and once the cat was away, the mouse would have . . . I can't even think about what this smart, well-connected cat could do. He admits as much. I feel sick. I know that this is the end. It's over. Like a porcupine who's lost too many battles, I have no quill left to erect in self-defense. I ball up, clatter my teeth, and just like a nocturnal animal on which one suddenly floods a strong light, on short trembling legs, I beat a quick retreat. I'm out.

Kevin Bishop has grown up now, he has been placed in a small private college, undetectably hidden within the folds of Manhattan, not far from his parents' house. A Sunday, on my subway ride to Central Park West, from where I'll head to my lesson with him, I notice that one of the only four passengers scattered comfortably on my same train car is reading an old book, which looks like those put out for free at Community Centers, churches, or Alcoholics Anonymous meetings. Intrigued by the fact that the guy with the book doesn't seem to fit your typical reader profile, I want to see what book has captivated this man's interest so intensely. But I am seated too far for a clear view. I lopsidedly squint, I pretend to tie my shoelaces, I deliberately drop a pencil on the ground, I do all types of contortions to put into focus the spine or the damaged front cover: it is a biography of the boxer Jack "Whitie" Cassidy, written by Debbie Spizzichino Cassidy. That *must* be the name of Debbie's biological father! She has never made a mystery of the fact that Cassidy, who genuinely loved her like a child of his own, legally adopted her and gave her his name. But she has never disclosed anything about her biological father. Such a deliciously Jewish-Italian name! I wonder how much James Bishop knows about his mother-in-law's and his wife's past . . . *And he must have thought he married down into Irish Catholic stock! I wonder, did the Roman Jewish Ghetto feature at all in the story they sold to James?*

This little subplot drives my imagination wild. I love Debbie, and now, because of this secret, because of this skeleton in the closet, I like her even better. Her mother must have been a force of nature. I admire them both. Perhaps one day I will ask her something more directly. I still don't know if she trusts me. Perhaps she too has lost respect for me because she thinks I should have made it to where she and her friends made it to by now. Perhaps even for her, there is something mysterious and disgusting in the fact that despite my class, cosmopolitanism, multilingualism, multi-ethnicism, education, and diplomas to sell, I hold real jobs and choose to live with a musician who's going nowhere. *What's the catch?, she too is asking herself.* It seems to me that there is a friendship between us waiting to grow; it has taken on small roots, hampered only by the employer–worker contract that binds us. There is an ocean of pure generosity in Debbie that unfolds in great, incontinent waves toward me. I see Debbie's affection in a tide of loving gestures: her gifts for the holidays, our funny chats on the phone (that start with a problem with Kevin and quickly turn to gossips about the rich VIPs of the Upper East Side cheating or being cheated upon, the results of someone's bad plastic surgery, someone else's unpardonable faux pas at a best friend's wedding, and so on). We go more and more often out for lunch together, Debbie and I, and those are for me moments of great happiness that pump up my courage for the rest of the week. She is very supportive and very direct. The Bishops even invite us to spend a weekend in their centennial home at the Hamptons—despite her overt disapproval of Philippe (not *per se,* but *for me*). With elegance and superiority, everybody's dislike is put on hold for the occasion. I am grateful for this and a thousand other expressions of her affection.

Despite Philippe's frustrations and the *châteaux* in the air, Kevin's hysterical bouts (by now more comical than frightful), the seven freelance jobs a week on top of multiple teaching commitments at four universities, I begin to distinguish at the horizon the end of graduate school. A better day may be about to dawn.

A certain air of excited anticipation begins to fill the atmosphere around me. Even Philippe is nudged by an invisible, and certainly unexpected, force to look toward the future. This new awareness in Philippe doesn't get embodied in trivial, practical, obvious forms such as marriage, a new house together, a lucrative music-related activity (and "Farewell to the purely artistic phase!"). No, this new awareness in Philippe shapes up into a final resolution to move back to Europe. To persevere in the purely artistic phase, postponing or ignoring completely the other occurrences of bourgeois life. His problem is *not* what he does, but *where:* "*Poupette,* we must leave New York," and sink back into the frigid breast of Paris, *chez nous.*

*Chez lui,* I'm not going.

I am *chez moi.* I am in Noyorc.

Lately I forget more and more often to repeat the apotropaic mantra "*Who knows, will I be in a relationship with Philippe for ten years?*" The ten-year mark is almost here anyhow and there's no reason to interfere with a dream that had no problem in materializing itself, independently from my magic formula, and that, in fact, is still so present to be almost cumbersome. No, I am *not* falling out of love. This is *not* disenchantment. On the contrary! There are two phases in any true and worthy love story: the first, when two people's minds, bodies, and souls can't stand separated not even for a second, when they burn and waste themselves like a wick soaked in gasoline, for fear that the darkness of the world they left behind may come back and swallow them for good; and the second phase, that of stability, when two lovers can devote themselves passionately to the "sensible" rest of their lives. The latter blissful phase is where we are.

Dr. Weber, my psychoanalyst, and Debbie Bishop, my friend, continue to hope that as the thread binding Philippe to me extends over time, the thinner it gets, the sooner it will snap. I continue to hope for things to stay as they are between us and be happy with him forever.

Life goes on, and I win the equivalent of the lottery for a graduate student. I apply for a competitive national fellowship and get it. A fellowship of thousands of dollars that will allow me to leave all my jobs and devote myself exclusively to writing the dissertation. Things are looking up.

It is spring, and I don't consider even for a moment leaving any of my lucrative jobs: I keep the jobs, I keep the fellowship, *and* I write the dissertation. (I also keep Philippe, the Bishops, Dr. Weber, and the few dear friends I hope never to lose again.) No problem. I have seen far worse days. If this would seem a Homeric undertaking to most, to me it is like slicing a cheesecake with an ax. Bring it on!

One can't deny a certain cosmic imbalance, though. Philippe and I are a bit like the two plates of a scale: the more one of the two goes up, the more the other, by the laws of the asshole who invented the scale, goes down. But I am convinced that Philippe will succeed, that together we will defeat the rules of physics, and we will revolutionize the principle of balance. We will both go up, distinct, yet tied together.

However, I am wrong.

She is an intelligent woman, Dr. Weber, about fifteen years older than me. She is not married but didn't let that stop her family planning. She went to China (twice) to adopt two girls, on her own. I see the happy photos of Dr. Weber with her two daughters on the white office shelves. She is positively happy. A purely good and happy person. I owe her. Without her, I don't think I could write my dissertation. I tell her my most painful secrets: she doesn't flinch. She smiles back and makes them look so small, unthreatening now.

During one particular session with her, I tell her of an episode upon which I hadn't reflected for years and about which I had never told a living soul before. When I was at Brandeis, in full crisis, I had sought the help of a psychoanalyst, hoping for the support needed to regain some balance, so as not to lose my mind. And I had been very lucky, I thought at the time, because the secretary at the students' mental health center on campus set me up for a consultation with the director himself. A PhD'ed clinician, not a graduate student training for his or her pre-practicum. The director, Dr. Stross, was a renowned scholar, *un professorone*, as my father would say (a "Big professor" *. . . what an old expression of undignified subservience*). He took me on for a full ten-session cycle, covered by my student insurance. Our meetings were rather pleasant, funny even: the guy was a fascinating man from all points of view. It took me all of one minute and forty-five seconds to understand that he liked me. But out of every painful story about the Criminal's behavior, Dr. Stross seemed to want to dig into the why and how I caused such reactions in this person who didn't matter *in himself* but only as a tool to better understand my subconscious mechanisms that were pulling out such actions from the Criminal. *Ok, it's a theory.* The doctor demanded as rich a detailed account as possible of the most carnal abuses . . . which I was reluctant to provide, both out of a sense of shame and because of the emotional pain that going over them caused me. But he craved those details: "Tell me, exactly *how* . . . ?" And "Do you like it if someone calls you . . . ?" "What were you wearing . . . underneath?"

Besides that, he was also very interested in hearing about Rome. Not in the sense of childhood memories or Freudian screens: but in Rome *qua* Rome. He sought advice on this or that type of restaurant; which places to visit for short day trips; in which neighborhoods it is better to take accommodation; the best night clubs; my advice on car rental or railways. My only knowledge of applied psychoanalysis comes from *Manhattan* ("You call your analyst, Donnie?! I call mine Dr. Chomsky . . . and he hits me with a ruler!") and *Bananas* ("I think I've had a good relationship with my parents . . . they started beating me on the 23rd of December in 1942 and stopped beating me in the late Spring of '44."). One thing that seems to be a recurrent trope is the total separation between oneself and one's shrink who must know everything about the analysand while remaining an impenetrable sphinx to the patient. Instead, Dr. Stross told me quite a bit about himself and was far from being unreadable to me. He told me of his travels to Europe, and, being familiar with my passions, he told me about his exclusive circle of friends in Venice where he had recently been at a party which, among other cultural brahmins, featured also Woody Allen . . . a *habitué* at his friend's house. *Why would he tell me that? I'd swear he's thinking of bringing me there.* Always directly from him, I learned that he wasn't married but cohabited with his partner with whom he had recently had a daughter—there was a considerable age difference between the two and he defined himself as a late bloomer.

He did not seem to think there was anything serious or urgent (*nothing to worry*) about my situation with the Criminal, or my psyche. There was nothing wrong with either. I left Dr. Stross consultation room, every time, shaken by his insinuations as to my culpability, but fundamentally I thought he was kind and it was probably in the nature of the "problem" that he couldn't do anything about the Criminal. No help from him on how to emotionally or legally fight back the Criminal. The words "restraining order" never passed his lips. Psychoanalysis is not a science of pragmatic action, but the art of cerebral illusionism. The important thing was that someone, detached, objective, with some authority, had finally been informed of the situation. I told myself: If they find me, say, dead the next weekend, I won't have to worry anymore: Justice will be delivered posthumously. The Criminal will pay for it. Dr. Stross will be my witness.

Instead, a couple of years later, I realized things would have gone rather differently had I been found dead in the attic at 69 Orange Street, Waltham, Massachusetts. In the midst of the apotheosis that followed my move to New Jersey and the brief marriage to the Criminal, while I was trying to gather the most credible documentation (*good character*) that could indict the culprit in a court of law (*and justice?*), I phoned Dr. Stross from Radio Italia offices (where I spent hours, hidden, long after everyone had left) to ask him for a letter confirming that as early as 1997 I had sought help for the anguish, torments, and punches my then boyfriend and now husband was inflicting. I brought him up to speed, giving him a quick synopsis of the current situation and, finally, after listening to me, *il professorone* pronounced, very quietly, almost as if he didn't want to be heard by other people in the room: "Fania, *you know* I can't write a letter for you. And *you* know *why*." I think I threw up in my mouth then and swallowed it. No, I had no idea what he meant, but it could not be a good thing for sure. I said in the respectful voice of an obedient *bambina:* "Ah, OK. No problem. Thanks a lot, anyway." Thanks anyway! How could I? How did I allow him to get away without a cogent explanation for his refusal and, as if that were not enough, I also *thanked* him for the insult! When I hung up the phone I had to run to the ladies' room and vomited my entrails out, crying myself blind all night until dawn and the first employees arrived.

From that moment on, I confess to Dr. Weber—who is staring at me with the wrinkled forehead of a crying *Mater Dolorosa*—"It is since that incident, not the violence or the abuses, that I entered a bewildered darkness from which I can't escape." Even as I say this, I feel my tone rise and my voice break,

I feel the panic surge like a tsunami. I can't hold back the quake that invades and waggles me from head to toe. I fold over, I fall off the therapist's couch, I let out the yelp of a tortured beast, in which is contained all the rotten horror of this tiny memory I accidentally disentombed. It was at the instant of that phone call between New Jersey and Brandeis that I realized I was alone, that no one would have any reason to believe me and even less reason to help me. That it would be very simple to pass me for a madwoman, *Gaslight* style.

In his soothing and calm voice, Dr. Stross had intentionally flickered the guilt switch. I was guilty, a priori, and this would have sealed my case against the Criminal as a case against myself. To win against injustice one must be without sin, never having committed an injustice—even if completely disconnected from the one in question. Like Joseph K. in Kafka's *The Trial,* I received my final sentence without having been able to defend myself and without being told the charges. The kabbalists suspect that the life we perceive is not the only existing reality. Somewhere beyond us, on a different plane (accessible in passing, by furtive glances, only in our dreams), there is a permanent tribunal in session, and for every living person, records are being gathered, kept, and scrupulously archived. We will never be consulted, the data speak for themselves, and one day an actual trial will take place, without us. The verdict will always be: Guilty. And the sentence ineluctably: Death.

I leave Dr. Weber's office in a state of pure upliftment. It's as if all this time I had been waiting on the gallows for the sentence to be executed and only now I figured out that I can slip my neck out of the noose and walk off . . . and I do! I slip my neck out of the noose, walk off the gallows, away, no one stops me. There's no one to stop me. I feel something has changed, viscerally. As soon as I close the door of the building behind me, I take a deep breath, I dry my eyes, and I feel *it is* truly over.

Aristotle said that banks do not protect rivers. Slowly, Philippe, like water, rejoins his natural channel and begins to flow home. He has tried, he has given it his all, but this city has rejected him with cruel severity and iniquity. He considers me the only thing worth staying for, but by now, even I can't hold him back, he just can't take it anymore. It doesn't even occur to me to stop him. I know the suffering his condition brings all too well. In fact,

I encourage him to follow his instinct. Who has the right to keep another chained? How can the unhappiness of one make another's happiness? I understand that Philippe is not leaving *me;* Philippe is leaving New York. And he doesn't vanish suddenly, like a cloud in the wind, without a trace. His traces surround me everywhere. They are a comfort. What he gave and leaves with me is more than anybody has ever granted me before. All his things remain around me at home, as he slips out of here and into a new world, far away, through longer and longer reconnaissance journeys. He goes to inspect the camp, he assures me, and as soon as he puts things in place, I can reach him. Like in the final dialogue between the Kikuyu servant Farah in *Out of Africa* and Baroness Blixen who is about to leave Kenya forever:

> *Blixen:* Do you remember how it was on safari? In the afternoons I would
> send you ahead, to find a place and wait for me?
> *Farah:* And you can see the fire and come to this place.
> *Blixen:* Yes . . . Only this time I am going first and I will wait for you.
> *Farah:* It is far where you are going? . . . This fire must be very big. So I
> can find you.

But this dialogue is not in Blixen's book, this dialogue didn't happen. Director Sydney Pollack invented it. I push forward, but without obsessively scanning the horizon for a smoke signal. I guess Philippe will simply ring me up.

Phone calls arrive copiously: from every public telephone in London or Paris, in the middle of the night, early in the morning, in the most unexpected moments. He even gives in to a cell phone, so that he can walk while describing for me the human scenes he steals on the boulevards and in the pubs. It's a bit like sitting together on the benches in Central Park. He tells me how horrid London has become since the last time he visited thirty years ago. Not so much the geographic distance as the mental difference between where he is and where I am seems tactile, palpable even through the phone receiver. We still laugh a lot, we always talk, there is always something to tell. But now, more and more often, I must cut our conversations short because, due to the time zones, Philippe catches me in the busiest hours of the day, between work, writing, private lessons, and chores. For the first time since we met, I even pretend not to be there.

That I may not answer Philippe's call seems unthinkable even to me. But this is New York, he knows this better than I. It is not Paris nor London nor Rome, where one has time to be human, to speak, to be a *flâneur,* to let a day extend to infinity. I have no time: I have to teach, I have seven different jobs a week, to which I added private language lessons for my thesis director Nancy K. Miller and her husband Sandy Petrey.

I selected my thesis committee. My choice of committee members didn't particularly please the department chair: neither did he like my choice for the first oral examination committee, nor the second committee for the second oral exam, nor my dissertation subject, nor my dissertation director. This is because there is bad blood between him and the rest of the female faculty body. My thesis director, Nancy K. Miller, is his antithesis, his nemesis, a primal antagonist. Seeing them together at a meeting is comical. She doesn't bend or relent. He stands, all puffed up, like an Emperor Penguin, machinating something in his strategic mind. This angry, insincere, resentful man is dangerous to me and all women.

He hates that I'll work on the Holocaust, he hates that I'll work on Jewish women, he hates that I'll work with Jewish women. I decided to write my dissertation about the relationship between Jewish mothers and daughters. When I say this to my female mentors, they immediately respond with a laugh of understanding and complicity. It is an ancient story, that of the animosity between mothers and daughters. . . and that too is all the making of the Fathers. My specialization doubles with a minor in the field of Women's and Gender Studies: when my students ask me how we say in Italian "gender" or "gender studies," they don't believe me when I roll my eyes and explain "we don't say it," we don't have the word. What Italian language indicates of our culture and mentality is a book that is still waiting to be written . . . although not by linguists, but by women, expats, or comedians.

Nancy and her husband Sandy are a couple from a page of the most humorous, but also quality, Russian literature: one tall, the other petite, one with a thundering voice, the other almost a whisperer, one introverted, the other hyper gregarious. Sandy has a brilliant mind that learns, absorbs, and remembers everything, with an extraordinary talent to summarize an impression, to distill it, in such a direct and precise way that an entirely new impression forms out of his genius observation; it's as if what he intends to tell you were a nut that he cracks open, showing you its true core and revealing, to your surprise, that what you had erroneously thought of as content was but mere surface, a fragile shell. Nancy listens more than she speaks, but when she does speak you better do as she says, because she has no patience for who waists her time and because what she advises you is always right and invariably earth-shattering. The two of them have impeccable tastes. From the furniture in their gigantic apartment on West End Avenue, to their clothes, books, music, the friends they surround themselves with, to the choice of vocabulary they use. Every gesture of theirs is like a dance choreographed by Balanchine. Even when they bicker—because one insists there was a flower shop at the corner of Piazza Grande in Genoa where they spent the summer, while the other replies dead certain that the memory is categorically false because that was a pastry shop—even in these moments they weld together more, their squabbles are the gears of their relationship. Without them, the mechanism would come to a halt, while with them it tires but it also continues to move forward. It's as if I observed them through a window in the night: me outside, them inside, in a well-lit room.

Sandy and Nancy are Baby Boomers (on the young side of the group, the side, to put it with columnist P. J. O'Rourke, born around the last year someone still liked Lyndon Johnson). They seem to me the last interesting people on Earth. A monument to the lost intelligentsia. I wish to turn into a tiny roach and hide under their sofa, or in a cupboard, and remain for the rest of my short verminous existence in that belly of *idées* and *finesse*. Nancy was a feminist revolutionary of the first hour. The mothers of the Baby Boomers were ancient by the age of thirty-five: their daughters, in their seventies today, are still the only ones with something interesting and subversive to say. And they don't wait to be asked. Today there is no student, researcher, or academic involved in the analysis of women's cultures, or the effects of male culture on women, who can exempt themselves from mentioning Nancy in their work. *She* is my thesis director.

Nancy and Sandy are like the characters in *The Big Chill*. I found them, finally. And yet, voices like that of Keith Botsford's (*you are a user, Pimpernel*) or my mother's (*of course you have friends, if you "buy" them!*) or of all the people I don't care to mention (*you will never make it, unless I let you*) force me to keep at a distance, to stay at the margins: I am too scared to be exposed for the insincere and inapt impostor I was told I am. For example, when Nancy takes me to parties with Gloria Steinem and other famous militants, with whom she has been an intimate friend for half a century, I am no longer the same twenty-year-old girl who in 1991 would have thrown herself into the "dance" with impetus and enthusiasm. The me of those days would have become one of the group, she would have given herself airs like an equal peer—because she believed she was—but all she had to contribute was her enthusiasm. The same one that met Saul Bellow in Boston in 1996, approached him joyfully and began to chat. But this was before a Criminal or a Keith Botsford or a Dr. Stross put her in her place. I am not twenty-one. I didn't make a name for myself in New York City as I had hoped I would, when I planned to come here and conquer. I did not conquer; I was defeated.

Twenty years ago I knew how to squeeze gold from a stone. If you asked me, "What do you do? Who are you?" you'd better have had three hours available because I would fill them up with my self-congratulatory reply of epic proportions and burn your ears numb. Today, I walk along the periphery of the rooms and halls, because I have no ammo in my arsenal to answer that same question anymore. I am not the one I was. On the other hand, I have no nostalgia for the one I was and if I met her again, that little girl (with flared teeth, big nose, majestic hair, Russian cheekbones) who chats cheerfully and without blushing about herself, about the languages she speaks, the places she lived in, the people she knows, and who gives you the whole laundry list of projects she's working on (all "unique," all "firsts"), I think I would slap her. Or worse, I would grab her by the wrist and drag her in front of the first famous man I spot in the room, and, thrusting her into his grip, I would tell him: "Here, take her! This one has a great hunger to please and to make it!"

Dr. Weber, upon hearing this, advises me to focus on the girl I was: she tells me, "Choose a picture of yourself when you were young, and put it on your desk, or in your wallet, wherever." I choose a photo of when I was four or five years old; we were all camping in Sicily and I must have been photographed minutes after waking up: I look straight into the lens of *zio* Adriano's camera who, faster than me, snaps it just a second before I turn the other way and ruin his shot. I look funny, mischievous, and totally adorable. I stick it on the fridge door.

"Whenever you feel you are missing the ground beneath your feet, when you think that the only solution is to jump into the abyss, look at that face and realize it is *still* you. That child *is* you. You will always be you. When you hate yourself, look at her: would you hate *her?* With those eyes so bright and astute, full of curiosity and cunning! You would protect her, you would tell her it's all right, don't worry. Protect that baby girl, she's not disappeared, she's not dead." I do as I'm told, obediently but unconvinced.

# 16

I am a bit melancholy now that graduate school is about to end and I will have to turn a new page; where this new lane will lead, I have absolutely no clue. The finish line is almost visible from where I stand, and it is natural for professors, colleagues, and acquaintances to talk to me about "the next steps": job applications, academic article submissions, conference papers. This is a particularly favorable moment for me, they repeat, because I also hold a full-time job as lecturer at Columbia University and stealing a scholar from Columbia University is something many institutions aspire to do. "Let yourself be fought over!" they joke, but quite seriously. That's right: I am at Columbia University. Unbelievable. It's as if fate is fooling around with me.

Galina has finally finished her doctorate at Columbia and has taken a job in a small but very prestigious private college in Connecticut—a few hours' drive from Manhattan. And now . . . now, everything points to a teaching job for me as well, to an academic career. I, a professor: "Those who can't do, teach. And those who can't teach, teach gym" says Woody Allen (*goddamn perv*) whom I never saw again . . . the Carlyle (where I never ate again) . . . Central Park (which is now just a shortcut to Debbie's house, a hindrance between Upper West and Upper East Sides) . . . Serendipity's (where you can no longer set foot because in 2001 they shot a romantic comedy for teenagers called *Serendipity,* and the discrete character it had has been altered forever by an unstoppable flow of tourists).

As I walk to Nancy and Sandy for our weekly lesson, I think back to all the fabulous ideas I've had which were supposed to generate fame and millions, especially in the early post-Criminal years when I was so desperate, when I had to rebuild everything. I can't fathom, given my state at the time, where I found the energy to come up with all that, patent my ideas, sell them, flood the markets with my genius. *Well, obviously, I didn't!*

(1) A progressive advertising campaign for the City of New York, which reinvents the symbol of the city as: The Green Apple. No longer the trite Big Apple, but an ecological, organic one. Keep the best known, most recognizable iconic image in the world, and simply recolor it. But my campaign wouldn't end there: it wasn't enough to let millions of people absorb its message passively through the huge posters in all the subway trains, on the Times Square billboards, on mugs, T-shirts, and other bric-a-bracs for tourists. My plan called for putting every New Yorker to work: "Let us know which public fountains are malfunctioning: Contact StopWaste@ greenapplenyc.org," or: "Let us know where recycling bins are missing: Contact StopWaste@greenapplenyc.org," and sweepstakes, awards, and the like. All I need is for the Mayor's office to give me a call.

(2) The electronic menu. Instead of passing the unhealthy germs among millions of people every time the waitress brings you those immense menus, why not computerize the table? That is, each table would feature a small computerized touch screen, imbedded into it (as many screens as there are places available at a given table), that the customers can use in order to browse what's available, select their choice, indicate special notes and requests which are then transmitted to a huge screen in the kitchen, received by the chef and staff. Touch-Menu: @, ©, °, ™ FANIA.

(3) Newlingual calendars. I tried to sell to Random House the idea of a calendar to teach foreign languages or, more correctly, something about foreign languages: "One Phrase a Day." An Italian phrase on every new day/ page, 365 sentences, or passages (with grammar rules). To be combined with this—sold together or separately in an exquisite box just in time for Christmas—"One Recipe a Day," 365 recipes from the Italian cuisine *in* Italian. For the pilot, I had practically already written them both. Patented idea, @, ©, °, ™ FANIA . . . run aground at ground-zero. (Random House never agreed to meet with me.)

But forget about all that. Here I am today: on a metaphorical train headed to . . . TEACHING . . . a place I had never wanted to visit. And I travel in third class to boot. Rightly so. Because the first class is occupied by the likes of Yonah and Galina, who give prestige to the academy, the likes of Cesare, who is now, with Francesca and the children, at the Loyola Law School in Los Angeles, and whose name one day I'll hear announced in the Nobel list. These are the people who have all the cards to be hired, while I am advanced in years and my curriculum exposes, unmistakably, the past of a person who hasn't given a thought to scientifically founded, experimentally solid principles in over three decades.

For the sake of mere survival, should I not land a teaching job or fail as *nouvelle-Malamud,* I could always open a private school teaching the Italian language. *Such a crass idea!* I would make a fortune. I have such an enormous amount of original material I put together over the years, that I could easily publish my own "exclusive" textbooks for the FANIA Italian Language Boutique—naturally, mandatory for the clients. . . *ka-ching!*

My mother used to derive a particularly sadistic pleasure from rehashing a certain parable every time I let my imagination take off as a small child and lose myself in my flights of fancy: "Miss Matilda is on her way to the market square, where she is bringing a small ricotta cheese to sell, which she carries balancing it on her head in the traditional peasant manner. She thinks to herself: 'If I am lucky, today I could sell my ricotta, and with the proceeds I could buy myself a small hen that every day would give me eggs to sell at the market, and if I sell all the fresh eggs she lays for me, slowly, ever so slowly, I could put together enough money to buy a young goat, healthier than Rosina, who is too old to even keep the grass in the yard under control. Then, later on, I could sell my goat and with the profits buy some tools to work the barren field that extends beyond the village borders, and soon I could use the money from the sale of the harvest to buy a very large . . . ' Matilda is so taken by her projects, and so intensely absorbed in her reveries, following which she has already come to be a queen, dressed in precious brocades, and with pretty and soft shoes—no longer barefoot on the hard cobblestones like she is now—when an acquaintance from the village sees her and greets her '*Buongiorno,*

*Signorina Matilda!* In response, Matilda, who is in the middle of fantasizing she is a rich noblewoman, makes a deep elegant bow and her ricotta slips off her head and plops on the ground, where a kitty rushes to eat it." This story didn't even have a title. It was enough for me to say that I wanted to do this, or to be that, for my mother's Pavlovian phrase to be unleashed: "Good morning, Miss Matilda!"—proffered with relish.

"Good morning . . ." a tentative voice from the outside world reaches me in the recesses of the chasm of memories and fantasies in which I plunged, insulating myself from everything and everyone around me, and it brings me back to reality . . . Broadway and 93rd. I am sucked back into a splendid daylight and crispy air, like a drowning man who at the last second is pulled out of the water onto land where he can breathe. "Fania, is that you?" Peripherally, I see a hand extending out of a dark coat sleeve as if to touch my arm and instinctively I shrivel and retract, self-protectively—it's New York, you never know. It's Yonah.

I can't say if the ricotta has just plopped on the ground or has instead developed into a castle.

The orange hues, already diffused all over, signal that autumn and a new festive season are here. The passersby are always in motion, in a hurry, from one side of the street to the other, yellow taxis can't satisfy the increasing demand, men are usually alone, women walk together, nannies gather with their employers' children at a street corner, or in the middle of a scrawny park in the dirty median, young people call each other from afar and make an appointment for the evening. Collars go up, hats make their first seasonal appearance, and so do heavier scarves; laced shoes replace sandals. And on the corner of Broadway and West 93rd, just steps from the European Bakery Café, for the first time in five years, between 10,000,000 people, Yonah and I cross each other. He's just finished a session with his shrink, nearby, and I am about to be late for my lesson with Nancy and Sandy. Me: "Do you still live in Washington Heights?" Yonah: "Do you still live by the Jewish Theological Seminary?" We'll have to leave further details for another time. We hurriedly exchange phone numbers. We promise to get together for coffee as soon as possible. We shake hands, awkwardly, and promptly reconsider, drop the formalities, and throw our arms around each other. As I begin to run in the direction of West End Avenue, Yonah manages to wedge in one last word: "Adina and I got divorced."

This time, we do meet at the Hungarian Café. This time, I don't lie when I say "I am single." I explain, by broad strokes, the long relationship with Philippe who is now in Europe. (*I don't specify that he is waiting for me, that from Philippe's viewpoint I may not be accurately defined as "single" . . . but Philippe's viewpoint is Paris, my view from Amsterdam Avenue is quite another.*) After our last meeting in 2002, Yonah and Adina, who opposed the idea of a divorce, tried a rapprochement that started and perhaps ended with the procreation of a second child—another male. (*Wow, an indomitable genetic starter, this Adina!*) *Baruch Hu.* And then the second definitive implosion. It is with great pleasure that one day I meet one of his sons. We go together, the three of us, to bring the boy's violin to a store for a small repair job and to find some suitable exercises for him to practice on. Afterward, they bring me to a giant M & M store in Times Square I knew nothing about. (*Childless people know nothing of where the other half of humanity, the childful one, goes for fun.*) We have such fun together: Fred is a polite child, well-behaved, already with a good head on his tiny shoulders, very intelligent, and naturally he can't believe his ears when he finds out that I, like him, speak Italian, just like his mom, and that at least the linguistic dynamics between him, me, and his father are not at all different from those at home.

I wouldn't define these meetings with Yonah as "dates." Our meetings are devoid of that adolescent anxiety to give a good impression, to put oneself at all costs in a positive light, to make sure that we sell ourselves successfully. And no time goes wasted in telling each other our whole pasts, because *we* are each other's pasts—and plus we did that already—and I'm sure Yonah remembers every bit of information, true or false, I ever gave him. But finally, I have nothing to hide or to be ashamed of. And these are not dates in the romantic sense either, because we don't even dare to hold hands: nothing physical happens. But perhaps exactly for this reason, the intimacy is all the stronger; we are like two old comfortable and sensible slippers that one can put on and walk in to the end of the world, without the footaches that always come from brand new shoes.

If I joined Philippe, what option would I have over there? Who would serve at the restaurant tables to make ends meet: The *grand maestro* or the other one? It is true that teaching had never been in my plans, but now it is, and it is a viable option—one precluded to me if I returned to Europe. The academic world is impenetrable over there. And now I learned to teach here, American style. I love being in the classroom. All big, small, trivial everyday problems vanish when I am in a classroom, and for seventy-five minutes there are only books and their relationship with . . . us! I teach about Botticelli's and Klimt's paintings, Wagner's and Beethoven's music, Kafka's novels and Sophocles's plays and what they intuitively foresaw of the future; visions from genius minds that encapsulate in words, colors and perfect rhythms, the feelings that the common mortal wouldn't know he has or, if so, how to express. With Dostoevsky, I can point out: O what grave is humanity digging for itself!

I have now deleted from my résumé those interminable lists of jobs I held between 1998 and 2001: instead, I choose to neatly list only my teaching positions and some of the subjects I cover: "The Hebrew Bible as Literature," "The Holocaust in Literature and Film," "Great Classics of the Western World (Part I)" and "Great Classics of the Western World (Part II)," "The Art of Writing (freshmen composition)," "Women Writers," and "Jewish Women Writers." And with this I would make a real bad waitress in Paris.

Yonah and I share stories about teaching, ideas for syllabi, bibliographies, and memorable teaching evaluations from our students. Just when I thought New York could not give me more, it gives me Yonah. Ten years too late: but perhaps this was the necessary path. *Like Odysseus's journey, who could very well have sailed from Troy to Ithaca in a couple of days and instead it took him . . . all of ten years.*

Here I am not alone anymore. I have Yonah again. I have new friends like Anastassiya, and Veronika; and old friends like Erez and Stephanie, Brett & Galina, and of course Debbie Bishop, who has grown to occupy a truly special place in my life. Same goes for Sandy and Nancy, whose affection and guidance are indispensable. A few years ago, I even came across Shira, my old Brandeis friend, as I was walking on the Upper East Side. After her master's at Brandeis, she didn't return to her parents in Baltimore (*I am sorry*

*I underestimated her*), but she moved to New York, where she has an interesting job, lives *unmarried* with a man who loves her very much, and she looks beautiful. From time to time, out of my Cracovian past reappears my dear old pal, Misha Davidovič Popkin, who stops by for a visit whenever he is in New York on business. He is a fulfilled capitalist and kosher-keeping Jew today and lives with his second wife and his mother—who has cost him his first wife—in Toronto. Recently, Brett & Galina have made their return into my life: they thrive more than ever in Connecticut, own a home and a car now, and are looking to buy a pied-à-terre in Manhattan. *Have they discovered the human face of capitalism—also known as "one's own bank account"?* I invite them for dinner at my place. We have a great time. Something inside of me wants to throw my arms around Galina's neck and never let go. I wish I could tell her how grateful I am for all the emails of encouragement and wise advice she sent me ten years ago. I would like to tell her that I know she was *there* for me, but that I could not hear her. But I don't mention the past at all. I make sure not to. Nobody dares. Here is today: here is me, now. In a few months, I'll be a PhD.

> Me: "This is nice, right?"
> Them: "Too bad Philippe is not here, we would have loved to meet him!"
> Me: "You would have liked him!" (Hm . . . as long as he bit his tongue about his ideas about extremist Muslims! Especially in France.)
> Them: "When is he coming back?"
> Me: "He won't." But have some tiramisù, I made it myself. Yes, I know, they divorced . . . Yes, yes, a second child, another boy . . . Yes, we see each other quite often . . . Come back, please! We can't let another ten years pass before we meet again!

I am *chez moi.* My friends are here.

Debbie tries only once to set me up with someone. She introduces me to a man much older, richer, and weirder than I would have expected. He is remarkably well-read, and, because of that, he reminds me of the Italian sexopath from centuries ago, Inferno. He is the owner of a small publishing house specialized in coffee-table books. He also happens to be physically repulsive. His is not a case of *Beauty and the Beast,* in which human, spiritual, and intellectual qualities overwhelm and cancel the physical ugliness. Nothing could redeem the overpowering disgust inspired by his slimy shapelessness. Yes, I let myself be taken to a Broadway show, out to dinner, and then to a weekend at his lake house, but only because there are always other people with us, friends of his he is so generous to share with me. Many of these are also friends of Debbie's. I'd never go alone with him. So, technically, these are not dates.

The lake house used to be Edith Wharton's: here slept Henry James. Beast bought and renovated it. I go there with a woman, former Playboy Bunny and wife of Hugh Hefner's business partner, and a few other friends. All very friendly and easygoing. A great crowd. The house, it goes without saying, is a dream. No, more than that: it's what I'd wish to be if I were a house. It is what I would want life itself to be. Of the three most beautiful places I have ever been, this lake house, Edith Wharton's, is the heavenliest. It is located in a wooded, semi-mountainous, exclusive area, thirty minutes from Manhattan and. . . . U N K N O W N. And gated. In Tuxedo, the town that gave us the homonymous piece of clothing. Ah, New Yorkers, always trying to beat one another to the best, the first of firsts, tomorrow's greatest new thing . . . trendsetters, envy-makers. But, hands down, Beast beat everyone out of the race here.

This house is on a lake, not in the sense of "along the shores that surround the lake," but in the sense of "over" it, built on a protruding boulder that extends over, *über* the lake. Hence its breathtaking terrace (not for agoraphobes) stretches directly above the waters that placidly swoosh at the base of this divine promontory. We, the guests, arrived all together from Manhattan, a merry company, like kids on a field trip. We all have a blast. When it's time to go home, the group comes together again to plan the return, and Beast, of his own initiative, announces, "I'll drive Fania back." I hear this for the first time myself.

I'll go out on a limb (on the ledge of this breathtaking terrace itself) and say that it must have taken years of tormented resentment, nursed in a lonely corner, nibbling on his nails to the quick, gorging on pints of chocolate ice-cream upon double-chocolate ice-cream, so much money, so much power and brainpower and never a soul to hug, before Beast formulated his genius plan of "Surprise Date with Lakeview" for his chosen victims. He barely nears his moist lips to mine, that I, in the gentlest way possible, juke aside with the alerted reflexes of one who's just smelled a vial of anal secretions, and as regal as a Katharine Hepburn who doesn't let anyone dictate her moves, I say "No." What a triumph if it ended there . . . but unfortunately I add a lame "Sorry." Hepburn would have never said sorry.

Beast drives me back home, as promised, in his convertible, and when I call him to thank him and make him understand that I am neither offended, nor angry, or outraged, but that I wish to put the awkward moment behind us and be friends because I admire him greatly, at first he doesn't take my calls, until one day he leaves a message on my answering machine in which, with a piqued tone, he tells me that he doesn't need friends, he already has plenty and doesn't want another. (*Especially me—he doesn't say this but, being the exquisite publisher that he is, it is printed in* BLOCK LETTERS *between his lines.*) "So, good luck and goodbye" the message concludes. From the height of my newly found ataraxy, I understand something that would have escaped me only a few years back: that the offence is not on me, but rather the defeat is on him. I am not the one supposed to feel hurt like a child whose actions were misinterpreted and has been punished for it nonetheless. (*My mother's philosophy of mistakes: Consider today's misguided punishment a down payment on the next mischief.*) It's not my fault. I don't think I have ever uttered those words in my life: IT'S NOT MY FAULT. They are so freeing! *It is time I too step out of my sepulcher, like Lazarus.*

I am not the only one awakening, but it seems as if a shroud has fallen off the body of the entire nation that lay entombed in a mausoleum of fear, hate, and poisonous discord and is now miraculously breathing again. Seven years of Pinocchio and Stromboli at the White House left the world scarred, disfigured, mangled in irrecoverable ways. The next president will not be a Republican, not even if the Elephant Party candidate is Jesus Christ himself! A light of hope is insinuating itself through every fold of society. We are finally at a turning point, we can finally open our mouths again, break our chains, open the cages, shove the guards aside, and rush toward the gates that open into the future: HOPE! It was indeed a monstrous time we went through. Politics itself was murdered: no president or government can be thought of any longer as the summit of power, the extreme point in the chain of command.

Above them now there are the corporations—entities without face, devoid of all human content, whose power to make and undo the world must be catered to, and appeased if necessary, by the politicians, who are pathetically naked and powerless now. They must offer the new avaricious gods more and more appealing morsels, ever greater sacrifices, until there is nothing left of the environment, first, and of our human traces in the end. These are the White Walkers from George R. R. Martin's novel *Game of Thrones*. But the most catastrophic consequence of the Caligula-style triumvirate, Bush-Cheney-Rumsfeld, is having made imbecility not only licit (no longer that unofficial socio-ethical crime of which even the idiots themselves were ashamed) but legitimate, as authentic as the American spirit. They have made it into an American value. As American as apple pie and obesity. The brand, if not the prerequisite, of true patriotism. Even before attacking the Axes of Evil, Bush-Cheney-Rumsfeld declared war on the Brain. "Intellectual" had already become a dirty word under Reagan, another great clown of the local historical Olympiads. In the Bush era, those who think are the enemy.

Hillary Clinton is the most prominent candidate in the Democratic Party and the one I consider most likely to make it. She has the full support of the State of New York. She also has the media on her like hunting dogs behind a wounded prey: they reduce her to the sum of her wrinkles, her choice of clothes, laughter decibels, and presumed frigidity. Finally a female candidate! Now we can overlook the politician's ideological positions and focus at last on what really matters: cankles. There is also another Democratic candidate in the race, Clinton's only true antagonist, but he seems a bit young and inexperienced. And if cankles are insurmountable for a woman, imagine being Black for a man! A Black president in the United States is as much a four-leaf clover as a Papesse in the Vatican.

Either way, the revolution is guaranteed.

Yonah and I watch the political debates in his Washington Heights apartment. We're good together. We both agree that, despite the fact that Barak Obama seems almost a biblical character, a David ready to knock down Goliath without even a slingshot, the nation is not ready for a jolt, but needs to take one step at a time: give us four years of Clinton first, and then the *coup de grace* with an Obama octennium. The whole city is glued to the television screens. You can hear shouts of support leaking out of cracked-open windows: "Yeah, baby!!!" "Yooohooo!" Whistles and cheers, with every well-crafted answer from Hillary. We too jump up from the couch and applaud some of her rhetorical pirouettes. I wouldn't have thought, but she is really great and so prepared. This is the worst nightmare for the Republicans, perennially married to the ontological law of noncontradiction: a woman and a Black man. Whatever happens, there is no "lesser evil" here for a Republican: they are two impossible possibilities.

At the primaries, I vote too. I am moved, happy, proud to be able to participate in this historic turning point. All of New York votes for Clinton.

Yonah still wears glasses and pulls up that inquisitive index finger when he wants to talk. I don't tell him because I wouldn't wish to make him self-conscious and lose this behavioral trait so characteristic and personal. And anyway, there are more important things to reveal to him.

I feel I always have something to reveal to Yonah, and it's never good news.

They just offered me a full-fledged university position. I sent out only one job application and it was accepted.

It is a tenure-track position as Assistant Professor of English and Jewish Studies at the University of South Carolina . . . full time, with benefits. In an empty academic market, and thousands of freshly minted PhDs hungry for any job, I got one of the rarest and sweetest. *Nah, I won't tell him just yet.*

I accept, of course. Nancy and Sandy congratulate me with tears in their eyes. At the Graduate Center, mine has already become one of those mythical stories that the new cadres of graduate students for generations will tell each other until at some point it'll be believed to be just an urban legend. With my friend Veronika, we have fun looking at houses for sale in South Carolina (*a place, by the way, I still can't find on a map*). Our jaws drop before the images of *actual* houses ten times bigger than ours in New York. *This can't be!* When they phoned me to make the offer, I wanted so much to call Yonah and ask him point-blank: "What do we do?" But that would be a different actress, another film. Yonah has two children now. In my film, my lips are sealed, I wait for him to ask me "So, what *do we* do?"

When I finally announce it to him, Yonah reacts in the most reasonable way: with great joy for me. He even leaks out a small indiscretion:

Jennifer—yes, that same Jennifer from our first Thanksgiving together in Boston, who appears to have moved to Queens in the arc of the last ten years—well, Jennifer had also applied for that same job. They chose *me*. Yonah is very happy *for* me. He doesn't ask "So, what do we do?"

Everyone congratulates me: I won the job market lottery. *Che fortuna!* *Lucky me.*

Things are looking up.

And I go South.

# PART 7

# The Shore

# 17

"The time has come," the Walrus said,
"To talk of many things:
Of shoes—and ships—and sealing-wax—
Of cabbages—and kings—
And why the sea is boiling hot—
And whether pigs have wings."

—Lewis Carroll

I load Milli in my brand-new Honda CR-V, at midnight sharp on July 9, 2008, locking the door behind us of an apartment emptied out of its bohemian furnishings and of the two of us who loved it so dearly. As I walked one last time through the corridor on my way out, I could have sworn that the apartment was letting out echoes of laughter, the aroma of cooking, the sound of water falling in the shower, of music, friends, love moans, phone rings, the kitty's nightly tip-taps on the wood floors, the crumbling *chateaux* in the air.

I load Milli, my violin, my old guitar, and my "lucky bamboo" (Veronika's gift . . . God knows I need it!). I program the GPS for 1411 Idalia Drive, Columbia, South Carolina 29206 and hear "Proceed to the highlighted route, then the guidance will start" in the unnaturally natural female voice I chose for my navigator: 750 miles, 17 hours, and 7 states to an unknown destination . . . unknown to me.

Paula Feldman, a colleague (to be) from the English department down there found a rental house for me, whose allure, apparently, is its enormous garden. She was out of herself as she explained over the phone: "You will love it! It has a giant ancient oak on the property! You've never seen anything so beautiful." Indeed, I have never seen an oak tree, or if I have, I haven't recognized it. Paula is a green-thumb gardener, a nature photographer, and an expert of English Romantic literature. I am none of the above. I tell her that I spent my life in insalubrious cities where the eye is trained to recognize only what type of a car is about to run you over, and that therefore I couldn't tell a giant oak from a plastic Christmas tree bought in a 99¢ store. She laughs it off and adds: "Believe me, you won't miss it." And I don't know if she is talking about sighting the tree or dying of pollution in a big city. "And, dear, it's not a garden: it's a yard," she also corrects me. I've no idea what the difference is either.

Milli begins to complain on the fifth floor of our (former) apartment building, continues all the way down the stairwell (possibly waking up the neighbors), and isn't assuaged at all by the pleasant interior and crisp leather seats of our new car. She lets me know by peeing in her carrier and forcing us to live with the stench until destination. She emits an angry "meee-aaaaaaaaaah" without taking a single breath between Riverside Drive and the George Washington Bridge.

*O George Washington Bridge! How long has it been since the last time I drove across! Today I intend to make it across! The days when I wished to drive off it, into the foaming waters below, are over.* Milli abruptly falls silent the moment the car wheels roll on the bridge. It's as if someone suddenly cut the wire of a wailing alarm. I stick my forefinger between the bars of her carrier to make sure she's alive. *Ouch. She's alive.* Her instinct must have told her that this is not a cab, and we are not going to the hated veterinarian clinic: this journey is conclusive; it has no return. I wonder why this was revealed to her only as we got onto the George Washington Bridge. Perhaps it is the silent and threatening presence of the Hudson River below us, the energy of this water boundary which completely erases the trail that leads back to our house, a trail she could sniff herself back to from anywhere on the island, but whose traces drown in this body of waves? We are turning our backs to 1264. *Twelve-Sixty-four Amsterdam Avenue, Apartment Five D, New York, New York one zero zero two seven, two-one-two-six-six-two-four-six-four-one, I repeat mechanically to fix the numbers in memory and to slow the present from becoming the past so quickly.* Once we get over this bridge, past these deep waves, invisible in the night (waves that once called to me, drew me, allured me into their embrace), neither Milli nor I will know our way back to 1264, we won't be able to return. Neverland, Macondo, Bengodi will vanish, and no one will ever believe us if we tell of our adventures on a strange island that will sound totally fictitious.

*I had a flat in New York City . . .*

The journey seems eternal, New Jersey (*rushed through*), Pennsylvania (*immoderately big*), Delaware (*ridiculously tiny*), Maryland (*oh, I see the sun rise*), Virginia (*by now I want to call it quits*), North Carolina (*gosh, it's huge and ugly*). As soon as I pass the South Carolina border, an apocalyptic rain starts pouring down like I've never seen before. I am here, and yet I swear I smell the slightly burnt American coffee and the greasy smoke coming out of the sandwich grill at the café on Amsterdam Avenue. I swear I still have some food remnants between my teeth of every single thing eaten in the last ten years, the dust collected from the street under my shoes and on my skin, the voices I heard are in my ears, I still feel the light touch of another lady's body who brushes against mine on her hurried way down the subway stairs.

I wonder at what point New York will start to fade. Maybe the extremities will fade first: I'll forget which subway takes you to J & R's in Wall Street. Then it will be the turn of the one-way streets: which roads run only from east to west, and which only from west to east? Which subway exits are always chained on Sundays, which are always accessible? Will the memories of half-dressed bodies lying down, as happily as dogs, wherever there's a beam of sunlight in Central Park vanish too? Will the most beautiful building, the Chrysler, and the ugliest, the Empire State Building, begin to merge into one until I no longer know the difference between East 45th and East 34th Streets? Will I be able to remember why exactly the only place I would eat a bagel from, for ten years, was Ess-a-Bagel on Third Avenue? Who will take my place on the ferry to Staten Island? I never failed to sail the 30-minute boat journey at least once a year, like the Holocaust survivor who taught me to celebrate our American arrival that way. Then the circle of darkness will become denser and ineluctably close in on the center: the particular weightlessness of the air on certain spring days when the buildings wrap themselves up in the turquois sky as a precious shawl for a big gala. Or the lampposts that automatically light up at the exact meeting point between day and night.

The darkness at this instant is almost total although it is only 4 PM and the wind is so strong that I feel my SUV (a CR-V SUV, I'm driving a double acronym!) levitate as if the air lifted it in its arms as you do with a bride on the doorstep. Maybe it's a good sign. I do as everyone does, I look at the other cars to understand how to proceed: the other cars stop, I stop. They don't panic, I don't . . . I panic less. Milli still doesn't stir, doesn't meow, doesn't drink or eat . . . And neither do I. I think I just drove through my first tornado.

We arrive at 1411 Idalia Drive passing through a tree-lined forest full of small houses. I seem to recall that my colleague referred to this neighborhood as Forest Acres. This is not like the periphery of Boston I remember: here between houses a third home could be built with wiggle room to spare! And between the street and the houses themselves there is a huge buffer, an isolating barrier made of wide, deep gardens full of shrubs and flowerbeds. A clue that people here don't live in full view but prefer to shield behind a bit of privacy, avoid unnecessary exposure. I approve of that.

I see the oak tree surrounded by pine trees before I even see the 1411 tag hanging from the mailbox: I make out a gray-trunked king, sinewy, knotted, with branches going up in the sky and branches resting to the ground as if taking a break from fighting gravity, covered in green moss and foliage. *That's gotta be it!* And a few meters away, tucked aside among more shrubbery, there lies the house of the third piglet: the one of bricks that the wolf can't blow away. Red bricks, a chimney that rises from the gable roof, tiny stoops up to the tiny door under an embracing portico, a side porch, a driveway. I am speechless! Three bedrooms, two bathrooms, kitchen, breakfast corner, formal dining room, large living room with woodburning fireplace, and between the kitchen and the third access door, the one on the back, there is an ample mudroom with washer and dryer . . . like the one in the basement in my New York apartment building, only better. So much better.

Milli can't believe her little legs, stiffened by years of roaming through non-existent spaces. Milli, I now realize with horror, doesn't know *space,* I think. I send her ahead (like soldiers do donkeys into a minefield): I follow her, just a few inches away from her erect tail, her upward-pointing ears, vibrating nose. She deliberately trots ahead, and I trot behind her: she sniffs the soft white carpet of the living room which she inaugurates by hastily sharpening her nails on it before moving on to the rest of the house paved in dark wood planks. This place is incredible. The lights go off and simultaneously an atrocious *boooom* explodes outside, like a cannon ball discharged from a meter away. Milli and I jump into each other's arms, (me) screaming and (her) digging freshly filed claws into my shoulder. The thunderstorm reached us here, and we must have lost electricity.

Immediately my mind conjures visions of old ladies in laced caplets, holding a white candle, entering through each of the three doors of this house that is perhaps built on an old cemetery (or worse, on a plantation) and now ghosts, still bleeding, will appear behind me in the reflection of the mirrors in each bathroom. In New York, I never had ghost fantasies. In New York, ghosts, if they are around, get pushed aside like anybody else who gets in your way when you are in a rush to reach the train station. Ghosts would get an inferiority complex, or feel useless, if they lived in New York. I can only imagine the conversation with their psychoanalyst: "you do have a bit of a morbid death drive, but, all in all, much healthier than most of my other, live, patients . . ." Plus, New York has pale, shabby, raggedy, bleeding people to sell! In New York you fear the lawless hoodlums. Oh, what I wouldn't give for one of those right now. A snappy, grumpy New York killer, but in the flesh! Here there is an unnatural silence . . . *No, wait . . . what's that?* The unholy wailing of the banshee?! Or an owl? (*Note to self: Never arrive at a new place at night, in the middle of an apocalyptic storm, when it is too late to make out old gravestones in the garden. . . . yard.*) The darkness is total. Not even the car or the oak tree outside are visible, except when lightning strikes, but that is also when I shut my eyes and withdraw my head like a turtle on the gallows. There are no public streetlamps. I am sure I saw other houses surrounding this one while I slowly rolled in my car along the path to 1411 Idalia Drive. What if they were an illusion created by the forces of the other world to deceive me? (*To-do: First thing tomorrow, find animal shelter and adopt fully adult, partly wild, German shepherd.*) Milli (*disloyal feline*) ran away to hide, but I remain stiffly seated in what I believe is the living room (I can feel the carpet beneath me), with my back to the wall, motionless, as wide-eyed as a colossal squid, and plan to stay there until the electricity returns. *Will it?*

I don't have a bed yet. I will sleep on the floor, but, not to worry, I have been prepared for this event for twelve years. Finally I can use the brown and orange sleeping bag from my camping days which, for incomprehensible reasons, I rolled up and squeezed into my suitcase when I left Rome in 1996 on my way to Boston—against everyone's advice. There! I knew it would come in handy one day. As soon as I unroll my sleeping bag, Milli reappears. Tomorrow, we'll see who laughs when I come through that door with a Husky! (*I'll show the disloyal feline!*) Speaking of Huskies, the inside of the house is deliciously glacial, despite the 96 percent humidity I felt outside, and the 103 degrees Fahrenheit the car's thermometer registered on the road this afternoon. They really like their houses chilly here.

In the morning, apart from a debilitating backache, everything is crystal clear. I would be lying if I didn't admit that I cried inconsolably last night. I cried so disconsolately that I must have dismayed even the owl on the tree outside that went silent for the rest of the time. But in the morning, with the dawn, a real miracle happened. I opened my eyes—awoken by the glow of the sun that penetrated from the countless windows all along the sides of my little brick house—Milli and I stretched side by side, and the first thought that occurred to me was *not* "Oh God, what have I done! This time I really gotta kill myself!" but . . . "*Oh my!*" a wave of tremendous happiness. Just like that. Total acceptance. And with total acceptance came a rush of gleefulness. No, I will not die because I didn't wake up at 1264 Amsterdam Ave.: I am excited to have opened my eyes exactly where I am right now, in this place.

I get up, I perk up my ears, as does Milli from her rolled-up position on the ground atop the sleeping bag: from outside, we are reached by an orchestral concert of chirps, yodels, warbles, tweets, screeches, purls, gurgles, as if all the existing species of birds had convened on the porch for a wild party. I do not hear a car, an emergency siren, or artificial music coming from neighboring houses, nor barking dogs, screaming men, or whining children. I hear only birds. I can almost tangibly perceive my essence adjust to the new environment in which it has been thrust: now that the space around me is so vast, my interior space dilates, expands, outspreads as if to finally stretch its limbs after a century of being bottled up. It's a little like being born: you don't know what it's like outside of a belly, neither are you particularly eager to find out, until they push and drag you out of there by force, and once you've been expelled from that cozy little bag in which you were just dandy—with a bare minimum that was, nonetheless, your "everything"—and in which immobility was the only option you knew, only then, only once you are spat out of there, you miss your breath for a moment, you deliver a loud cry of protestation, but then comes the realization that (1) you are huge compared to your size of only minutes earlier, (2) it's not so bad, the world has not ended but seems, for all intents and purposes, to have just begun, (3) you had been missing a lot of interesting shit spending so much time where you were, safely, curled up like a cat, sucking in whatever came down someone else's throat, and (4) you've already lost any desire to crawl back in there, you won't even think about it anymore. And anyway, now that your mass has suddenly tripled, there is no way to deflate, re-roll yourself up and push yourself back up there. The future has started its march: it is in this *now*, not *before*, that infinite paths of possibilities unfold before you. You've got to relearn everything anew because this life, just like the previous one in the slimy sac, is also life . . . only totally different. First thing: you must learn to move your legs, to walk, one step at a time. (*From there, though, it should all be pretty self-evident: uno due, uno due, forward . . . southward.*)

My furniture was packed and removed, once again, by the charming Israeli giants from a company aptly called Noah's Ark, and it will all arrive at Idalia Drive from New York in ten days. Mom and dad are busy preparing a package with a new wardrobe suitable for the South of their imagination: Yamamay swimwear (the sea, I was given to believe, is a few steps away), brand new lingerie from La Perla, floaty pants and linen jackets, and a large-brimmed hat that my mother considers essential for my new role in *Gone with the Wind 21st Century Edition* and which my father loses his mind trying to fit inside the parcel with his wife screaming hysterically next to him "*Attento!* Don't damage it!"

For the time being, Milli is the only one of us to have food . . . even if she's not touching her plate. I, on the other hand, about to starve, do give some thought to tasting Purina Beef Feast for Gravy Lovers.

I drive my car around for a reconnaissance trip but can't find where food is sold. I haven't spotted shops or supermarkets. The Time Warner technician will show up only next week to connect telephone line and internet, so for now no Google: no Google, no maps or information, no information, no food. Apart from the Danesi coffee and my Neapolitan espresso machine (that has already scented this house with a delectable caffeinated smell of home), I didn't bring with me anything else related to subsistence.

No one is around. The only noise that indicates a civilizing presence is the buzzing of a distant engine which I can't place. (I hope they are not deforesting Forest Acres!) Then, without warning, the first human makes his appearance: I am alone on my porch, drinking the first cup of coffee of the day, freshly out of bed, a bit disheveled . . . *say, the uglier version of Scarlet O'Hara* . . . and here I see a dried-up, tall Clint Eastwood, in blue jeans, T-shirt, and leather boots, emerge from a little house across the street and head toward my direction. Immediately, I jump to attention, wondering which way to run—all the worse, because I am still wearing my relatively see-through nightgown . . . more like a Yankee whore than the genteel Confederate lady. The guy stretches out his hand and introduces himself . . . but the moment he opens his mouth, something out of an untuned banjo that has no resemblance to the spoken English I assimilated in the last third of my life hits my uncomprehending ears. I don't understand a word. "*Dingidydin din din blengidyblen blen* eight riffles *blen dingy blen din din* mah truck."

Certainly the neighbor has seen a new cowboy arrive in town and came to demarcate the turf, like a dog pisses in the four corners of a room. He must have spied through the curtains of his wooden cottage every move of mine since I arrived. He must have counted and analyzed the objects I took out of the car because those, better than a police report, summarize exactly what kind of person he'll have to deal with: one without even a cooler for beer! He must have freaked out when he saw the musical instruments and a cat with a sensitive stomach instead of a snarling pit bull. "A liberal!" he must have immediately told himself, alarmed—maybe even a communist! And as a true

American, he took destiny into his own hands and came to check in person. However, confronted with, well, me, he must have felt sorry and decided instead to offer me his protection as a true Southern gentleman: "If you need anything, Miss, come to me any moment, I'll take care of it . . . I have eight rifles in the back of my truck . . . always loaded" was the tune the banjo was playing. *OK. I'm readjusting.* I get it: Here, from language to kinesics, it's all another planet!

I discover that that mechanical buzz I hear comes from lawn mowers and leaf blowers. I wonder what it means (and how!) one blows leaves off . . . Forest Acres. *It's a forest of sort . . . aren't leaves . . . hum, too many, no?*

I would like to call Yonah. In the twelve years we've known each other, I don't think I ever called Yonah. *He doesn't carry eight guns and never encouraged me to call him any time in case of trouble, like Clint Eastwood here.* New me, new rules: I call Yonah to give him my new address and let him know that I made it safe and sound. Distances, between people, possess a physical thickness beyond the geographical plane. On the other end of the line, I hear the city around Yonah. The unbearably humid July heat, the sizzling cement, apartments as hot as ovens, the human traffic in which he circulates, the acoustic background through which he hears my voice. And after my long car journey, now this distance is also measured in motorways, toll booths, gas pumps, between me and him . . . all of it makes the separation tangible. He is in the hustle and bustle, I am in quietude; he, in the heart of things, I at the extreme edges; he, marching to a thousand daily destinations, I, gently rocking on a swing on the porch without a care in the world. *Is it possible that this is what makes Fania happy? I'd swear I am actually well! Or is this "perceived" happiness just a trick to make do with whatever hand life deals me at this point? Am I like Aesop's fox that claims to dislike grapes just because it can't reach the vine branches?*

I also call Nancy and Sandy: Nancy is a purebred New York Jew, from her brilliance to her inability to operate an elevator's buttons, but Sandy was born in Alabama, a deeper South than even South Carolina, so he knows how to survive in the world. He'll help. The enthusiasm with which I narrate about my findings here makes my voice go up two octaves and I worry I am already sounding like a banjo myself, symbiotically, like Zelig, morphing into a mixture of Clint Eastwood next door and the birds in my garden this morning. I explain to them about the acres of land I have around, the magnolia trees so leafy that you can't see their trunks, of the third little piglet's house in which I live, and which has more rooms than I could furnish with a three-year salary. I take this opportunity to reveal to the trusted mentors the small setback I'm up against: "Problem is, there are no supermarkets!" I say with a few tears in my dismayed voice like a goat's bleat before the slaughter. From New York I am reached by a thunderous roar of laughter. As soon as he catches his breath, Sandy explains to me that, *in America,* where I seem to have freshly arrived, the stores are not by the road (*how am I to know?*) but removed two thousand feet from the street: they are gathered around what they call here a strip mall or a mall. (*I have no idea what he's telling me.*). "As you drive, you'll see signs to get off the road, turn into a kind of *piazza* and there you'll see various markets, shops, post offices, usually under little arcades." Sandy laughs, suspecting it'll still take me days before I find some food. He also admonishes: "Don't ask for 'shops,' ask for a "strip mall." ("*Strip*" . . . "*stripper,*" *same word? Same verb?*) "Welcome to America!" He laughs cheerfully before adding, "Look for a sign that reads WALMART. Wherever there is a Walmart, the rest follows."

I hang up and head out. This time, I come back with my SUV packed to the roof with food, Brita filter carafes, bird feeders and seeds, and most of all a queen-size inflatable mattress and a manual pump (*Mistake No. 1*). While shopping, I came across the new rabbi in town. How bizarre! I was in front of the yogurt section and, one thing led to another, a gentleman standing next to me, wearing a fedora clearly not in keeping with the southern headdress style of baseball caps, made a very witty joke, and we struck up a conversation. Him: "Where do you come from, your accent isn't from here." Me: "I just got here from New York." Him: "I also just arrived from New York!" He from Broadway and 122nd, me from 122nd and Amsterdam. A "Jewda" in the South! I chuckle thinking of Gene Wilder in *The Frisco Kid.* This is my first Friday in South Carolina and I already have a rabbi, a *shul* to go to, and a *comunità* to join. Who would have thought things would fall into place so smoothly?

I'm back at the third piglet's cottage, I sit on the porch, and I let the birds' chirrups lull me while I drink a small espresso. I also attempt a small experiment—I probably shouldn't: I lift Milli in my arms and set her down gently on the grass just for a minute. I want her so much to experience for once in her lifetime what it's like to be out here, what nature is like. She looks at me resentfully. But then she takes three cautious steps toward a random green tall grass growing by the porch and starts chewing on it. What made her know to do that? I gently carry her back inside and she positions herself by a bay window from which she keeps an eye on me and meows desirously at the birds. *Et in Arcadia ego* . . . We are so well.

At night, after I almost lose a leg pumping air in the inflatable bed, I finally lie down on more than mere hard floor, *hmmmm* . . . divine. A minute into this bliss, I hear a hiss . . . *psssssssssssssssss*. . . . I hiss to myself "Idiot!" It didn't occur to me (Mistake No. 2) that Milli would claw her way up to curl next to me on the deflatable mattress.

> *"A loaf of bread," the Walrus said,*
> *"Is what we chiefly need:*
> *Pepper and vinegar besides*
> *Are very good indeed—*
> *Now if you're ready Oysters dear,*
> *We can begin to feed."*

The most august disasters caused by tornados are usually due to the action of a "family" of twisters, never of a single isolated nucleus. But this is an irrelevant detail, when, in its wake, this destructive breath of nature leaves behind 695 dead, as happened in Missouri in 1925: what difference did it make to the survivors or victims the kind of tornado that hit them? Machiavelli spoke of end and means, but I don't know which one is more pressing when one is weighing one's moves in life, or drawing conclusions from one's own disasters: end and means, or cause and effect? Even with tornadoes, the cause–effect relationship is neither predictable nor necessarily proportionate. Causes and effects are inextricably linked, yet the effects are attestable, while the causes can only be presumed or inferred. Can we always say with absolute certainty what comes first? Karl Popper ruled that the only effective way to test a theory is to try to deny it. Let's say that the present is an effect of the past: between cause (past) and effect (present), the connector element necessary for the existence of both would be memory. But what master does memory serve? Whose side is it on? The present or the past? And if memory makes a mistake, how is our perception of both affected?

All in all, the South is a surprise. Nothing I learned in the last twelve years prepared me for this America. Now I understand that only Debbie Bishop had got it right when she warned me of the "steel magnolias," talking about people down here. The magnolia, queen of the local plant kingdom, is outwardly the incarnation of an ideal daintiness, genteelness, domestication, but, inwardly, unmovable, unbreakable, in fact indomitable. But of course, what Debbie Bishop meant was: they are so false. "Bless your heart!" the ladies here tell you, with perfectly coiffured hair at all hours of the day, with nickel-plated cadences in their voices, when in reality they mean to say "Bug off!" And you, naive, smile and thank them, thinking they just offered you a blessing. The South, where the first question everyone asks upon meeting you for the first time is "Which church do you go to?"–and they don't care whether it's a monotheistic tabernacle, a pagan shrine, or a heretical chantry as long as *you have a church* or are prepared to produce one on the fly if you don't want to be looked at sideways forever by the entire neighborhood. No church, and they immediately frame you as a subversive. "Oh, I love your accent!" I hear repeatedly from every cashier, waiter, hairdresser, mechanic, electrician, policeman, insurance agent, plumber, postman, and secretary as soon as I open my mouth for as little as a "Hello." At first, I thought it was the truth. Then I realized that it's just a different way to announce, "Watch it, I got my eyes on you." The South, where Sunday is the Lord's Day and it is forbidden by law to sell, hence, to buy, alcohol, but it is perfectly legal (in some states, or if you get permission from your pastor) to enter church with a rifle. The South so amicably segregated, in spite of the Civil Rights Act of 1964. *Bianchi* and *Neri* coexist harmoniously, smiling, with friendly "Goooo' mornin'!" held apart by a brutal police force and invisible borders known by both sides and never trespassed. *But was it not the same in New York? Even if differently set up? Maybe more subtly, but oh so visibly!*

South Carolina is the state of Bernard Baruch, the Jewish guy who gave us the phrase the "cold war." *Which I suspect he pronounced drawling the words, since I discovered that the Jewish accent down here is nothing like it is in Brooklyn.*

No muffins from the neighbors, no invitation to Thanksgiving or 4th of July BBQ for Fania in South Carolina. Here I have to learn from scratch the rules of the game: the gestures, the body language, the speech tones are all different from, if not the opposite of, the signals I got accustomed to in the north.

Here I am a stranger in the same way a refugee from Eritrea or the undocumented Mexican gardener is a stranger. In the sophisticated cities of the northeast, the word "Italian" elicits a jolt of admiration and excitement, it makes a New Yorker skip a breath. But in the "real" America, the interlocutors don't even make the effort to recall to mind the vaguest silhouette of the globe in order to place you in the country you call home. When they ask you where you are from, their ears are programmed to register only two kinds of responses: "Here" or "Not from here." From which part of the "not from here" you are doesn't make any difference: you're not American, you're not one of them, you're not from "here," where you are from is inferior to here, and so better to keep an eye on you. The nonurban mentality knows neither admiration nor pity, only mistrust.

Here I am again, cast onto a new planet, adjusting to a new world, totally unprepared but this time around, at least, without the illusion of ever "belonging." I didn't mean to be here. This time I am a stranger even to myself. This version of me—*Fania in the Deep South, one with nature, assiduous worker in a noble profession, law abiding citizen*—wasn't my making. *Or was it?*

I feel like Alice fallen through a deep tunnel of mysteries (and wonders, I hope), but I can't swear that at the end of the story I will resurface.

My colleagues say encouragingly, "You'll see, you won't die of hunger here!" The people of the South take boundless pride in their food culture. Fish is omnipresent, and inexpensive, and the basic accompaniment for everything is grits (polenta, I think it is), or rice, of which, in centuries past, the South Carolina plantations were among the largest producers. And there is no food that, according to the local culinary wisdom, can't be fried with excellent results. "No New York-style pizza, though." *I want to cry.*

Before I left New York, my friends Erez and Stephany told me to cheer me up that the universe had made a mistake and corrected it: when it sent me to Columbia University, it actually meant for me to go to Columbia, South Carolina. They hoped that I might enjoy the idea that I was finally fulfilling my fate. Let's hope the universe hasn't messed up again, I tell myself, and meant for me to be in Colombia, the South American State of Gabriel Garcia Marquez and the cartels that murdered Pablo Escobar.

While the universe hopefully prepares an apology to me, I better roll up my sleeves and start figuring out how to get on track for this new race . . . needless to say, over hurdles. This is what I've gathered: If one wants to be promoted (as the only alternative to being fired), one must publish a book, a minimum of two academic articles, get five-star reviews from students each semester, establish a good collegial rapport with everybody from the university president to the cafeteria waitress (*good character!*) and a name for oneself through local, national, and international recognition. All of this, within the six-year trial period. Bugger! And mind the gap . . . literally, a one-year gap! Because when they hire you and mention the "six-year tenure period," they forget to mention that in fact the years available for you to do the impossible are five, not six, as your tenure file must be submitted a year ahead of time for the various committees and subcommittees to analyze it and come to a decision about your life or death. My tenure clock starts ticking. I have until 2013. Bugger!

If I stop to ask too many questions, to double guess myself, it's the end. I can only go forward. There's no stopping this snowball. They put you on a tricycle, you start pedaling; they throw you into the water, you learn to swim; they catapult you to South Carolina, what do you learn? To pedal and swim simultaneously as fast as possible to get your sorry ass out of South Carolina, I guess? I'm panicking. This is not good. I need to sit on the porch, to get some air, to have a drink, to fight the tears back. Clint Eastwood, shoot me now!

I land on Moriel Yarkan's couch: Moriel is the local cantor and doubles as the local Israeli psychoanalyst. I start my first session with her even before I get a real bed at Idalia Drive.

Moriel is a woman in her late fifties, extremely spiritual bordering on mystical, a mother-earth type, with floating clothes, meaningful necklaces and rings, silvery hair cascading over her shoulders, a wide bosom that comforts you with every hug, and an office space full of incense smoke, cushions and red, yellow, blue fabrics, apotropaic trinkets, including two extremely therapeutic dogs I love caressing while they doze off next to me on the couch, loaded with a persuasive energy and healing cuteness for body and mind. Freud would excommunicate her.

First, Moriel shares with me her cheesecake recipe. For my birthday, I bake myself a masterpiece identical to the New York Carnegie Deli one. I am in love with Moriel. Second, Moriel prescribes I contact a medium. She has just consulted her herself and tells me the details of the results. This medium is not a reader of the future (*whom I'd really need right now*) but of the past (*whom I so don't need*) and even the remote past (*why would anyone need it?*). An expert in drawing up the map of the tracks followed by each one to arrive at the present incarnation. To what end, I am not sure. I don't believe in reincarnation. I don't believe *period*. But I am also incapable of denying my analyst's wishes. I contact the medium.

I feel obliged to do so in order to be able to show up at my weekly session with Moriel again, who places so much hope in what I can bring to the table from three lifetimes ago.

The first thing the medium says is that her revelations can shock people, so be prepared. How do I prepare? She doesn't say. If I am not satisfied with any aspect of the procedure, she'll refund me entirely. *Wow, a repayment for a bad past life? That's neat. How about for the current one?*

I'm a bit on edge as those who don't believe in this stuff usually are as they know they might be about to be proven wrong.

My first life dates back to ancient Greece, where I was the queen of Mycenae, patron of the arts. The medium dwells on this story, with ornaments and frills, because, she warns me with a lugubrious tone, "This is as good as it got." No subsequent life was this good. "It was by far, of your lives, the most enviable: in your kingdom [*easy to say if you're the queen*] as in your personal existence [*easy to pull off if you are the queen*]." OK, I wasn't Clytemnestra, at least. (*Please, please, please, tell me I wasn't Hitler either!*) Then I vanish from circulation for a thousand years. I occasionally reappear in Europe . . . ethnically speaking, I maintained an impeccable consistency through the eras, it seems. After the fun Mycenae part, all I want is to call it a day, but the medium won't relent. The non-fun parts are not fun. In the seventeenth century I was born in America, though, where "you died accused of witchcraft in Salem," she says. *I had forgotten Salem! Salem: a few miles from Boston. Salem: that I had refused to go to visit as a tourist. Salem: where the Criminal insisted he wanted to take me, every time we passed the road sign, while I looked the other way.*

If it's a game, it's supposed to be fun. This is not fun. "You were young, unmarried, tied to a boy with whom you hoped to start a family. But," the medium says hesitantly, "there's a man I keep seeing in all your previous lives. A man who is persecuting you. He is more or less your age, in love with you and obsessively jealous. It is he who falsely accused you and sent you to your death." Clearly in my New England Puritan past I was much more puritanical than I am in the present incarnation. Today's me would advise the pious Pilgrim me to give "it" to the lethal guy, without thinking twice, at the first whiff of sulfur (or whatever they used for their matches three hundred years ago). "The thing that upsets me," continues the medium, "is that this man comes back all the time . . . I have never seen anything like this before!" While I expected the medium to be weird, I begin to have serious doubts on the sanity of my psychoanalyst.

Milli, during all this, brushes against my legs, jumps on my lap, and lets me caress her and kiss the top of her soft head. I, in 2009, a woman with her cat. It's gotta bring good luck, right? It's good witchcraft!

After the Salem episode, which the medium describes as particularly traumatic and painful, I took a break for a couple of hundred years. At which point, I reappeared in New York, late nineteenth century, the only daughter of a cruel mother, from a high-ranking family. *Oh, the Edith Wharton's environments . . . sounds nice.* "You died young, early twenties, also in that life." *Disease? A genetic flaw that can be transmitted from one incarnation to the next? I wonder in anguish.* But the way I died doesn't interest my spiritualist, who instead is flabbergasted by another quite unusual (her words) phenomenon she saw in that life: "Your mother in that life is the same mother in your present life." The New York mother was possessive and despotic, jealous of me *(it squares):* we had ferocious fights *(darn, definitely her)* in which she threatened me, psychologically abused and blackmailed me (*sounds right*). I wanted to go where the artists were, attend night clubs, dance and listen to music deemed indecent by the reactionary élites like the one I belonged to. She wanted instead to parade me with pride through the soirées of the New York's "Four Hundreds," families on par with our own; she wanted me to marry one of the grandees of her choosing and secure a family line. *Pursued in each life by a man who can only have me through brutality, and a mother obsessed with me to the point of sadism. This makes my old flirtation with suicide less palatable: what's the point if I'll still have to deal with them as soon as I come back for another round?*

My shrink is extremely amused by these stories. (*At least, I wasn't Hitler.*) I announce to her that it's the last time I let her force such a crazy thing on me. With her strong Israeli accent, or perhaps a Jewish mother inflection, she responds: "Don't worry! In this life, *I* will teach you how to survive."

# 18

For the first few months in South Carolina, I still feel surrounded by the affection of those I left behind, or who let me go: my friend Veronika expresses in superlative terms her gladness for me; Debbie, I think, expects me back—though, I know, it is meant for my own good; Nancy and Sandy promise to visit very soon. I must resist the temptation of hopping on a plane every few weeks. If I split myself between worlds, I'll end up inhabiting neither. And I'll lose the necessary focus to do the work I'm supposed to be doing (*tenure clock is ticking*). It's a challenge, I've accepted it, I intend to win it.

My first semester at the university comes to an end. One of the two courses I teach has only one student. Four originally registered, but by the second week into the semester three withdrew. It's a course on European and American Jewish writers. (*Note to self: Next semester come up with a sexy title [must include "comics" and "bible"] even if it has nothing to do with the contents. Rule No. 1: lure students into your net, first, and then, pray that Rule No. 2 works. Rule No. 2: Charm them on the first day of classes so that they'll forget whatever false promises the title explicitly made.*)

I spend winter break at home, on Idalia Drive, where for the first time in my life I try my hand at kindling a fire, which Milli adores. "Time spent in the company of cats is never wasted," said Sigmund Freud. I look at Milli, who is looking languidly at the wood-burning fireplace curled by the warm hearth. We both love this.

Yonah writes at long intervals—out of discretion, I'm sure. What if I finally asked something of Yonah? But what? "What are your intentions, young man? Come out with it, if you have a wish to share. Declare yourself!" I'm not cut for asking. Plus now he has two children, and they are of an age when stepmothers are notoriously as welcome as onion juice in your eye.

Philippe, for his part, calls at all hours to make sure that I am well. What should I ask of Philippe? To wait for me? Or to grant me a year to figure out what I want to do? Philippe didn't feign admiration for my new South Carolina condition: no "You are going to be alright!" from him. He genuinely fears my collapse. And therefore, he tries to remain within my orbit, affectionate, sweet as ever. I assure him that there is no reason for me to miss New York. After all, what would I do there that would be more exciting than what I can afford to do here, including a fire in the fireplace—*I could roast chestnuts!* . . . *if only they existed in America.* And before this year fades into history, as a last cosmic stroke of irony, I receive the following email:

Dear Fania,

I am writing to you on behalf of Janusz Budulec, who is spending now a few days in New York.

He is leaving on Saturday and he would like to meet you before Saturday.

His mobile is: +48 501 35 30 35.

Best wishes,

Magda Szukalska

Speak of bad manifestations! Or at the very least, untimely. "My" Polish love, after more than fifteen years of silence, found a way to reemerge but lacked the good taste to do it in person. While the ghosts of tortured orphans, bitter old ladies, or other vampiric figures buried under the foundations of this house never appeared in the tarnished mirror of the bathroom, the ghost of someone who is alive and not from around here suddenly manifests himself. The echo of that first love of my life reaches me electronically, indistinct, and mediated by a secretary who doesn't even know who I am and in what relationship I stand with her boss.

*In the beginning* . . . In the beginning there was him, and in the end, upon turning all the written and unwritten pages of dreams and nightmares, of failures and successes, he demands to be here to close the circle, personal and geographical, of all loves found and lost. Right time, right place. And what about me: wrong time, wrong place? I start to laugh uncontrollably. Stephen Colbert is right: you can't laugh and be afraid at the same time.

I feel like a new person. I am not. I am simply the best version of me I've ever been.

I am a person from the North. A mental North, of course. The North is sophistication, superiority and cosmopolitanism. Wherever *I* am, *there* lies the North. Tel Aviv? North. Rome? North. Krakow and Warsaw? North and North. New York? Good God, North's North! Columbia, South Carolina? Not even my presence can turn it into the North. It's hard to be more South than this. Ironically, only once transplanted here, I heard the idiomatic American expression, "to go south" that is to say, to capitulate to a total failure, to make a mistake, to literally take the direction—where else?—SOUTH.

You know you are in the province of the provinces when not even IKEA wastes its particleboard to open a branch in your State and when, next to the name of your city, the capital to boot, you must always add the state, because otherwise people would think of any other Columbia but the unknown place you are referring to. British Columbia? District of Columbia? Columbia University? You mean, Colombia, Latin America? Columbia Records? There is at least one small town called Columbia in the states of Virginia, West Virginia, Texas, New York, Indiana, Tennessee, South Dakota, Pennsylvania, North Carolina, New Jersey, New Hampshire, Missouri, Mississippi, Maryland, Maine, Louisiana, Iowa, Alabama, Illinois, California, Connecticut, and Kentucky.

Columbia, South Carolina, a place of cement, streets without sidewalks, under a hammering sun unchallenged by tree crowns or other verdant leafage, because anything taller than a Japanese maple has been downed to make room for empty parking lots and more cement. Columbia, South Carolina, which in 1865 General Sherman sacked and burnt to the ground (to dot the "i's" on who was winning the Civil War) and never completely recovered. A city that in the urban vision of the political-technocrats of the 1960s had to be built in the least fluid way possible in order to discourage people from congregating—to deflect any revolutionary attempt. This ungraceful splash of land was therefore designed for exclusively utilitarian purposes: a university, hospitals, sports facilities. Not much else. No room for fun. No room for daytime or nighttime flâneuring about . . . especially nighttime.

Another thing South Carolina is not famous for is its speed. Slow ways, slow driving, slow cooking, and even the speech patterns are so slow. It takes Job's patience to reach the cashier in a supermarket without bursting into hysterical spasms! While fifteen people submissively queue awaiting their turn, the cashier attendant takes her jolly time to chat with each customer about the heat, the blossoming azaleas, and the shrimping season. At Zabar's, this would bring the grumpy octogenarians to the brink of a riot.

White people here speak with the Southern drawl, that is, they mumble the words, lengthen them, and emit them through their noses, slowing down the rhythm of each sentence. It is a very different accent from that of Black people in the same region: more rounded, pectoral, full of sorrowful notes like the Blues.

Here, honking is a capital offense. I don't even understand why they still manufacture horns in cars destined for the American market. All drivers keep in single file, one after the other, and sometimes out of three lanes they use only two for fear of being perceived as aggressive toward other drivers. Bikers and motorcyclists don't zigzag, don't use the sidewalks, and never, ever, wiggle their way to the front of the line to be first at a traffic lights. Car drivers turn on their signal at the exact moment they start to turn: they don't warn you that they will turn, they simply tell you they *are* turning, and as they do so they may decide to practically stop, think about it a moment, and then slowly slowly get out of your (impatient) way. Worse still, when they are about to turn (unannounced) they have a habit of making a 180-degree curve in the opposite direction first, which is, they swing out, broadly, they practically veer in the opposite direction in order to aim head on at the new road, rather than simply taking it by cutting the corner tightly like everybody else on the planet.

They do stop for pedestrians, though, even for those who haven't yet reached the zebra crossing and will not do so for the next ten minutes. They'll stop and patiently wait for the ninety-year-old lady who is still at the cashier inside the store and won't cross the road before turning ninety-one. And you can't honk at the extremely kind driver in front of you, lest they shoot you.

If you pass by someone on your walk, you raise your hand to signal "Hi there": pedestrians greet motorists, motorists greet pedestrians, pedestrians greet pedestrians, motorists greet drivers . . . and those sitting with a beer watching the traffic from their porch greet everyone and everyone greets them. When my parents (who never fail to visit every place I move to) come to South Carolina for the first time, I have to instruct them to wave at everybody we meet on our walks. My father, who is happy to comply, is also careful to perform the gesture by raising his hand up to his chest a bit awkwardly to do the right American thing while avoiding reproducing the fascist salute.

Woods and forests abound outside of the city center: chestnut trees are missing, and the innumerable pine trees do not yield pine nuts. It's a weird place.

My house is the only one in the dark at night: the neighbors' homes have the lights on even when and where there is no one. At the first sign of the sun's departure, all the lights on the porches and the many garden lamps turn on automatically. Kitchens are permanently lit. Visibility must be total. I try to conform and buy a tiny safety light to plug into the wall, softer than the emergency lights on an airplane, not to upset my neighbors and, like them, to signal to the murderers cruising the neighborhood "There's someone in this house!"—although I suspect, since there are no murderers around and everybody behaves because everybody else has eight rifles in their trucks, that the electric overconsumption is not about fending off the enemies as much as to declare, "I can afford it" or "I don't give a damn about global warming." Far more American, if you ask me.

The meter they use here to measure a person's decency is the appearance of his or her front yard. In no other realms does American control freakishness manifest itself more plainly: they obsess over their gardens, which they obdurately refer to exclusively as yards. The grass must be kept very short, like the military shearing of a Marine. You must collect all the leaves and pine needles as soon as they touch the ground . . . or better still, if you truly wish to belong, in midair before they reach the ground. It is not uncommon, from January to December, to be woken at 8 AM by the continuous and deafening noise of a leaf blower which rages for hours against each petal, each pine needle, each acorn, each pinecone, guiding them as a herd of sheep into a corner of the yard. What I affectionately call plants, here they call weeds, to which they declare a ruthless war that consists in poisoning them, mowing them, hatcheting them down, uprooting them with special tractors, sucking them out with industrial aspirators. Ivy is considered a danger to humanity. "It'll take down your house!" cry the neighbors, horrified by the sight of the foliated vines that warmly embrace the red bricks of my house.

Garbage collection is four times a week: religiously, at dusk, the night before, citizens pull their garbage out of their garages and, with as much dignity and elegance as possible, expose it to everybody's scrutiny. On Mondays, kitchen waste; Wednesdays, furniture and appliances; Thursdays, garden debris (mountains of them!—magnified by the juxtaposition to the little mummified twigs I sometimes deposit by the curb to give the impression "I am as against nature as the next fellow!"); Friday, recyclables. What state are your bins in? How much wear is enough before you throw away your furniture? Do you get rid of vogue designer chairs or of the yellow-orangey checkered armchair Archie Bunker style? I learn it is fundamental to clean the gutters, and I learn of their existence altogether . . . but must look them up first. The front yard is the prologue to your personality. Through it, we read what kind of neighbor you are. A backyard is the yard in the back of the house and therefore it's one word: front yard is two words, I surmise, because it is not the yard in the front of the house but a "front," your frontispiece.

I buy a pair of heavy-duty galoshes, work gloves so thick that I can't bend my fingers, and a gardening hat with UVA-UVB-SPF 70+ protection. A very curious thing I learn is that all this work to clean, fertilize, sterilize, tame, and decorate the front yard has a purely aesthetic purpose: it showcases the ethical fiber of the owner but not the owners themselves who don't do anything on their perfect front yards. They don't eat on it, they don't sit in it for a chat, they don't play ball nor sunbathe (God forbid!) on it, they don't lie down to read a book in the cool front yard either. The front yard is that room of the house that you ask the maid to clean every week even if no one is allowed to enter it, except on special occasions once a decade. I gave up reading the *New York Times* on the bench under the shade of my oak tree, when I noticed that passersby waved their hands hello in that hesitant and over-the-lines way one uses to keep a madman calm, while the nurses sneak up behind him ready with a straitjacket. I immediately dragged the bench into the backyard.

To its notorious slowness the South combines a chronic laziness, the most American quality in general. Americans love comfort. Only New Yorkers immolate themselves, neurotically, on the altar of unstoppability. The rest of America has no qualms in minimizing an effort. The drive-through, not only for fast foods but for all restaurants, is the epitome of this fantastic tendency: you don't have to get out of your car to retrieve the food that you have someone else cook for you, but they'll throw it at you—like a meatball to a dog—directly through your car window without you having to inconvenience your body with any unnecessary movement. Since, I estimate, ironing boards dropped out of the market around 1969 here, all clothes, sheets, tablecloths and so on are created "wrinkle free," and to boot, given that Americans have no memory of what is an ironed piece of clothing, their sense of fashion has evolved, following a Darwinian law, to like only wrinkled things. Want a dog? Yes, but the effort to play with it is too much? More and more often, I see dog owners use a device consisting of a long handle that ends in a mini-basket which allows them to collect, without bending their knees, the ball from the ground and throw it at the desired distance for Fido to fetch. (I imagine that only 60 percent of Fidos go to fetch it though, because a recent study revealed that 40 percent of American dogs are obese.) No reason to be shocked: after all, this is the country that gave the world the escalators . . . and the battery-powered fork that spins the spaghetti for you. South Carolina, however, confirms the general rule that the more you climb on the social scale, the more the scale dials drop, and vice versa: weight is indirectly proportional to class. The real Southern ladies have the physique of little girls, all ribs, twiggy legs, stiff necks, and sharp eyes even at ninety. Their service women barely fit through the wide colonial doors.

Truth be told, it is reductive to see it as simply laziness. It is not just laziness but an art: the art of making life comfortable. The apex of this propensity is embodied in the "Return policy"! No one believes me back home when I talk about it. You can return everything here, from clothes (GAP takes back your blue jeans after you've worn them a year) to foods (chewed and . . . "Nah,

I don't like it. Here, take it back"). In Italy, they would directly call the police on you if you tried. The three most loved words of the American vocabulary: No questions asked.

Yet here in this beautiful paradoxical South, I've shed so much of the fear that was asphyxiating me. Here I feel strangely free. I love driving around, exploring the magnificent coastline. I cannot fix, let alone redeem, the South. I can only open up to it and watch. This place welcomed me. I am healed and humbled by its sublime landscapes, so little spoken of up North.

I fall in love with the Lowcountry, the area between Pawleys Island, Charleston (the film location of *Gone with the Wind*), and Hilton Head. Since the short-lived honeymoon on the Jersey Shore, I haven't returned to US beaches anymore (and without Philippe, my tropical life is over too). Touching the water again, feeling the sand under my feet, opens my eyes to the fact that perhaps, by ethnic-cultural formation, I am more connected to the sea than I had imagined. I get drunk on happiness.

In South Carolina, and especially along the coast, the weather is always good, and when it isn't good, it is so bad that you stare the end of the world in the eyes. There is no middle ground between an unperturbed sunny sky and the killer hurricane that follows leaving you a handful of seconds to run for shelter. It's a risk, but I learn to love that, too. Every weekend, every holiday, every excuse possible, I rush to the coast to enjoy the change of pace (yes, even slower there!), the change of seasons that occurs in colors more than in temperatures, the warm waters, the skeins of Spanish moss hanging indolently in the wind, decorating the branches of the ancient oaks or the birds' nests. The alligators soundlessly crawl by, hummingbirds vibrate in the breeze, and the humidity is so heavy that even the mosquitoes can't lift themselves up in the air.

I investigate every inch of the Lowcountry. I find Fripp. A tiny little island, a couple of hours drive from Columbia, at the estuary of the Harbor River. A place unknown to most people, a dot on only the most detailed maps, yet the inspiration of many a book by Pat Conroy, a native of this place. Half the plot of *The Prince of Tides* is set on this island and the other half in Manhattan. When I saw the film with Barbra Streisand and Nick Nolte, in 1991, all my attention had gone only to the New York half of the story. At the time I had never even seen a tide. And wasn't sure, to be frank, what the word meant in the title.

Tides revolutionize the coastal landscape four times a day, every day slightly differently than the previous one. It's a show that knows no curtain. There are times during the year when the tides are so low that all that remains is a lunar landscape of gray craters blissfully decorated by the intense blond-green hues of the spartina which grows everywhere. Let six hours pass, and if you saw this view for the first time you'd never guess that there is any grass at all underneath the high waters which overflow onto roads, underneath houses, half way up some trees. If you are on the beach, you see the sea retreat so far, kilometers even, from the shoreline that (at least it was this way for me the first time) one cannot but suspect an incoming tsunami. On the other end of these flows, during the high tide, the beach may disappear altogether . . . and that's when from the deck of your house (usually built on stilts many feet off the ground), you can see dolphins swim, jump, feed, play undisturbed. Dozens of pelicans fly above them, and so do the black-headed seagulls, with their inelegant croak, always afraid to be missing a bite. When the tide is so high, the blue herons are the least happy, as they need to be planted on solid ground to fish their dinners out of the waters: imperiously, they sit on the tree branches waiting, in the breeze that ruffles their grey, bluish and white plum-age, for the tide to go down again. It's just a matter of hours, an ineluctable fact . . . the planet will turn, and so will the bad luck of the blue heron. As the tide recedes, it leaves behind a gargantuan feast of small and big fishes trapped in small puddles or stuck in the mud. The most skilled fisherman there is, the heron, runs the prey through with its beak used as a spear. He is the last to be served, but his perseverance is amply rewarded. That's the beauty of it: that nature is capable of such admirable patience.

When I decide that this is the place, and nowhere else, where I will build my nest, the real estate agent I hired to help me find a nest for sale on Fripp Island didn't trust my resolve and worried that I could change my mind once I realize how unknown, small, and uneventful this corner of the world truly is. So she tried to make it more interesting by telling me of all the legendary an-ecdotes about the island and the nearest town, Beaufort. For instance, that the corsair Barbarossa had installed on this island, when it was still uninhabited, eleven young girls whose task was to wait for his return from his exploits out at sea, and among these there was his favorite, red-haired Maria, who (evidently) not being particularly patient, or cautious, entertained herself with another pirate. When Barbarossa found out, he cut off the rival's hand, threw him to the sharks, and sent the hand in a box to Maria, who died of sorrow. On a moonful night, the figure of a pale maiden, with long hair like flames in the wind, is said to be regularly seen pacing back and forth along the beach as if she were waiting for the sea to give back what's hers. Film director Robert Zemeckis filmed the Vietnam war scenes from *Forrest Gump* in this little island's jungle. Not far from here, there is a colony founded by former enslaved people, where, to this day, the locals managed to preserve with great effort the old customs, rites, foodways, and dialect (Gullah) of their African ancestors. This county, I also learn, is part of a larger area called Parris Island, which was the first place to be colonized in the South: first by the French, quickly replaced by the Spaniards who were slaughtered by the Native nations who wanted their territory back, and finally by the English. It seems that Colonel Alexander Parris, who bought Parris Island in 1715 and gave it his name, was the brother of the Reverend Samuel Parris, a pastor of the church in Salem, Massachusetts, and the judge presiding over the witch trials.

The agent wishes to entice me with prospects of fishing, hunting, and endless rounds of golf and is evidently shocked at my contrariness with regard to these pleasures. She scratches her head and pulls out one last factoid she probably fears will make her look totally stupid at this point: "Have you ever heard of the movie *The Big Chill?*" The real estate agent cannot tell what the expression on my face truly signifies: "It was shot entirely here. In Beaufort."

I go alone to see the big white plantation home from the film location, with its front yard and views over the gorgeous blond-greenish marshes. Now, technically, I can no longer complain of not having found "The Big Chill" in America. Clearly, this is the universe finally sending its heartfelt apologies.

To the real estate agent's great relief, I buy a property on the island: a type of bungalow, called by the locals "a tree house" because it is an octagonal structure built on a thick elevated base which makes it look like a giant mushroom. The day of the closing, the agent explains one last detail: the owners left the keys for me in a key box by the door . . . the combination to open it

("Write it down," she commands) is 1264. No need to write it down. I could hardly forget. It was the same as my address on Amsterdam Avenue. The universe has spoken again.

I feel at peace with myself when I am on my island. My nest is tucked away, easy to miss even if you know it is here, impossible to find if you don't. I bought my corner of maritime paradise with the profits from the sale of 1264 Amsterdam Avenue. The co-op board didn't allow me to rent it out. Out of a house that had meant so much to me, another equally significant was born. Jokingly, to those who ask how I ended up here, I say that "This is a gift from New York." This tree house is my personal eye of the storm; the last station of a long journey that has finally come to an end; here I'm at my destination. There is nothing beyond this place.

From the west-facing deck of my house, where I love to sit and watch the fog rise in the morning and the sun fall in the evening, I enjoy an unobstructed view over endless salt marshes, interrupted only five hundred meters from me by a wide tidal creek that flows between north and south, where dolphins regularly come swim, fish and play . . . and who knows whether they hear me call excitedly from my balcony in Italian "*delfini!*" to summon and welcome them.

I am back on an island. In all, the exact opposite of Manhattan. Was my destiny to be surrounded by water? Or have the gods had fun packing me into this geophysical metaphor of what life ultimately is?

I haven't met many Princes Charming since I've come here, and the feeling of being at the center of the world has evaporated. Being in New York meant feeling permanently, even when I wasn't conscious of it, at the center of the universe; what happened in New York happened to the world . . . albeit not vice versa: instead, from where I am today, New York appears to me as the atoll that it actually is, not as big as the whole world, nor so connected to it as I had believed.

My main residence is in Columbia, of course, because of work. I used to live in a big metropolis, New York City, on a street that bore the name of another illustrious big metropolis, Amsterdam: today I live on streets with bucolic anonymous names like Idalia or Northlake Road. Around me the human rustle has abated, replaced by the slow parades of neighbors who wave hello as they pass by with their dog and exchange friendly pleasantries. Certain memories are so intense as to have an almost physical quality to them: such are my memories of Central Park, for example, and its iron lampposts, lit up in the snowy evenings. These don't vanish, but next to them I was able to squeeze new sensations and awes. Perhaps thirty years too late, I discover the joy of having a dog. I rescued my Chester, and now, with Milli, he is the faithful companion to every moment of my day, every walk and Netflix binging session on the couch. We have our own park now: it's a giant natural reservation called Sesquicentennial State Park, around the corner from where we live when we are not on Fripp, and where Chester and I go for long hikes through a buzzing landscape full of colors with continuous surprises from its majestic beauty. I don't know a thing about fauna or flora, granted: to me, everything that swims is a fish, anything in the air is a bird, and whatever grows out of the earth is generically a plant. I couldn't sufficiently describe anything I encounter on my walks. All I can speak to is the happiness it provokes and the gratitude I feel for this sense of safety I experience only in nature. Yes, I am aware—well aware!—that an alligator might have me for dinner or a bear (*are there bears in South Carolina?*) may jump out of a thicket and . . . well, I wouldn't live long enough to find out what the bear would do to me. But that's totally OK. I want to write a document to be used in court that says that should my life be taken away by a wild animal, I leave as my will that no harm come to the poor thing. *Should the Criminal show up at my door, I will however ask any Clint Eastwood type neighbor to lend me a rifle. Call me impartial.*

Today, like Tim, my housemate in Boston, I compost my leftovers in the back of my garden, and like Camilla Criscitiello I recycle everything, I send my thank you cards exclusively via email, I reuse shopping bags, I use only cloth napkins, I scrimp on paper towels, and I declared war on plastic bottles. Now I know how to prepare for Halloween, and year after year, I begin to recognize the neighborhood kids and enjoy seeing them grow up. In New York, I got trick-or-treaters knocking on my door only once, when I lived on Seaman Avenue: it was a small group of teenagers, who stepped inside my apartment and, ignoring the basket of American (properly wrapped) chocolates I offered them, spotted in the kitchen the Ferrero Roche and Belgian bonbons I had just gotten out of my parents' gift package from Rome, and helped themselves to those, and on the way out muttered a blasé "Thank you." It hadn't occurred to me that, unless you have a strong death wish, you don't open the door to whoever knocks in New York. The exact opposite happens in South Carolina: the neighborhood committee writes you down in a secret blacklist if their grandchildren report that they passed by your house, and you pretended not to be there. In South Carolina, I had to learn to look left and right before crossing the street, while in New York, or Rome for that matter, there's no point in looking . . . you jump in the middle of Sixth Avenue at rush hour and hope for the best. This is because in a city where no one follows the rules, everyone is always on alert and everybody is attentive to what others do; in South Carolina, on the other hand, if you as much as motion toward the edge of the sidewalk when *it is not* your turn, when the light is still green for the cars, you will throw the drivers into total bewilderment and cause a chain collision.

My home in town and my writing retreat on Fripp Island are still fully decorated and furnished with my stuff from so long ago: all things, this time, I was able to bring with me. On my daybed, I still wrap myself in the quilted comforter I bought in Boston that first autumn in the freezing attic of Orange Street, now faded and frayed; out of the hundred coffee cups accumulated over the years, every morning I still use the ceramic one I bought in the Bronx, near Salvatore's house, in 1998; my breakfast nook now features beautiful inbuilt cupboards, and through their glass doors, I see my collection of Fishs Eddy milk jars, mugs, and ramekins. Veronika's lucky bamboo is thriving here, like me.

The plants both at home and in the garden have become a source of great satisfaction and encouragement: I am making an effort to get acquainted with nature, from which I stole a corner for myself. I don't kill anything, if I can avoid it: I kindly, albeit squeamishly, accompany all intruders outside the house when they penetrate uninvited . . . including snakes (*which I do with a special tool and the accompaniment of my uninterrupted high-pitch shrieks that make the poor thing shrink to the size of an earthworm*). Of course, the fact that unlike my neighbors I don't use pesticides or other deterrents means that my backyard is a jungle swarming with life but also destined never to see a

strawberry or a blackberry ripen: practically I cultivate for the squirrels' benefits. The wild rabbit that has made its den right under my wisteria happily
eats all my parsley and when I try to distract it by hand feeding him (I want
to say it's a boy rabbit) carrots, he eats the carrots and then, to clean his palate,
goes back to the parsley. My plum tree yielded two pieces of fruit and by the
time I ran inside to fetch my camera and immortalize the miracle, something
had gotten there before me and left a few bitemarks all over them. I now master the recipe for homemade hummingbird syrup, and I learned the hard way
(may karma forgive me this one!) that the fish I put in my little garden pond,
which have quintupled in size in just a few months (and sweetly eat out of my
hand), do not appreciate competition, so when I gleefully came home from
the pet store with a bag of ten tiny little fishes to join the lucky company, the
big guys devoured them without mercy.

Gardening has replaced both psychoanalysis, the gym, and the yoga. Lucille Roberts, the fitness guru, died at the age of fifty-nine of lung cancer in
2003, although she never smoked. Her house ended up on the postmortem
market for a record amount of $95,000,000. The *New York Times* obituary
editor Douglas Martin, whose name owes its last shred of interest to the fame
of the newspaper on which it appears, has lapidarily defined her as "the Mc-
Donald's of health clubs." Not surprisingly, a gym exclusively for women, and
for women who can't afford *not* to go to McDonald's, escaped the understanding of this man.

Today, after decades of silence, Monica Lewinsky is beginning to make
timid public reappearances again. She is beautiful and sweet, and tears come
to her eyes when she speaks about those traumatic days and confesses that she
indeed thought of killing herself. In a sense, Lewinsky has never left us: forced
to disappear, yet forced to remain present in every dirty joke, in every mastur-
batory rape fantasy of the nation, and cited in at least forty rap songs. At a recent public talk, she was approached by a young man who tried to seductively
charm her with the phrase: "With me, you would feel twenty-two again." To
which Lewinsky retorted that she is the only forty-one-year-old in the world
who absolutely has no desire to be twenty-two again. Monica is still paying for
"Blowjobgate"; Hillary is still paying for her husband's sexual peccadillo; Bill
sleeps like a log at night.

I owe the South a lot: I owe Fripp Island everything. Anything I achieved, or rather anything *I* consider an achievement, happened here; it was possible because of my island, of my yurt on stilts in the marsh. I now enjoy every day, I take care of everything with a thrill of excitement. When my parents come for a visit, I see how out of place these curious Italians are in this Southern context. (*They love it, by the way—but then again, they've always loved America.*) On the way to Fripp Island, we stop to admire the tiny town of Frogmore, and I say to them: "You know, someone told me that here Martin Luther King Jr. came to write his last book, in 1967." They gasp. My father dabs his wet eyes with his white hanky.

They still look so funny to me, the American, and do everything so patently wrong! But I am not ashamed anymore. I kind of enjoy the clashing differences in action. I like to stand at the intersection of all these extraneities of which I can proudly consider myself the most conspicuous one, for both cultures.

My father laughs and points out: "You have become so American!" I don't know what the decisive factor was in my becoming "so American." Perhaps my move to South Carolina? It coincided with a historic presidential election here. We have this in common, Barack and I: 2008! Such a fundamental year in our lives.

I wanted America so much. And here I am. In America.

I arrived twenty years ago, and today neither America nor Europe are the same as they were then. Would I leave Italy today? Twenty years ago, there was no Euro currency and barely an EU itself. Ethnic diversity? Zero. Twenty years ago, there was no Barilla in Boston and no crème fraîche in New York. Between Florence and Taormina, very rarely you'd meet someone who spoke enough English to sustain a prolonged and coherent conversation. Today when the BBC reporters interview folks in France, Spain, Italy, or Greece, they almost never need to use a translator. Twenty years ago, there was no web, no Google, androids, tablets, iPads, or anything more than rudimentary cell phones: no Skype or WhatsApp. There was no Halloween in Italy: no one could even spell the word correctly, and few would have guessed what it was because the only ones familiar with Halloween were those, like my mother and me, who were assiduous readers of *Peanuts* comics. For years, my mother and I, obsessive dairy gourmets, thought that Snoopy and his cousin Spike melted cheese on skewers on the desert campfire—a kind of cowboy fondue. Only recently, I caught a colleague eating one of those fluffy snow-white sticky balls and asked him if they were the same cheese cubes Snoopy roasts in the fire: he roared with laughter and handed me a piece: "Yes, except. . ." He didn't have time to finish explaining that they are not made of cheese because my horrified expression (and haste to the trash bin) plainly told him that I had just figured it out myself: "Marshmallows," he said wiping his tears. An abominable skein of sugar that don't melt when roasted but take on the stink and color of burnt truck tires. On the other hand, I also always wondered all my life why Linus was waiting for "Il grande cocomero" in October, in an orange field of squashes. Nobody explained to us, fifty years ago, that the Italian translator of the comic strips had taken the liberty of rendering "The Great Pumpkin" with something he thought would sound more familiar to his audience: "The Great Watermelon."

Today marshmallows, muffins, and donuts have invaded the diets of every Italian kid. They tell me that even pizza in Italy is now home delivered (*oh, I should have been born now!*) in a box, with the plastic table in the middle so as to prevent the cardboard lid from collapsing on the pie toppings. We didn't have MFA or Women's and Gender Studies programs, and we still had numerical marks instead of "credits" at La Sapienza when I was a student there. I didn't know what a "mall" was because it didn't exist in the world I left in 1996, and I had to move to South Carolina to be forced to shop in one. Now my mother goes *"alla mall"* to buy me pretty much everything. As all Italians who talk to me notice, I use incorrectly the new American terminology that infiltrated Italian language while I was away: I use the word "email" as a feminine noun because it translates as *"posta elettronica"* in Italian, which is feminine—but the nation, while I wasn't there to correct them, decided that email should be a masculine noun. If a quorum was met on whether to say *il muffin* or *la muffin, il mall* or *la mall,* I have no idea.

Students find my American adventures quite hilarious. Like the story of the New York cat who fell silent upon crossing the George Washington

Bridge. Or that of my encounter with the South Carolinian fisherman: I met the guy on the tiny pier by my house on Fripp one day and thought of showing off my best southern behavior by striking up a small conversation with the man. I asked him if he had caught something yet (*knowing all too well that I wouldn't recognize any species of fish he was going to mention anyway*). He held up a bottle full of a piss-colored liquid, and answered me with his Southern-banjo voice, what I thought was, "Uh gu' whun." I squinted my eyes as if to put into focus a microbe swimming inside that murky liquid, but seeing nothing, I inquired humbly "One of what?" "Uh gu' whun," he repeats shaking the bottle before my nose. I ask again, with the tone of diligent pupil, "One of what?" But the man sticks to his answer, as if the sheer repetition of it would suddenly make it clear. "Uh gu' whun" he says at least three more times. And then a large lady sitting in the shade of the wooden gazebo at the top of the pier, who's been following the scene between two idiots from two different villages with amused interest, understands what the problem must be and, bursting into a dehydrated laugh, she clicks her tongue in my direction while explaining to her fellow countryman "She's not from here" and then to me "He's tellin' ya, he's got wine." I make the students crack their ribs with my stories of a troublemaking Martian visiting this incomprehensible planet of theirs. My weaknesses in the classroom become my strengths; the literature we study together only corroborates this point—that is, our vulnerability unites us, not a false sense of heroism they hear so much about, but which, in reality, doesn't seem to be of this world.

In the classroom, I am the queen of a peaceful and happy kingdom: I use my power to do good and there's so much satisfaction in this simple act. I use my power to protect them, not to destroy them, to inspire them, not to demoralize them. I have the power to ensure that nobody in my classroom makes a derogatory comment against a peer or against the opinions someone else expresses. I give them extra points on the final grade if they do group-study sessions for the tests, or if they exchange textbooks and notes. They'll have plenty of competition to deal with in the world out there; I better give them a taste for cooperation and support while they still can learn from it. When students, male or female, of any ethnicity, gay or straight, come speak to me during my office hours, I stop them from closing the door: "No, leave it open," I say kindly. I hope they'll understand one day that that gap is our salvation, theirs and mine. That I will not abuse them behind a closed door, where and when they can't defend themselves or run away easily. That I know the vulnerability of being face to face with a person of authority behind a closed door, where the outside world cannot reach us.

Foreign students always ask me, lowering their voice: "How did you stay in America?" My mind goes to the default: "I came for seven days and ended up staying for seven years!" But I say instead: "Mine was a special case." I unequivocally reassure them that they oughtn't worry because there are so many alternative ways to receiving a green card other than marriage, that they shouldn't do anything silly because they'll be able to stay without having to compromise their happiness. In the end, they always expect a hug from the eccentric Italian professor of Jewish literature, with a quaint British accent, who wears only trousers and, despite the southern heat, always a scarf and a hat. They tell me "I love the way you talk" and not "I love your accent" (and therefore I believe them). When I speak of myself, and of the world "out there," outside the narrow confines within which so many of them have grown, I always throw there a casual "*You know,* I lived in New York City" and add a studied gesture that says, "Ah, don't make me start . . ." and I see their eyes grow bigger, their attention perk up. I tell them to go, to leave everything behind, to try something new. "There is always time to return 'home,' if you understand you made a mistake." But what I omit to tell them is that "home" won't be there any longer, because the journey changes us radically, and if we are no longer ourselves when we return, the home we return to can't be ours anymore. This I let them discover for themselves.

When a road bifurcates, you can only take one of the possible paths, as recalled in Robert Frost's by-now cliché lines:

> Two roads diverged in a yellow wood,
> And sorry I could not travel both
> I shall be telling this with a sigh
> Somewhere ages and ages hence:

Two roads diverged in a wood, and I—
I took the one less traveled by,
And that has made all the difference.

Alice doesn't stay in Wonderland, nor does Dorothy in Oz, or Karen Blixen in Africa. After New York, should I have gone back to Rome? Retreating can be a first step toward victory. (Certainly some Russian general must have thought as much as the Napoleonic troops were advancing.) Problem is, I still lack a good definition for victory: or, to be generous, let's say that it changes from decade to decade. I want to believe that it is LIBERTY: but I fear that, more frequently than not, it was "fear of being outed" (not sexually . . . but each has her or his own closet). If Descartes had not already taken Ovid's maxim for his own tombstone, I would have loved to claim it for my own: *Bene qui latuit, bene vixit*—He who concealed himself well, has lived best.

Philippe used to sing to me:

*If they asked me, I could write a book*
*about the way you walk and whisper and look*
*I could write a preface on how we met*
*so the world would never forget.*
*And the simple secret of the plot*
*is just to tell them that I love you a lot.*
*Then the world discovers as my book ends*
*how to make two lovers of friends*

To this day, when I listen to it, it melts my heart. I still cry when I think of him, of our perfect love in an imperfect life. We managed to fix our lives, but the cost was us. After a few years in Paris, Philippe found a companion, a Japanese woman who, unlike him, wanted to get married and have children. So she fell pregnant and, just moments before delivering the baby, finally convinced him to lead her, if not to the altar at least to the municipal office in Paris, where the mayor performed the rite. He sent me a picture, which illustrates the nine-month pregnant bride (shaped like the dome of the Sacré Coeur), beaming with joy, and himself in a suit without a tie, with the cheerless air of someone who's marching to the guillotine.

Yonah has remarried for the third time. He announced it in an email, specifying "an American this time!" not without humor and a bit of pride. They had an adorable daughter soon after.

The soundtrack of my days today is more Nina Simone than Paul Simon. Music is very adaptable. My imagination still sees New York in every song: but when I make the effort to tune into the present, I can hear a new music here, in South Carolina, too. My soundtracks don't conflict, the old music slips into my present and I hear it a little differently.

I often associate people to music. Each person is his or her own special tune. No one ever told me what melody I am. But I have an idea. The year I was born, William Bolcom composed a series of musical tributes to the forgotten ragtime tradition. I would ask those I'll leave behind one day to remember me by the notes of Bolcom's *Graceful Ghost Rag* in his own transcription for violin and piano. The most American piece of music of all.

The problem with gardening is that it is enslaved to permanence. Thoreau unforgettably says that one can't kill time without injuring eternity. Planting a tree in the garden is like taking on a long-term commitment—it's not a matter of a day or a summer. Trees, bushes, and flowerbeds don't take root in a season. It takes years of care, love, and out-loud conversations; before they begin to bear fruit, before their trunk thickens, before they learn to survive the changes in weather, or before the flowers bud up and burst open, they must feel comfortable and safe in the new environment. Nature lasts longer than we. The Central Park trees are still there where I left them—the same can't be said of me. Does it make sense, I ask and torture myself every time, to spend money, energy, and hope removing the brushwood, digging holes, mixing the earth clods, fertilizing, transplanting, renewing the soil, and spreading mulch, and all of this at the risk of not being here to witness the flowering of the azaleas, to celebrate the birth of the first leaf on a peach tree, to never know what happened to all my hard work? Should I be forced to flee again, I could pack all my animals in the car and go. But gardens are tacitly crueler: they challenge you to stay. In order to make plants live we must become one ourselves: we must take root, face the wind and the change of seasons that become more ferocious and unnatural from year to year, risk even death without being able to run away for our life. The lesson from gardening is that you grow where you are, make an effort, plan as much as feasible, but for the rest, accept chance and rely on your own innate qualities. Roots are not for sissies.

I still keep the photograph of when I was about four years old pinned on the fridge with a magnet of Alice in Wonderland's Cheshire Cat. The little girl, whom Dr. Weber had commanded me to love and to protect, has split into myriads. I am not talking of parthenogenesis. I am talking about my students. I learned to recognize her, myself, in the hundreds of young students I encourage, support, love, and protect every semester. Bernard Malamud has one of his protagonists, Sy Levin, say "What does a teacher teach if he can't teach what he is?"

Sometimes I look at that picture and scold her, jokingly, "You made me do laps!" The expression on the child's face clearly indicates that she is still metabolizing the world around her and, stubborn, she's trying to grasp as quickly as possible all its mechanisms without anybody's help. "What else do you want?!" I whine. She stares back at me with her eyes as brown as autumn and, with a little mischievous twinkle, she replies: "Chestnuts."

# ACKNOWLEDGMENTS

I owe so much to Fripp Island and the friends I made there. From its healing beauty, I received nothing but happiness.

My heartfelt thanks go to: Sandy Petrey, my favorite reader—*Grazie, professore*!; to Chris Holcomb, who convinced me this book *had to* happen; to Lucio Martino, for helping in the most generous and elegant way; to Katherine Barbieri who always cheered me on; to Barbara and Grant Sullivan for enveloping me in their friendship; to D. V. S., you've been a real brick; and to the anonymous peer-reviewers of the manuscript—I don't know your names, but I know that you are some kind of angels (the best kind). Last but not least, of course, to Ehren Foley, at University of South Carolina Press: among those in this country who gave me a lifesaving chance, you will always have a special place in my heart.

# NOTES AND TRANSLATIONS

*Part 1*

**I**

About the banning of the word "tornado": Howard B. Bluestein, *Tornado Alley: Monster Storms of the Great Plains* (New York: Oxford University Press, 1999), 2.

About the fate of the Pottawatomi tribe: T. P. Grazulis, *The Tornado: Nature's Ultimate Windstorm* (Norman: University of Oklahoma Press, 2001), 146.

About the elephant twister of 1876: David J. Wishart, editor, *Encyclopedia of the Great Plains* (Lincoln: University of Nebraska Press, 2004), 315.

Laura Ingalls Wilder, *These Happy Golden Years* (New York: Harper Collins, 1971), 257–58.

*He'll build a little home...*: from *The Man I Love* by George Gershwin (music) and Ira Gershwin (lyrics).

*Oleh chadash,* pl. *olim chadashim:* (Hebrew) Diasporic Jew who emigrates to and becomes citizen of Israel.

*Fame:* (Italian) hunger.

**2**

*Mozzarella in carrozza:* (Italian) fried mozzarella-stuffed bread.

**3**

About George Barnard and the Cloisters: Sara Dodge Kimbrough, *Drawn from Life: The Story of Four American Artists Whose Friendship and Work Began in Paris during the 1880s* (Jackson: University of Mississippi Press, 1976).

About diners: Richard Gutman, *American Diner Then and Now* (New York: Harper Collins, 1993).

*Part 2*

4

Henry James, *The American Scene* (New York: Harper and Brothers Publishers, 1907).

About the Plymouth landing: Michael Krondl, *Around the American Table* (Holbrook, Massachusetts: Adams Publishing, 1995); Charles Panati, *Extraordinary Origins of Everyday Things* (New York: Harper & Row, 1987).

*Alef* e *gimmel, kof, lamed* are respectively the first, third, nineteenth, and twelfth letter of the Hebrew alphabet.

*Pilpul:* (Hebrew) Talmudic debate.

5

About Durgin-Park and Union Oyster House: James C. O'Connell, *Dining Out in Boston: A Culinary History* (Hanover: University Press of New England, 2017); Steve and Linda Bauer, *Recipes from Historic New England: A Restaurant Guide and Cookbook* (Lanham: Taylor Trade Publishing, 2009); Jean Kerr, and Spencer Smith, *Union Oyster House Cookbook: Recipes and History from America's Oldest Restaurant* (Brooklin, ME: Seapoint Books, 2008); and the restaurants' information leaflets and menus.

*Matchmaker, matchmaker, make me a match . . . :* from the film *Fiddler on the Roof,* directed and produced by Norman Jewison.

69 Orange St, Waltham, MA 02453: Through a past letter, dug out of a dusty corner in my mother's house and found in a box with letters and other stuff I sent them at the time, I was able to confirm that this was indeed the exact address at which I lived.

*Part 3*

6

*Kezayit:* (Hebrew) The amount of matzah we are allowed to eat at the Seder, which is no bigger than an olive.

*Incubo americano:* (Italian) American nightmare.

7

*Cavolo:* (Italian) For crying out loud.

*Felice 1997:* (Italian) Happy 1997.

*Nie, dziękuję:* (Polish) No, thank you.

## 8

*Kiddush:* (Hebrew) Blessing over the wine. The wine is poured in special cups used only for this ritual purpose.

*Mozzarella in carrozza, supplì, fiori di zucca fritti:* (Italian) fried mozzarella-stuffed bread, fried mozzarella-stuffed rice balls, fried mozzarella-stuffed zucchini flowers.

*Primula Rossa:* (Italian) Scarlet Pimpernel.

*Cazzo:* (Italian) interjection, "Shit!"About Monica Lewinsky: Andrew Morton, *Monica's Story* (New York: St. Martin's Press, 1999).

*Quella vera:* (Italian) the real thing.

Alan Alda, *Things I Overheard While Talking to Myself* (New York: Random House, 2007), 16–22.

## Part 4

### 9

*Sabes que haser. . . . Ocupate de ella*: (Spanish) You know what to do . . . take care of her.

*Uno due, uno due*: (Italian) one two, one two . . .

### 10

*Bastoncini cinesi:* (Italian) Children's game Pick-up sticks.

About the Jewish Hollywood moguls, the Hollywood studios and the role immigrant Jews played in creating them: Neal Gabler, *An Empire of Their Own: How the Jews Invented Hollywood* (New York: Anchor Books, 1989).

About Jews in *blackface* or *redface* and the Yiddish version of the song *Home on the Range*: Peter Antelyes, "'Haim Afen Range': The Jewish Indian and the Redface Western," *MELUS* 34, no. 3 (Fall 2009): 15–42.

*In culo alla luna*: (Italian) in the middle of nowhere, but literally "in the moon's ass."

*Buona condotta*: (Italian) literally "good conduct" or good behavior.

About Pietro and Giovanni Delmonico: William Grimes, *Appetite City: A Culinary History of New York* (New York: North Point Press, 2009).

Philip Hone, *The Diary of Philip Hone, 1828–1851*, Vol. 1 (New York: Dodd, Mead and Company, 1927), 32–33.

## II

About the history of chestnut trees in America: Susan Freinke, *American Chestnut: The Life, Death, and Rebirth of a Perfect Tree* (Berkely: University of California Press, 2007).

*Je ne suis pas d'accord . . .*: (French) The full French quote reads: *Je ne suis pas d'accord avec ce que vous dites, mais je me battrai jusqu'à la mort pour que vous ayez le droit de le dire,* which means "I disagree with what you say, but I will fight to my last for your right to say it."

*Il gioco dell'oca:* (Italian) children's board game, known in English as The Game of Goose or The Royal Game of Goose.

Daniel Denton, *A Brief Description of New York, Formerly Called New Netherlands* (New York: William Gowans, 1845), 19, 21.

### *Part 5*

## 12

*Mossadnik*: (Hebrew) Israeli Mossad secret agent . . . think of it as a Jewish James Bond.

*Parle-moi en italien*: (French) Speak to me in Italian.

*I met my old lover. . .*: from the song *Still Crazy After All These Years* by Paul Simon.

## 13

*La poupette:* (French) a term of endearment equivalent to the English "my baby doll" but not as creepy and condescending as it sounds. Philippe remembered his grandfather calling with great love and in all seriousness his rather robust wife "*ma poupette.*" When he didn't call me "poupette," Philippe called me "Féfé."

*It's very clear . . . :* from the song *Our Love Is Here to Stay,* music by George and Ira Gershwin.

*Verweile doch, du bist so schön:* (German) "Stay a while, you are so beautiful" from *Faust* by Johann Wolfgang Goethe.

*¡No se detengan en Limón!*: (Spanish) Don't stop in Limón!

*Los negritos peligrosos*: (Spanish) Dangerous black people [racially offensive].

### *Part 6*

## 15

*Kashrut:* (Hebrew) Jewish dietary laws.

*Shemah Israel:* (Hebrew) the opening words of the founding prayer in Judaism, "Hear Oh Israel!"

P. J. O'Rourke, *The Baby Boom: How It Got That Way . . . And It Wasn't My Fault . . . And I'll Never Do It Again* (New York: Grove/Atlantic, 2014), xvii.

## 16

*Baruch Hu:* (Hebrew) "Blessed be He [God]."

## Part 7

### 17

About tornadoes: Richard Bedard, *In the Shadow of the Tornado: Stories and Adventures from the Heart of Storm Country* (Norman, OK: Gilco, 1997).

Karl R. Popper, *Conjectures and Refutations: The Growth of Scientific Knowledge* (New York: Basic Books, 1962).

### 18

Henry David Thoreau, *Walden* (New York: Barnes & Noble Classics, 2003).

Bernard Malamud, *A New Life* (New York: Avon Books, 1979), 266.